IN A TIME OF WAR

"[A] significant work and worthy of reading . . . [A] heartbreaking tale of the shift from youth to death in the blink of an eye."

—*Austin American-Statesman*

"In these days when most of America glides along, more and more oblivious to the conflict overseas, it is a remarkable achievement for any storyteller to reveal the tight, committed subculture that contends with war every day. Our military community—isolated, insulated, and, indeed, emotionally segregated from the rest of the nation—is fighting, suffering, and, at times, dying. *In a Time of War* has paid attention and done so simply, beautifully, and honestly. And attention is due."

—David Simon, writer and producer of HBO's *Generation Kill*

"Murphy tells the story of the class of 2002 with subtle passion and eloquent compassion. What emerges most clearly is an unforgettable group portrait of service and sacrifice—haunting and uplifting at once."   —Military.com

"Here is the unforgettable story of the West Point class that bore the full burden of American policy in Iraq. Bill Murphy Jr. captures young officers at war in a classic account that is powerful but not overdrawn, and hauntingly sad yet never saccharine—just straight and true."

—David Maraniss, author of *They Marched Into Sunlight*

"Verdict: This powerful, skillfully written and moving book sheds a personal light on the wages of war. Highly recommended."   —*Library Journal*

"Brilliantly reported and elegantly written. *In a Time of War* is a story of courage, but it will also break your heart."

—Bob Woodward, author of *State of Denial*

"Stands out from much current military reporting by avoiding editorializing about war. [Murphy] confines himself to a skillful journalistic narrative of events that are gripping enough to hold any reader's attention."

—*Publishers Weekly*

Praise for *In a Time of War*

"Alternately inspiring and heartbreaking . . . At the ground level, wars are fought by painfully young men and women—and by the junior officers who lead them. *In a Time of War* movingly profiles some of those officers, and as combat veterans grow more rare in American society, books like Murphy's become more important."   —*The Washington Post*

"What Rick Atkinson did for the West Point class of 1966, Bill Murphy Jr. has had the courage, talent, and dedication to do for the class of 2002. With pencil, boots, and tape recorder, Murphy has performed a national service: He sends the reader out among some of the bravest, most inspiring young people in the country, at one of the most pivotal times in our history. Prepare to be moved and amazed."   —David Lipsky, author of *Absolutely American*

"They serve. Was there ever a word more descriptive of what a group of women and men do? 'Serve': It works. Soldiers march and shoot and dig ditches and climb mountains and build bridges and clear roads, but what they really do—in that khaki-colored tent of a verb that spreads out over all the rest of the activities—is serve. Never has that been made any clearer than it is in Bill Murphy Jr.'s *In a Time of War*."   —*Chicago Tribune*

"A powerful, penetrating tale about the young officers who bear the burden of our twenty-first-century wars. The themes of *In a Time of War* are timeless: duty and sacrifice, love and death, heroism and fate."
              —Rick Atkinson, author of *The Day of Battle* and *The Long Gray Line*

"An astonishingly well written and compelling tapestry . . . Most extraordinary is how [Murphy] manages to avoid histrionics. . . . Murphy is invisible here, and allows the simple yet eloquent words of the soldiers and their loved ones to take center stage; the book is more powerful for his restraint."
                                                          —*Grand Rapids Press*

"Bill Murphy Jr. has captured the idealism and the courage of the 'Golden Children' of our wars in Iraq and Afghanistan, West Point's bicentennial Class of 2002. Readers will be moved to tears and fierce pride by their spirit and sacrifice. *In a Time of War* is a heartfelt portrait of war and family—a book that tore my heart out, and one that I will never forget."
              —Lt. Col. John Nagl (ret.), author of *Learning to Eat Soup with a Knife*

IN A TIME OF WAR

OF WAR

THE PROUD AND PERILOUS JOURNEY OF
WEST POINT'S CLASS OF 2002

· ★ ·

BILL MURPHY JR.

A HOLT PAPERBACK   HENRY HOLT AND COMPANY   NEW YORK

Holt Paperbacks
Henry Holt and Company, LLC
Publishers since 1866
175 Fifth Avenue
New York, New York 10010
www.henryholt.com

A Holt Paperback® and ® are registered trademarks of
Henry Holt and Company, LLC.

Library of Congress Cataloging-in-Publication Data
Murphy, Bill, Jr.
    In a time of war: the proud and perilous journey of West Point's
class of 2002 / Bill Murphy Jr.—1st ed.
        p.   cm.
    Includes bibliographical references and index.
    ISBN-13: 978-0-8050-9085-7
    ISBN-10: 0-8050-9085-1
    1. United States Military Academy—Biography.   2. Military cadets—
United States—Biography.   3. Iraq War, 2003—Biography.   4. Soldiers—
United States—Biography.   I. Title.
    U410.MIA38 2008
    355.0092'273—dc22   2008019465

Originally published in hardcover in 2008
by Henry Holt and Company

First Holt Paperbacks Edition 2009

Maps by Paul J. Pugliese
Designed by Kelly S. Too

Printed in the United States of America
1   3   5   7   9   10   8   6   4   2

To my parents,
William T. Murphy and Patricia Murphy,
and
to Natalie, Savannah, Maggie, and Julia—
and all the children of the Golden Children

A BRIEF CHRONOLOGY OF
RELEVANT WORLD EVENTS FROM 2001 TO 2007

SEPTEMBER 2001: Al Qaeda terrorists hijack four U.S. airliners and crash them into the World Trade Center in New York, the Pentagon in Washington, D.C., and a field in Pennsylvania, killing nearly three thousand.

OCTOBER to DECEMBER 2001: The United States launches Operation Enduring Freedom and, along with anti-Taliban forces within Afghanistan, deposes the Taliban. After the Battle of Tora Bora, Osama bin Laden and other Al Qaeda leaders escape.

JUNE 2002: At the West Point graduation, President George W. Bush announces his preemption doctrine, under which the United States reserves the right to attack its enemies before threats to America fully materialize.

OCTOBER 2002: Congress votes to authorize military force in Iraq.

MARCH 2003: U.S.-led coalition invades Iraq. Within three weeks, the force takes Baghdad.

MAY to JULY 2003: President Bush declares that "major combat operations in Iraq have ended." U.S. Administrator for Iraq L. Paul Bremer orders that Ba'ath Party members may not work in government, and disbands the Iraqi army. Looting begins. The first improvised explosive device kills an American soldier. By July, U.S. military officials in Baghdad concede they're facing a "classic guerrilla-type campaign."

DECEMBER 13, 2003: Saddam Hussein is captured alive by U.S. troops in Tikrit, Hussein's hometown.

APRIL 2004: Moqtada al-Sadr leads an uprising of Shiites in Sadr City and elsewhere in Iraq. Later that month, photographs of American soldiers torturing and humiliating inmates at Abu Ghraib prison are made public.

JUNE 28, 2004: The United States transfers sovereignty to Iraq's government in a secret ceremony, two days ahead of schedule.

OCTOBER to NOVEMBER 2004: Afghanistan holds its first presidential election since before the Taliban. In the United States, President Bush wins reelection. After a fierce battle in the Iraqi city of Fallujah, Marines and soldiers reestablish control.

JANUARY 30, 2005: Iraqis vote in the first truly democratic elections for parliament in fifty years.

FEBRUARY to MARCH 2006: The al-Askari shrine in Samarra is bombed and severely damaged, triggering a new round of violence in Iraq. Sectarian murders multiply as dozens of bodies are found executed on Iraqi streets daily.

JUNE to AUGUST 2006: Abu Musab al-Zarqawi, leader of Al Qaeda in Iraq, is killed in a U.S. strike. The top American general in Iraq, General John Abizaid, warns Congress that Iraq could slide into civil war.

NOVEMBER 2006: Saddam Hussein is convicted of crimes against humanity and sentenced to death by hanging. In the U.S. elections, Democrats take over the House and Senate. Secretary of Defense Donald Rumsfeld resigns.

JANUARY 10, 2007: President Bush announces that he will send additional troops to Iraq, a strategy he calls the "surge."

SEPTEMBER 10, 2007: The new commander in Iraq, General David Petraeus, testifies to Congress that the United States is meeting most of its military objectives and advises against a large reduction in the number of American soldiers serving there.

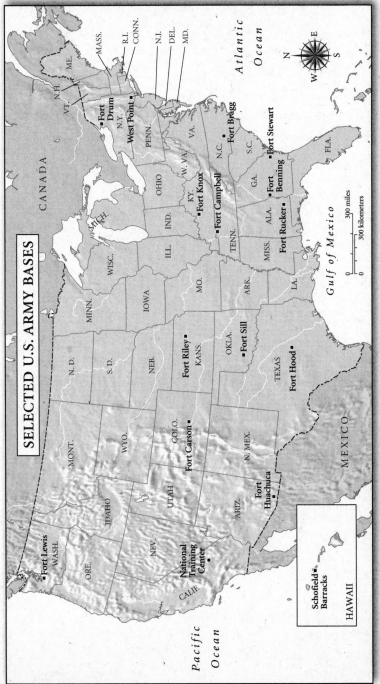

SELECTED U.S. ARMY BASES

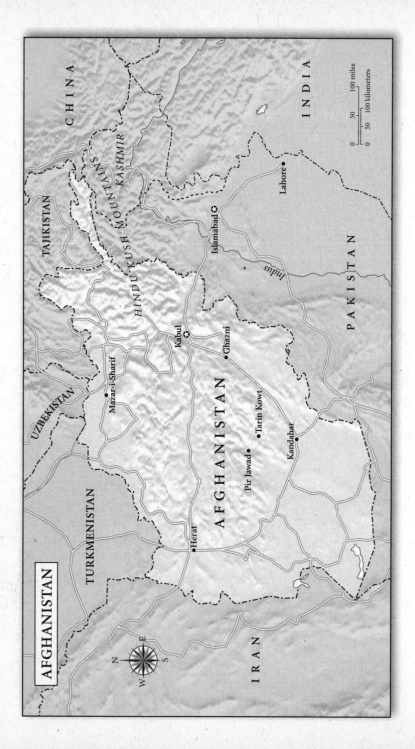

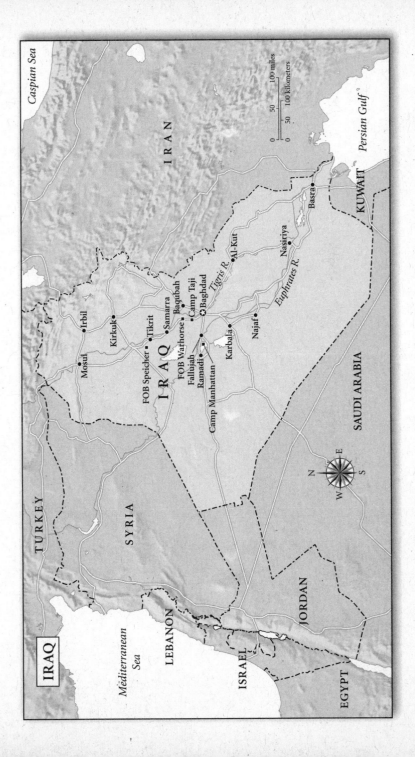

IN A TIME OF WAR

He was laid-back and blond, a surfer dude in manner if not literal truth, a California kid who believed a double-double burger from In-N-Out was nature's perfect food. Five foot nine and stocky, he was known in high school for decent golf, mediocre football, better grades, and outrageous pranks. He was sentimental, even sappy, a romantic who was confident in his charms. When he wanted to take a girl he hardly knew to the senior prom, he armed himself with a dozen roses, drove to her house, and asked her in person. (She said yes.) Most of all, he was mischievous. On days off from school, he and a friend would cure their boredom by wandering the mall or the shops of their hometown, competing to see how many stores would kick them out. When all else failed, a game of one-on-one basketball in the sporting goods department usually did the trick. Perhaps his most famous high school prank was the time he sneaked in before marching band practice and swapped a porn movie for the videotape of the band's most recent performance. The band director fumbled with the VCR for the longest fifteen seconds of her life.

But there was another side to Todd J. Bryant, West Point class of 2002: He had practically been born in uniform. Though he was born on January 14, 1980, the tale of Todd's life had truly begun two decades earlier, when his mother, Linda, visited the United States Military Academy on a family vacation. The year was 1959, the height of the Cold War, not even two years after Sputnik. Linda was eleven, a small-town Indiana girl, daughter of conservative and patriotic parents. As she walked the gray stone campus on the banks of the Hudson River north of New York City, she instantly fell in love. There was something so honorable and compelling about West Point—the tradition, the uniforms, the utter crispness of the place. It moved her deeply. How wonderful it would be, Linda thought, to one day stand as part of the long gray line of West Point graduates.

Seventeen years would pass before the American service academies admitted women, and so when Linda went home to Indiana, she limited herself to collecting military memorabilia. She grew up, went to high school in a class that included future vice president Dan Quayle, and earned a degree from Indiana University. Still, she thought about the military. She had high school friends who had died in Vietnam, and she felt that as an American she was in their debt. When the Air Force started commissioning women as regular officers in the 1970s, she joined up. She married a fellow officer, Larry Bryant, and they served together for more than a decade.

She loved the military life as much as she had hoped, but it all came to an end when she started having children. Especially after Todd was born, Linda had trouble losing her pregnancy weight. Her annual evaluations dripped with sarcastic comments and faint praise about the truly admirable effort she was making to slim down to military standards. She was passed over for promotion, and by the mid-1980s, when her husband left active duty for a civilian job at the Jet Propulsion Laboratory in Southern California, the writing was on the wall. She cried as she turned in her military ID card, and as she scraped the Department of Defense parking sticker off her car.

TODD, THE YOUNGEST of the three Bryant kids, grew up in a five-bedroom house on a cul-de-sac in the desert suburbs an hour east of Los Angeles. He and his sister, Tiffany, went to school an hour away, near Pasadena, the Rose Bowl, and their parents' work. It was a long commute but a good life.

Riverside County was right-wing California, flush with military retirees and civilians working in the defense industry; Linda and Larry fit right in. Their kids grew up understanding that it was important to serve in the armed forces, to repay their country for the freedoms they enjoyed. Barely three years after Linda left the Air Force, there was a Bryant back in uniform. Tim, Todd's big brother, nine years older than Todd was, enlisted in the Marine Corps Reserve and went off to college on a Naval ROTC scholarship.

Then it was Tiffany's turn. Pretty and blond, she had towered over Todd for most of their childhood, and tagged him with the teasing nickname Poco, Spanish for "Little." But in truth, Tiffany thought of herself as more of a second mother to Todd than a sister. Nearly three years older than Todd, she was trendy and rebellious, about as unmilitary as could be imagined. Convincing her even to spend two years part-time in the National Guard, Linda and Larry thought, would be a major accomplishment.

But again, the subtle lessons sank in. Even if Linda and Larry never recalled saying it explicitly, their kids understood that military service, especially as a commissioned officer, was among the highest positions one could aspire to. Tiffany came home from high school one day talking about enlisting in the reserves. She also mentioned wanting to study architecture in college, or civil engineering.

"You know," Linda said, "the number one civil engineering school in the country is West Point."

"What's West Point?" Tiffany asked.

Linda was incredulous. How could her daughter not know about the world's greatest military academy?

United Air Lines had a special over the July Fourth weekend that year, $60 or $70 each way, direct from Ontario Airport in California to Newark. Linda, Tiffany, and Todd flew out on the red-eye. They drove straight from the airport to the academy, the first time Linda had been on campus since her childhood visit thirty-five years before.

In later years, Tiffany and her mother would remember things differently. Linda would recall that after a daylong tour, her daughter stood apart from her brother and mother on the academy's storied parade ground, known as the Plain. "Okay," Linda recalled her announcing. "This is where I'm going." Tiffany recalled being much harder to convince. Regardless, she applied, and though she did not get in at first, the academy offered her a sort of tryout, a year at the U.S. Military Academy Preparatory School in New Jersey, to see if she could get her grades up to West Point standards. Tiffany thrived at Prep. She felt she'd had a much stricter upbringing than many of her peers, and despite all the Army discipline, she felt freer at the Prep School than she ever had in her life. At the end of the year, she was admitted to West Point as a member of the class of 2000.

TODD HAD BEEN fixated on Notre Dame since he was a kid. His bedroom was decorated with Fighting Irish wallpaper, and a football signed by Coach Knute Rockne rested on his bookshelf. Some of his high school football teammates had even nicknamed him Rudy, after the title character in a 1993 movie about a low-talent, high-desire Notre Dame football player. Though his parents figured Todd would probably apply for an ROTC scholarship like his older brother in the Marines, they also presumed his path would travel through South Bend, Indiana.

But then Todd visited Tiffany at West Point for a weekend during her freshman year—her "plebe" year. She loved it there, and Todd could see why: There was just something amazing about the place. It represented a challenge. *I can do this,* he thought to himself.

"That's where I'm going," he told his parents when he got back to California.

"What?" Linda replied. "West Point?" She was truly surprised. "What about Notre Dame?"

"Forget it."

Still a high school junior, Todd enlisted in the Army Reserve and went through basic training at Fort Sill in Oklahoma the summer before his senior year. He wrote letters home to a girlfriend, waxing on about how grown-up he felt at seventeen, and wondering what it would be like if the United States ever went to war again. By the time he came home to California at the end of the summer, he had slimmed down and was in the best physical shape of his life. He broke 1500 on his SATs and banged out his West Point applications.

Do you have a part-time job? the form asked.

"Yes," Todd wrote with evident pride. "I am a private in the United States Army Reserve." That was a big part of his identity now. He even wore his dress blue enlisted soldier's uniform to the prom later that year.

What do you see yourself doing ten years from today?

"As a captain in the United States Army, I expect I will be commanding an armored cavalry unit."

Why do you want to attend a U.S. service academy?

"I seek the opportunity to protect the freedoms we cherish," Todd wrote. "And if need be, to fight and die for my country."

Todd's course was set. His congressman sponsored him. West Point accepted him. He didn't apply anywhere else.

TODD BRYANT AND HIS CLASSMATES in the West Point class of 2002 were the heirs apparent to a military in crisis. In the wake of Vietnam, the leaders of the first army in American history to lose a war faced a stark strategic choice. They could study the war intently, learning and applying its lessons so they would never be caught flat-footed again. Or, they could decide that Vietnam was simply the product of a strange confluence of unfortunate geography, misguided tactics, and a lack of political will at home: an unnerving episode, but unlikely ever to be repeated. With a few notable exceptions, the leadership of the late-twentieth-century U.S. military chose the latter, more comfortable course. The Army set aside its Vietnam-style missions against insurgents and guerrillas, and instead prepared almost exclusively to fight the hordes of Soviet tanks that they expected would one day invade western Europe.

Most of the West Point class of 2002 had been born in 1979 or 1980; while they slept as infants in their cribs, two events unfolded that would profoundly affect their lives. The first of these was the 444-day Iranian hostage crisis, which began in November 1979; the second was the Soviet invasion of Afghanistan the following month. Turmoil in the Middle East was a dire threat, and President Jimmy Carter quickly announced the U.S. policy that would stay in place for a generation: Any attempt to gain control of the Persian Gulf would be treated as an assault on America's vital interests and would be "repelled by any means necessary, including military force."

When Todd and his peers were in grade school, the Berlin Wall came crashing down, and the Soviet Union broke up. The great invasion of Europe never came. But in the 1991 Persian Gulf War, the Army used the tanks and tactics it had developed to fight the Soviets to annihilate Saddam Hussein's Iraqi army in a hundred hours of one-sided desert combat. In its wake, the ghosts of Vietnam were finally exorcised, and the Army's planning seemed vindicated. America stood more than equal to all rivals. There were dangers in the world to be sure, but they appeared inchoate. The biggest challenge the U.S. Army faced seemed to be simply figuring out where the next military threat might come from.

THE DEAL AT WEST POINT IS THIS: a taxpayer-funded, four-year college education in exchange for five years of service as an officer on active duty in the Army, and three more in the reserves. Like their peers at the Naval and Air Force Academies, West Point cadets pay no tuition, no room or board. The academy touts the education it provides as being on a par with the finest universities in the country. Most applicants in the class of 2002 had top grades and impressive extracurricular activities, and were the kind of kids who could have chosen Harvard, Yale, or any elite college. Of twelve thousand applicants, 1,246 were admitted. There were team captains and Eagle Scouts, leaders and academics. More than one hundred of the new cadets who took their oaths with Todd on the academy football field in the early summer of 1998 were ranked first or second in their high school classes, and fully three-quarters had graduated in the top fifth. They were an accomplished, impressive group.

On the whole, cadets were likely to be the sons and daughters of alumni, or at least to have grown up in families with a tradition of military service, and in that respect they reflected American society as a whole. In the era of the all-volunteer Army, the common measure of civic responsibility had shifted. A great gulf had opened between those who served in the military and those who didn't. Americans no longer believed they had to serve to be good citizens. Instead, they simply had to "support the troops," whatever that might mean. As the class of 2002 arrived, West Point was grappling with how to remain relevant in that environment, in a post–Cold War world with a smaller Army and no obvious international adversary. How could the academy keep a steady supply of America's best high school graduates streaming through its gates?

The academy hired a public relations firm in New York City, and reporters and filmmakers were welcomed to campus. When Todd Bryant and his classmates sat nervously in the bleachers of the football stadium on Reception Day in 1998, listening to welcoming speeches and taking their first orders, a few of the people among them were actually incognito actors playing cadets in a movie. West Point's top generals even convinced the editors of *Rolling Stone* to do a story on the academy. The article was the longest the magazine had ever published.

As it happened, the academy looked on the class of 2002 with special favor: Its graduation would coincide with the two hundredth anniversary of West Point's founding, and the cadets' arrival inaugurated a four-year opportunity to mold the academy's image. The bicentennial class was constantly touted as the new face of West Point, linking two centuries of tradition with a bright American future. As a result of all the attention, the class of 2002 was quickly nicknamed the Golden Children by the envious cadets ahead of them. They were celebrated at every turn, the upperclassmen complained, but the only thing special about them was the year they were born.

THE FIRST SUMMER and first year at West Point are legendarily tough. The system was designed to disorient new cadets, to make them feel "a little like Dorothy did when she landed in Oz," in the words of the academy commandant, a one-star general named John Abizaid. New cadets were allowed to speak only when spoken to, and then only with one of four scripted responses: "Yes, sir"; "No, sir"; "No excuse, sir"; or "Sir, I do not understand."

Todd and his new classmates were like actors now in all the classic military movie scenes: Long periods of standing at attention. Sixty-second buzz cuts at the cadet barbershop. Upperclassmen in starched uniforms, imitating the Marine Corps drill instructor in *Full Metal Jacket*. The new cadets were made to look uniformly foolish on the first day, issued and quickly dressed in gray West Point T-shirts, black shorts, calf-length socks, and dress shoes. Each wore a light blue note card around his or her neck—a USMA Form 2-176—with a checklist of stations, as if the new cadets were kindergarteners who couldn't be expected to remember their home addresses or phone numbers. One by one, they made it through the stations—"ID Photo"; "Lunch Meal"—as unsmiling upperclassmen unceremoniously checked them off, subtly reinforcing their new status. The new cadets never touched the cards or opened their mouths.

By early morning on Day 2, they were doing push-ups and sit-ups with their squads in formation. In Armyspeak, working out was "PT"—"physical training"—and besides keeping the new cadets in shape, it provided a healthy outlet for stress and anxiety. The new cadets marched, ran, camped, worked, memorized, and sweated. Most of all they followed, for a fundamental precept of "America's premier leadership school," as West Point humbly touted itself, was that one could never dream of being able to lead before learning to take direction.

Summer gave way to fall and then winter, and for the first-year cadets the days became a blur, a nonstop regimen of more academic assignments than could likely be done in a day, coupled with still more PT. Cadets who screwed up badly enough faced a time-honored punishment: marching in uniform for hours, rifles cradled across their shoulders. But while tradition ran deep, some things had evolved. Just before Todd and his peers arrived, West Point had instituted a series of reforms so sweeping that they were referred to simply as "the Changes." "Demanding but not demeaning" was General Abizaid's catchphrase. A member of the West Point class of 1973 and a combat veteran of the 1983 U.S. invasion of Grenada, Abizaid was a different kind of officer. After the academy, he had studied at Harvard and in Jordan, and he spoke Arabic. (Abizaid played down his fluency in later years, but he was certainly among the few U.S. officers of his time who knew his *as-salaam alaikum* from his *inshallah*.) He had a reputation for modern thinking and new ideas, and under his reign, much of the hazing, meanness, and abuse that had long been part of West Point life were gone. Creature comforts that would have brought scorn and punishment in years gone by were now officially sanctioned. Cadets could watch movies on computers in their rooms, for example, and had cell phones in their barracks. The older classes and some alumni grumbled that the Corps of Cadets had gone to hell. But as they worked their way through their first three years at the academy, the class of 2002 believed they were being better prepared for success in the Army than their predecessors, who had trained as much for the idiosyncrasies of West Point as for real war.

TIFFANY BRYANT GRADUATED from the academy in 2000 and was stationed in Korea, and so when Todd had to pick an Army internship a year later, just before his senior ("firstie") year, he put in for a U.S. base near the Demilitarized Zone, forty miles north of Seoul. Why not let the Army pay for a trip to visit his sister? he reasoned. In less than a year he would be commissioned as a second lieutenant, and he still planned to serve in "armor," as a tank commander, just as he had written in his West Point application. It struck him as the perfect assignment, in one of the real warfighting branches of the Army, at the heart of the action. Plus, you rode into battle. Todd wasn't a big fan of PT, and he absolutely hated running. In a tank unit, he reasoned, who needed to run five miles a day?

But if he was certain about branching armor, Todd was no longer sure what he wanted in the long term. Though West Point had traditionally prepared cadets for twenty-year careers as Army officers, its official mission statement now proclaimed that graduates were expected to perform "a lifetime of selfless service to the nation." The language provided a moral escape clause, and cadets were quick to recognize that there were other ways to serve. Todd often spoke about his dream of one day serving in Congress, or even running for governor of his beloved California. But he also loved history, and he imagined that after his five-year active duty obligation, he might teach high school and coach football. Sometimes he even thought that his true calling was stand-up comedy. Growing up in Southern California, he'd been a child model and actor, and had appeared as an extra on TV shows like *Family Ties* and *Beverly Hills 90210*.

But the answer to the question of what form his service might finally take lay in the far distant future; in the meantime, Todd was looking forward to the real Army. West Point, the joke went, offered a free, quarter-million-dollar education, shoved up your ass a nickel at a time. Todd complained constantly, and he was fond of saying the view of the academy he looked forward to most was the one he'd see in the rearview mirror after graduation. But it was obvious to everyone who knew Todd that he admired the place. Yes, his mother could drive him batty with her exuberant devotion to West Point and all things military, but he had come to love its tradition and honor every bit as much as she did. And he had made friends who were as close as any he could imagine.

In his final year now, Todd was rooming with Tim Moshier, a tall, gentle, quiet cadet who had grown up in a suburb of Albany and who towered over Todd by at least eight inches. Tim was a good student and a talented writer, but he preferred subjects like science and engineering, in which mathematical certainties could be attained. He was still very much a kid, with large, expressive eyes and a broad smile that masked his natural shyness. His friends teased him regularly about his affinity for sitcoms and his insistence on watching the teen drama *Dawson's Creek* every Tuesday.

West Point divided its cadets into regiments, and again into companies, each carefully filled to reflect the statistical diversity of the academy as a whole. Todd and Tim were assigned to Company D, 1st Regiment. Go back forty years and D-1 had been "Dogshit-One," reputed to have the meanest upperclassmen and toughest officer-instructors. But the academy was a little more family friendly now, and D-1 was known simply as the Ducks. Traditionally, classes "scrambled," meaning cadets were reassigned to new companies at the end of their second year. But in a rare show of democracy, West Point had put the usual practice to a vote for the class of 2002. Overwhelmingly, the cadets had preferred to remain in their current companies, so Todd and Tim had lived with the same group of friends for three years. They were exceptionally close.

As roommates, they were terrible mutual influences, chronic slackers who debated endlessly whether to hit the gym, study, or clean their barracks room—and then did none of those things. Other cadets would marvel as they ordered and wolfed down giant, grease-soaked takeout pizzas called B-52s, topping them off with a pint each of Ben & Jerry's ice cream. Their room was a sty by West Point standards. Less than a month into their senior year, their cadet platoon leader had no choice but to write them up for it, the only room he had to cite that semester. But Todd and Tim were hilarious together: Their friends would compare them to classic comedy duos, everyone from Abbott and Costello to Fred Flintstone and Barney Rubble, with Todd as the frenetic jester and Tim as his willing straight man. Even when Tim was the butt of Todd's jokes, he never seemed to mind. The consummate team player, he was happy to have found a place where he fit in.

Todd could walk down the hallway, past one identical room after another, and point to a close friend in each. Will Tucker, from Haleyville, Alabama, population 4,182, was one of the closest. Will's father ran a bait-and-tackle shop and his mother taught junior high; Will was the salutatorian of his high school class. He was a tough, quiet kid. In a football practice during his sophomore year of high school, he had broken his femur, but held on to the ball until the end of the play. Later, as a sixteen-year-old, Will had taken a job that involved overseeing work-release prisoners from the local jail. He'd drive the van, watch as they worked, and take them on illicit runs for cigarettes and Burger King on the way back to the lockup.

Will was as tight-lipped as Todd was gregarious. Partly it was a matter of his personality, and partly it was because he took so much crap for his thick southern accent. Todd ribbed him mercilessly, but that was different; Will barely minded. After three years together, in what Todd sarcastically referred to as their "happy Hudson home," they were as close as friends could be. Will had a sister back home in Alabama, but Todd was like the brother he'd never had.

This, for Todd, was the essence of West Point. "Duty, honor, country" was the academy's motto, and everyone talked constantly about honor and commitment, loyalty and patriotism. All that was true and good, but stripped of its pomp and circumstance, the place was really about love. Love of your country, love of your classmates and friends, and love of the future officers you'd someday serve with. Most of all, West Point was about learning to love the soldiers you would someday lead, the privates and sergeants, knuckleheads and heroes alike, who might, just once, in a life-justifying moment, look to you for leadership in some great battle on a distant shore.

IN 2001, THOUGH, Todd was thinking about a different kind of love. Jen Reardon was a blond-haired, blue-eyed biology major in her junior year at Boston College. They had met online through a mutual friend, a girl named Ryan Poe who had grown up across the street from Todd in Riverside and who worked with Jen at the college bookstore.

"What made you decide on West Point?" Jen typed in one early instant message.

"My sister told me I had to," Todd replied.

"Oh, good reason."

"I never cross my sister," Todd continued. "For safety reasons."

Before long, they were up until two or three A.M. most nights, chatting on the computer. Theirs was a brave new twenty-first-century relationship in which they talked daily, grew close, and shared their innermost secrets before actually meeting in person. Finally, in April 2001, Todd headed up to Boston for a weekend to meet Jen. He was eager and nervous. Their intense interaction had an element of escapist fantasy, and it was weird suddenly to encounter each other as living, breathing human beings. With some of Jen's college friends, they went to an Irish bar called Kinvara, a dive where they were pretty sure Jen's improbable fake ID would work. (She was twenty; it said she was twenty-six.) Slowly, the ice melted, as they talked, danced, and sang along with the 1980s cover band. When they finally kissed, it was as if they'd been together for months.

Todd's spring had gone by in a blur—his fast-moving romance with

Jen, raucous road trips, wild parties, and an episode involving the Boston College police department, smelling salts, and a trip to the hospital emergency room. And then the academic year was over, and Todd had left, first for a service project in Seattle and then for his assignment in Korea. He called Jen at the end of nearly every workday, and the phone would ring late at night at her mother's house in Pennsylvania where she was staying for the summer. Todd wrote long letters, once scribbling on the backs of pages from a "Far Side" calendar so Jen could read the cartoons if she was bored by what he had to say. That seemed highly unlikely, and by the end of the summer, he was pouring his heart out. "I dreamt that some day I would find a girl that could make me as happy as you do," Todd wrote. Then, on second thought, he scribbled out "dreamt," and replaced it with "prayed."

Now, in August 2001, Todd was back at West Point, and Jen drove up from Pennsylvania to greet him. It was her turn to be nervous. Todd was a great guy—funny, good-looking—and he made her feel special. But their relationship was intense. Who knew where this might lead?

"Those West Pointers," warned one of her roommates, a girl whose father had graduated from the academy, but whose parents' marriage hadn't lasted. "Their goal their firstie year is to find a wife that will follow them around the Army and cook and clean for them. You have to beware of that."

Todd wasn't allowed off campus during Jen's visit, and she couldn't even hug him, since public displays of affection were prohibited when a cadet was in uniform. It was her first visit to West Point, and she was surprised to find the place so cold and gray, even at the end of summer, nothing like the pretty campus at Boston College. All around were reminders that Todd owed a half decade of his life to the Army. True, no West Point class had graduated into conflict since Vietnam, years before either of them had been born. But still, there would be months of training, and an assignment to some distant military base—maybe Germany, or South Korea again. Todd could even be sent away for six months or more on a peacekeeping deployment in Bosnia. If only he weren't in the Army, Jen thought, things would be so much easier.

Todd led Jen down Flirty Walk, the one place on campus where he was allowed to walk arm-in-arm with a girl while in uniform. As he talked about the academy's history and traditions, he spoke with such passion and reverence that Jen—against her better judgment—grew fascinated. The campus seemed an irony-free oasis, both severe and beautiful, apart from the rest of America. The academy made her proud of her country, proud of her boyfriend's military service, proud that he loved America and wasn't afraid to say it.

A couple of weeks later, Todd called Jen at Boston College with a plan. Her birthday was coming up, and he wanted to do something special. Pack a bag, he told her. Bring something nice to wear. He drove the two hundred miles up to Massachusetts in his Chevy Suburban and whisked her away over Labor Day weekend to the Diamond District Inn, a bed and breakfast north of Boston. It was romantic and wonderful, intoxicating for Jen. Before the weekend was out, Todd started talking about getting engaged.

"You're out of your mind!" Jen replied. Marriage? She was crazy about him, but she was just a kid, and they'd known each other for only a few months. She'd hardly seen Todd since Korea, and just a few times before that. She did her best to ignore him, pretending he hadn't said the word.

"I'm not going to pressure you. I'm not going to push you," Todd replied. But sooner or later, he promised, "You're going to realize what you already know in your heart. It's just your stubborn head that won't cooperate."

The first Drew Sloan ever heard of West Point was in a Tom Clancy novel. There was no military tradition in his family to speak of, certainly no pressure for him to go into the Army. The Sloans were political liberals, the kind of parents who wouldn't let their son play with toy guns as a kid. Drew's mother was a high school history teacher, and his dad was a professor at the University of Arkansas–Fayetteville. They'd been casual friends of Bill and Hillary Clinton's in the early 1980s, when the future First Couple taught at the law school there. Drew's mom, Vicky, liked to tell a story about when she was pregnant with Drew, and Hillary was expecting Chelsea. They'd gone water skiing, of all things. Vicky nearly hit Hillary with the boat.

Though Drew had two older half-sisters from his father's first marriage, they lived out of state, and for all practical purposes he was an only child. Vicky was diagnosed with Stage IV Hodgkin's lymphoma when he was in sixth grade, and she'd had to go to Texas for long-term treatment on his birthday that year, the first of many such trips. Drew seemed to collect stand-in mothers as a result, and his notion of family expanded beyond blood relatives. That first time Vicky had to leave, a friend's mother brought doughnuts for his class, just to make sure someone remembered his birthday, and Drew remembered the act of kindness for years.

In school, he was popular enough but never really part of the in crowd—neither the bullied kid eating lunch alone in the cafeteria, nor the one invited to every party and after-school event. He was a bit of a loner; he studied, and by his freshman year in high school he was working as a gofer at a law firm.

The idea of the academy grew on him slowly. An older kid in his Boy Scout troop was accepted, but nobody else he knew seemed particularly impressed. As Drew's interest in attending West Point increased, it set him apart, and that, in turn, was part of its self-perpetuating appeal. For a kid growing up in a liberal university town, the idea of going to one of the most regimented and disciplined colleges in America could be an ironic act of rebellion.

On paper, Drew's credentials were worthy of West Point, but he was his own hardest critic. The academy wanted scholars and leaders. He had good grades and had taken advanced placement classes; he'd earned his Eagle Scout credential. But he wondered whether he was truly a leader. The academy also wanted athletes. Drew had played baseball, or at least held a roster spot, but he was, in a word, scrawny. Standing five foot seven in high school, he topped the scale at maybe 140 pounds. He recognized he would need to work to get into West Point; he'd also need a bit of luck.

Work he could handle. Drew was a natural striver, and he was methodical about achieving goals once he identified them. He put himself on a program: He went to the university gym every day and, working with a trainer, built muscle until he could breeze through the academy's physical fitness entrance test. He benefited from the fact that his parents had held him back for a year before sending him to kindergarten. Now he was a year older than many of his grade-level peers. Moreover, Drew realized, he was fortunate to be from Arkansas—a small state, and one where there didn't seem to be as much competition for academy slots.

In his senior year, Drew applied to West Point and got in. At the last minute, his mom ran interference, encouraging him to look at other colleges. If joining the military was important to him, Vicky Sloan argued, he could try the Reserve Officer Training Corps. Drew applied to several, and it eventually came down to West Point or Vanderbilt. But one afternoon in the spring of his senior year, while his mother was still at work, he called the officer in charge of ROTC there. Drew thanked the captain for offering him a scholarship, but turned it down.

He'd made up his mind, Drew told the captain. "I'm going to West Point."

THE ACADEMY MADE DREW SLOAN. He looked different. For one thing, he'd kept growing until he reached six feet. And he filled out, too. But there was much more to it than that. Though he would visit Arkansas occasionally, in all the ways that truly mattered Drew had left home for good. He'd even changed his name. Up until West Point, he'd always been known as Andrew, but he didn't like the way it rolled off the tongue. *Andrew Sloan*. People were always shortening it to "Andy," which he hated, and at the academy gates he realized he could call himself whatever he wanted. The first time anyone asked him his name, he made a decision. "Drew," he answered.

He stumbled a bit at first. In retrospect, he realized that despite his teenage fixation on West Point, he'd known almost nothing about the place. Unless you had a sibling or a parent who was an Old Grad, as alumni were known, unless you'd grown up hearing about plebe year, Beast Barracks, Ring Weekend, and parades on the Plain, how could you know?

Academically, Drew did fine. He took tests that first summer to qualify out of some of the plebe-level courses, and eventually, his uniform collar bore gold stars signifying that his grades put him in the top five percent of the class. But he was socially immature, and a little awkward. He also had a habit of bringing trouble on himself. His most egregious mistake was writing a snarky e-mail to friends criticizing the upperclassmen in their company, which he accidentally sent to all the other cadets. Changes or no Changes, the yelling and hazing had lasted for hours.

That first year, the academy assigned Drew to room with two other cadets, one a six-foot-ten-inch basketball player, and the other a prematurely bald twenty-one-year-old Army veteran named Dave Swanson. Dave had spent three years as an enlisted soldier, and he had come through the West Point Prep School. He lived by a hardworking, blue-collar ethic. Though Dave was intelligent, he'd barely opened a book in high school, and he took a perverse pride in his dubious distinction of having had the lowest SAT scores in the history of the Prep School. He ruefully recalled his first math class, when he'd asked the professor to explain the meaning of a symbol she'd written on the board.

"This thing?" the professor asked in disbelief, pointing at the square root symbol and sending the class into hysterics. It turned out that Dave's high school had allowed him to graduate with only a seventh-grade understanding of math. But his commanders in the Army had seen raw leadership ability in him, and he was motivated. Dave was a truck driver's son and West Point was his only shot at college, so he buckled down, studied dozens of extra hours of remedial math each week, retook the SATs, and socked away his Army salary each month, saving $10,000. Now Prep was touting him to prospective students as a great success story.

Dave and Drew's company was H-2, which had a reputation as a lucky, easygoing, fun-loving unit. Formerly "Happy as Hell," the company had recently taken on the innocuous moniker "Highlanders." They benefited from the fact that the companies in their barracks were arranged alphabetically: Upperclassmen from other companies had to climb six flights of stairs to harass them, which was hardly worth the bother.

Dave fell in with some of the older cadets who had also been enlisted men, while Drew counted a Massachusetts native named Ryan Beltramini—a classmate in a series of honors courses during plebe year—among his best friends. But a West Point cadet's company is his home, and everyone in H-2 got along well and grew close. By the end of their third year at the academy, Drew, Dave, and a dozen of their company mates had gotten matching tattoos on their shoulder blades, a twisty, artistic rendering of the letter "H" and the number "2." "H-2 rolls deep," the Highlanders liked to say. It wasn't unusual for a half dozen H-2 guys to road trip together, to Manhattan and Atlantic City, or up the New York State Thruway to Montreal. When one of Drew's closest H-2 friends, an Army brat named Brian Oman, started dating a girl at Marist College in Poughkeepsie, he was expected each time he visited her to bring some of his fellow cadets along so they could meet girls and escape the West Point grind. Drew tried to expand their horizons on a few weekends, leading road trips to Vassar College, a notoriously liberal and nonconformist school, geographically close to West Point but metaphorically a world away. The experiment was a failure, and it was rarely repeated.

In August 2001, as firstie year began, Drew felt he had come into his own. He was enjoying the best time of his life. He held one of the highest ranks in the Corps of Cadets, and was now one of eight battalion commanders. Though his mother had never quite warmed to the idea of her son serving in the Army, when she came to visit one weekend and watched him leading five hundred cadets in a parade on the Plain—"Second Battalion," the announcer intoned as they marched by, "commanded by Cadet Captain Drew Sloan of Fayetteville, Arkansas"—she beamed with pride in spite of herself.

Drew had spent part of the summer with an Army unit in Texas, which had been difficult at times but had confirmed his desire to be in the infantry. Army officers served in branches that were divided into three classes. Furthest removed from fighting were the "combat service support" specialties like the quartermaster (supply), adjutant general corps (personnel and administration), and transportation (truck drivers). Next up was "combat support": military intelligence, the signal corps (communications), and the like. But the core of the Army was "combat arms"— infantry, armor, artillery, and air defense artillery. And infantry was first among equals. The foot soldier, the grunt, the proverbial "man on the ground with a gun": The rest of the Army existed primarily to support him. It was almost a moral failure, Drew believed, for a male cadet to go through four years at the academy only to ask to be assigned to anything other than the infantry. (Female officers could be judged by a different standard, since they were banned from combat arms.) Okay, he would admit, perhaps if his eyes had been better he might have thought about aviation— becoming a helicopter pilot—but Drew had always worn thick glasses or expensive contact lenses. But bad eyesight aside, Drew had a dream. West Point's favorite sons were Airborne Rangers, infantrymen who jumped out of perfectly good airplanes and had survived the grueling sixty-day infantry tactics course known as Ranger School. Drew wanted to be one of them.

Over the summer, Drew had had another important experience. Like Todd Bryant, he'd been assigned to spend a few weeks involved in a service project. Drew worked at an elementary school in Chicago's Chinatown, and through the project he met an Old Grad from the class of 1972 who made it a point every summer to host an elaborate party for cadets working in the city. This year's party was at the city's Shedd Aquarium, and it was there that Drew first laid eyes on the Old Grad's nineteen-year-old daughter. Chloe Hayes, a petite, brown-haired city girl, was witty, flirty, and lots of fun. She was a college journalism major, smart and well-read. To Drew, who'd been more or less cloistered in the Army, and who at twenty-two had never had a serious girlfriend, she was intriguing and exotic.

He saw her a few times during those few weeks in Chicago, though always in a group, with several fellow cadets and Chloe's girlfriends. Drew made little headway, but he was enthralled. Now that he was back at West Point, the thousand miles between him and Chicago were an undeniable hurdle to pursuing her, and active service would soon beckon. But Drew couldn't help himself. He summoned his nerve and called Chloe, inviting her to New York. The first big milestone in the school year was Ring Weekend, when the cadets would get the jewelry that would make them stand out instantly in the real Army as academy men and women. The activities on that September weekend included a formal dance, he explained. Would she be willing to come as his date?

The invitation floored Chloe. She'd hardly expected ever to hear again from Drew, or from any of the cadets she'd met over the summer. But she had grown up hearing about West Point from her father, and in her mind, Ring Weekend was a glamorous and important event; this was almost like being asked out of the blue to go the Oscars or a presidential inaugural. She accepted Drew's invitation and made plans to travel to West Point with a group of friends and sorority sisters, some of whom would be going as blind dates with Drew's buddies. When she landed in New York on the Friday morning before the dance and stood in the airport waiting for Drew, she panicked.

Oh my God, she thought, suddenly very nervous. *I have no idea who this guy is.* She wasn't even sure she would recognize him. She pulled out her cell phone, but just then Drew walked up to her. Drew knew exactly who she was: There was no way he could have forgotten what Chloe Hayes looked like.

The ring ceremony late that afternoon was storybook: the banks of the Hudson River; a beautiful, sunny day; and a thousand proud cadets in dress whites. Getting their rings was the first real suggestion that the academy thought they would graduate, that they were being groomed not just as leaders but also as future Old Grads. The cadets were ecstatic, and Chloe grew sentimental as she watched them, imagining that exactly thirty years before her father had done the same thing in the same spot.

Chloe and Drew went back to Manhattan that evening with their friends, enjoying a cruise around New York Harbor. The next day he went to pick her up at the on-campus Thayer Hotel for the Ring Weekend dance. Chloe looked utterly gorgeous in her long, black strapless dress. It was one of the best weekends of his life, he thought. Absolutely perfect.

TIM MOSHIER'S PARENTS had come down for the ring ceremony and a luncheon afterward, leaving their video camera behind with their son. He filmed constantly for the next week or two, like a kid with a new toy. He burst in on some of the female cadets in Company D-1, and filled the tape with the "hellos" and awkward "What do I say now?" comments of friends suddenly on camera. Another cadet turned the tables on Tim at one point, catching him with a half-empty pizza box on the floor of his room and watching an episode of the TV show *Just Shoot Me* on his computer. "They got the machine fixed," Todd Bryant explained in another video segment, slurring his words. It was late evening, and he and a female D-1 cadet named Kara Pond had just returned from the on-campus bar known as the Firstie Club. By "machine," Todd meant the bar's frozen-daiquiri maker. "We had to test it out," he said, a goofy smile on his face.

Tim, like Todd, had a serious girlfriend now. He had gone to high school in upstate New York with Katie McKee, but they had moved in different circles—Tim had been a quiet brain; Katie was more of a social butterfly. They'd bumped into each other back home at a New Year's Eve party during winter break in Tim's third year at West Point, traded e-mail addresses, and flirted online, trying to figure out whether they were friends or something more. Not long after they met, Katie drove five hours in the snow from her college in Pennsylvania to visit, only to learn Tim was also seeing another girl. They went out to eat anyway, at a little Italian restaurant called Schade's, right off post. During dinner, Katie's car windows frosted up, and she grew furious at Tim when they left the restaurant, as he climbed cluelessly inside the car, turned on the heat, and watched her scrape the ice. Still, she was persuaded to come back a few weeks later, and she hung out with Tim and Todd at the Firstie Club.

"You should date her," Todd started telling Tim after a few drinks, right in front of Katie, saying she was a big improvement over his other girlfriend. They were off and on for a bit, but when Katie went away to Spain for a summer semester abroad, Tim had realized he was smitten. They'd been together ever since.

Katie had been thrilled when Todd started dating Jen Reardon seriously, just so there was another noncadet girl to be friends with in the D-1 Duck social network. West Point was so Cinderella, Katie thought, belonging to a bygone age, and it helped to have someone else around to provide a civilian reality check. The academy buildings were big and elegant, and she heard constantly from Tim and other cadets about the distinguished lineage of West Point graduates. But the place was a little odd. Some of the cadets seemed so socially awkward. They were brilliant and motivated, yes, but not always wise to the ways of the world. Put them all together, though, and they fit perfectly, like a four-thousand-piece puzzle. And Katie was impressed at what West Point had done for Tim. The shy, retiring kid she'd known back in high school was emerging as a confident, self-assured man.

Todd was thrilled that during his penultimate semester he could finally focus on the classes that interested him most. Most promising was "Congress and the Legislative Process," a small seminar taught by a visiting professor, David Kozak, from Gannon University in Pennsylvania. Now fifty-six years old, retired from the Air Force, Kozak had been a missile officer, "the guy with the key around his neck," as he put it, at Strategic Air Command in the 1970s. But he'd managed to spend most of his active duty career teaching, first at the Air Force Academy, and then at the National War College in Washington.

For someone like Todd, with budding political aspirations, the course was a joy. One of Kozak's claims to fame was that he attracted high-end guest speakers to the classroom. At the National War College he'd brought in the chief justice of the U.S. Supreme Court, and former presidents Nixon, Ford, and Carter. Now his contacts were people more like the governor of Pennsylvania, Tom Ridge, and the highlight of the seminar would be a twenty-four-hour cadet trip to Washington to tour the Capitol and interview congressmen and journalists.

Kozak loved being at West Point, and he quickly noticed a handful of cadets with great potential. Among this group were Todd Bryant and Joe DaSilva, a diminutive kid from outside Boston. Earnest, motivated, and easy to talk with, Joe was the son of Portuguese immigrants and the first person in his family to go to college. He'd been elected president of the class of 2002 at the end of their second year, and with no further election scheduled, that pretty much made him class president for life.

Neither he nor Todd was a top academic—they were B students, mostly—but they had sky-high emotional intelligence. They "got" people, which made it much more likely that they would become exceptional leaders. Kozak felt qualified to make the prediction, for in thirty years in college and graduate school classrooms, he had taught some of the military's best leaders. The chairman of the Joint Chiefs of Staff, General Hugh Shelton, and West Point's highest-ranking general, a three-star officer named Daniel Christman, had both been his students. In fact, at one point in the 1990s, Kozak had realized that of the six officers then sitting on the Joint Chiefs, five were his former students. In any event, Todd and Joe were likable people, winners, the kinds of students Kozak was happy to see coming down the hallway to talk with him about a class discussion or ask for his help with an assignment.

One gorgeous September morning, Joe DaSilva was doing just that, heading up the stairs of Lincoln Hall to ask for Kozak's thoughts on a paper he was writing for class. As he came to the doorway he could see his professor was on the phone, nearly beside himself.

"My God!" Kozak practically shouted, still holding the phone. "Did you hear what happened?"

"What's going on?" Joe asked.

"A plane just hit the World Trade Center," Kozak exclaimed. He locked eyes with Joe. "This is going to change your career forever! This is going to change your career forever!"

For their grandparents' generation, the shared moment was the attack on Pearl Harbor. For their parents', it was the assassination of President Kennedy. For the West Point class of 2002, and for all Americans of their generation, the shared moment was the morning of September 11, 2001. The first hijacked jet had flown directly over the academy, just a few thousand feet off the ground, following the Hudson River to Manhattan.

The cadets' families were frantic, worried that the home to four thousand future Army officers might be the terrorists' next target. West Point went on lockdown. Drew Sloan's father sat in his university office in Arkansas, trying over and over to get through. In Boston, Jen Reardon called Todd every few minutes. The academy had cut off all civilian phones, and while Todd had a cell phone, reception was terrible in the old stone buildings. Finally, he reached Jen by instant message.

"I'm all right," he wrote. "As soon as I can call you, I will." Jen had never spoken with his parents, but he sent her their phone number and asked her to call. He was worried about his brother and sister, already serving in the military, and wondering what all this would mean for them.

"AND NOW, A BRIEF MESSAGE from the president of the United States, Todd J. Bryant."

The voice, off camera, was most likely Tim Moshier's. He had the video camera out again, and Todd filled the frame, sitting solemnly behind his desk in their dorm room.

About fifteen hours had passed since the attacks. It was late now, and the cadets were angry, eager, and still shocked. News had spread that a company mate of Drew Sloan's in H-2 had a brother who had worked at Cantor Fitzgerald at the World Trade Center; he was presumed dead. The cadets were grateful that they were in the military, proud that they were part of the mighty force that would guard the country and exact revenge on whoever had done this.

But first, Todd had to be Todd.

He sat at the desk, channeling President George W. Bush. In the coming days, Bush would give the best speeches of his political career, but in the hours after the attack, his words had seemed hesitant and uninspiring. Todd thought he understood how it should have been done.

"My fellow Americans," he began solemnly, as if addressing the nation from the Oval Office. "To the people of New York and to all Americans who are hurting at this tragic time, you can rest assured that anything and everything that can be done to ensure the safety of our country will be done. This is the greatest country in the world and we will get through this trying time. Now is the time for all people to set aside our differences and show the world that no one or nothing can destroy the fortitude of the American people."

He had it down perfectly, the pacing, the tone, the gaze just perceptibly off camera toward an imaginary TelePrompTer. "To the people responsible for today's tragedy," he continued, "I say this . . ."

Todd leaped from his chair, sliding the desk forward and lunging toward the camera. "Are you fucking kidding me?" he screamed. "Do you know who you are fucking with? Americans are so hungry to kill, we shoot each other every day! We are dying to have new targets. Have you forgotten what happened to the last people who started fucking with us? We slapped them all over the Pacific!"

He was on a roll now. "Go ahead and try to hide, bin Laden. We are America! We kick ass! This is what we do!"

Then he sat back down in the chair, regaining his composure and channeling Bush once more.

"Thank you," he said calmly. "And God bless America."

DREW SLOAN HAD been in a tiny office updating the information on his Army life insurance policy, of all things, when he first heard about the

9/11 attacks. Now he thought back to the night before the Ring Weekend dance, to being with Chloe Hayes and her friends on New York Harbor. He remembered staring straight at the skyline of lower Manhattan, how beautiful it was. But he didn't remember the Twin Towers. He had had no reason to notice them until they were gone.

A week after the attacks, the West Point schedule called for the firsties to rank the branches they wanted to serve in. Drew was still set on the infantry, but he wanted to learn enough about the other branches to make intelligent second and third choices. His old roommate, the practical-minded Dave Swanson, put in for military intelligence. He could always request to be loaned to the infantry in a "branch detail," and the idea of leading men in combat appealed to him. But he figured he'd learn marketable skills for the civilian world in a more technical branch, in case he decided to leave the Army after five years.

Todd Bryant had never wavered from his plan to be a tank officer. Will Tucker was set on branching armor as well. The two friends had once watched a documentary about armored warfare in Desert Storm, and they often talked about what it would be like to roll across an open desert and level America's enemies with the awesome firepower of their M1 Abrams tanks.

Tim Moshier wanted to fly helicopters. But another close friend from D-1 was having a tough time deciding. Eric Huss, an athletic Wisconsin native with an easy smile, had roomed with Todd during plebe year. He and Todd had matching tattoos on their left biceps: "SPQR," the mark that Roman legionnaires had worn two millennia before. The letters stood for "Senatus Populusque Romanus," or roughly, "The Senate and People of Rome." Originally the tattoo had enabled easy identification of military deserters, Eric had read, but over time it grew to represent the ideal of giving up one's freedoms—one's very self—for the greater glory of the state.

"We, too, are the poor saps who have given up our freedom for the glory of the state," Todd always said. Technology had changed, people had changed, even the nation-states to which they gave themselves had changed. But that fundamental social phenomenon, the honorable place of the professional soldier, endured.

Now, Eric was torn. He'd been just as eager as Todd and Will, talking—fantasizing, really—about the giant tank battles of the Persian Gulf War. But he was also contemplating the infantry. It was Tim Moshier who came up with a simple way to decide.

"We're going to flip a coin," he said. "Heads, you're going infantry. If it comes up tails, you're going armor."

It came up tails. Armor.

"All right," Eric agreed.

Tim was excited. "If you'd hesitated and said, 'No, let's do two out of three,' I would have told you to go infantry."

It was a great decision-making technique, Tim explained. He'd seen it on the TV show *Friends*.

IN THE DAYS following the terrorist attacks, rumors about how the academy would respond ran rampant. Some cadets believed the class of 2002 would graduate early, as had happened in World War II. Professors refocused their courses, quickly understanding that what had happened in New York, at the Pentagon, and in rural Pennsylvania would affect their students' futures far more than almost anything on the normal curriculum. Though the West Point superintendent volunteered the entire Corps of Cadets to head down to Ground Zero in New York to help out, more helping hands weren't needed on the site. Word came back about what was: socks. Firefighters and emergency workers changed their socks several times each shift as they got wet, and they were running out. So the cadets launched the Mother of All Sock Drives, gathering thousands of pairs.

All kinds of plans were put on hold, as academy security remained tight. Todd Bryant wanted to go to Boston to see Jen again, but he was told that this was now impossible. (Drew Sloan got special permission that same weekend to fly to Los Angeles for a wedding—H-2 really was luckier.) But as the weeks went by, an odd normalcy returned. The United States sent troops to Afghanistan to overthrow the Taliban and search for Osama bin Laden, and soon there was a sense that the fighting would be over by the time the class of 2002 graduated and really entered the Army. After they received their diplomas in the spring, they'd attend officer basic courses to learn the nuts and bolts of their Army specialties; they wouldn't actually reach their units until 2003 at the earliest. Besides, the United States hadn't fought a war that lasted more than a few months since Vietnam.

As the fall wore on, people remained on edge, but daily life plainly continued. "Tactical patience" became the superintendent's watchword. West Point's job was to do just what it had always done: prepare America's future officers to fight its future battles.

"Don't worry," some members of the class of 2001 wrote teasingly to their friends still at the academy. "We'll have this all taken care of by the time you graduate."

WEST POINT'S FOOTBALL GAME the Saturday after 9/11 was postponed, and the schedule was road-heavy after that. Not until several weeks later— after a 31–10 drubbing at the hands of Boston College, which Jen Reardon teased Todd about mercilessly—did the team play another game at the academy's Michie Stadium. Tim Moshier's parents, Jim and Mary Ellen, loved making the trek down from Albany for most home games, so they could tailgate with the D-1 Ducks. In fact, Tim had first visited the academy for a game back when he was in junior high. Hanging out with their son and his fellow Ducks, who called them Mom and Dad Mosh instead of Mr. and Mrs. Moshier, made for some of the best times of Tim's parents' lives. They'd slowly adopted his friends over the years, and when they set up their food and beer at the Army game against the University of Houston in October, it was a subtle sign that life was getting back to normal.

For lower-level cadets, football was one of the few sanctioned respites from academy life—mandatory fun, really—but as firsties, Todd, Tim, and the rest of them could drink beer legally and relax. The football programs at West Point and the Naval Academy had once been among the most powerful in the country; generations ago, the annual game between the service academies had occasionally doubled as the national championship. But those days were long gone. The first weekend of December, when virtually the entire Corps of Cadets headed to Philadelphia to watch their team take on the Naval Academy, it was a battle between a 2–8 West Point squad and an Annapolis team that had lost all of its games.

Still, Todd loved Army football. He almost seemed hurt when his friends didn't get into it quite as much as he did, or cheer quite as loud, even when rooting to beat the winless Navy squad. (That fall, Army did win, 26–17.) When Jen thumbed through his spiral school notebooks, she found them virtually devoid of class notes. Instead, they were filled with creative football plays, and even a schematic drawing of an SUV designed specifically for tailgating at games.

"How do you even pass your classes when there's no notes in here?" she said.

"It's all right," Todd said with a smile, tapping his forehead. "It's all up here."

PROFESSOR KOZAK NEARLY CANCELED the long-planned Washington trip for his class. Besides the 9/11 attacks, letters containing anthrax had been sent to the offices of prominent journalists and Democratic senators, and five people were dead. In that environment, with the U.S. Capitol on virtual lockdown for months, Kozak doubted he could arrange the high-level visits to members of Congress and senior administration officials that he had counted on. But West Point's top generals and the department chair encouraged him to go ahead. He bused thirty of his students down to Washington—Todd among them—and checked them all into the Hyatt Regency hotel on Capitol Hill.

That evening, Kozak walked them to a spot in the shadow of the Supreme Court and the Senate office buildings, where they could look up Pennsylvania Avenue to the west and see the White House. It was a remarkable vantage point, and as the group of cadets stood there in the crisp dark air, within view of the symbols of all three branches of government, they were awed. The next morning, they had a tight schedule, starting with a tour of C-SPAN and interviews with the author of the book they'd been using in class. Then it was off to the Capitol to meet with a handful of representatives, and the House sergeant at arms.

Though they were only in Washington for a day, Todd was in heaven, soaking in the aura of the nation's capital. He bought a postcard with a photograph of the Capitol Dome from the reflecting pool on the National Mall, and addressed it to Jen in Boston.

"Here is a picture of where I hope to be working someday," he wrote. "I promise to take you there. Of course, that may lead to a session of me talking your ear off. I miss you sweetie and I can't wait to hold you again. You're getting a big hug at the train station, and a kiss or 50. I love you."

He signed it "Always, Your Todd."

☆ 3 ☆

Jen Reardon went out to California with Todd for the Bryant family Christmas in December 2001. They hit Disneyland, and an annual California military ball that Linda and Larry liked to attend. Todd's sister, Tiffany, surprised her family by coming home from Korea, and the fact that Jen knew all about it before Todd but kept the secret—the parents of Todd and Jen's mutual friend, Ryan Poe, had picked up Tiffany at the airport—earned her points in Tiffany's book. Todd and some other California cadets marched in the Rose Bowl Parade near Todd's high school on New Year's Day, and they were in the stands for the national collegiate football championship two days later.

Todd was still talking marriage, and Jen almost expected to fly back east with a diamond ring on her finger, but he hadn't saved enough money to buy one yet. He gave her an Irish Claddagh ring as a promise ring; as it happened, she'd bought him a very similar one as a Christmas present. Neither of them had any real doubt about what was coming. Back at school in the start of 2002, they talked constantly, and they saw each other every other weekend. They would instant-message for hours each night, and Jen saved every transcript in a Microsoft Word file. Occasionally, her computer would crash, and she'd ask Todd to e-mail the transcripts to her.

"Why?" he complained. Sentimental as he was, this seemed over the top. "It's going to be so boring to go back and read them."

No, Jen replied. When they were old and gray, they'd be happy to have them. Their kids might someday appreciate being able to look back and see what their parents were like when they were young, silly, and in love. "It will be fun," she told him. "You'll see."

BY FEBRUARY, Drew Sloan knew he had his infantry slot. So did Joe DaSilva. In fact, in the wake of 9/11 the Army had given infantry to each of the more than two hundred West Point cadets who put it as their first choice, bumping ROTC cadets around the country into field artillery and military police. General Abizaid had moved on from the academy to command an Army division, but his replacement at West Point, a one-star general named Eric Olson, gave a rousing pep talk the night the cadets learned their assignments. "It is freedom that works miracles in the United States of America," said the new commandant. "And it is freedom that is being threatened, that is under attack. It's freedom that you are sworn to defend. And tonight you take another decision on the path to serve this nation, to protect that freedom."

There wasn't an unmotivated cadet in the hall afterward. A thousand firsties opened white envelopes at the same time to find the insignia that indicated what branch of the Army they were going into. Todd Bryant, Will Tucker, and Eric Huss got tanks, and Tim Moshier got his shot at flight school. Dave Swanson got his second choice, signal corps, but he put in for his branch detail with the infantry. For all intents and purposes he'd be a ground-pounder, going through school at Fort Benning, Georgia, and leading an infantry platoon.

Now, on another cold night in February, the cadets broke up into smaller groups to find out where they'd be stationed. Firsties chose their posts in order of their standing in class, and Drew—still sporting the stars on his collar that signified his high academic rank—had a good shot at going anywhere he wanted. His first choice was one of the least popular, though: Fort Hood, Texas. Drew's mom, Vicky, had grown up in Houston, so he had a family connection, but it was more that he'd simply liked the place during his short time there in summer 2001. The sprawling base an hour or two northwest of Austin was home to two large divisions, and there were plenty of places for lieutenants.

Drew's friends thought he was crazy. Why go to Fort Hood when you could head for the beaches of Hawaii, or pack up for Italy or Germany and spend every long weekend in Paris or Prague? Drew tried without success to convince his closest friends to go with him to Texas. In the end he changed his mind, and put in for Hawaii and the 25th Infantry Division, a unit that hadn't seen combat since 1971.

Because Tim Moshier got aviation, he didn't get to pick a post. He was headed to Fort Rucker, Alabama, for a year and a half of flight school; only when he was a qualified pilot would he be assigned to a unit. Todd, Will, and Eric sat in another large classroom among the 117 firsties who had been assigned to the armor branch. In a perfect world, Todd wanted Germany, and he knew that Jen was excited about the possibility of living a glamorous life abroad for a few years. But with a B average and a middling class rank, an assignment in Europe was a long shot. Todd, Will, and Eric were ranked within a half dozen slots of one another. They had little chance at the Army's best posts, but a decent likelihood of being assigned together.

The first-ranked cadet in the room stood up.

"Germany," he said, to cheers and groans, and an Army officer crossed off a slot on an overhead screen. One by one, the firsties picked their stations, and soon the glory posts disappeared. Finally, it was Will Tucker's turn. Fort Stewart, Georgia, wasn't supposed to be a bad place, home of the 3rd Infantry Division and not far from Savannah, a city of maybe 130,000 people. Will picked it—and so did the couple of cadets behind him. By the time Todd and Eric got their turn, Fort Stewart was gone.

"Do you want to go to Fort Hood?" Eric asked Todd just before he picked. "Or do you want to go to Fort Riley?"

Riley was in Kansas, pretty much the absolute middle of nowhere, home to units in the 1st Armored and 1st Infantry Divisions. Nevertheless, Todd had heard from someone that it was a decent post, "the best-kept secret in the Army."

"I have no desire whatsoever to go to Texas," Todd said. "Let's go to Riley."

EARLY MARCH BROUGHT 100TH NIGHT, a countdown of the days to graduation and the biggest social event of the cadets' careers. There was a formal dinner and dance, but the highlight was a sort of all-cadet revue, a roast making fun of their four years at West Point and the officer and cadet personalities they all knew so well.

Drew Sloan had kept in touch with Chloe Hayes, but she was a thousand miles away, so he went to the dance with a fellow firstie. Drew and Shannon McCartan had first met while she was dating a friend of his during the summer of 2001, and they'd later seen each other again when she came to the H-2 Halloween party. Shannon was from Pittsburgh, an American politics major and another of Professor Kozak's favorites. Any relationship between Drew and Shannon had a practical expiration date, though, since Shannon had landed in military intelligence and would be heading to Arizona for training after graduation.

Todd Bryant, meanwhile, had much bigger plans. Jen came down and they took a room at the Waldorf-Astoria in Manhattan the night before the event. The next morning, he led her on a walk around the city, stopping at a Dunkin' Donuts for a quick breakfast, and nonchalantly suggesting that they eat in nearby Bryant Park, behind the New York Public Library. As they sat on a bench, Todd pulled a blue box with a white ribbon from his pocket. He had finally saved enough money, and his hand was shaking.

Jen just sat and stared.

"If you don't open it," Todd said, "I can't ask."

He dropped to one knee and asked Jen to be his wife. She held out her hand, tears streaming but still speechless, as Todd slipped the ring on her finger.

A voice from another bench, pure New Yorker, called out, "I can't tell if she said yes!"

Jen laughed, leaped forward, and threw her arms around Todd.

"Yes!" she screamed.

She was his focus now. Again and again for the rest of the semester, they traveled between West Point and Boston. Jen was the great joy of Todd's high-spirited life. They had been raised in different religions—Todd had grown up Presbyterian, and Jen was Catholic. But Todd understood it was important to Jen to get married in her church, and so he arranged for them to take the required "Pre-Cana" marriage preparation course through the Catholic chapel at the academy before he graduated.

In one of his academic courses, Todd was assigned to write a series of reflections on who he believed he was and what he wanted his role to be in the world. A running theme was his desire to emulate the Tralfamadorians of Kurt Vonnegut's *Slaughterhouse-Five*, an alien race born able to see every scene of their lives, but also able to focus their attention on the best moments. Todd's plan was to "have as many fun experiences as possible," he wrote, "and not let the bad experiences get to me."

In the same essay, he wrote about his siblings in the military and his realization that after 9/11, the Army would be different from what he had once envisioned. He no longer imagined "sitting behind a desk, hoping for a chance to lead," as it seemed an entire generation of officers before him had done. Instead, he foresaw that he would likely be "seeing the world through the sights of a 120-millimeter cannon," the main gun on the M1 Abrams tank.

But his life had been changed most by the fact that he was now engaged to Jen. "This means I have had to become less selfish with my life goals," he wrote, "as the 'us' is more important than I am."

With just a few weeks left at West Point, Todd wanted Jen to experience as much as she could of what his life had been like at the academy. She even sat in on some of his classes. One afternoon, she attended Professor Kozak's seminar.

"You're a pretty lady, but I question your judgment," Kozak told her in front of the class. "Is this the best you could do? I recommend you live some place cold, with a lot of snow, because he's not very bright. But he can shovel snow. You might as well get some work out of him." Kozak had been meeting cadets and their fiancées for more than three decades, and he waited for the laughs he knew would come from his playful jokes at Todd's expense.

"No," he continued when the class died down. "He's a first-rate person. You've got a great guy there. I hope you guys are as happy as my wife and I are."

The de facto West Point rule about bringing buddies to visit girlfriends at distant colleges was still in effect, and so when Todd went to visit Jen now, Will Tucker was his most constant road-trip companion. On one of the last weekends of firstie year, Todd, Jen, and Will kicked back in Jen's apartment watching the 2001 movie *Pearl Harbor*. The film's improbable plot involved a soldier who winds up with his best friend's girlfriend, after he and the girl mistakenly believe the friend has been killed in action.

The story seemed completely ridiculous, and Todd kept up a running commentary, reacting indignantly to each melodramatic line of dialogue.

Jen turned to Will. "If Todd went away to war and didn't come home," she started to ask, teasingly—

"No," Will quickly said. He didn't like the joke, didn't like even contemplating that anything could happen to him or his friends. He started to give her a longer answer, but Todd jumped in.

"You make sure you see a body before you do anything like that!" he bellowed at Jen in mock indignation. Then he spun toward Will: "And you! You keep your hands off of her!"

But later, back at West Point, Todd took Will aside for a more serious conversation along the same lines. Graduation was now only weeks away, and as unreal as it might seem, they could be at war themselves within a year.

"If anything ever happens to me," Todd told his friend, "I want you to make sure Jen is okay."

TODD HAD BEEN ASSIGNED as a member of his cadet battalion staff in the class of 2002's final semester. Tim Moshier was assigned as a cadet platoon leader—ironically, this made him the man who had to inspect other cadets' rooms—and he reported in turn to Tricia LeRoux, the cadet company commander.

The Army was filled with soldiers who had followed their fathers into the service, but Tricia, a long-distance specialist on the academy swim team, was part of a rare demographic: a female cadet whose mother had served, but whose father had not. Her mom had taken a direct commission in the Army Nurse Corps in 1989, part of a plan to help her family move on from their small hometown. They'd traded Wisconsin winters for Hawaiian sun, and her mother now planned to stay in the military until retirement. Tricia wore a perpetual smile that belied her inner toughness, and she was well regarded as a natural leader. She had chosen to serve in the Army Medical Service Corps after graduation, primarily because she figured it was one of the few branches in which a female officer could be virtually assured of leading a platoon for a long time.

Todd and Tricia had been close friends since plebe year, when Todd and Eric Huss had lived in the room directly above Tricia and Kara Pond. Tricia found Todd hilarious. She marveled at the fact that during Christmas break of their junior year, he had traveled nearly one hundred and forty miles round-trip from Riverside to the Los Angeles airport when she had a layover on the way to Hawaii, just so he could take her to the drive-through at In-N-Out Burger and prove to her that in California, even the fast food was better.

With only a few weeks to go until commencement, anticipation was high, but so was the cadets' dread that something might happen to derail their graduation. Tricia and her close friends were rarely in any real trouble, but as company commander, she had to stand in mid-May with the active-duty Army captain in charge of D-1, disciplining four cadets who had been caught downloading enormous amounts of pornography over the academy computer servers. Their punishments would include "walking hours," and since two of the cadets were firsties who had to clear up all of their disciplinary infractions before they could graduate, the scramble was on to figure out how to fit all the hours in before the end of May.

Tricia listened awkwardly as the captain read the details of the cadets' formal offenses to them, including the names of the websites they'd been caught visiting. Some of the sites sounded mild—they evoked pictures of girls in bikinis reclining on the hoods of sports cars—but the names of others were so explicit that she could barely bring herself to read them.

One underclassman's computer logs revealed he had visited hundreds and hundreds of porn sites in a single evening.

"How is that even possible?" Tricia wanted to know.

"Pop-ups," he explained sheepishly.

BOTH DREW SLOAN'S PARENTS and his maternal grandparents had divorced during his time at West Point, and Graduation Week was the first time he had to juggle his newly splintered family. To make things even more awkward, his father, his father's parents, his mother, and the friends his mother had brought with her all landed in New York on the same flight. There was Drew, meeting them at the airport, suddenly an adult. He hugged his mom hello and made sure she got her rental car, and then drove back with his dad and his paternal grandparents.

So many parents and friends wanted to throw so many parties and dinners for the graduating cadets that it was soon clear why Graduation Week had expanded into a ten- to fourteen-day affair. That night, Drew and his dad attended a dinner at the restaurant at the Culinary Institute of America, with some of Drew's best friends and their families—among them Ryan Beltramini, who had been in all the honors plebe-year classes with him. Vicky Sloan had wanted to host something huge. But Drew was running out of days, and so she co-hosted a big party the following night with one of Drew's mentors, a retired Air Force colonel and West Point benefactor named John Kelly.

A Vietnam veteran and former C-130 pilot who had left the military after twenty-three years for a successful career in business, Kelly had a quasi-official role making sure that the handful of West Point cadets who were taking their commissions in the Air Force instead of the Army had some exposure to that service's culture before they made the choice. Kelly had met Joe DaSilva and another infantry-bound cadet named Carter Smyth at a West Point football game in the first half of the year, and soon it seemed he was acting as a counselor and guide to half of the highest-ranking firsties in the cadet chain of command. He offered them his season tickets when the New York Yankees were in the American League playoffs, and it was Kelly they'd call for advice on where to buy a diamond ring if they decided to get engaged. In the patriotic aura that had descended on America after the 9/11 attacks, being around West Point felt good, like being part of the military again. Kelly was the type of man who seemed never to have met a stranger, and he had a lot of respect for the cadets—younger versions of himself—who had volunteered to train and lead the next generation of soldiers.

Drew was a charter member of the Colonel John Kelly fan club, and the colonel and his mother hosted a phenomenal dinner, at an Italian restaurant in Tarrytown, about fifty miles from the academy. What with Drew, Carter, the other cadets, and their friends and families, Vicky Sloan and John Kelly wound up splitting a check for forty people.

THE NEXT DAY, the Friday before graduation, Jen Reardon sat in the stands watching as Todd and his class marched in their final parade. The entire Corps of Cadets—four thousand strong, plebes through graduating firsties—marched in front of their family and friends, and stopped. Then the class of 2002 marched forward, separating from their fellow students and taking a symbolic step toward their new lives. Jen was so proud of Todd and what he had accomplished. She could barely pick him out in the great mass of gray uniforms, but she knew he was probably choking back tears and trying to remain stone-faced.

That evening brought still another big dinner—white dress uniforms, gold tablecloths, red roses—this one with New York City mayor Rudy Giuliani as West Point's guest of honor. Drew finally had both parents together at one table, along with a cousin who had flown in from London and was more like a sister to him. Todd, Will Tucker, Tim Moshier, Eric Huss, and their families were stuck way in the back, so they couldn't actually see Giuliani as he spoke, but his stature post–9/11 was so high among the cadets that they were honored just to be in the same room. Besides, they were having a blast. Afterward, the Ducks and their families kept the party going until late. They hit a middle-of-nowhere bar that Todd and Eric had first discovered during an illicit off-campus trip their second year, and stayed up half the night.

Because he was on the battalion staff now, Todd had lived away from the Ducks from January to May, and so Tim had roomed with Eric for their final semester. Eric ran their room like boot camp, pushing and cajoling Tim to work out and go running or swimming virtually every day. This was a welcome change for Tim's girlfriend, Katie, who appreciated seeing her man in better shape.

Tim and Eric had packed up and everything they owned into their cars that last full day, right down to their wool blankets, and parked the cars in a secret spot where they were pretty sure West Point security wouldn't bother them. Only two sets of uniforms remained unpacked: the gray cadet garb they would wear in the graduation ceremony, and the green polyester-blend Army "class As" that they would put on a few hours later for their commissioning ceremonies. The plan was to get their room inspected immediately after graduation and then leave campus as fast as possible, thereby avoiding being stuck in line behind dozens or even hundreds of their classmates. It had all seemed perfect, until they woke up on the chilly morning of June 1, shivering and stiff, with their arms aching from pulling the thin sheets over their shoulders all night.

Todd's parents, his brother and sister, and Jen were on campus almost before dawn. The Moshiers, along with Katie McKee, had awakened at four A.M., anticipating lots of extra time for security, crowds, and the long walk to Michie Stadium, where the commencement would take place. Linda Bryant was beaming and excited to be at her second West Point graduation in two years, and to realize that by the end of the day, every member of the Bryant family would have served as commissioned officers in the U.S. military. "Very right-wing, patriotic, and conservative," as Linda described herself, she'd been less thrilled in 2000, when the speaker at Tiffany's commencement had been Vice President Al Gore. But she was happier today, for President Bush would address Todd's class. By tradition, the commander-in-chief gave the speech at one military academy each year, but as a post–9/11 security precaution, West Point hadn't confirmed until two days before that

Bush was coming. The rumor was that Army and Navy had traded speakers for 2002 so that Bush could address the bicentennial class.

Tim Moshier's mother walked down the hill toward the stadium feeling a bit anxious. For four years, she had thought of the academy as a serene oasis, walled off from the dangers of the world. As long as Tim was here, she felt he was safe, away from the Army and from all the trouble he could have gotten into at a civilian college. But today things seemed so different, and the security enhancements for the president's arrival were unnerving, with hovering helicopters and sharpshooters on the roofs. A contingent of U.S. Army Rangers was fanned around the field, adding an extra layer of protection. And she was worried by more than physical danger. What might witnessing the horrors of war do to Tim's gentle personality? It was a gift to be so easygoing and to see the world as Tim did, and she hoped he would never lose it.

Mary Ellen Moshier reached the metal detectors and had a sudden fright, as she realized she was carrying a corkscrew in her purse. She could almost see the headline in the next day's paper: WOMAN RUNS OUT OF CROWD, CORKSCREW IN HAND, TO ATTACK THE PRESIDENT. She breathed deeply as she watched the guards confiscate baby formula from the woman in front of her, but they barely even looked in her purse, and she walked right in.

THE CADETS GATHERED by eight in the morning, a gray sea in the large field just south of Michie Stadium. In their heavy wool uniforms, with the sun beating down, it felt much hotter than the official temperature. Hungover firsties held on to one another, trying hard to stay upright.

An officer called the roll, nearly a thousand graduates. Word trickled through the formation that some poor soul in the first battalion had learned only then that he wasn't getting his diploma. "Cooperate and graduate" was one of the West Point clichés, the idea that all the cadets were in it together. But at this late date, the rest of the class just huddled under the sun, trading jokes and memories, and thanking God the unlucky one wasn't them.

Air Force One touched down at a nearby Air National Guard base, and after a quick greeting to the small crowd, President Bush and the First Lady were ushered to a helicopter for the short trip south to the academy. The cadets marched into the stadium and took their places on the field, a few yards and four long years from where they'd been sworn into the Army for the first time together as scared new cadets. As the president and Mrs. Bush walked onto the stage, the band played "Hail to the Chief." When it became clear that they wouldn't reach center stage before the tribute was done, the band simply played it a second time. Finally, Bush reached the podium, to thunderous cheers. A contingent of spectators began to cheer, "U-S-A! U-S-A!" Later, when the official transcript of Bush's address was released, it included thirty-two interruptions for applause.

In the wake of 9/11, George W. Bush had enjoyed some of the highest approval ratings any president had ever had. Though the numbers had slipped a bit, more than seventy percent of the American people still said in surveys that they approved of the job he was doing. His speech was epic, by design. His speechwriter, Michael Gerson, thought it was the most important thing he'd ever worked on. Gerson normally watched Bush's speeches on television, but today he'd come with the president because he wanted to see and hear history live, as it happened. Bush's advisers had picked the locale carefully: West Point was the perfect venue for Bush to deliver one of his most important addresses, in which he would fundamentally challenge the American foreign policy mind-set that had dominated since the end of World War II.

After congratulating the "Golden Children of the Corps" to great cheers, he started into his speech. "In your last year, America was attacked by a ruthless and resourceful enemy," Bush said. "You graduate from this academy in a time of war, taking your place in an American military that is powerful and is honorable. Our war on terror is only begun."

Jen Reardon was exhausted, and it frustrated her that once again she had a hard time picking out Todd from his classmates, all identically dressed in gray. Until now, she'd barely listened to a word Bush had said, but then she was suddenly alert. Those five words echoed in her brain: "In a time of war . . ." She had always been able to imagine that there was a difference between the West Point Army that Todd served in—with its dress uniforms, parades, and formal dinners—and the Army of tanks and camouflage that fought in places like Afghanistan and might now be called to fight somewhere else. The president of the United States, of all people, had shattered her illusion.

"For much of the last century, America's defense relied on the Cold War doctrines of deterrence and containment," Bush continued. "But new threats also require new thinking. Deterrence—the promise of massive retaliation against nations—means nothing against shadowy terrorist networks with no nation or citizens to defend. Containment is not possible. . . . If we wait for threats to fully materialize, we will have waited too long."

Jen was listening to every syllable now. "The war on terror will not be won on the defensive. We must take the battle to the enemy, disrupt his plans, and confront the worst threats before they emerge. In the world we have entered, the only path to safety is the path of action. And this nation will act."

DOWN ON THE FIELD, Bush's words barely registered with most of the cadets. They were tired, lightheaded, and baking in their high-collared uniforms. Besides, they had been living with the likelihood of war since 9/11. Most had presumed "war" would mean fighting Osama bin Laden and the Taliban in Afghanistan, but if the plan was to strike at terrorists somewhere else, so be it.

A cadet dropped his Army-issued ceremonial saber on the metal benches, making a horrendous racket. Other cadets strategized how to beat the long line to return the sabers after the ceremony. A few decided simply to buy the damn things at $200 each, rather than wait an hour or more in line.

The sun beat down, and some cadets seemed to be falling asleep. But among the throng, a few realized the importance of what Bush was saying. Eric Huss was one. He stopped applauding and paid rapt attention, sucking in the meaning behind the rhetoric. The longer the speech went on, the louder and clearer was its message. The president was signaling a voluntary war. And he and his friends—Todd, Tim, Will, and the others around them—would be doing the fighting.

ON STAGE AS CLASS PRESIDENT, Joe DaSilva had extra duties. He'd been Mayor Giuliani's military escort at the graduation dinner the night before, and now he would present the class gift to the president. He could hardly believe how close he was to history, and he was excited and proud. Bush finished his speech—again to riotous applause—and DaSilva marched forward to give him one of the cadet swords.

"God bless you for what you do," Bush said as he shook Joe's hand. "Be ready."

Joe was suddenly overcome with the understanding that he was now a second lieutenant in the U.S. Army, and that the commander-in-chief had just given him a direct order.

The cadets marched up one by one to receive their diplomas. Bush was scheduled to greet only the first hundred cadets, but he remained onstage and shook hands with all of them. Tim Moshier was surprised to find that he towered over the president. Bush looked a lot taller on television, Tim thought.

"Go get 'em," Bush repeated to the cadets again and again as he handed them their diplomas. "Take care of those soldiers."

"We're ready to go where you need us, sir," one graduating cadet told him.

"That's good, son," the president replied. "Because we're going to kick their asses."

"Mr. President," another new lieutenant asked, "could I give you a chest butt?"

"Bring it," Bush replied, and braced himself. He and the young officer, a former enlisted paratrooper in the 82nd Airborne, leaped at each other, crashing sternums like NFL players celebrating a touchdown. The crowd loved it.

· ✦ ·

THE ANNOUNCEMENT of each classmate's name launched an artillery barrage of emotion and half-forgotten memories for Drew Sloan. He perked up as he heard the name of a girl he'd had a crush on in his second year, and laughed when he heard the announcement for "Timothy . . . J. . . . Moshier . . ." Tim had been in honors plebe English with Drew and Ryan Beltramini. For some reason, the professor had gently teased Tim all semester, referring to the most intense, passionate variety of romantic love in literature as "Capital L Tim Moshier Love."

But it also struck Drew how few of his classmates he actually knew. Cadets had their little worlds, their groups of friends and acquaintances. Who you got to know was, to a large extent, utterly random. Take Drew and his plebe-year roommate, Dave Swanson, who sat next to him now. Because of the system by which the companies were arranged, he and Dave would be third and second to last in the entire class to be called to get their diplomas. If not for an accident of the alphabet, and the fact that West Point had more or less arbitrarily put them in a room together, would they have even known each other?

Dave was too preoccupied for that kind of reflection. His Ford Escort was packed to the gills and parked illegally; he'd relied on nothing but the good graces of campus security to prevent it from being towed away. Now he was having second thoughts about the wisdom of where he'd left it. With each second the ceremony dragged on, it seemed less likely his car would still be waiting for him.

Finally Drew's name was called, and then Dave's. Then the last cadet in the long gray line, Emily Wnuk, one of 123 female graduates, shook the president's hand and got her diploma.

THE CLASSIC FRONT-PAGE NEWSPAPER photograph the next day would be of the cadets launching their caps in joy and relief at the end of the ceremony. Most had bought new hats for the occasion, and they stuck money, notes, and other trinkets in the linings. Kids would charge the field to pick up the tossed caps; it was yet another tradition. Tim Moshier was an exception. Early that morning, he'd realized he was broke—he had packed his money with everything else in his car—and he had nothing to put in his cap.

"Cheapskate," Katie McKee said after he told her.

The ecstatic graduates threw their caps, and they seemed to freeze in the air for just a millisecond, separating the before in the new lieutenants' lives from the after. Then they fell, and the glad-handing grads were joined on the field by a throng of children, snatching up the minor treasures.

After the ceremony, Tiffany and Tim Bryant stood in the stands, both wearing full dress uniforms, scanning the field and trying to find their brother. Tiffany looked very official in her paratrooper uniform with a maroon beret and jump boots—she was assigned now to the XVIII Airborne Corps at Fort Bragg, North Carolina—and she hopped over the fence and onto the field. But Todd found her first, jumping on Tiffany's back as soon as he saw her. A little later, Major Tim Bryant of the Marine Corps swore Todd into the Army. He and Jen Reardon each pinned a gold second lieutenant's bar—a "butterbar," in Army slang—on the shoulders of his uniform, as Linda and Larry Bryant watched with pride. Tiffany followed, pinning the last remaining insignia of rank on his cap.

Dave Swanson flat-out missed his commissioning, having run off to check on his car. Sure enough, it had been towed, and he spent half the day trying to get it out of hock. One of his favorite professors stood there waiting on the banks of the Hudson with Dave's gold bars, and he didn't find out for two years what had happened.

Drew Sloan and his H-2 friend Brian Oman were sworn into the Army by Brian's father, a colonel in the air defense artillery who had nearly twenty-five years in uniform. A few hours later, around four P.M., Brian and his girlfriend, Ellen, set out for her parents' house in Poughkeepsie. As they drove up Storm King Mountain on Route 9W, he asked her to pull over. It was the last and highest point on the road from which you could see West Point.

Brian got out of the car and looked back at the campus, the left half of his face sunburned after facing in the same direction under the sun in Michie Stadium for so long. He couldn't remember when he had felt so free. He couldn't believe it was over, finally over.

But it wasn't over, not for any of them. In fact, it had only begun.

★ **4** ★

West Point cadets were prohibited from getting married, so every year the academy's chapels ran back-to-back-to-back ceremonies starting right after graduation and all through the day Sunday. Two of Drew Sloan's friends' weddings were scheduled at the same time. He went to the ceremony for one at the Catholic chapel, and then hurried over to the other friend's reception. Todd Bryant flew to Fort Lewis, near Seattle, where Tricia LeRoux would be walking down the aisle. He'd told her he'd make the three-thousand-mile trek on two conditions: She had to have an open bar, and she had to let him be the one to slap her on the butt with his saber as part of the ceremonial sword arch, a military tradition.

Tricia and her new husband, Toby Birdsell, a quiet, intense classmate destined for the infantry, had had a short and intense courtship. They'd met on an internship in Washington the summer before firstie year, and had gotten engaged by Christmas. After training, they would begin their military careers in Germany. Both twenty-two, they were among the older West Point couples. One 2002 West Point graduate married the nineteen-year-old daughter of a professor the day after graduation.

One reason so many lieutenants married young was West Point's cultural experience, with its four years of indoctrination in the values of tradition, honor, and commitment. But another reason was pragmatism. The Army had strict rules about its soldiers' personal relationships, and it didn't legally recognize boyfriends, girlfriends, significant others, or even fiancées. (When the Pentagon announced a blanket ban on dating and sex between officers and enlisted soldiers in 1999, unmarried couples were offered a choice between breaking up and getting married "prior to 1 Mar 00.") So, if the new lieutenants wanted any support for their love lives, they had to get hitched. Officers whose brides were civilians (it was a rare female officer who married a civilian man) got extra pay and upgraded housing, and soldiers married to other soldiers could usually arrange to be stationed together.

After graduation, Todd moved temporarily into Jen Reardon's apartment at Boston College. She had another year of school, and their wedding was still in the early planning stages. Tim Moshier came up for the Fourth of July; they went to the Boston Pops concert, and Todd and Tim teased Jen in front of a crowd at Kenmore Square by serenading her with "You've Lost That Lovin' Feeling," imitating the scene from the movie *Top Gun*. Tim's parents had a house on Cape Cod; Katie McKee came out for a visit, the first time she'd ever really hung out like that with Tim's family. They all got along fine. When Todd and Tim came back from a round of golf, they found Katie, Jen, and Tim's mom and sister laughing and buzzed after a day of beach and booze. The party kept going, culminating with late-night skinny-dipping in the Atlantic Ocean.

Still, every once in a while something would remind them all of the line of work Todd and Tim had chosen. There'd be a story on TV about the death of a soldier in Afghanistan, for example. And then one of their West Point classmates, a well-liked cadet named Zac Miller, was killed in a training accident at Fort Benning. Later, especially when they were out with friends who weren't military, someone would always ask Todd and Tim about the war in Afghanistan, or whether they thought the United States would invade Iraq, or just how dangerous things might be for them and their friends. Todd would answer quickly, and then just as quickly change the subject. He was a Tralfamadorian, after all, and he refused to spend his few weeks of freedom worrying about things he couldn't control.

DREW SLOAN HAD KNOWN Zac Miller well. They'd spent many hours at West Point talking about the Army, religion, and the meaning of life. Drew and Zac had both been interested in Shannon McCartan, and they'd sparred a bit in the final weeks of firstie year, although they had a long talk the night before graduation and parted as friends. Even at a competitive college like West Point, Zac had stood out. Top of his class in math, and captain of the Army rugby team, he'd been at Fort Benning so soon after graduation only because he was leaving for Oxford as a Rhodes Scholar in the fall, and he wanted to get through Ranger School first.

Drew's summer had been hectic. He and Shannon had had a rocky, on-again, off-again relationship. Now they'd started dating for real, but Drew wanted to pack in as much fun as possible before he began his life in the infantry. New lieutenants picked the day they would start officer basic school on the basis of their class rank; Drew was taking sixty days of leave before reporting to Fort Benning, the maximum allowed. He and Ryan Beltramini went to Cape Cod as well, where John Kelly, the retired Air Force colonel, had invited some of his favorite graduates to spend a few days vacationing together. It took about an hour (or, as Kelly put it, "about three beers") to cruise to Nantucket from Kelly's house on the coast, and he loaded the cadets and their girlfriends—Drew was with Shannon, and Ryan was with Alisha Wassenaar, a student at Texas Christian University whom he'd met at a West Point football game—in his twenty-eight-foot Bertram Flybridge cruiser. Ryan and Drew disappeared with the girls almost as soon as they docked, while Kelly and a couple of the single cadets—Carter Smyth and another new officer who had cross-commissioned in the Air Force—hit some of the bars downtown. By the time they bought a case of beer and made it back to the boat, they found Drew and Ryan genteelly sipping wine with their girlfriends.

"Let me ask you something, Carter," Kelly said, loud enough for Drew and Ryan to hear, and pointing at the other cadet with the case of Heineken on his shoulder. "Which guys are going in the Army, and which are going in the Air Force?"

From there, Drew toured Greece for ten days with his mother. Then he climbed into his dark red Toyota 4Runner, still loaded with virtually everything he'd ever owned as a cadet, and drove to Pittsburgh to meet up with Shannon once again. She'd been traveling with her family in Ireland while Drew was in Greece, and they now planned to drive cross-country together. Drew would drop Shannon off at Fort Huachuca, in the southern Arizona desert, where she would start her military intelligence training, and then head back east to Fort Benning for the infantry officer basic course.

They learned about Zac Miller on the road, when Shannon's mom called in tears. The McCartans and the Millers were from the same part of Pennsylvania and knew each other well. As Drew and Shannon flew back east for the funeral, information about what had happened began trickling in. Zac, they learned, had been found dead from dehydration on a land navigation exercise. The idea that somebody in their class—let alone Zac—could die of such a vague cause was deeply disturbing. Shannon had sent Zac letters of encouragement while he was in training, but now she learned that they had all been returned to her mother's house as undeliverable. She talked with the funeral director, who let her slip the letters inside his casket. Many of Zac's friends flew in for the service, a mini-reunion of West Pointers just a month after they'd left school. They tried to be strong together, but when one of them started crying, that was it; everyone did.

Afterward, Drew and Shannon started thinking about themselves and their relationship differently. They spent a few weeks together in Arizona, and life seemed much shorter and more serious than it had. The possibility of marriage was mentioned. Virtually everyone they knew was doing it, and they got along and had fun. But there was a geographic problem. Shannon was due to be stationed at Fort Hood, while Drew would be training in Georgia before leaving for Hawaii. Shannon put out feelers for any Hawaii-bound lieutenant who might, for some odd reason, want to give up the assignment. To her great surprise, she found a taker. Another

West Point classmate had decided he wanted to try out for the elite 75th Ranger Regiment, and he figured that the quickest way to get a shot at it was to volunteer first for a one-year "hardship" tour in Korea. Drew left for Georgia, and the next month, Shannon had news: When he got to Hawaii, she'd be waiting for him.

TODD, WILL, AND ERIC reached Fort Knox in July. Armor school was a breeze compared to West Point, the first time in four years they had been able just to relax and have fun together, without some assignment or academy requirement hanging over their heads. They were mixed with new ROTC officers, and settled into a fairly leisurely lifestyle, with barbecues and pickup football games every evening around the bachelor officers' quarters.

They took road trips. Eric had a brother in Cleveland whose wife was a law student at Case Western Reserve University. It was just a six-hour drive, Eric reasoned, practically nothing for guys who'd spent their college careers commuting to other cities when they wanted to have real fun. Eric made the trip alone in late September, and he hit it off with one of his sister-in-law's classmates. Things got serious quickly, so much so that the girl, Julie Niehoff, drew a line in the sand. She wasn't going to be an Army wife, following Eric around from post to post. It was his choice, she said, but if he was planning on going career military, they should think twice about taking things further. For now, they left things unsettled.

Todd and Jen once again had to settle for a virtual relationship. Most mornings, Todd would get up extra early to e-mail her, so that when she woke up in Boston she would have something to read. He was a good writer, if sometimes a bit over the top, and he'd send her the most heartfelt love notes, interspersed with pragmatic questions and comments about everyday life. Jen even started thinking about joining the Army herself. Todd's mother sent her an e-mail pointing out that it wasn't too late: in her senior year, she could still apply for ROTC. Jen's parents had both been enlisted in the Army before she was born, and they didn't like the idea, but it was tough to imagine any other career that would allow her to follow Todd to Fort Riley and perhaps other faraway bases.

Besides, she told Todd on the phone, she didn't think his mother would ever like her if she didn't serve in the military. Jen was majoring in biology. "I could do something in the medical corps," she suggested.

"No," Todd replied. "I know you could do it, but I also know it's not for you. Your strength is teaching. That's your dream." Jen had her own ambitions, and he didn't want her falling into the trap of following someone else's plan for her life.

FIVE HUNDRED MILES TO THE SOUTH, Tim Moshier reported for flight school. Katie McKee was with him. She'd decided almost as soon as Tim chose aviation that she loved him and was going to go with him to Fort Rucker, Alabama, to see if their relationship could work. "Either I move or we break up," she told a friend.

The base was in the middle of peanut country, far from everywhere. Even small cities like Mobile, Tallahassee, and Pensacola were a two-hour drive away. Tim had a bit of free time before he began the eighteen-month course, and Katie threw herself into trying to find a job. She had no luck at all, and she was nearly ready to try on the blue smock of a greeter at the nearby Wal-Mart on Boll Weevil Circle when she saw an ad for a Spanish teacher. Dothan High School, "home of the Tigers," was about forty minutes away. Katie had majored in Spanish in college, but she had no state certification. She was pessimistic about her chances but she replied to the ad.

The school called her in quickly, and the principal led her upstairs to meet one of his teachers.

"Just talk to her for a minute," he said.

Katie introduced herself in Spanish, and after a brief conversation, the teacher turned to the principal. "Yep, she looks good," she said.

"Can you start tomorrow?" the principal asked. School, he explained, had already begun, and Katie was the only applicant for the job. She thought of the $450-a-month townhouse she and Tim had rented, with all their things that hadn't been unpacked.

She negotiated for one more day and then left, thrilled to have a job.

But a thought occurred suddenly to her: She had no idea what she was doing.

FLIGHT SCHOOL FINALLY STARTED. The Army ran it in blocks of instruction, an hour for this, four hours for that, almost like shift work. Half the time Tim was home before Katie was done with school. Almost everyone in his class who had chosen aviation had come to flight school at the same time, and there were just a handful of ROTC lieutenants and warrant officers mixed in. Everyone was eager to get in the air, but they first spent a lot of hours in the classroom, learning about all the bizarre and scary things flying could do to the human body. The abrupt movement of fluid in a pilot's head could lead him to perceive up and down as reversed—a dangerous phenomenon to learn about for the first time in the air.

After two weeks, the course ground to a halt: The flight school administrators were short on helicopters and instructor pilots. In the meantime, Tim and his classmates became glorified day laborers. Each morning they were assigned temporary duty, from cleaning the post to providing the honor guard at Army funerals. The deceased were older men mostly, veterans of World War II and Korea who were entitled to a military salute and a flag. A lieutenant would learn the day before a funeral that he was going to be in charge, and he'd practice a few times with a team of enlisted soldiers, folding flags and getting the steps of the ceremony down. But with just a few hours of training, they weren't exactly the Old Guard at Arlington Cemetery. Once, Tim drove six hours for the funeral of a farmer who wanted to be buried at home, and they held the service with all the dignity Tim could muster in the middle of the farmer's fields. Tim didn't mind the duty, but he wished that they had a little more time to learn to do it well.

Other matters weighed on him. Tim was a little bit lost, starting over in the Army without Todd, Will, and Eric, although the presence of another D-1 Duck at flight school helped. Pat Killoran was from rural Northern California; he'd escaped with Tim, Todd, Will, and Eric to Tim's parents' house many weekends, raiding the refrigerator and the liquor cabinet. Now he lived within sight of Tim and Katie's place, and he spent a lot of time with them. But otherwise, it was Katie, the naturally ebullient one, who made most of their new friends.

ONLY A LITTLE MORE THAN half a decade later, it can be difficult to recall exactly how events unfolded on the world stage in 2002, how a U.S. invasion of Iraq seemed inevitable and yet was simultaneously the subject of passionate public debate. Opinions and statements that at the time seemed pedantic, alarmist, or outlandish later took on enormous significance.

Unbeknownst to the new West Point alumni, President Bush had ordered Defense Secretary Donald Rumsfeld to update the military's Iraq invasion plans in November 2001, just two months after 9/11. Several months later, a Rumsfeld ally published a jingoistic op-ed in *The Washington Post* predicting that such a war would be a "cakewalk" and "the greatest victory in America's war on terrorism." The summer after the class of 2002 graduated, another op-ed—this one in *The Wall Street Journal,* by the Republican former national security adviser Brent Scowcroft—was headlined DON'T ATTACK IRAQ, and warned that an invasion "very likely would have to be followed by a large-scale, long-term military occupation."

As Katie McKee interviewed for her teaching job, and as Drew and Shannon tried to figure out whether they had a future as a couple, Vice President Dick Cheney stood before a convention of the Veterans of Foreign Wars and asserted, solemnly: "Simply stated, there is no doubt that Saddam Hussein now has weapons of mass destruction. There is no doubt he is amassing them to use against our friends, against our allies, and against us." A few weeks later, as Todd was talking Jen out of joining the Army, President Bush addressed the U.N. General Assembly. Iraq was "a grave and gathering danger," Bush said in a speech on the first anniversary of 9/11. "To assume this regime's good faith is to bet the lives of millions and the peace of the world in a reckless gamble. And this is a risk we must not take."

By October 2002, nearly every U.S. senator was being secretly warned by members of the Bush administration that Saddam Hussein had not only chemical and biological weapons but also unmanned aerial vehicles—drones—that could be launched from ships to attack U.S. cities. And on October 16, 2002, as the first members of the West Point class of 2002 prepared to graduate from officer basic school and join their Army units, Congress voted overwhelmingly to authorize the use of military force in Iraq.

AS THE FIRST WEEKS at Rucker had passed, it started wearing on Katie McKee that she was virtually the only girlfriend who had moved down for flight school with her soldier-boyfriend. Everyone else was married, or at the very least engaged. In the rural Deep South, the fact that she and Tim were unmarried was not something people accepted without comment. Teaching in Dothan was almost like going to church every day, she felt, with everyone judging her, asking when she and Tim were getting engaged and looking askance when she didn't have an answer. The minor humiliations and annoyances caused by the Army bothered her more and more as they accumulated. Every time she drove onto the base, she had to stop and fill out a visitor's pass, because she had no legal status in the military's eyes. She couldn't go to the on-post grocery store, the commissary, without Tim coming along to sign her in. And one night they went to a reception for new flight students. Tim introduced Katie to a major and his wife.

The major's wife quickly turned to Tim. "This nice girl moved all this way, and you haven't put a ring on her finger?"

Tim turned beet red. In truth, he had been thinking about proposing since before Alabama. A Catholic, he'd never been completely comfortable with the idea of simply living together. And so, when Katie went away to visit some friends one weekend in October, he went to the jewelry store and bought the ring he knew she liked—platinum setting, a diamond just over a carat, smaller diamonds on each side. He hid it in his sock drawer to await the right moment. For the rest of his life, he figured, people would be asking about when he and Katie got engaged. He wanted the story to be a good one.

In November, he found his opportunity. He read in the local newspaper that the following night would feature a brilliant meteor shower, the

Leonids, and that rural Alabama would be one of the best places in the world to see it. He set the alarm for three A.M., woke Katie up, and cajoled her into the car. They drove down to a driving range where the sky opened wide above them.

They watched for a minute before Tim got down on one knee and took the ring out of his pocket.

"Will you be my best friend forever?" he asked her.

"Yes!" Katie said immediately, overjoyed and relieved. When they went home she insisted on calling her sister and parents. Tim thought it was crazy to call in the middle of the night, but it was a life-changing moment, and she wanted everyone in her family to know the good news right away.

After buying the ring, Tim was a little light in the wallet, and flights back to New York ran several hundred dollars. So he and Katie drove six hours north to spend Thanksgiving with Will Tucker's family in the tiny town of Haleyville, Alabama. Armor school was nearly over, and Will knew that the unit he was assigned to, the 3rd Infantry Division, would be going to Kuwait soon after he joined it. On paper, they were supposed to be on a six-month rotation as a sort of trip-wire force defending Kuwait from Iraq. But with all the saber rattling, it was clear he might well be part of an invading army. Will was nervous about heading to war so soon, but this was what he'd been training for. So many officers had served their entire careers in the military without ever leading soldiers in combat. It was almost too good to be true that he might be doing it as a brand-new second lieutenant.

The Tuckers were decent, salt-of-the-earth people who embraced the South's slower lifestyle but observed both their hometown's virtues and faults with clear eyes. It had been the best place in the world to raise a family, Will's father, Randy, observed, but he still encouraged his kids to leave as they grew older, for there wasn't much economic opportunity. The main industry in town had been mobile home manufacturing, but that business was in trouble.

Like their son, Randy Tucker seemed to enjoy it when stereotypical Yankees (like Tim and Katie from upstate New York) were taken aback by how different things were in the South. Tim and Katie marveled at how, as you drove through the town on the way to the Tuckers' house, people on the side of the road stopped and waved—though they obviously couldn't and didn't know them.

How's it going, teaching Spanish to those Alabama kids? Will asked Katie when they all sat down for dinner.

Spanish? Katie joked. With their southern accents, she could barely understand them when they spoke English.

JEN REARDON FLEW OUT to see Todd and his friends graduate from armor school in December, and they drove together from Kentucky to Fort Riley, Kansas. Tiffany Bryant had just left for Afghanistan with the XVIII Airborne Corps, and there was talk that their big brother, Tim, might soon be heading for Kuwait as part of the Marine Corps contingent of the expected Iraq invasion force. When Todd reported to Riley, he learned he would likely ship out as well. There were no official orders, but one of the first sergeants he talked with told him when he checked in that he would be going to Kuwait in early 2003.

The Army gave him ten days in a Fort Riley motel while he looked for a place to live, but he and Jen had a hard time finding anything suitable. Money was tight. They planned to attend a wedding the day after Christmas—another D-1 Duck, Reeves Garnett, was marrying a girl he'd met through Tim Moshier and Katie McKee while up at West Point—and they couldn't afford to fly to California to be with Todd's family or to Pennsylvania to be with Jen's, and still make it to New York for the wedding. So they ate Christmas Eve dinner together at a Denny's restaurant (Todd had the country fried steak and eggs; Jen had the turkey with mashed potatoes and stuffing), and snuck a seven-foot Christmas tree into their motel room.

With only two days left in 2002, Todd and Jen decided to hurry up and get married. They would have preferred a big church wedding, but it seemed foolish to leave hundreds of dollars on the table every month, the difference between what the Army paid a single officer and a married one. And if Todd was truly going to war, he wanted the Army to respect Jen as his wife while he was gone.

On December 30, they walked into the courthouse in Manhattan, Kansas, hoping to get a waiver for the two-week waiting period. The judge turned out to be a Naval Academy graduate, and Todd hid his West Point ring. Interservice rivalries notwithstanding, he took pity on them.

"Do you have two witnesses to sign the marriage license?" the judge asked.

"No," Todd said. "We don't know anybody here."

The judge's secretaries stepped in for a fee, and within minutes, Todd and Jen were married. But after thinking about it, they decided to keep the whole thing a secret, and didn't refer to each other as husband and wife even when they were alone. They would still have a religious wedding, with family, friends, and flowers—and, of course, an open bar. This exchange of vows had just been "signing papers," Todd said, "like signing your tax return."

Two days later, on New Year's Day, Todd had a voice mail from his brother, Tim: He and his girlfriend were on the way back from Las Vegas, and Todd should call. He said he had big news.

"They think they beat us!" Todd said when he heard the message. He called back, but Tim wasn't calling to announce an impromptu elopement. Tim's weekend away had been cut short because he'd been ordered to Kuwait immediately. If war came, it looked as if the Bryant brothers would invade together.

DREW SLOAN AND RYAN BELTRAMINI hung around Fort Benning the first week of January like convicts awaiting execution, killing time in Army lodging until the start of Ranger School. They'd more or less breezed through infantry officer basic school that fall, but now Ranger would be the real test. The nine-week course was designed to simulate the stress of combat and small-unit warfare. Whenever the military used euphemisms like "simulating stress," Drew and Ryan knew that things were going to suck.

Ranger School was a rite of passage for infantry officers; a lieutenant who showed up at his first infantry assignment without the arched Ranger tab on his left shoulder would be in for a rough time. Most

Ranger candidates had to repeat at least one section of the three-part course—there were phases at Fort Benning; in the mountains of northern Georgia; and in the swamps of Florida—so it often took a lot longer than the scheduled nine weeks. But that just made it more important to persevere.

Ryan's wife, Alisha, came out to Georgia to see them off, and she helped her husband and Drew shave their heads before heading back to her family in California. Part of Ranger was about deprivation—candidates got by on little food and less sleep—and so they tried a preemptive attack on hunger. The night before the course began, Drew and Ryan headed to a restaurant called the Mediterranean Café in a redbrick strip mall, where they ordered huge portions of chicken parmesan. Then, too nervous to eat, they sat in near silence before heading to the motel for their few remaining hours. Drew called Shannon just to hear her voice one last time, then dozed fitfully before he met Ryan in the parking lot at midnight, and drove way out into the Fort Benning boondocks. The temperature was below freezing, and neither man really bothered to try to hide his anxiety. The hour was so early that when Ryan called Alisha in California on the way to say a last good-bye, she hadn't gone to bed yet.

Instructors corraled everyone, ordering them gruffly to form up into three even-sized companies. Though Drew and Ryan could barely see in the darkness, they could just make out some of their West Point classmates, running around looking scared. There was Joe DaSilva, the 2002 class president, charging toward the lines as they'd been ordered to do. Most had heard that for some reason A Company was the most easygoing, sort of the H-2 of Ranger School, and so nearly everyone tried to push into one line, with two scraggly little groups of leftovers who either hadn't heard the rumor or just didn't care. Then people started rushing to the third and smallest group, thinking that maybe the instructors might get wise to the ruse and, instead of designating the companies A, B, and C, do just the opposite. Drew and Ryan both wound up in the real A (for-Alpha) Company, but soon it seemed they'd been obsessing about nothing.

The first few days of Ranger, the Ranger Assessment Phase—again, the Army's ear for dry euphemism was a thing of beauty—comprised a series of physical tests and skills qualifications; traditionally, more candidates washed out at this point than any other. For days and weeks beforehand, candidates had watched one another practice push-ups and sit-ups, making sure their form was pristine; they'd heard a Ranger instructor might send them home for the smallest imperfection. The rumor was that Ranger was chronically oversubscribed, and that instructors kicked students out on the first day just to cull the herd. In fact, Drew and Ryan learned that exactly that had happened to Drew's plebe-year roommate, Dave Swanson, only a week or two before.

"Are you fucking kidding me?" Dave had yelled at the instructor who failed him less than an hour into the first night at Ranger. In eight years in the Army and at West Point, he'd never failed a PT test. "Eight more!" called out another instructor. Sure enough, eight of the fifteen candidates behind him failed as well.

RYAN AND DREW PASSED Ranger Assessment, only to wonder what kind of hell would come next. Joe DaSilva wasn't so lucky. He made it through the first morning, but a test in the Fort Benning swimming pool that afternoon changed the course of his military career. It was simple in theory: Candidates had to dive into the deep end fully suited for battle, sink to the bottom, and strip off all their equipment before coming up for air. But Joe's hand broke the surface before he'd gotten all his gear off. Immediate washout.

Joe packed his things and headed with a bare shoulder to his assignment: Fort Campbell, home of the 101st Airborne Division. He tried to force self-pity from his mind. He'd known the standard, he figured; it was his own fault he'd made a silly mistake and failed to meet it. In war, silly mistakes could get people killed.

Still, Joe was disheartened. He reported to Fort Campbell and was assigned to 1-327 Infantry, a storied brigade whose lineage went back to World War I. Sure enough, the conventional wisdom was accurate. Everyone he met cast nonchalant glances at his left arm, looking for the tab. "So, what happened in Ranger?" they'd ask. He told the story over and over, listening respectfully to officers' admonitions about how important it was for a brand-new infantry officer in his position to go back and give it another shot. Even his new battalion commander, Lieutenant Colonel Marcus DeOlivera, gave him the left-shoulder peek, but the colonel had bigger issues on his mind. As it turned out, Joe's timing had been impeccable. He'd reached the Kentucky Army post on January 31, 2003, just a day after the 101st Airborne received its orders to go to Kuwait. Suddenly there was a very good chance that, instead of fighting fake battles in Georgia and Florida, Joe would soon be going to war.

The division was scrambling. Everyone in Joe's new battalion was locked into the positions they'd held on the day the order came down. Platoon leaders would stay platoon leaders, and staff officers would stay staff officers. With no real job open for him, the colonel explained, Joe would be assigned as a sort of second-lieutenant-at-large on the battalion operations staff.

"I know you're worried because of the Ranger thing," Colonel DeOlivera said. "I think it's important." But, he added, "How you carry yourself professionally and tactically—that's how I'm going to judge you."

Within a couple of days, Joe was standing in the damp cold and snow of the Fort Campbell rail yard, weighing vehicles so they could be loaded on ships and sent across the Atlantic Ocean. It was miserable duty, but he had promised himself he'd adopt a strict no-complaining policy. As it happened, it was his twenty-fourth birthday, a fact he mentioned to no one.

Todd and Jen finally found a little house near the fraternities and bars of Kansas State University. Their few remaining days together before she went back to college in early January were filled with errands, trying to furnish their place, and filling out the endless paperwork required for the Army to recognize Jen as Todd's wife. Todd was psyching himself for war, but as Jen posed for the picture on her military ID card and headed to Boston, he learned that Fort Riley's personnel office had done some reshuffling, and he was now assigned to a unit that wasn't going anywhere. In the chaos, he found another Fort Riley tank unit that was short of lieutenants, where at least he would get to be a platoon leader right away, and he switched the unit patch on his uniform to the 1st Infantry Division. It seemed like a better home. His new unit was the designated reserve for Korea, but given the intense preparations for war with Iraq, it could be assigned a new mission at any time.

Captain Pat Chavez, the commander of Charlie Company, 1-34 Armor, didn't know what to make of his new platoon leader. In their first meeting, Todd struck him as extremely formal: Every other word was "sir." *Maybe this is just what West Point lieutenants are like,* thought Chavez, an ROTC officer. But then Chavez thought back to his own time in armor school, and how important they'd told him it was to make a good impression on his company commander. It was funny to think that just a few years ago he'd been in Todd's boots.

A platoon leader's job had few analogies in the civilian world. In a tank unit, a new officer, often just twenty-two or twenty-three years old, would usually have less experience in the Army than many of the sixteen soldiers he'd be leading. And he would almost certainly know a lot less than his troops about how to maintain, operate, or even fight with the platoon's four M1 Abrams tanks. The platoon leader's position was a learning assignment and a lot of lieutenants screwed things up at first, not knowing how to balance the technical authority of their rank against the practical personal dynamics required to lead a team and accomplish its mission.

Chavez gave Todd his company's 3rd Platoon, and told him he'd be on his own for a few days because his platoon sergeant—the experienced noncommissioned officer who would be his right-hand man and guide him as he learned to lead—was attending a training course out of state. Todd walked alone over to the motor pool where his new soldiers were working on their tanks. A few of them had been in the Army since the days when Todd was getting kicked out of sporting goods stores and dreaming of going to Notre Dame. West Point prided itself on preparing cadets for exactly this moment, when a young officer addressed his troops for the first time, but Todd's soldiers were leery of lieutenants, especially the West Point variety, who had a reputation for acting like they already knew everything. Todd seemed to grasp that instinctively. He won them over with humility.

"I don't know anything," Todd said after he introduced himself. "Whatever you guys want to teach me would be great."

IN EARLY FEBRUARY, Eric Huss pulled up in front of Todd's house with a U-Haul trailer and just about everything he owned in the world. Eric had been one of the few armor officers early in their basic course to express a strong interest in going to Ranger School, and he'd endured extra PT each morning at Fort Knox for the privilege of giving it a shot. That had meant he'd spent the entire month of December waiting for the course to begin, with no official duties, working out constantly, drawing a paycheck, and loving his life. But ten days into Ranger, he lost his map and scorecard on a land navigation exercise. He searched in vain for two hours in a knee-deep marsh. Just like that, he was out of the course.

He drove to Cleveland to see his girlfriend, Julie, watched the Tampa Bay Buccaneers win the Super Bowl, and then drove on to Fort Riley. Todd never mentioned his secret marriage, but Eric was quite amused to see how quickly he had become a sort of Home Depot househusband, painting the little place and trying to get it ready for Jen. Eric crashed with him for a few days, and Todd asked his battalion's personnel officer whether they could pull Eric into the unit. But the Army had other plans, and the reassignment wasn't approved. Eric found out why when he reported to his new battalion and saluted his colonel for the first time.

"I hope you have your bags packed," the commander said. Their unit was sending its tanks and equipment to Kuwait that very day. The soldiers would soon follow.

One by one, Todd's family and friends in the military left for the Middle East. His brother was already in Kuwait. Tiffany was in Afghanistan, fighting last year's war, but at least she was playing a part. Will had gone sort of radio silent, but he was scheduled to head over soon. And then it was Eric's turn to go.

He and Julie had continued to talk about whether they had a future together, but now Eric decided to break things off. They had great chemistry, but Julie was far from convinced of the wisdom of the invasion, and it was tough for Eric to be part of the war if his girlfriend opposed it. Even if she had felt otherwise, it seemed unfair to leave her hanging on while he was fighting overseas. Her life would and should continue without him. Besides, God only knew when he'd return. And though he didn't like to think this way, Eric had to admit there was a possibility he'd never come home.

He and Todd hung out in Eric's brand-new apartment the night before he was supposed to fly out, having a few drinks and watching a rented movie. A blizzard delayed them for twenty-four hours, but when the weather cleared, Eric and his unit boarded a chartered plane in Topeka, flying first to Rome and then Kuwait, where they would wait for war.

WILL TUCKER HAD been assigned to the 3-7 Cavalry when he reached Fort Stewart in December, and they'd left for the Middle East in a hurry. It was colder in the desert than he'd expected, and they slept in tents in a barren desert camp, without heat or electricity. From there things had only become more austere, as they moved to a staging area where they bundled up and slept in the open on their tanks.

As a young leader, Will was usually content to keep his mouth shut—to watch, wait, and learn. Everything was intensified by the fact that he'd taken over his platoon and then they had left almost immediately for the desert. At least one of his soldiers had been in Desert Storm back in 1991, but even among those who hadn't seen combat, Will had some experienced noncommissioned officers. First among them was his platoon sergeant, a sergeant first class named Tony Broadhead. Their platoon was part of a heavily armed troop, with nine tanks and thirteen Bradley Fighting Vehicles—thirty-ton tracked, armored troop carriers equipped with powerful 25-millimeter cannons—and the squadron of which they were in turn a part had a daunting mission: They would be among the first soldiers to cross the border into Iraq if the invasion came, spearheading the entire U.S. Army in its fast march to Baghdad.

They spent their days now shooting their weapons, and planning and rehearsing the exact moment when they would burst through the giant berms that lined the border between Kuwait and Iraq. The engineers working with them found a similar earth, wood, and concrete structure about ten miles from the border. They practiced over and over again how they would blow a hole through the berm and burst through, with the tanks leading the way and securing the far side of the berm so that the more lightly armored Bradley Fighting Vehicles could follow.

But as the days stretched into weeks, they began to wonder if the order to invade would ever come.

JOE DASILVA was now at Camp Pennsylvania, a mass of tents and wire in the Kuwaiti desert named not so much for the state itself but for the 9/11 airplane that had crashed there. Scud missile warnings were issued frequently, and the troops walked around with chemical protection suits in backpacks, gas masks hanging on straps by their thighs. They drilled constantly, and it was common to see troops sprinting to bunkers while trying to pull on their charcoal-lined overalls, heavy boots, and masks.

Joe was working hard, determined to make up for his lack of a Ranger tab. He was eager to get a platoon, but as the junior officer on the battalion staff, he was little more than a glorified gofer, diligently executing whatever mini-mission needed a warm body. After three weeks in the desert, though, Colonel DeOlivera called him into his tent.

"Joe, you're fired," the colonel told him.

"Sir?"

"We're going to move you over to Delta Company, and you're going to take a platoon." Though the colonel didn't explain, Joe was the last in a chain of officers in the battalion to suddenly get new jobs on what was now pretty obviously the eve of war. A higher-ranking staff officer had been reassigned to the brigade headquarters, which meant another officer had to be pulled in to replace him. That meant another officer down the ladder had to be reassigned in turn. And so on, and so on, until they reached Joe.

Joe could hardly speak. "Sir?" he said again.

"Delta Company," DeOlivera repeated. "Talk to Captain Anderson. He'll have more for you."

"Okay, sir," Joe said. "You know, there's a war that's supposed to start in a few days."

"Yeah. You sure have good timing."

Captain Eric Anderson, the Delta Company commander, was talking in his tent with his first sergeant, Jim Plowman, a thirty-seven-year-old, two-hundred-pound ox of a man, when Joe found them. They did not look happy.

Plowman ushered him outside. "It's not the most optimal conditions to have you come to the company," the sergeant said. They would be crossing the berm in a few days. "You're going to have a lot to learn," Plowman added. It was an Olympic-class understatement.

He brought Joe over to meet the outgoing platoon leader, Captain Clinton Cunningham, a familiar face: Cunningham had been a firstie in Joe's cadet company when Joe was a plebe.

"It's a great platoon," Cunningham said, clearly trying to keep his own spirits up after being promoted out of his leadership position. He took Joe to meet the soldiers, paying special attention to two tough-looking sergeants: Terrence Jack and Ramón Melendez, both from California. They were physically imposing guys, a little rough around the edges, and Cunningham spoke as if they could run through concrete. They greeted Joe cordially enough, but they were obviously nervous about getting a brand-new butterbar on the eve of war. Joe had no time to worry about that. There was so much to be done—he'd have to inventory the platoon's property, draw ammunition, and most important, figure out where they were going to get their Humvees and trucks for the march into Iraq.

MANY YEARS OF METICULOUS work had been invested in the plan for the American-led invasion of Iraq. The latest version was the product of thousands of the military's best minds. It envisioned a race to Baghdad that would bypass most cities; assuming all went well, the invasion force would capture the capital and topple Saddam Hussein's regime before he could unleash biological or chemical weapons. The plan originally called for two avenues of attack, with the 4th Infantry Division invading from Turkey in the north while a second force came up from Kuwait in the south.

The 4th ID would be sending most of its equipment and vehicles to Turkey on ships, and soldiers were needed to guard the cargo. That mission was assigned to the 1st Infantry Division, which passed it down several levels until it landed in Captain Chavez's lap. Soon, Todd Bryant's platoon was out at the Fort Riley swimming pool, practicing man-overboard drills and floating with a hundred pounds of equipment. It wasn't much, but if this was their chance to be part of the war, they'd take it.

Jen Reardon hadn't intended to return to Kansas until her spring break in March, but Todd's assignment pushed things up. She was ambivalent about the idea of invading Iraq to begin with, and she was frustrated that from her perspective, the Army didn't seem to be able to decide whether to send Todd or not. Now that he had a role, even a tangential one, the tension was almost too much. She ran around to her professors trying to get permission to take an early week off in February. Most readily agreed, but her calculus professor didn't believe her story about being married to a soldier going overseas, and scheduled a test for when she'd be gone. When Jen went anyway, he failed her.

Todd was venting one evening to Jen about all he had to do to get ready—the equipment he needed, the things he had to do for his troops. He rattled off the vaccinations he had to get: anthrax, smallpox, tetanus—

"Wait a minute," Jen interrupted. "Smallpox?" Todd had been treated for a minor dry skin condition, and Jen was sure she remembered something worrisome from one of her classes. "You can't get the smallpox vaccine if you have any kind of skin disease," she continued. "It can be lethal."

"No, no," Todd said. "The medic told me I was fine."

Proud that her biology classes were coming in handy, Jen insisted that he get a doctor's appointment anyway. Sure enough, Todd couldn't get the vaccine until his rash cleared up. And if he couldn't get the vaccine, he couldn't deploy. Jen was relieved when she heard the news, but Todd was embarrassed. Some of his sergeants gave him a hard time, insisting that because Todd looked so young it must have been diaper rash.

Worst of all, another platoon went in their place.

THE TURKS REFUSED to allow American units to invade Iraq from their territory, and the revamped war started a day earlier than planned, on

March 19, 2003, with a U.S. air attack on a palace complex outside Baghdad where intelligence suggested Saddam was hiding with his family and some of his top commanders. Early the next morning, the American-led forces got the word that they'd be crossing the border that night. Will Tucker's unit was near the very front of the line. After so long in the desert, he and his soldiers were tired, covered in sand and grime, and feeling almost as if they'd already fought the war. As the day wore on, he could hear American artillery pounding targets on the far side of the border. The 3-7 Cavalry rolled forward as they'd trained, ready to blast through obstacles originally meant to keep the Iraqis out: deep antitank ditches; hundreds of miles of razor wire and electric fences; and the berms that the U.S. Army had spent twelve years helping to build. But at the last minute, their orders changed. Instead of fighting their way through, they crossed through a U.N. border checkpoint. Though their tanks were among the first to enter Iraq, camera crews had crossed ahead of them, turning their cameras behind and filming the whole thing like a Hollywood movie.

The 3-7 Cavalry moved northwest toward their first objective. The Iraqi army, and the resistance they'd expected, were nowhere to be found.

JOE DASILVA'S PLATOON was part of a brigade that was scheduled to move out a couple of days behind Will Tucker's unit. His troops were understandably nervous, and Joe thought hard about how he should respond. At West Point, they had done case study after case study on leadership, and now, Joe realized, he was a living case study. He called his platoon together. "I don't know what awaits us on the other side of that berm," he told them. "But I'll tell you this. If I have to give my life for any of you I will do it in a heartbeat."

Dawn broke as they waited, and fierce weather rolled in over the desert. They had hardly seen a drop of rain since they'd reached Kuwait, but now the skies filled with dark gray clouds. Thunder and lightning cracked, hail fell from the skies, and a brutal sandstorm raged.

It was ominous, almost biblical. *What is God trying to tell us?* Joe thought as he sat in his Humvee. Just then his gunner crouched down next to him.

"Hey, sir," the gunner said. "Can you imagine if you were an Iraqi, and you're looking at this? 'They're bringing this weather with them! This is horrible!'"

An order came down from Colonel DeOlivera to take the doors off their soft-skinned Humvees. The doors wouldn't provide any protection but might get in the way when they tried to return fire. Given the miserable weather, though, Joe made an executive decision to keep his doors on. The brigade moved out, rolling across the desert, hundreds of vehicles following one after another with the violent weather raging around them, soaking the soldiers in open vehicles and making them miserable. Colonel DeOlivera came over the radio, making fun of his own order.

"Who's the jackass that said no doors?" he asked, in mock indignation.

WILL TUCKER'S UNIT had made great progress and had run into very little resistance. Over the radio Will could hear snippets of reports that other American forces were taking fire, but so far he had seen nothing. They reached their first major objective—Samawah, a southern city of about 250,000 people—just about the time Joe DaSilva was entering Iraq. The city stood about a hundred miles from where they'd crossed the border, and was still another 140 miles southeast of Baghdad. Samawah was key because it was the location of two major bridges over the Euphrates River, which the Americans would need to control. As they reached the outskirts of the city, early on the morning of March 22, a group of small pickup trucks with mounted machine guns raced toward the convoy, and the pilot of a Kiowa scout helicopter patrolling overhead radioed that he was about to open fire. Before he squeezed the trigger, however, he recognized through the dust and haze that the trucks were flying giant American flags off their tailgates.

The trucks belonged to an American Special Forces team that had been hiding in Samawah for several days. While the intelligence Will's unit had heard so far suggested the city was virtually undefended, the

Special Forces soldiers reported now that not only was the city defended by members of the Iraqi militia known as the Saddam Fedayeen, but also that one of the most wanted members of Saddam Hussein's defense establishment was hiding there: a former general nicknamed Chemical Ali, who had ordered a chemical weapons attack on Iraqi Kurds in the late 1980s.

Will's commander sent Sergeant Broadhead toward one of the bridges that they had to control, leading a team of two M1 Abrams tanks and three Bradley Fighting Vehicles. Will was to stay about 150 yards behind, with the rest of his troop. Broadhead's soldiers moved beyond where Will could see them clearly, and Will strained to watch, filling in the picture by listening to the reports Broadhead and his men gave on the radio.

Broadhead rode with his head sticking out of the hatch of his tank, and as he approached the bridge, he saw a small group of Iraqi men just standing there, not wearing military uniforms but carrying AK-47 rifles. Broadhead waved to them, and the men ran toward his group, opening fire. The armored vehicles were impervious to rifle fire, but now wave after wave of men in civilian clothes charged impotently at Broadhead's tank and the Bradley that was closest to him, only to be mowed down. Another Iraqi man stepped out in the open with a rocket-propelled grenade—the kind of weapon that had been used to shoot down a Black Hawk helicopter in Somalia in 1993—and fired. An RPG was unlikely to destroy a tank, but as it impacted on the side of the Abrams, it knocked the man who had fired it back hard, apparently killing him.

Still more than a football field's length away, Will stood in his tank with only his head sticking out of the hatch, watching the battle. A mortar exploded overhead, and he watched with an odd curiosity, realizing that, like the RPG, it wasn't anywhere near powerful enough to harm a tank. If whoever fired it knew what he was doing, however, he would use the location of the first explosion to readjust his aim, then follow up with more rounds. Sure enough, a series of mortars landed near the tank, one just a hundred feet away. Feeling oddly invulnerable, Will barely flinched. It was the first time he'd been on the receiving end of real fire, and it didn't quite click in his head that someone was trying to kill him. Finally another round landed very close, and the shrapnel and flying rock slammed into the side of the tank, ricocheting and hitting him in the left arm.

Will ducked down quickly into the hatch of his Abrams. The wound was barely a scratch, but he realized he'd been very lucky. He ordered his tanks to move, rushing out of the line of sight and the range of the mortarmen.

The gloves were now off, and Will's unit called in artillery on the parts of the town they'd been attacked from. By the time it was over, Broadhead and the other soldiers reported that they had counted 221 dead bodies piled around their armored vehicles.

JOE DASILVA'S BRIGADE had been ordered to take the Iraqi city of Najaf, roughly halfway along the Euphrates River between Samawah, where Will Tucker had fought, and Baghdad, about sixty miles to the north. The original American plan had been simply to bypass Najaf, but now Iraqi raiders were using the city as a base to attack U.S. supply lines. The brigade surrounded the city in the last days of March, preventing anyone from coming or going without their permission. Tanks rolled in, occupying a college campus just to get a foothold somewhere. The unit started doing "thunder runs" through the city, showing the flag so that the people would see that the Americans were present in force. After a day or so, another group of U.S. Special Forces soldiers who had been hiding in Najaf linked up with Joe's brigade commander, Colonel Ben Hodges. Most of the city was pro-American, the Special Forces soldiers reported, but there were pockets of enemy fighters. They also provided locations of suspected weapons caches.

That night, Joe's battalion was ordered to send a platoon to serve as personal security for Colonel Hodges. It seemed like a safe assignment, and thus a sensible task for a platoon under the leadership of a brand-new butterbar who didn't even have his Ranger tab. But Joe's soldiers were pissed. They'd trained for war for years, and had thought of themselves as the top platoon in the company, if not the battalion. Clearly they were being sent to do this job only because they now had the untested, weak-link lieutenant. Joe didn't like it much either, because the assignment put him in a tough spot with his new soldiers.

"We're going to do any job we get," he told his troops, trying to boost their spirits. "It's not like it's going to be over tomorrow."

He took half his platoon with him as the brigade commander ventured into Najaf for the first time. Besides Colonel Hodges's truck and Joe's two trucks—one with a .50-caliber machine gun mounted on the roof and the other with an automatic grenade launcher—a fourth truck carried a military camera crew and civilian reporters.

At first everything went smoothly, though it was a bit nerve-racking for Joe, since he was now responsible for the life of his boss's boss's boss. People stood in the streets, waving and cheering. Every time the colonel got out of his truck, Iraqi men and women ran up to hug and kiss him and his soldiers, and Joe felt the sinking nervousness a Secret Service agent must experience at a campaign rally.

They drove on, passing an industrial yard of some sort with a big collection of broken vehicles inside. Suddenly Colonel Hodges came over the radio. "I saw a truck in there," he said as they kept moving at forty miles an hour. "A garbage truck filled with weapons." He ordered them to turn around.

How could he have seen that? Joe thought. None of his guys had noticed anything either. They headed back and came to a halt on a sidewalk. The yard was surrounded by a fence, and now they could see half a dozen men running around inside. Sure enough, Joe saw the garbage truck, its back filled with AK-47 rifles and rocket-propelled grenades.

The colonel and the camera crew climbed out of their Humvees, and Joe hopped out as well, jogging up to them. He heard a loud cracking noise. It took a second to register. *Hey*, he thought, *these guys are shooting at us!*

Now all kinds of fire began coming from the yard, and Joe spun on his heel, completely exposed. He lifted his rifle, lined up one of the armed Iraqi men in his sights, and squeezed the trigger. He had done the same thing many times in training, shooting at practice targets of paper or metal. The man dropped quickly to the ground.

"Sir!" It was Sergeant Melendez, in the turret of one of the Humvees.

"You crazy motherfuckers! Get back in the vehicles!" Melendez opened fire with his automatic grenade launcher, and seconds later the grenades started falling rhythmically into the yard with a series of dull bangs. Sergeant Jack's driver rolled their Humvee onto the median of the road so that he would have a clear shot into the yard. He opened fire with his .50-caliber machine gun, a weapon that was not only deadly but also loud and intimidating. If anyone was still alive inside the yard, they had to be flat on their stomachs.

The Americans quickly pulled away to regroup. One of the military photographers was wounded—he'd taken a bullet in the foot—but everyone else was okay. Colonel Hodges was all over the radio, trying to call in Apache helicopters to destroy the vehicles in the yard. But now the pilots couldn't find them.

"Mad Dog Two-Six, this is Bastogne Six," Hodges called to Joe as they turned around.

"Roger, sir."

"Okay, Mad Dog. We're going to go back and I'm going to drop smoke right in front of it. So, Sergeant Jack, you don't slow down for a second."

They raced by as fast as they could and Colonel Hodges threw a smoke grenade out the window, marking the spot so the helicopters overhead could find it. The Iraqis were waiting, and the fire coming back out of the yard was intense enough that the driver of the third vehicle in the American convoy slammed on the brakes, cutting the convoy in half. But the smoke marker worked: The Apaches saw it and fired everything they had at the yard.

Three of the Iraqis tried to escape, jumping in a white four-door sedan. They raced out the front gate toward the Americans, firing out the windows with rifles. Sergeant Jack lit them up with his machine gun. They died quickly, and suddenly Joe's first combat experience was over.

The four-vehicle convoy continued driving through the town, finishing the colonel's tour almost as if the battle hadn't happened. A few hours later, Joe's platoon headed back outside the city to the 1-327 Infantry headquarters.

"I put you on that so that you wouldn't get shot at!" Captain Anderson said, shaking his head and laughing. But Joe's soldiers were excited: They had been the first in his battalion to see real combat.

ERIC HUSS'S SITUATION had been similar to Joe DaSilva's at first. As the newest lieutenant in his unit, he was designated to lead a specialized, ad-hoc headquarters platoon—not a particularly desirable assignment, because instead of riding a tank, he was issued two M113 armored personnel carriers, tracked vehicles that had first seen action in Vietnam. The M113s had upgraded armor, and his had a .50-caliber machine gun mounted on top, but that was nothing compared to the big gun on a tank. His main mission was to protect the battalion's medics, who were traveling in another M113 and had no weapons at all except for their pistols. Eric had never even been in an M113 until he and his small platoon picked them up in the Kuwaiti desert, but now he'd see the war from one.

His battalion had been something of an orphan. They had been attached to the 3rd Infantry Division—Will's division—during the early days of the invasion, but although he and Will were within a few miles of each other many times, they never crossed paths. In April, however, they had been switched to the 101st Airborne—Joe DaSilva's division—as if in a mid-season football trade. Eric's unit met up with the grunts they'd be fighting beside, and together they worked on tactics. The infantry commanders wanted their soldiers to ride on top of the tanks, so that when they encountered the enemy they could take cover quickly in the drainage ditches that ran along all the roads. The plan was that the tanks would stop immediately—so as to avoid running over the grunts—and then fire away with their big guns.

The first battle had started almost at once, and the 101st Airborne troops dove to the sides of the road as planned. Quickly, they realized that the infantry and the tankers were on completely different radio networks and couldn't talk with each other. The Army had spent God knew how many millions to develop a combat radio system that would scan through half a dozen frequencies every second, so nobody could eavesdrop, but the 101st Airborne and 2-70 Armor radios weren't synched properly. Eric and his tankers did the only thing they could. They watched which way the infantrymen seemed to be shooting, turned their guns in the same direction, and blasted away.

The M113s turned out to be a little better than Eric had expected. The upgraded armor worked well, although there were little sliding doors made out of Kevlar that weren't very secure. They stopped AK-47 rounds, but shrapnel went right through. Eric and his men kept as close as possible to the tanks, using them for cover.

After the first couple of battles, Eric realized that the fear of death didn't bother him much, but he was deeply disturbed by the feeling of killing. In the heat of battle, he would be so pumped up with adrenaline, just trying to keep himself and his troops alive, that he went on autopilot, and did what he had to. But later it would sink in. It haunted him. They rolled into one city, driving over dead bodies in the middle of the road with the tracks of their armored vehicles. He was ordered at least once to stay put after a battle before heading north to the next objective. The heat set in, and the dead Iraqi bodies on the battlefield bloated up. Packs of dogs came around and started to feed on the rotting flesh. The carcasses popped as gases escaped. They began to smell like rotting garbage, and worse. Nothing in the world could prepare you for that.

LATER IN THE IRAQ WAR, American soldiers would have widespread access to telephones and the Internet and could stay closely in touch with family and friends despite the distance. They could write daily e-mails, post videos on YouTube, write blogs, and describe in great detail what their lives were like. But in the first months after the invasion, the soldiers were almost completely cut off from the rest of the world.

In Alabama, Will Tucker's parents were glued to the television. A CNN reporter was embedded with one of the nearby units, and the cable channels provided a steady stream of grainy video clips and flashy graphics. But the news was like eating funnel cake, all empty calories and no nourishment. They would hear each morning that a certain number of troops had died, but had no idea whether their only son was all right.

In Cleveland, Julie Niehoff had free access at her law school to Lexis-Nexis, the online legal and news database, and she ran a search for newspaper articles about Eric Huss's unit. Story after story came up on the screen, with details of fierce firefights. Though they had supposedly broken up, Eric thought about Julie just as often, and when some of the soldiers in his battalion came up with a clever way to call home—they had a radio that could reach Kuwait, and a contact there who would hook the radio receiver up to a telephone—he called her before he tried anyone else. After twelve seconds the line went dead, but at least they had heard each other's voices, and Julie knew that Eric was still alive.

Jen Reardon flew down to see Todd at Fort Riley much more often than he came up to Boston, since she had more flexibility in her schedule as a college student than he had as an Army officer. But the trips were expensive, and she was a full-time student, while Todd was taking home just a little over $2,000 a month. By the time she came back down for Easter, on April 20, she found he was completely preoccupied with the war. From Boston it all seemed over but the victory parades. They had watched on television as Marines helped Iraqis pull down a giant statue of Saddam in Baghdad, and although the cable networks showed footage of widespread looting, Americans were assured that it was simply a "transition period between war and what we hope will be a much more peaceful time," in the words of the chairman of the Joint Chiefs of Staff. One Fox News commentator offered a cogent summary that suited the dominant mood of the television coverage: "The final word on this is hooray."

But Todd was getting a much more complex picture of the war. He was having a hard time "understanding himself," he told Jen, and it wasn't until she was alone with him in their little house near Kansas State that she began to comprehend. Todd, Will, and Eric had talked for years about how much they wanted to go to war, how freaking cool it would be to fight in a giant tank battle like the Army did in Desert Storm. But now

Todd was playing a role he hadn't really envisioned—that of a garrison soldier, clamoring for real news about his brother and his many friends who were in the fight. He and Jen had scheduled their church wedding for Labor Day weekend, the two-year anniversary of Todd's impulsive marriage talk at the bed and breakfast in Massachusetts. But now he was wondering if they should put the wedding on hold. He had no idea when his friends might return. And he couldn't imagine getting married without his big brother, Tim, as his best man.

"What if . . ." Todd began, but he couldn't finish the sentence. He started to cry, something Jen had never seen him do before. It was embarrassing for him, but she knew what he was trying to say. What if Tim or one of his friends didn't come back? What if they don't get out of there alive?

Todd's parents came out to Fort Riley to visit. Linda and Larry were immensely proud of having three kids in the military, two of them at war. While they were visiting, Tim called from Iraq: He was coming home, and he'd be landing at Camp Pendleton in California in a few days. As Todd's parents prepared to leave the post, they could tell that Todd was disappointed that he hadn't gotten a chance to be involved in the fighting. How could he not be? On television, President Bush had landed on an aircraft carrier off the coast of San Diego. Standing before a giant banner reading "Mission Accomplished," he announced to the world, "Major combat operations in Iraq have ended."

"It's going to be over," Todd said to his mother as they left. "The war's going to be over and I won't get in."

RANDY TUCKER GOT in touch with Todd Bryant in early May to say he'd finally received a letter from his son. Will hadn't written before, he said in the letter, because mail service was sketchy. He sounded frustrated. He was in Baghdad, living near the airport. His squadron had seen more battles, and now that the fighting seemed over, it was sinking in that the targets he had shot with the .50-caliber machine gun on his tank had been real people. The enemy, yes; men who wanted to destroy him and his men—but human beings nonetheless. Will didn't regret killing them, but he didn't like that he'd had to do it.

It was hot now in Baghdad, Will wrote—at least 100 degrees every day, sometimes as high as 125. His troops had spent weeks subsisting on two prepackaged meals and only a quart and a half of water a day. They had heard about Bush's "Mission Accomplished" speech, and his soldiers were asking him when they'd be going home. But Will didn't know, and he and his troops felt that the politicians in Washington were jerking them around. Meanwhile, word started circulating that their departure probably wouldn't be until at least October.

A few days before, Will had run into a former professor of his from West Point. Major Peter Kilner was in Baghdad as part of a team interviewing soldiers for the official U.S. Army history of the invasion, and he made a recording of his interview with Will for the project. Years from now, Kilner asked Will, when he was an old ex-soldier sitting around the bar at the Veterans of Foreign Wars, what did he think he'd recall as his biggest accomplishment in combat?

"I brought eighteen soldiers over here, nineteen counting myself," Will replied. "We all survived the fighting, and unless anything major happens in the however much longer we're here, we're all going to go home and be with our families. Considering what we went through, and the type of fighting we ended up having to do, I think that's a major accomplishment." He'd never quite thought that he or any of his troops was going to die, Will added, but he and Kilner laughed when he explained why: "I guess part of it is being in an Abrams tank gives you a sense of invincibility."

But the letter to his parents showed that Will's attitude had clearly taken a hit. "I'm really worried about my soldiers," he wrote. "We've all hit rock bottom in the morale department." A few days before, when he'd been in Baghdad with his troops, buying ice, "some Iraqi kid kept bothering me and wouldn't go away. So I cussed him like a dog. Even worse was that no one thought that it was unusual."

He didn't like admitting it, but Will had had it with the Army, and he decided for sure to get out as soon as possible, after his five years were up.

As a captain or higher rank, he might just be a part of a broken system, he wrote. He was no longer sure he wanted to be a part of it.

BACK AT FORT RILEY, Todd's mixed feelings and low morale were evident, and one of his bosses in the battalion, a 1988 West Point graduate and Gulf War veteran named Major John Nagl, who had a puckish sense of humor, assigned him a mission designed to cheer him up. The battalion had no solid plans to go anywhere, but it had been ordered to put a single company of tanks on call to go to northern Iraq on short notice, if needed. This presented a major logistical challenge. They couldn't just drive a convoy of sixty-ton tanks down Interstate 70 to Topeka International Airport. Every step of the journey had to be considered, with subplans for contingencies that would almost certainly never come about.

So Nagl put Todd and one of his fellow platoon leaders, an ROTC officer from Pennsylvania named Matt Homa, on a reconnaissance mission, ordering them to scope out everything they could possibly need on the sixty-mile trip—and specifically instructing them to include all of the strip bars between Fort Riley and Topeka. Both lieutenants called their wives ("Honey, Major Nagl said we *have* to do this"), and set out on a meticulous inspection tour.

Todd was glad for the diversion, and he put together a PowerPoint presentation for their report to Nagl, including a handy reference guide to the sizes of the strippers' breasts. But inside, he was still struggling. He wrote Jen a long letter, trying to explain. He was full of guilt and concerned about his classmates, but he was also envious of them because they were getting the chance to lead men in combat. Sometimes he even felt guilty about being eager to go to war, because he knew that his going would have put Jen through an emotional wringer. For most of the country, it seemed, there was no war, at least no war that really affected them. Others could express their support for the troops with magnetized yellow ribbons on the backs of their cars—only, perhaps, to peel them off one day, when patriotism was no longer fashionable. Todd also knew it bothered Jen that he didn't sound very excited when she talked about wedding plans. But he just couldn't help it: With a war on, it didn't feel right to get excited about normal life.

"I think about the guys who won't be coming home and that their fiancées don't get to plan a wedding anymore," he wrote. "I think about the fatherless children, and I wonder if it was worth it. I question my profession and everything I stand for. I play the good soldier, the proud patriot, with doubt in my mind and my heart."

⋆ 6 ⋆

Drew Sloan had three things going for him in Ranger School: He could keep his mouth shut; he could carry a lot of weight; and he had good friends from West Point who were going through the ordeal with him. They slept three or four hours a night at the very most and ate rushed meals, consisting mostly of prepackaged MREs, "Meals Ready to Eat." People got injured on the long marches and exercises, or they washed out. While the Ranger instructors reminded them that nobody ever earned a Ranger tab on his own—it required meticulous teamwork—the lack of sleep and food and the intense stress meant everyone had low moments. Drew quickly realized that some of his peers had better basic military skills than he, and others were more natural leaders of men. And so he did what he could to fit in and help out, volunteering on long patrols to carry his unit's fifteen-pound Squad Automatic Weapon (known by its acronym, SAW), which was twice as heavy as the rifle he'd otherwise have.

Outside, the war seemed to have been won—the statue fell in Baghdad; Bush landed on the aircraft carrier—but the Ranger students were almost as cut off from the world as the soldiers in Iraq. One big difference was that they got mail, although they often had little time to read it or write back. Ten, twenty, or thirty minutes of free time to eat, clean and assemble gear, and read or write a letter if they could—that was pretty standard. Drew and Shannon McCartan had been nervous about whether their relationship would survive the extended separation, but Shannon was clearly doing her part to try to make it work. She was a fantastic long-distance girlfriend. Virtually every time Drew's training unit was allowed to receive mail, he had stacks of letters from her. In one Ranger company, an instructor allowed his students a few minutes with a newspaper one day, giving them at least some notion of what was going on in Iraq. Several students dropped out, saying they hoped to get to their units before combat ended. Those left behind suspected that they were using the war as an excuse to quit, and that they were missing the point. They weren't skipping their generation's war; Ranger School *was* their war. Earning the arched tab was arguably more important for a young officer, especially in the infantry, than actually serving in combat. Besides, they figured, if it wasn't Iraq, it'd be somewhere else; they would get their chance to fight.

Ryan Beltramini had to repeat the first phase of Ranger, but Drew was one of the few who made it through the whole course in sixty-three days, without having to repeat a section. As a result, he finished a few weeks before Ryan. Shannon McCartan flew out for his graduation, and even brought her mother and grandmother along. Drew's mother couldn't make the trip, but his father, David, flew out to watch as Drew was awarded his black and gold Ranger tab. Drew was so proud.

But that afternoon, he went to the Lieutenant Transition Office on post and called the personnel office at the 25th Infantry Division in Hawaii, where both he and Ryan would be assigned. The division was generally seen as a stay-at-home unit—it hadn't been to war en masse since Vietnam—but Drew was hoping that he might arrive just in time to find an order to deploy overseas. Now was the time to get into combat— while he was young, unmarried, and motivated after Ranger School, and while the United States was fighting a two-front "good war," in response to the terrorists who had attacked on 9/11.

The captain in the personnel office had good news and bad news: Drew and Ryan would be deploying all right, he said. But they'd be going straight back to West Point, where they'd run summer training for cadets.

Worse still, they had been assigned the mission only to free other units from the 82nd Airborne and the 10th Mountain Division for war.

It was the most deflating moment of Drew's life.

AS A NEW armor lieutenant at Fort Riley, Todd Bryant had to qualify on his tank, and sometimes he felt like a sixteen-year-old applying for a driver's license. Two of the three other men assigned to his M1 Abrams were fellow Californians, and they nicknamed their tank "California Dude," stenciling the letters along the barrel of the main gun. (The tank's driver, a Chicagoan named Luis Gutierrez, was outvoted.)

One of the grizzled staff sergeants at the gunnery range where they had to qualify was a terror, the kind of guy who had managed to make his own little area of responsibility into a kingdom. All of the privates and even the other sergeants were afraid of him. One evening as they were wrapping up for the day, Todd realized his platoon was holding ammunition that they'd have to turn in for the night, only to draw again in the morning. The sergeant would be at the range overnight, so he could save the platoon two trips by guarding the ammunition. Todd walked up to ask for his help.

"I don't have to do shit!" the sergeant barked, dismissing Todd as if he were dirt, and turning his back. Todd was flummoxed, momentarily stunned and intimidated. Such a blatantly disrespectful response had to be a joke, some kind of hazing or rite of passage for the new lieutenant.

Todd's gunner, a thirty-year-old sergeant from Sacramento named Earle Bundy, ran over. "Sir, if you let him get away with that, everyone in this platoon is going to walk all over you," Bundy insisted. He liked Todd and wanted him to succeed, and he recognized that this was one of those times when a sergeant with a few years in the Army could coach his lieutenant and show him the way. The platoon was watching. "You can't do that," Bundy continued. "You *cannot* do that."

Todd didn't answer, but he stormed over to the staff sergeant and ordered him to parade rest. The staff sergeant stopped almost in shock, as if trying to decide what to do. After an instant, he locked his body as he'd been ordered, hands clasped smartly behind his back, feet shoulder width apart, staring straight ahead as Todd got in his face. Bundy had never seen anyone turn it on like that, suddenly going from laid-back, casual guy to angry officer, brimming with confidence and authority. Todd seemed to channel every war movie he'd ever seen, every drill sergeant he'd had at Fort Sill, every firstie on Reception Day back in 1998, every ass-chewing he'd ever received. He spewed it all right at the insolent soldier. The goddamn sergeant would goddamn well watch the goddamn ammo.

"Was that good?" Todd asked Bundy after the other sergeant left with his tail between his legs.

"Perfect, sir," Bundy said. "Just remember that, sir. You're an officer. You've got to stand up for yourself."

The qualification course itself was fun, shooting at pop-up targets in all kinds of combat scenarios. Todd had some trouble with it early on, but after a pep talk from Major Nagl, and especially after his friend and fellow platoon leader Matt Homa failed the first time out, he was well motivated. His platoon passed, which meant Todd was now allowed to wear distinctive-looking tanker boots, black with large straps around the outside. He was thrilled with himself, and he had more good news, which he recorded in a small brown journal.

"What a great day!" he wrote. "Jen got a job offer!" She would be teaching general science to ninth-graders at a public high school not far away. It was a big relief, since Todd felt guilty about dragging her away from a big city like Boston to live in the middle of nowhere in Kansas. Though he had never worn his religion on his sleeve, he found that when he was out in the field training with his troops, he felt closer to God. "I have done a lot of praying these last couple days," he wrote. "I feel like my prayers are being answered. This job sounds like a wonderful opportunity for Jen. I am so proud of her."

DREW REACHED HAWAII in May, a few weeks before Ryan and Alisha or any of his other West Point classmates who were assigned to the unit. As it happened, he arrived on the eve of a big, formal dinner that the unit was hosting. The result was that the first time he met many of his soldiers they were all wearing dress blues. He sat there quietly for a while, not knowing anyone or even aware of which of the hundreds of soldiers in the room were assigned to him. After a little while, a conspicuously drunk man with the shoulder stripes of a sergeant first class and a nametag reading "Seaver" ambled over. He stumbled through a few sentences that Drew could barely understand, but four words stood out: "I'm your platoon sergeant."

Another sergeant also came over and introduced himself. "Hey, sir," he said, introducing himself as Rob Felts. "Here's a beer from me for all the hell I'm going to put you through in the next year." They talked for a few minutes, and Drew liked this guy immediately.

A few days later, before Drew had even finished signing in to the division, they went out in the field on a training exercise. His platoon was in a company led by Captain Rich Ducote, a 1997 academy graduate, and Ducote laid out the timetable for heading back to West Point for the summer. Without almost no time to find an apartment on Oahu and get his things in order, Drew moved in temporarily with Shannon McCartan and her housemates.

Drew and Shannon were excited to be together after several months apart, but what both assumed would be a great time turned out to be a complete disaster. Shannon had been in Hawaii since finishing her military intelligence course in December. She had been an incredibly sweet and thoughtful girlfriend while Drew was at Ranger, but the separation had taken its toll. Shannon was well settled in Hawaii, with housemates and friends who had been in previous West Point classes or were ROTC officers. She felt like Drew and his 2002 infantry officer buddies were less mature than her friends who had been out in the real Army and the world for a few years. For his part, Drew felt that Shannon had decided to grow up way too quickly. And it unnerved him when she began talking about settling down together when they were so young and at the start of their careers. Then, as it became clear that they were going in opposite directions, Shannon grew angry with Drew. After all, she had left her closest West Point friends behind in Texas—an assignment they had picked together—to be with Drew in Hawaii. Gradually, though, she came to understand that they'd both been immature and foolish to think that a couple of months of dating during the intense summer following graduation was really enough to build a future on. Both of them were hurting, and by the time Drew left for West Point, after barely a month in Hawaii, they were obviously on shaky ground.

JEN REARDON GRADUATED from college in May 2003 and flew to Kansas for good. She was thrilled finally to be with Todd and to get their long-awaited chance to start their lives together. They continued fixing up their little fraternity row house while they waited for one of the nicer old brick townhouses on Fort Riley proper to become available, and formed a close social circle of twentysomethings among the other lieutenants and their wives. Matt Homa and his wife, also named Jen, were among their closest friends. Todd had taken to Matt quickly, and constantly ribbed him for being a week junior in rank because Todd had reached Fort Riley first. They'd experienced many of the same emotions as the war unfolded; like Todd, Matt came from a military family and had a brother in another unit who had been part of the invasion.

One night not long after Jen arrived, Todd called Matt around three in the morning. "I need your help," Todd said urgently. "I'm about to die."

Without asking any questions, Matt raced to Todd's house and found him bracing a 130-pound clothes dryer against the basement stairs. He'd been working nonstop since they'd finished for the day, and he was near the end of his physical strength. Now, seeing him trying to move the dryer to the basement by himself, Matt had to control his laughter before he could help.

Jen threw herself into her new life as a military spouse. She and Jen Homa signed up for a softball team made up entirely of Army wives, and Todd and Matt would sit in the bleachers, arguing intently about whose wife had less talent on the field. Jen joined the battalion's Family Readiness Group, an organized community of military families, led by the spouse of the highest-ranking officer. In 1-34 Armor, that meant Vanessa

Swisher, whose husband was Lieutenant Colonel Jeff Swisher, the battalion commander. Jeff and Vanessa had been classmates at West Point; Vanessa had left the Army after her five-year active duty commitment expired in the summer of 1990. A month later, Iraq had invaded Kuwait, and Jeff Swisher had left for the Persian Gulf War. Though twelve years had gone by since then, Vanessa remembered vividly what it had been like to be left behind, a civilian for the first time in her adult life with two kids to take care of.

Jen went to the first FRG meeting after she'd arrived, only to hear the announcement that the entire battalion would be leaving Fort Riley in July for a three-month rotation at the National Training Center at Fort Irwin, California. It was such terrible timing, and Jen could hardly believe it. Todd had been in Kansas without her for six months, and now he'd be stuck in the California desert until long after Labor Day, when their official church wedding was scheduled. Training rotations like this one were treated like combat deployments, and Jen was certain that no soldier would ever be allowed to leave for something as personal as a wedding. She was beside herself.

Todd promised to ask if there was any way he'd be able to leave NTC over Labor Day weekend, if he absolutely, positively swore he would come right back afterward. He went over to Colonel Swisher's house one evening and put the request directly to him and his wife. The colonel was surprised and impressed that a young lieutenant like Todd would have enough self-confidence to knock on his door. Todd was respectful, but the Swishers could see how anxious he and Jen were. It wasn't just a matter of wanting the wedding on a particular day: They didn't have all that much money, and they'd already put down deposits. Colonel Swisher decided to let Todd go. What good was all the rhetoric about the importance of soldiers' families, and how the Army itself was a family, he thought, if he didn't help a young lieutenant like Todd when he could?

JUST HOVERING IN A HELICOPTER required extreme coordination, like rubbing your stomach and patting your head while standing on top of a basketball, and it turned out that Tim Moshier was a natural pilot. Flight students at Fort Rucker wore colored baseball caps, known colloquially as Skittles caps, to distinguish them from their instructors. After they completed their first flight alone in a TH-67 helicopter—a craft that looked more like an Action News chopper than a machine made for war—they were allowed to sew on solo wings; Tim wore his with pride. Too big to fit in the standard trainer for the course in basic attack aviation, Tim had to fly a special Vietnam-era Huey. But again, he excelled. He was always convinced before each qualification that he wasn't going to make it, but then he'd pull it out easily.

Pilots were either commissioned officers—lieutenants and captains— or warrant officers, a special grade comprising technical specialists, who ranked above the highest sergeant but below the most junior second lieutenant. Tim's talent began attracting attention: Too bad he was commissioned, one of his instructors commented in private, because if he stayed in the Army he'd eventually be pulled out of flying jobs and assigned as a staff officer. Warrants got to fly for their whole careers.

Life as the fiancée of a flight student had grown on Katie. She had come home in tears every day early in the school term, but after that rough start, her fledgling career as a Spanish teacher had improved, and by spring break, she'd decided she liked the work enough to sign on for another year. She made friends easily, and Tim's circle slowly widened. The pilots and their wives would go to the beach, have parties, and hang out at one another's houses. Best of all, they were together, and unlike their friends who had gone into different branches of the Army, Tim had no chance of deploying to war anytime soon. It seemed almost impossible to imagine that the war in Iraq would still be going on as late as 2004, when Tim was to report to his unit.

By spring 2003, the young pilots were given the opportunity to pick which of the four Army helicopters they wanted to specialize in. The largest group would learn to fly transport and cargo helicopters like Black Hawks and Chinooks. Others would train to fly the little Kiowa scouts. But for Tim, there was a clear, obvious first choice: the Apache, the true attack helicopter in the Army's arsenal, a two-seater machine brimming with powerful weapons. Attack aviation was all about taking the fight to the enemy, laying waste to those who would want to hurt you or your loved ones. Apaches had big, beautiful cockpits; the gunner would aim the 30-millimeter main gun using an eyepiece mounted to his helmet and fire high-explosive bullets with a four-yard blast radius. It was so freaking powerful, Tim thought, so freaking cool.

Apache pilots were the guys with swagger and style, the real daredevils. Everyone knew the old aviation joke: You walk into a bar and there are three Army helicopter pilots. How do you know which one flies Apaches? He'll tell you. Not to take anything away from UH-60 Black Hawks, Apache pilots would say, but those were just glorified airborne buses, transporting people and cargo—"ass and trash"—wherever they needed to go. And the Chinooks with their twin rotors just looked goofy. "Two palm trees fucking a dump truck" was the common putdown.

To those who did not know him well, Tim didn't seem like the prototypical cocky Apache pilot, but Katie understood right away that flying the intimidating helicopters was exactly what he wanted. Near the top of his class as always, Tim had first pick. He was a video-game addict, and flying an Apache was about as close to a real-life video game as you could get. Personally, Katie would have preferred that he sign up as a Black Hawk pilot, just because there were more assignments for Black Hawks in interesting places like Alaska and Hawaii. But Apaches were complex and cool, and they would challenge his skills the most.

Most of the Apache pilots looked like Tim—young, eager, male, and white—but one lieutenant in the group stood out. Holly Harris was thirty years old, one of the very few African-American officers in the entire flight school, and the only female to choose attack helicopters. She was the single mother of a ten-year-old son, she'd been an enlisted soldier before going to college, and she had been commissioned through ROTC. The rest of the flight school class seemed to have known one another for years, to have gone through the same West Point experiences, and to have the same inside jokes. Nobody intentionally excluded Holly, but almost inevitably, she was often the quiet student on the periphery of every one else's little groups.

Tim appeared to have little in common with her, but he understood what it was like to be an outsider and to want nothing more than to be a part of a team. One day that summer, Holly was picked to lead a class exercise where they had to figure out the timeline for repairs and maintenance on a helicopter unit, a boring but essential logistical exercise. Within a minute of getting the assignment, all the students sat down with their buddies, ignoring Holly, who was supposed to be leading the group. She stood struggling at the board in front of the class, obviously feeling very alone.

Tim walked to her side. "All right, Holly," he said. "Let's do this."

It was a simple gesture, but those six words were among the most beautiful and welcome she had ever heard. Tim's large physical presence, and the fact that he had marched up so ostentatiously and indicated that she was in charge, transformed the room. She practically wanted to hug him, though that wasn't exactly the way to fit in at flight school.

Thank you, she thought. *Thank you for reaching out.*

AS MANY OF THE FORMER D-1 Ducks as possible descended on upstate New York for Tim and Katie's wedding over the Fourth of July holiday in 2003. Todd and Jen wouldn't have missed it for the world, of course. But Will and Eric were still in Iraq, as was Reeves Garnett, whose wedding Todd, Jen, Tim, and Kate had attended the previous December. Tricia LeRoux Birdsell—she'd adopted Toby's last name but continued to use her maiden name as well—couldn't make it; she'd been in Germany for six months, and Toby had just joined her there after Ranger School. But Kara Pond, Tricia's friend and West Point roommate, was there. Kara had a beautiful voice, and Katie asked her to sing in the ceremony.

Tim and Katie got married at St. Thomas the Apostle, the church Tim had attended as a kid, in Delmar, the town where they had grown up. Both had large extended families, and nearly three hundred people crammed inside, sweltering in the July heat. With so many good West Point friends in Iraq, they blew up poster-sized cutouts of Will, Reeves, and Eric's West Point yearbook photos and put them on sticks, so they could be remembered and included.

At seven o'clock on the morning after the wedding, Tim and Katie were on the first flight back to Alabama. Tim had to return to flight school immediately. Todd and Jen headed right back to Kansas as well, as Todd was scheduled to be out in the field, training with his platoon all week. When he returned to the house early the following Saturday, Todd was thrilled to find his older brother, Tim, and Tim's girlfriend, Niki, who had arrived for an impromptu visit. Safely back from Iraq, Tim was en route from California to Virginia in his new Corvette, to attend a school for the Marine Corps. It was a great reunion, the first time the two brothers had seen each other since Todd's West Point graduation.

Todd took a badly needed shower, and then he and Jen took his brother on a tour of Fort Riley. Having been a Marine for most of his adult life, Tim had seen more than his share of military bases, but he still thought it was pretty cool to see his baby brother's platoon area and his "California Dude" M1A1 Abrams. Then the two brothers left Jen and Niki at the house, talking about wedding plans, while they took the Corvette out on the highway. The road was deserted on the weekend, or so they told themselves, and Todd got behind the wheel and opened it up.

TODD GOT THE OCCASIONAL LETTER from Will now, and a few brief phone calls came from Eric Huss—always, it seemed, in the middle of the night. But details of both friends' experiences were hard to come by.

Eric's war had changed a lot since he crossed the border back in March. By July, some of the soldiers in his battalion, 2-70 Armor, had been assigned to guard duty in the predominantly Sunni city of Abu Ghraib, whose people had been in the upper class under Saddam, and who were not at all happy about the presence of the Americans. The duty was dangerous, albeit not as intense as the combat they'd seen during the invasion. About a quarter of the U.S. soldiers killed since "Mission Accomplished" had been shot or blown up while performing exactly this kind of static guard duty. Eric's companion unit was guarding a building that had come under fire by rockets, flares, grenades, and countless small arms. The Americans were like "sitting ducks," one soldier in the unit told a *Washington Post* reporter.

In the early morning hours of July 19, 2003, one of 2-70 Armor's platoon leaders, a second lieutenant named Jonathan Rozier, was standing outside that guard post just a few feet away from the building. There was a screeching whine, the telltale sound of a rocket-propelled grenade. The RPG sailed through the post without hitting anything, but the fin on the back of the rocket caught Rozier in the shoulder, tearing him up badly. He bled to death on an operating table.

Eric had known Rozier—not well, but enough to know who he was, and to say hello. Married, and with a child at home, he was twenty-five, from Texas, and had been the platoon leader for only a few months. Now Eric was called in to take over for him.

He was scared. How could he simply step in and take charge? He'd had plenty of leadership training at West Point, wargaming what it would be like when one day he assumed a real tank command. But Eric couldn't remember ever talking about the scenario in which he'd take over as a platoon leader because the previous platoon leader had just been killed. Worse still, the platoon had lost a number of other soldiers as well—none were dead, but several had been wounded badly enough that they had been evacuated to Germany and Walter Reed Army Medical Center in Washington.

The commander of the 101st Airborne Division, Major General David Petraeus, West Point class of 1974, flew down for the memorial service in Rozier's honor, and Eric was due to take over the platoon immediately afterward. As the service ended, he spotted Lieutenant Rozier's driver, an eighteen-year-old private who had come to Fort Riley right out of high school, and who had grown very close to Rozier in the last few months. He was a good kid, Eric thought, but young and scared, no older than Eric had been on his first day at West Point five years before. Tears rolled down the kid's face. Eric draped his arm around him, and they mourned together.

RUMORS FLEW like startled pigeons around Fort Riley. The training rotation in California was being scrapped, the soldiers and their families heard, and they were going to Korea instead. No, another rumor said, they were going to Iraq. In late July, Jen went to another FRG meeting, where they gave out the mailing address and a schedule for the NTC rotation, letting the women know when their husbands would be able to call home. Despite Colonel Swisher's assurances, she was still nervous, but she flew to Pennsylvania anyway for some serious wedding planning.

Over the course of the summer, Todd's battalion had had a rash of drunk driving arrests. At least once, Todd was awakened by the news that one of his soldiers had been locked up. The issue was coming to a head, and so when the brigade commander—one level above Colonel Swisher—called a full formation one afternoon in late July, many of the soldiers expected a long lecture about the evils of driving while intoxicated.

"We've been alerted for you all to go to Iraq," the brigade sergeant major said abruptly after they'd been called to attention.

The whole formation quickly abandoned military decorum, with troops talking excitedly over one another. Todd and Matt Homa stood next to each other in front of their platoons, straining to hear what else the sergeant major was saying. They were going! They missed the part about the deployment lasting six months, but that didn't matter. A few minutes afterward, Colonel Swisher called the officers and senior non-commissioned officers of his battalion together. Get your families ready, he told them. And, he added, "forget this six-month business. Plan on a year."

Todd took a deep breath and called Jen in Pennsylvania. She had just come back from putting the finishing touches on her selection of wedding flowers, and she was very excited.

"Sweetheart," Todd began. "I have to tell you something."

Jen knew. Maybe she heard it in the tone of Todd's voice, maybe it was her fear, but she knew what he was going to say. NTC had been just a smokescreen, she was sure. He was going to Iraq.

"No!" she said, hoping to change the truth by pure force of will. "No! I don't want to hear about it."

7

Drew Sloan and Ryan Beltramini reported to West Point for training duty just in time for the 2003 graduation. Only twelve months had passed, but it felt like ten years. This time the commencement speaker was Vice President Cheney. "If there is anyone in the world today who doubts the seriousness of the Bush Doctrine," Cheney said, meaning the preemption strategy that Bush had outlined a year before, "I would urge that person to consider the fate of the Taliban in Afghanistan, and of Saddam Hussein's regime in Iraq." Nearby, as Cheney spoke, a 2001 West Point graduate sat in a wheelchair, wearing dress blues. Lieutenant John Fernandez was Cheney's guest; he had lost both his legs just two weeks into the Iraq War. (Months later, Fernandez would learn that he had been the victim of friendly fire: An Air Force jet had accidentally dropped a laser-guided bomb on his unit.)

Drew Sloan hadn't been to war, but he had his Ranger tab, and he couldn't imagine coming back to the academy without it. It would have been demoralizing and ridiculous for a cadet to be taught by an officer who hadn't earned one. Just as Joe DaSilva was still finding in Iraq, Drew and Ryan would have had to endure a constant, day-in, day-out series of left-shoulder glances. But with their tabs, Drew and Ryan were among West Point's favorite sons, the kind of lieutenant every high-speed cadet aspired to be. Drew loved the feeling.

Drew's platoon had two important jobs. First, they taught land navigation and how to avoid and react to land mines. Second, they ran live-fire exercises; this was a high-profile and somewhat dangerous assignment, with a thousand cadets firing weapons. The mission was pretty intense, which took some of the bite out of being called to run it only to free up other units for war.

Most of Drew's work went well, but as the weeks went by he began to have a problem with his platoon sergeant. Sergeant First Class Seaver was an alcoholic, and since the platoon was living together, sleeping in one large, open bay while they were stationed at West Point, his problem was soon obvious. Drew shared a bunk bed with him—Drew on the top, Seaver on the bottom—and the sergeant came back to their barracks each night absolutely hammered.

As a twenty-two-year-old second lieutenant, Drew didn't quite know how to handle the problem. Over time he decided simply to push Seaver aside and let his squad leaders take on more responsibility. The sergeant wasn't breaking the law: He was of legal age, Drew had never caught him driving a car while intoxicated, and he always managed to do at least the bare minimum required. But he wasn't the kind of sergeant you could trust, or that you'd want to go to war with.

Meanwhile, two important things happened that overshadowed the Seaver situation. First, Drew and Shannon finally broke up. It had become increasingly obvious to both of them that their relationship was going nowhere, and now it was official. And second, the commander of the 25th Infantry Division, General Olson, the same general who had been the commandant of West Point during Drew's senior year, and who had given them the motivating speech on the night they picked their branches in the Army, visited the battalion at West Point with an important message. They'd finally get their chance. It was only a six-month deployment, and they were being sent to Afghanistan, not Iraq. But at least they were going to war.

· ✴ ·

ERIC HUSS WAS STILL OPERATING in and around Abu Ghraib, where his platoon was now facing a new threat: "improvised explosive devices," or IEDs, makeshift bombs that somebody—who, exactly, was the question—used to attack American patrols. As a result, most of Eric's missions were now "IED sweeps," a euphemism for heading out before dawn on the major highways around Baghdad in tanks and Bradleys, lumbering down the road, and trying to find, drive over, and detonate the IEDs that had been hidden the night before. No IED yet seen could really damage a giant tracked and armored vehicle, but they could wreak havoc on Humvees and trucks. Eric hated the missions, especially after one of his tanks was hit with some sort of molten projectile that blew through the supposedly impenetrable armor and nearly killed two of his soldiers. The Army couldn't figure out what kind of weapon it had been, who had fired it, or from where.

Very little of this kind of information made it back to Fort Riley in the summer of 2003. Todd Bryant and Matt Homa spent long hours with their platoons, trying to get their tanks ready for battle. The tanks were already Iraq veterans, as the maintenance records revealed; Major Nagl's peers had ridden them into battle in the Gulf War. Matt's tank was a real piece of work, with a turret mechanism so screwed up that a person standing next to the tank could grab the gun barrel and spin the turret like a pinwheel. Todd's was better, but there was no getting away from the fact that the tanks were two decades old, older than some of the soldiers in his platoon.

They worked twelve- to fourteen-hour days, six or seven days a week, but still spent as much time as they could with their wives. Once, Todd and Jen were in a bookstore in Manhattan, Kansas, and Todd picked up a copy of a book called *Absolutely American*. Todd recognized the name of the author, David Lipsky; the *Rolling Stone* journalist who had written about West Point at the invitation of the academy's top generals had expanded his articles into a book. Todd flipped through it, stopping at a photograph.

"I'm in this book!" he exclaimed.

A woman nearby overheard.

"That's me right there!" Todd told her, pointing to a black-and-white photo of an academy gym class. There he was, in the background but recognizable, standing behind a female cadet who was one of the book's main characters.

"You're such a dork," Jen told him, embarrassed. "You're going to make this woman think this whole book is about you."

Occasionally, Todd would hear disconcerting suggestions about what the war in Iraq was now like. Matt Homa's brother Tony, an Army sergeant, had been in the invasion and was still in Iraq. He managed to call Matt a few times, and once Matt took Todd aside to relay a disquieting story Tony had told him. Some of Tony's soldiers had been on guard duty when a ten-year-old girl had approached the base with her arms crossed in front of her, hiding something. They yelled at her to stop but she kept coming, and they shot her. As she fell to the ground, her arms flew open, exposing the grenades strapped to her chest. Later, Tony learned that the girl's family had been taken hostage and threatened with death if she didn't sneak the grenades into the base. Todd didn't say a word when Matt told him the story, but the look on his face said it all: This is for real.

IN EARLY AUGUST, Captain Chavez gathered Todd, Matt, and the company's other leaders for lunch at a Chinese restaurant near the local Wal-Mart. Todd had long since perceived that his captain was every bit as laid-back as he himself was, but today Chavez had an edge. Something was wrong.

"There's been some thinking about our tanks," Chavez said when they finally got down to business. "They're not great in urban environments. They're too imposing. They scare civilians." Then, as calmly as he could, Chavez told them they would be going to Iraq without their tanks.

He might as well have told them they were going to war without their pants. Everyone immediately grew agitated and anxious.

"This is stupid," Todd said bluntly. "Why would an armored unit not take tanks?"

Chavez agreed with Todd completely, but he felt he couldn't let on.

Earlier in the day, he'd been sitting in another meeting, playing exactly the role that Todd was now playing, when Colonel Swisher let him and the other captains in on the change in plans. Chavez later looked back on the moment as one of the saddest of his military career. He'd devoted his professional life to the Army, training for years to go to war as a tank commander. Now, at the last minute, they were taking his tanks away from him.

For that matter, Major Nagl was just as shocked. And Colonel Swisher had also been surprised and concerned when the brigade commander, his boss, called him in. Swisher had tried bargaining, asking at least to bring a few tanks from each of his companies. But the order had come from far above any of them, and the idea itself had almost certainly originated with some faceless bureaucrat or staff officer at the Pentagon. Once the lowly brigade and battalion commanders received the order, they had to put on brave, team-playing faces and pass it down the chain.

Nobody around the table was eating anymore, and Todd's questions came fast and furious. If they weren't taking tanks, what would they be taking? Not soft-skinned Humvees, he hoped, like the ones they used to drive around Fort Riley? And what was their mission going to be? How could they possibly train sufficiently before they were scheduled to leave in about a month? What did it mean for the Army that they were being retasked like this so quickly? What did it mean for the war?

"Todd, I can't answer those questions," Captain Chavez said, sounding subdued. Frankly, Chavez liked the fact that his West Point lieutenant was asking the right questions. "But," he added, "that's what we're doing."

AS THINGS PLAYED OUT, the battalion's Alpha Company got to keep its tanks, but the rest of the unit, Todd's platoon included, was supposed to pick up new-style armored Humvees in Kuwait. This was troubling news, for tank tactics and infantry tactics were completely different. The unofficial motto of the armored corps was "Death before dismount," meaning that tankers never, ever, ever got out of their tanks. If they had six months with the Humvees, they could become proficient, but with just a few weeks, their soldiering would be half-assed no matter how hard they trained. The battalion did the best they could, clearing out a space in the motor pool so they could simulate storming into buildings, and at least making sure that everyone had a chance to shoot the machine guns and grenade launchers that would be mounted on their vehicles. Todd and Matt and their platoons were nervous about being used as ersatz infantry like this, but they assured one another it was nobody's fault—at least nobody they were likely ever to meet. The decision, they said to one another, had been made at an echelon higher than God.

As the arms room officer, Matt Homa issued shotguns and M-16 and M-4 rifles more suited to infantry missions than what they normally carried. Todd, meanwhile, finally got his smallpox vaccination. The entire battalion was called into an auditorium where someone gave them a briefing on IEDs; few of them had ever heard the term before. The message Todd and Matt got was that these were crude bombs, something to look out for but not really that big a threat. But Todd wasn't convinced, and neither was his platoon sergeant, Sergeant First Class Verle Wright. A thirty-eight-year-old West Virginian who had been in the National Guard since 1982 and the active Army since 1986, Wright had brought along three brand-new lieutenants before Todd, and had two teenaged sons serving in the Army.

"Expect contact everywhere we go," Todd and Sergeant Wright told their platoon repeatedly. For all the encouraging talk they were now hearing about the enemy in Iraq being nothing more than ineffectual "pockets of dead-enders," they had a strong sense that they were heading into the unknown. When Todd and Sergeant Wright were alone, they talked about their families and missions, and the bits and pieces they had heard from their friends and relatives who were already deployed. But most of all, they talked about how important it was to bring everyone home alive. Anything less, and they would have failed.

The battalion's departure date was now cast in stone: September 9, 2003. Todd was frantically trying to convert the permission he'd received to leave NTC for his wedding into a pass to leave Fort Riley for those few days in the first weekend in September, so he and Jen could officially be married before he went to Iraq. Captain Chavez and Colonel Swisher had no objection, but there were all kinds of concerns at higher levels. It wasn't just a training exercise anymore. What if he was in a car accident? What if he went AWOL? What if he came down with some disease?

Yeah, well, he could fall off the steps going up to the plane as we're loading, too, Chavez thought. Eventually Todd got his final permission: four days off, but back in Kansas for work bright and early on Labor Day, September 1, 2003.

August sweltered by. Todd and Jen crept up the housing list, and finally they gave up their Kansas State fraternity house and moved into a brick townhouse on post next to another officer and his wife. Toward the end of August, Jen started teaching freshman science at the high school in Abilene, Kansas. She would come home exhausted after standing all day, and Todd would sit on the couch with her, massaging her feet. She and most of the other young lieutenants' wives would stay at Fort Riley while their husbands were gone. They had put a lot of effort into setting up lives in Kansas, and it made little sense to start over again somewhere else on short notice. Besides, they clung to the hope that if the war went well, Todd and the others might be home in six months.

The week before the wedding, Jen set out in their silver Toyota Camry for her hometown, Pittston, Pennsylvania, a twenty-four-hour drive. Todd flew in on Thursday, and he and his male friends who were in town went out for a bachelor party. Tiffany was back from Afghanistan, and she pulled in from her base in North Carolina just in time for the rehearsal dinner on Friday night. Hurrying to the restaurant, she spotted Todd outside. She jumped on his back, just as he had jumped on hers at his West Point graduation. Poco marched into the restaurant, carrying his Big Sis.

A lot of the D-1 Ducks were there, and the reunion was great fun. Most important to Todd, Will Tucker was home from Iraq. Todd was very happy to see him and to know that he was safe. Will had only been back for a few days, and nobody really knew much about what he'd been through. Todd and the others had seen the news reports about the combat 3rd ID had been involved in, but Will had offered little bits of information in his few brief letters; he had had little access to e-mail or a phone. But for now they would focus on the future—Todd's wedding and the happy times ahead. Years from now, when Todd and Will were drinking beer at the bar at the Veterans of Foreign Wars—as Will's West Point professor had phrased it in Baghdad—that was when they could tell their war stories.

Still, Todd was so proud of Will, and he bragged to everyone about his friend who had just liberated Iraq, the soldier who had been the tip of the spear during the invasion. Will was just plain embarrassed; it was Todd's weekend, not his. So he smiled, said little about the war, and tried to turn the focus back to Todd and Jen.

THE NEXT MORNING, Tiffany went to Jen's hotel room to help her get ready. Tiffany's cell phone rang as she entered the room. It was Todd.

"Do you know where my shoes are? And my cover?" he asked, using the military term for a hat. "And my bow tie and my gloves?" He'd left them all in the restaurant the night before. Sure enough, Big Sis had collected them.

"Is something wrong?" Jen asked, realizing Todd was on the phone.

"Oh, he's just wondering if he should go through with this," Tiffany joked.

She drove to the church, where Todd was waiting with only half his uniform and a pair of civilian shoes. West Point degree, lieutenant's commission, sixteen soldiers waiting for him back at Fort Riley—even so, he still needed his Big Sis to mother him.

The wedding was military in tone and style. Once again, Kara Pond sang. Outside St. John the Evangelist Catholic church, Will, Tim Moshier, Tim Bryant, and a few other military friends performed the traditional sword arch. Cars stopped on Williams Street in front of the church to watch. Jen had three sisters who hadn't met Will before. When he put on his Stetson hat—the traditional headgear of cavalry units—and danced in the center of the reception hall to "Sweet Home Alabama," every single woman at the reception wanted to know who he was. With Eric Huss still in Iraq, they recycled the picture-on-a-stick groomsman they'd used at Tim and Katie's wedding the month before.

And yet, for all the joy and excitement, there was an undercurrent of anxiety. Many of the guests learned only at the wedding that Todd would be leaving for Iraq so soon. And Todd had only told his parents for the first time at the rehearsal dinner that his unit would be going overseas without its tanks. That development worried Linda Bryant deeply, but with so much going on, she and Larry had little opportunity to talk with their son about it. Will tried to reassure Todd's parents and Jen that Todd would be okay. He didn't want to tell them too much about his own experience. It was war; it had been rough, and he had encountered plenty of danger. But Will could tell them honestly that his entire squadron—1,248 men—had survived, and now he was standing there with them. Still, he understood that nothing he could say would truly reassure them.

"I'm not happy at all that he's not going in his tank," Linda said to Jim and Mary Ellen Moshier when they said hello and asked how she was dealing with her son's imminent departure. Few people held the institution of the U.S. military in higher esteem than Linda Bryant, but she felt the Army was dropping the ball here. They were sending her son on a poorly defined mission that he wasn't trained or equipped for.

The end of the reception was tough. It almost didn't feel like a celebration anymore, with everyone sad that Todd and Jen would be separated so soon after their wedding day. Todd's sister and brother hugged each other and cried. As much as she tried to enjoy herself, Jen couldn't stop thinking that in less than eighteen hours she would put her husband on a plane back to Fort Riley.

Kara Pond hugged Todd good-bye, tears streaming down her face. "Be careful," she said.

JEN DROPPED TODD off at the airport in Philadelphia the next day, Sunday, and got on the road immediately, retracing her steps to Kansas in the silver Toyota, now decorated with streamers, balloons, and a "Just Married" sign. Other motorists honked their horns and waved, but got puzzled looks on their faces as they pulled alongside—Where was the groom? Perhaps they wondered whether she was a runaway bride.

She had reached Interstate 70 in Ohio when her cell phone rang.

"You're never going to believe this," Todd said, clearly livid. While changing planes in Atlanta, he'd called Charlie Company to report that he was on his way. During the call, he learned that his unit had Labor Day off, which meant he didn't have to go in the next day after all.

"What?" Jen exclaimed. Todd could have been sitting in the car with her at that very moment, but nobody had bothered to call and tell them about the last-minute day off. Jen pulled over and broke down crying. She was just so angry—angry at the Army, angry at their friends in Kansas who had known where they were and hadn't thought to call, angry at the world. Angry at Todd, even. She had asked him to check in before they left, on the off chance that schedules had changed and he wouldn't have to go back right away. But Todd felt that he had asked a lot just by leaving so soon before the deployment, and he hadn't wanted to do it. Years later, Jen's face would still tighten with irritation when she told the story.

Now Jen drove even faster, ninety miles an hour in the lefthand lane. She reached Terre Haute, Indiana, around eight P.M., and steeled herself to keep going late into the night, stopping at a motel only when a tornado warning came over the radio. Every extra minute she was on the road was a minute she couldn't spend with her husband before he went to war. She was back on the highway at six in the morning, and by early afternoon on Labor Day she reached Fort Riley. Todd was waiting for her at the brick townhouse as she pulled in, and he carried her over the threshold.

DREW SLOAN HAD a wedding to go to, as well. Ryan Beltramini and Alisha had "signed papers" quickly and in private before a justice of the peace so that the Army would recognize Alisha and pay to ship her things to Hawaii when Ryan was assigned there. But twice already they'd had to cancel their plans to hold a formal church wedding near her childhood home in California—first when Ryan had had to recycle during Ranger School, and again when he arrived in Hawaii only to be sent back to West Point for the summer with Drew. Now they decided just to hold a smaller ceremony, with about forty guests, in a church on the very southeast tip of Oahu. Drew was one of the groomsmen.

The next day, Drew got on a plane for Rome. His father, the University of Arkansas history professor, was leading the college's study abroad program there for a semester. The chance to visit was too good to pass up, and Drew also understood that it was better to go now, before the training and preparation in advance of his deployment to Afghanistan in summer 2004 really heated up.

After his time at West Point leading his troops and training cadets, Drew told his father when they met in Italy, he really loved being a platoon leader. He felt bad for Ryan—after only five months in charge of a platoon, his friend had learned he would soon be reassigned as the executive officer of a company, a much more administrative and paperwork-intensive job. Ironically, Drew was coming to realize, the fact that Sergeant Seaver was so ineffective had benefited him, because he'd been forced to learn quickly how to lead. And Ranger School, as difficult as it had been, had been misery with a mission. He could feel that he'd grown as a leader in just a few short months.

They talked about the academic work Drew's father was doing in Rome. David Sloan was focusing on the history of early Christianity, and he'd been struck by how completely Roman Christians—once they had gone from persecuted sect to privileged state religion—had sought to wipe out all human memory of religions that had gone before.

The early Christians spent thirty years destroying books and wiped out a large part of the record of the classical world, David Sloan explained to his son.

It all reminded Drew of the Taliban in Afghanistan, and of how the religious rulers of that country had dynamited two immense Buddhist statutes—more than a hundred feet tall and fifteen hundred years old—in March 2001. Drew was looking forward to going there, he told his father. It was a great relief finally to have a real-world mission, and learning of their deployment had been a great morale booster for his platoon. But he was more than just excited about finally getting the chance to do what he had trained for for so long. He would be going to war in the service of a cause he believed in.

8

Even with only sixteen soldiers in his platoon, Todd had hundreds of things to do in the days before they left for Iraq. Several of his soldiers were married, which meant that Todd was dealing with two people for each one actually in the Army. Another soldier was busted for drunk driving, creating all kinds of headaches. He was all over his troops: Have you filled out your paperwork? Does your wife know what to do if anything happens? What are you doing about your taxes if we're not back by April?

He called Will Tucker a few times, asking for advice, but his old friend's experiences, recent as they were, did not seem all that relevant. Will had fought mostly during the invasion, and the war was more like an occupation now. Despite all the action Will had seen, he had for the most part felt secure, because he had fought from inside a sixty-ton Abrams tank. Todd's situation would be very different. The one thing Will could offer was to promise to check in on Jen while Todd was gone.

Todd made his good-bye phone calls to his brother and parents. Linda was very concerned about Todd's unit going to war with Humvees instead of tanks. She and Larry had given Todd and Jen money for a honeymoon, and now Linda suggested that they take one quickly—in Canada.

"I could never do that," Todd told her. Linda wasn't surprised.

Todd reached Tiffany on her cell phone at Fort Bragg as she drove to work. "Trust your sergeants," she told him. She said she loved him, was proud of him, couldn't ask for a better little brother. Finally, she added her most important bit of advice. In Afghanistan, she said, she'd seen too many soldiers neglect their spouses. "If you even think about calling us before you've called your wife," Tiffany said, "I will come over there and kick your ass."

The night before Todd left, he and Jen finally talked about some of the really hard issues. Jen had heard from some of the older wives in the unit that she should expect Todd to change during his year in Iraq. She should do everything possible to help them stay close, they'd advised. Too many military families drifted apart, and that was how loving Army couples wound up divorced. She and Todd promised each other they would write, call, and e-mail as often as they could. They both felt that the content of the communication was as important as the frequency.

"Don't spare me from what's happening," Jen told Todd. She insisted that he promise to tell her everything.

Todd walked her through their banking and investments. Late that evening, they broached the most difficult subjects imaginable. What if something happened? What if Todd were wounded, or even killed?

"You need to tell me what you want," Jen said, meaning funeral arrangements and the like. They had to talk about it, just this once. Todd said it would be an honor to be buried in Arlington National Cemetery. "But when it comes down to it," he said, "bury me someplace nice. Bury me where you would want me to be, where you'll feel comfortable."

He started to tell her that if something did happen, she should move on, and continue living her life. But Jen cut him off.

"I honestly don't think I'll be able to survive," she said. "I don't think I can survive without you."

Todd dropped the subject. They stayed up all night together, holding out against the morning's arrival.

· ✮ ·

CHARLIE COMPANY ASSEMBLED early with their families, and Jen Bryant—she had adopted Todd's last name now—tried to be strong. One soldier's wife was six or seven months pregnant. Little kids clung to their dads, dressed in desert camouflage. Todd's fellow platoon leader Matt Homa was stuck issuing weapons most of the day. He finally sent someone down to get his wife. "If they want to throw me in jail for having you in here," he told her, "that means I don't have to go to Iraq." As they kissed good-bye, Matt completely lost it. He cried hard for ten seconds, fitting all his anxiety and sadness about parting into one burst. Then he shut it off.

Time dragged on, a half hour, an hour, more. Nobody seemed to know when the buses would come to take the soldiers away. One of Todd's troops, a sergeant named Ken Wyma, came over to Todd and Jen.

"It's going to be all right," he told Jen. "I'm going to see if I can get my LT some medals while we're over there."

"I don't care about medals," Jen said. "Just bring him back."

Finally the buses arrived. Jen clung to Todd, but with his big, bulky vest and all the equipment hanging off his harnesses and belts, she felt she could hardly give him a proper hug. He was inside that warlike shell somewhere, but she couldn't quite feel him.

A sergeant called the formation. The troops lined up. And with their families watching, they turned their backs, climbed aboard the buses, and drove away.

IN TOPEKA, flight attendants pushed the officers and senior sergeants to the front of the chartered jet, and guided the lower-ranking soldiers toward the back. The five buses' worth of soldiers boarded in record time, but the plane then sat on the tarmac for four hours. Todd and Matt went back into the coach section and brought more soldiers up to first class. Finally, the plane took off, and the crew started the first movie: *What a Girl Wants*, about a fourteen-year-old who discovers she is the long-lost daughter of a British politician. Bad enough that they were showing a movie about a teenage girl, Matt Homa thought. They could at least have picked one who was over eighteen.

They cruised over Boston at about thirty thousand feet, and Todd scribbled his first war letter to Jen. "I don't know what to say except this sucks. I mean, really, really blows," he wrote. "I miss you so much already. I can't stand it."

KUWAIT WAS BLAST-FURNACE HOT. A sign at the airport mess hall read "No weapons allowed," and Todd laughed as they ignored it and walked in armed for war. Their battalion boarded buses for a vast camp of tents and prefab buildings near the Iraq border. They had been traveling for twenty-nine hours. It was about five thirty in the morning, September 11, 2003.

"All this sand and no water," Todd said to one of his soldiers as he looked around the desert. "I guess we'll have to learn to surf the dunes."

He found a phone and called Jen, talking briefly because there was a long line of troops waiting. Later he wrote her again in longhand, reflecting on the road that had led them from the attacks exactly two years before to where he was now. He didn't see "the Iraqi link" to 9/11, he wrote. "I didn't really think we would wage this war." But mostly, he wrote about what—and whom—he'd left behind. "I hope you realize how much I miss you and I love you. You are everything to me Jen," he wrote. "I can't wait to hold you again."

Major Nagl sent his battalion's lieutenants to pick up their armored Humvees, telling them to hurry and grab the best trucks, those with working air-conditioning. Todd and Matt hitched a ride with a group of 82nd Airborne paratroopers, riding in a convoy of six Mercedes buses driven by South Asian men who spoke very little English. The paratroopers egged the drivers on, urging them to go faster and faster, headlights off and flying across the two-lane desert road. When they hit a ditch, their helmets flew off the luggage racks. Todd and Matt had a blast.

But later, they had something for each other: "the letters," as they call them, addressed to their wives back home, in case the worst happen Matt's told his wife that he loved her and that he'd always be around e if he were killed. It's all right for you to get married again, he wrote. He said good-bye to her and to his parents and brother and family. He handed his letter to Todd, and took Todd's in return. There were no jokes now, no cynical jabs at what they were facing. Matt looked down at Todd's envelope. It was addressed, "To My Jen, My Everything."

THE DRIVE INTO IRAQ took three days. They reached their destination, a former British air force base on the Euphrates River that they named Camp Manhattan. The base was in Anbar Province, the heart of the so-called Sunni Triangle; it was spooky, but surprisingly beautiful in spots, with thick vegetation. Giant palm trees lined the roads. A botanical garden grew near large colonial buildings that the soldiers soon nicknamed the British Mansion and the British Hotel. Though the Americans knew almost nothing about the base, it had a long history. Among the Royal Air Force fliers who had served there during World War II was Roald Dahl, who would later write *Charlie and the Chocolate Factory* and *James and the Giant Peach*, among many other books for children.

Before long, Todd and Matt ran into Noah Hanners, another member of the West Point class of 2002. Noah was a platoon leader in the 3rd Armored Cavalry Regiment, serving with Drew Sloan's good friend Brian Oman, whose father had sworn Drew and Brian into the Army after graduation. Todd and Noah had moved in different circles at West Point, but they had gotten to know each other a little at Fort Knox. Noah had been in Iraq since shortly after the invasion. His unit was not even half the size of the 1-34 Armor battalion that was now slated to replace them, although Noah's soldiers were in tanks, not Humvees. For weeks, his troops had been expecting to get the order to go home, but now they were starting to realize they might be in Iraq for a year or more.

Noah's platoon's main job had been escorting convoys to and from Fallujah and Ramadi, and acting as a quick reaction force to swoop in whenever coalition units were attacked. Just after he celebrated his twenty-fourth birthday in June, he told them, things got crazy. His platoon had lost one soldier in July. Just a few miles from where they stood, Captain Josh Byers, a 1996 West Point graduate, had been killed by an IED. Recently, they'd begun noticing all kinds of material disappearing from a nearby weapons dump. The place was huge, almost eight square miles, and held just about every kind of weapon imaginable—rifles, machine guns, missiles, bombs. But they didn't have anywhere near enough troops to guard it. Every morning there were more drag marks in the dirt, showing where people had scavenged weapons and brought them into the nearby town.

"What's that?" Matt asked, pointing at Noah's map, which was covered with tick marks.

"That's every time we got hit," Noah said.

COLONEL SWISHER CALLED HIS COMPANY commanders together, Pat Chavez among them, just a few days after they arrived. "Expect a casualty," he told them. It was only a matter of time before one of their soldiers was wounded or killed by an IED. At the beginning of the last full week of September, Todd's platoon left Camp Manhattan en masse for the first time. Matt Homa's platoon was on the mission as well, with Noah Hanners's troops escorting them in their tanks.

Sergeant Wyma, the soldier who had promised Jen Bryant he'd bring Todd home with a chest full of medals, was the gunner in Todd's vehicle, manning the .50-caliber machine gun. Sergeant Wright, the thirty-eight-year-old platoon sergeant from West Virginia, was in the passenger seat, and Todd sat just below Wyma in the back. They headed out toward the north, touring the area that Charlie Company would be responsible for, driving down a road with tall earthen berms on either side. Soon they heard a loud cracking sound.

"Is that gunfire?" came a voice over the radio.

Inside Todd's Humvee an intense debate ensued.

"No, that's gravel," someone said. "The truck's hitting gravel."

Red flashes flew by in front of them.

"Contact to the left!" yelled Sergeant Wright, recognizing the tracer rounds. The war they'd been waiting for had arrived. Bullets flew everywhere, loud pops and snaps followed by the sound of rounds rico-cheting off the armored Humvees. In the turret, Sergeant Wyma couldn't see anything, and he realized the firing was coming from behind. Sud-denly he felt a hot pain in his arm. He tried futilely to spin his machine gun around, but it was too heavy.

"Stop bleeding on me!" Todd yelled from below. He grabbed Wyma and pulled him into the Humvee.

"Oh, shit!" Wyma yelled, realizing he'd been shot.

"Sergeant Wright!" Todd called out. "We need to move! We need to move!" He grabbed the cloth cover from the machine gun and wrapped it around Wyma's arm, trying to stop the bleeding. They called out over the radio and described what had happened.

Matt Homa, a few vehicles away, had a medic riding in his Humvee, a twenty-year-old from Texas named Anuar Valdez. Valdez jumped out, sprinting so fast that after a few steps he fell flat on his face in the road. He picked himself up and kept running. Todd leaped out to make room for him, and ran back to Valdez's spot in Matt's truck, covered in blood. Bul-lets were still flying, and the noise was so loud that Matt couldn't hear what Todd was saying.

"Are you all right?" Matt yelled. With all the blood he thought maybe it was Todd who had been shot. Todd nodded, and they hit the gas. The tanks led them off road, plowing down guardrails. They hauled ass back to Camp Manhattan and drove straight to the helicopter pad.

Sergeant Wyma's arm was badly damaged, but he would be okay. He was soon medevaced to Baghdad and then Germany, and eventually back to Kansas. But Todd was very upset that one of his soldiers had been in-jured, and during their first real battle, no less.

"I would rather die than have one of my guys get hurt," he said to Matt.

Not long afterward, Todd lay down on his green canvas cot. He wrote to Jen nearly every day now. He hadn't heard back from her yet, and didn't know whether she was even getting his mail, but it helped ease his mind just to write his wife.

"Some of the other guys won't tell their wives what we're doing in an attempt to keep them from worrying," he wrote. But that made little sense to him. He was afraid, and he could feel his fear changing him—for one thing, Tralfamadorians didn't waste time worrying. Todd liked who he'd been, and if he was going to change, he at least wanted to chronicle it, to understand what was happening. He crammed his feelings into envelopes and sent them methodically home. He needed Jen to know.

"I promised I would tell you everything," Todd wrote. "Like coming home, that is a promise I intend to keep."

NOAH HANNERS and the 3rd Armored Cavalry Regiment moved on after less than a week of combined operations, and the intense fighting that had begun with the attack in which Sergeant Wyma had been wounded continued in earnest. It seemed that the enemy—whoever they were—was well aware that a new, larger unit had arrived and wanted to make its presence known. Virtually every time 1-34 Armor left Camp Manhattan now, they were shot at or hit with IEDs or both. Todd wrote home to Jen with undisguised relief that the armor seemed thick enough to withstand whatever the enemy could dish out. Riding inside the Humvee was surreal—sometimes they saw bullets bounce off the windshield.

The gunners in the turrets were in the greatest danger. A few days after Sergeant Wyma was shot, another gunner was injured when an IED went off, catapulting a rock into his arm and breaking it. Then another platoon from the company was ambushed on the same route where Todd's platoon had been hit. A soldier was shot in the head when he opened the window to return fire with his rifle. Miraculously, he survived and later returned to duty.

"That's Iraq," Sergeant Wright said. "A guy breaks his arm, he's evacuated to the States. A guy gets shot in the head, he comes back a week later."

Most of the troops rode down below, protected by the armor. But everyone volunteered to switch off up top to share the risk. Even Todd and Sergeant Wright took occasional turns, both to lead from the front and to get a different perspective on their surroundings. They made split-second decisions, so it was impossible to be right every time. On one patrol, the gunner who replaced Sergeant Wyma in the turret of Todd's truck spotted a white Toyota driving suspiciously, apparently trying to hide in some bushes. They tried to flag it down; the car took off, and the gunner lit it up. It turned out that it was simply a scared group of Iraqi civilians. The shooting was justified under the rules of engagement, but the gunner was distraught. Sergeant Bundy, the Californian who had coached Todd to stand up for himself back on the gunnery range, took over for him in the turret.

On another patrol, Matt Homa's gunner lined up a car in his sights when he saw someone pointing a firearm out the window, a clear case. But he hesitated, and they saw that the hand holding the gun was that of a little girl, maybe eight years old. She never fired, and the troops later realized that it was a Wednesday, wedding day in that part of Iraq. The girl almost certainly was carrying the weapon so she or one of her relatives could fire it in celebration, a dangerous but common Iraqi custom.

Both these incidents illustrated the troops' ever-present dilemma. They didn't know who the enemy was, but they also had to worry about becoming trigger-shy. Nobody wanted to be the one to kill an eight-year-old girl celebrating a wedding. But neither did anyone want to get his platoonmates killed because he hesitated to shoot at a real threat.

Charlie Company's sector was north of Camp Manhattan, and every time they went out the gate they had to cross the Euphrates River, following one of only two or three possible main routes. They would drive as fast as they could to get to the start of the sector, about forty-five minutes away. Usually they traveled in a convoy of four Humvees, and they'd spend four to six hours at a time driving the roads, patrolling and looking for IEDs. As whoever was placing the bombs grew better at hiding them, Charlie Company grew better at spotting them. From one day to the next they'd notice the smallest differences on the road: a dead animal or a pile of trash that hadn't been there the day before.

Todd was amazed at how the body got used to even the strangest and most stressful conditions. Their mission and doctrine didn't seem to envision that they would come under attack anywhere near as often as they did. They drove around their sector, tried to identify who was attacking them, and returned fire if they could. The running joke now was that their training back home had been remarkably realistic. They felt like they were back on the gunnery range at Fort Riley—only now *they* were the pop-up targets.

A NEW LIEUTENANT had to choose between two leadership styles. He was obliged to follow his commander's orders, of course. But he also had to decide whether, at his core, he was going to be his platoon's envoy to the higher brass, or the higher brass's man embedded with the soldiers. Todd chose the former style, and most of his soldiers considered him one of them. He was their guy, advocating on their behalf to the people making the decisions that controlled their lives.

As the battles outside the wire intensified, an urgent debate developed about how 1-34 Armor should adapt. Nowhere was the tension more pronounced than in the differences between Captain Chavez and Captain Mike Taylor, a thirty-one-year-old ROTC officer who had grown up an Air Force brat, and who would soon be taking over from Chavez as Charlie Company's commander. The new plan, as Chavez understood it, was to be more proactive, take some risks to pacify the area, and thus, in theory, reduce the risks in the future. But Chavez didn't see any reason to go looking for trouble. He hadn't seen any good intelligence, and he felt that the battalion just didn't have the manpower to patrol everywhere all the time, which was what it would take to create that kind of pacified environment. There were no Iraqi security forces to speak of—the local police were simply barricading themselves in their police stations—and the grind was taking its toll on morale.

This is not a thinking military, Chavez thought. *What kind of person gets hit and goes back to the same place to get hit again?* And so, on some of what he felt were the most dangerous missions, where he couldn't see the point, he would simply decide not to go. He would say, "Yes, sir" to the commander, but he wouldn't take his troops there.

Matt and Todd were trying hard to keep a brave face for their soldiers, but it was no use bullshitting. The two young lieutenants were like an old married couple, griping, teasing, and watching out for each other. They made it a point to seek each other out before missions, to say good luck and be careful. A new worry was a recent report in the Iraqi media, which claimed that Americans were shooting at innocent people for no reason.

"These people don't want democracy," Todd wrote to Jen after he heard the report. "It is totally against their culture. They do, however, want capitalism." He also told her that the Army planned to let most soldiers in the battalion go home for two weeks of leave sometime between December and July. "So it remains," Todd wrote. "Plan for a year and pray for six months. Honestly I don't know if I can do a year. I just want to be with you. All we do every time we try and start our lives together is hit a snag."

IN OCTOBER, a mail convoy traveling to Camp Manhattan was attacked, and all the letters and packages it was carrying were lost. "If only they would tell us which convoys had mail," Todd said, "we would all probably volunteer to leave the base and guard them on their way in." A few days later, he was finally able to call home and speak to Jen for ten minutes. He tried a few more times later that month, and Jen lived for those calls. But she also felt terribly guilty because she would break down in tears every time, the stress and worry flowing out freely as soon as she heard Todd's voice. So many of their conversations consisted of him listening to her cry, and saying over and over, "I'm okay, sweetheart. Things aren't as bad as you think. I love you."

Sometimes they got cut off; sometimes, Todd would tell Jen at the end of one call when he'd try to call again, only to spend four hours and all his free time in line for the phones and have them go dead before he was able to make the call. Jen got to the point where she didn't want to leave her house. Cell phone reception was poor in rural Kansas, and the one time she missed his call, she felt sad for hours.

A month after Todd left, Jen received the first of his letters, the ones he'd written in Kuwait. Colonel Swisher would talk with his wife and Jen would occasionally hear brief reports about what he'd said. But very few details about life in Iraq made their way back to Fort Riley. When Sergeant Wyma came home after being shot, the wives descended on his house, desperate for news. He'd been wounded on their first patrol, so he didn't know much. He said simply that the situation was out of control.

Jen's mother came out to stay with her for a couple of weeks; Jen would cry in the shower, trying to hide her tears. Rumors swept through the base all the time, and the other wives in the platoon would call her, presuming that since her husband was an officer she must know something. She and the other lieutenants' wives reached out to one another. They were all frustrated at having no control over anything and almost no knowledge of their husbands' lives besides the bare fact of danger. At least the men had some idea of what was going on every day. At least they knew each day whether they were alive.

$\star$ **9** $\star$

One evening in mid-October, Todd called Matt Homa into the room he shared with Sergeant Wright and some of the other senior sergeants.

"Here, you need some mouthwash," Todd said. Linda and Larry had sent him a Listerine bottle filled with contraband Jack Daniel's. Later that night, Matt got through to his wife on the phone for the first time. It was a short conversation, but he was still feeling good about it when he woke up the next morning and got his platoon's assignment for the day. Matt's soldiers sat at the ready point in their Humvees; just before they rolled out, his gunner yelled down to ask whether they could switch places with the last truck in the convoy. The tail gunner always had to face backward, covering the rear, and for once the soldier who usually rode there wanted to be able to see where he was going.

"Fine with me," Matt said. Anything to break the monotony. They moved to the back of the convoy and rolled out. Matt called the battalion headquarters as they passed through the gate.

"Centurion X-Ray, Cobra Two-One. SP," meaning starting point. "Time now. Five vehicles and sixteen personnel."

They headed west and drove under a bridge. One of his soldiers happened to have a video camera in the truck, and was recording the scene. Something odd—a small bottle in the road—caught Matt's eye.

"Go left!" Matt called out. "Left! Left! Shit!"

A 155-millimeter artillery shell buried in the road exploded. The triggerman had been using the bottle in the road to help him time when to set off the bomb.

Bright light, family, floating away—Matt saw it all. He felt he'd been transported and was sitting on the bed in his childhood room. Then he was lounging on the couch in Kansas with his wife. Then, just as quickly, he was back in Iraq, sprawled in the front passenger seat of a blown-out Humvee, covered in blood.

"I'm hit! I'm fucking hit!" Matt yelled into the radio mike. Specialist Roger Ling, his driver, leaned over, holding him in place. Within seconds Specialist Valdez, the medic who had treated Sergeant Wyma, was at his side.

"My arm," he said to Valdez. He was in shock. A piece of his hand was missing just below his right thumb.

"Roger," Valdez said. "It's all right, you just broke your arm."

Suddenly, Matt felt as if his lungs had been shut off.

"I can't breathe!" he gasped.

Valdez tore open Matt's flak jacket, and the young lieutenant's lung flopped out of his chest cavity, completely exposed. Later, doctors determined that the shrapnel had hit him in the small part of his torso not covered by his body armor. It had punctured one lung, expelled the other lung from his body, and missed his heart by a quarter of an inch. Matt went into shock, but he was still semiconscious, asking again and again, "What's wrong with me? What's wrong with me?"

Valdez kept Matt alive and Ling manhandled the Humvee back to the base with four flat tires and a gaping hole in its side. They rushed Matt into the aid station. He grabbed one of his sergeants by the hand.

"Tell my wife I love her," he said.

"Bullshit," the sergeant said. "You tell her yourself."

Matt suddenly considered that he might live through this. He realized he was naked, like Adam in the Bible, even as his internal organs were exposed on the table. He asked for a towel to cover himself, which the doctors took as a good sign. After stabilizing him, they flew him to an Army hospital at a bigger base and rushed him into surgery. At one point his vital signs dropped to zero and he was considered clinically dead. A doctor called Matt's wife in Kansas, waking her in the middle of the night. Your husband has been very badly injured and probably isn't going to make it, he told her. It would be better for her financially if Matt were to die as a medically re-tired veteran than on active duty. He needed her permission to retire him.

Matt went through thirty units of blood, but eventually the doctors brought him back. Three days later he was at Walter Reed Army Medical Center in Washington, D.C. He learned that the lead doctor in Iraq had been named Mulligan. Matt found that hilarious. He'd been given a Mulli-gan—a golf term for a do-over—on life.

Back in Kansas, Jen Bryant heard the news about Matt and felt full of dread. She wanted so badly for Todd to call her. Matt Homa had been doing the same job in the same place; it could so easily have been her husband.

Why doesn't he call me? she thought. *I know he needs me right now, and I need to hear from him.*

She was right. Todd was hurting. He wanted to call, but the phones rarely worked, and when they did the lines of waiting soldiers were long. As badly as he wanted to hear Jen's voice and comfort her, he felt he had to stand aside and let the lower-ranking soldiers call home first.

CHARLIE COMPANY LOST all semblance of sympathy for the Iraqis after Matt Homa was hit. Soldiers came out to gawk at the wrecked Humvee, and to marvel that Specialist Ling had been able to drive it back to base. They laid sandbags on the floor of their trucks to provide a little extra protection and wedged their armored vests in between the seats and the doors. Soon Todd's platoon was out on patrol again, and another big IED went off, dangerously close. Nobody was hurt, but the blast shook his troops up badly. Sergeant Bundy unloaded in the turret, firing the .50-caliber machine gun across the river at a car that had been driving suspiciously just before the blast.

"Cease fire!" Todd yelled at him. "You need to calm down!"

"Calm down?" came Bundy's response. "These people are trying to kill us, sir! Screw them!"

With Matt gone, writing to Jen was Todd's last remaining outlet. Venting his feelings was the only way he could stay sane. He had no way of knowing when she might get his letters, but he wrote to her every day.

"I am coming back to this letter after just going out on a mission," Todd wrote one day. "An IED went off right in front of the truck in front of me. I was scared. I hate this place." He didn't have the time or energy to write about everything that happened, but he had promised to tell her everything and he was trying to fulfill his pledge. "I am so thankful to God to be alive, to have lived a good life and I pray for many more years. I will come home safe, I promise."

But in truth he wasn't so sure.

"Hey, sir," Todd called out to Captain Chavez one night on the base. "I did some calculations. Looking at the number of times soldiers have gotten hit in the last two weeks, some of us are going to have to be shot twice."

"What?" Chavez said as he walked over.

"We only have about seventy people in this company. At this rate, a hundred and twenty-five people will get shot," Todd explained, presuming 1-34 Armor stayed in Iraq for a full year. "So some of us are going to have to get shot twice."

"Todd," Chavez said, "how does your mind work that you could come up with something like that? I hope you're not telling your platoon."

"No," Todd said.

"That's not a statistic I really want to think about," Chavez said as he turned away. But then he stopped. *Typical Todd Bryant,* he thought. "Thanks, Todd," he added out loud. "That's not good."

TOWARD THE END OF OCTOBER, Captain Taylor took over Charlie Company; the ceremony was held on an old British parade ground. That night, he called his lieutenants and sergeants together. They lit Cuban cigars.

The task force needed more infantry, he told them, and with nobody else to fill the role, they would do it themselves. He was relying especially on people like Todd, who had at least some basic exposure to infantry tactics at West Point. Todd had just received a written evaluation, and it turned out that Colonel Swisher thought he was one of the two best lieutenants in the battalion. Now he would have to step up. They would ask Special Forces teams in the area for help training, Taylor explained, and reach out to the handful of infantry platoons that were attached to the battalion. It would be on-the-job training—"not the preferred method," Taylor acknowledged— but it would have to do. If they could get on the offensive, Taylor said, they might be able to cut down on the number of IEDs. Heck, if they were going to get hit every time they left the gate anyway, they might as well go on the offense. It would boost morale simply to take the fight to the enemy.

Todd and Jen talked briefly on the phone a few days later. "The sound of your voice and hearing you say 'I love you' heals and strengthens me," Todd wrote after talking with her. "You are the best wife in the world and I love everything about you."

As usual, rumors about the Army's plan for their battalion were abundant. One had 1-34 Armor heading home in six months. Another had them sticking around Anbar Province for six months, but then moving to northern Iraq for another half a year. His soldiers felt totally helpless, and Todd figured they wouldn't really have any real idea about what was going to happen until February.

"I will do everything in this world to be home by March outside of shooting myself," Todd wrote to Jen. "Maybe in the foot wouldn't be so bad."

ONLY FIFTEEN OR TWENTY MILES to the east, Eric Huss and his soldiers were still going out on patrol, getting shot at, and setting off IEDs with their tanks. Eric was geographically close to Todd, doing very much the same job, but the two friends never had an opportunity to talk with each other. One of Eric's jobs on Friday mornings was to take his platoon into Abu Ghraib with an interpreter, record what the imams were saying over the loudspeakers, and get translations. Around the last week of October, the imams' tone changed markedly.

"Ramadan has begun," said one message, wailing through the city. "The gates of hell are now closed to anyone who slays the infidel."

Havoc now reigned on patrols through Abu Ghraib. People took potshots at the American forces wherever they went. They'd drive under an overpass and someone would drop a grenade on them; it wasn't enough to blow up a tank, but it was more than sufficient to let them know they weren't welcome. They were always fearful of the mysterious tank-piercing rockets, like the one that had hit them in August.

Eric started having nightmares that people he knew were dying. In one graphic dream, a friend, someone very close to him, was dead. Finally, he got some welcome news. No, they weren't going home, but the Army had opened a training and gunnery center out in the desert, south of Baghdad and away from the fighting. Eric's battalion was one of the few armor units that had been in Iraq since the invasion, and they were therefore the first to be taken out of action for a few days. It was like a mini-vacation: Nobody was shooting at them. Eric was almost happy.

"ANOTHER DAY BEHIND ME," Todd wrote to Jen on October 27. "One day closer to stepping off that plane and back into your arms."

His platoon was feeling the effects of Ramadan as well, taking fire on virtually every patrol. "Got some RPGs fired at us," Todd wrote. "Luckily they missed us by a good bit." The insurgents would always run off, and Todd's soldiers were rarely sure that they'd hit anyone in return. He spent another four hours waiting in line for the phone, only to have the lines go dead when it was his turn. But not everything was terrible; he was heartened that his soldiers would be using "soft power" soon, handing out candy and soccer balls to young Iraqi kids and trying to win their hearts and minds. His platoon got a welcome break for a few hours one afternoon, playing football against the battalion staff, although the game was interrupted by the sound of a huge explosion when an IED hit a civilian truck. It was the first of eleven bombs that day.

"These people just frustrate me," Todd wrote to Jen. "They don't want our help here and we could probably never 'win' this war. The key is just to bring all my guys home safe. The good news is that is what I plan on doing."

The next day was a long one. Todd's platoon went out on an early-morning mission, and when they got back to Camp Manhattan they had to stand guard for four and a half hours. Later, the mail came, with six letters and a package from Jen. "Wahooo!" he wrote her that night. "I have the best wife in the whole world." She'd sent him the first pictures from their wedding. It seemed so long ago.

Looking at those brought back so many memories. I miss you so much. All your letters were wonderful and totally made my whole week and will probably carry me into November. Perfect timing on the Halloween card as it is tomorrow. I think I will dress up like an armor officer.

Todd was lying on his green canvas cot now, ending the day his favorite way, writing to his wife.

I was reading your letters and thinking about some of what you wrote. One part [was] about me not replying, and I am sorry that I don't always answer all your questions. It is only that they come in waves so I read them all in a frenzy and then often forget some of the questions you asked. I will sit down in my next letter and do my best to answer everything you asked. Some of the questions about Matt and stuff may be tough for you to read but I will answer them. As my best friend and soul mate, I would give you no less. I can answer one thing before going to bed cause I am beat. I promise you I will come home safe. . . .

I love you with every fiber of my being. I miss you sweetheart. I keep you always in my thoughts and prayers.

Love Always,
Your Todd

Charlie Company's plan for the following morning, October 31, called for a much larger force than normal, taking them out past the area where Sergeant Wyma had been shot and where Matt Homa had been injured two weeks earlier. The force would include Todd's platoon, Matt Homa's old platoon, and Captain Taylor and the company headquarters element. This gave them twice as many Humvees as normal, plus a couple of M113 armored personnel carriers, the Vietnam-era vehicles like those Eric Huss had ridden in the invasion. They'd be trading speed for firepower, since the personnel carriers couldn't go anywhere near as fast as a Humvee, but they would also be able to fight back with a vengeance if anyone attacked them.

Captain Chavez was temporarily working for Major Nagl while he waited for permission to leave Camp Manhattan. Todd stuck his head into the office. It was about six in the morning.

"Hey, you know where we're going, right?" Todd said.

Chavez responded hopefully. "Maybe we've come to the point where they're assuming we're not going to go back there," he said. He could see the discomfort in Todd's eyes.

"Yeah," Todd said, and paused. "You wouldn't do this."

He was right. But Chavez was no longer in command. He looked at Todd, not knowing what to say.

"Hey, sir," Todd said, filling the silence. "I'll talk to you when I get back."

The convoy headed out, moving much more slowly than normal. The day was hot, and the strong smell of diesel fuel from the Humvees mixed with the stench rising from the river. Men stood on the side of the road scowling. Women seemed to shy away. Some little kids waved and cheered, but others appeared to be cursing. A few threw rocks.

Todd's Humvee was second in line. He sat in the front passenger seat. A private named Taylor (no relation to the new commander) was driving. Bundy was in the turret. In the backseat sat another private, Ted Wheeler, along with Specialist Valdez, the medic who had saved Matt Homa's life two weeks earlier. Valdez had been on this very road the day before, traveling with 2nd Platoon, when they'd been hit yet again by an IED.

"I don't know about him," Todd said after a while, referring to Captain Taylor. They were all nervous, driving through the most dangerous part of their sector at fifteen miles an hour. Normally they did at least forty. "He's going to get somebody killed. He doesn't know what he's doing. He's too gung-ho. I don't know what has to happen for him to realize what's going on here."

The first Humvee cleared the bridge over the Euphrates River and began a hairpin, 180-degree turn back toward the riverbank. Todd's Humvee followed about a hundred yards behind.

"Slow down," came a call over the radio. The M113s were having trouble keeping up.

The lead truck turned left again, driving east, parallel to the river, which was perhaps twenty-five yards to the south. Small trees and brush lined the road. Again, Todd's Humvee followed. They were now within a hundred yards of where Valdez's truck had been hit by the IED the day before.

Bundy called down from the turret to say that there were two guys sitting by the side of the road and pointing at them. "They're doing something," he said. "We should stop and pick them up."

We don't have time, Todd replied.

"Watch out," came Captain Taylor's voice over the radio. "Second Platoon got hit in that area."

Todd turned around. "What did he say?"

Valdez started to answer. "He said watch for—"

"BLUE ONE, this is Blue Four!"

It was Sergeant Wright on the radio in the third Humvee. Todd's truck was gone. There was only a huge cloud of dust and smoke.

"Blue One, Blue Four!" No response. "Blue Two!" Wright yelled, now hailing the first Humvee in the convoy. "Turn around. Do you got eyes on the LT? Do you have eyes on One?" He yelled at his driver: "Punch it! Get up there!"

The dust was thick; visibility was almost zero. Racing forward, Wright saw another Humvee headed right toward his. This was the first truck in the series, which had spun around and come back. Both trucks slammed on the brakes. Sergeant Wright scanned the landscape frantically, at last focusing on a ditch to the left, where Todd's Humvee had come to rest.

GODDAMN, THAT'S ONE HELL *of a fucking rocket*, Sergeant Bundy had thought just as the explosion went off. Something had hit him in the back of his legs, buckling him from behind. His memory wasn't very precise, but whatever pushed him down as the vehicle lurched and slid down the hill almost certainly saved his life.

The world had gone dark in an instant for Specialist Valdez, though he came to again even before the Humvee stopped. This was a bigger blast than any he'd seen yet. He couldn't hear, couldn't see very well. He had a sense of not being able to control his body, a dim understanding of just how helpless he was. Valdez had never thought of himself as a religious person, but even as the Humvee was flying through the air, he'd heard a voice: "It is not your time. Other things await you." He thanked God and took a deep breath.

Sergeant Bundy shook his head and opened his eyes. His ears were ringing and he felt warm blood flowing down his face. *I'm hurt bad,* he thought. The roof of the Humvee was half torn open, and he could see daylight. In the front seat, the driver, Taylor, lay against the steering wheel. His helmet was gone, but he was alive and moving. Valdez lay on the ground outside with just his foot inside the truck. Private Wheeler started screaming. He was stuck in the back, with heavy boxes of .50-caliber ammunition on top of him.

"Calm down!" Bundy called out to him. "Where's Lieutenant Bryant? Where the fuck did he go?"

It took a minute before Bundy realized that he'd fallen into the front of the Humvee and was almost on top of Todd.

"Sir!" he called. Todd's helmet was gone and his eyes were closed. He grunted, but otherwise did not seem to be conscious. His legs were wedged underneath the metal structure holding the radio in place. Bundy saw bone sticking out. *Fracture,* he thought. *Okay, let's get everyone out of the truck.* He grabbed Todd's armored vest and tried to pull, but couldn't get any traction.

From behind, Bundy felt someone pulling him. Mack McCarroll, a hulking medic, had reached inside. He quickly manhandled Bundy out of the wrecked truck.

"I can't get out!" Wheeler called from the back. Another soldier, Specialist Nania, yanked him out of the truck, and then crept up to the front of the Humvee, where Todd was still stuck, unconscious and unmoving.

Valdez was slightly more alert now, and he stood next to the destroyed Humvee, dazed and semioblivious, with blood in his eyes and a big hole in his leg. He climbed slowly up the embankment toward the road and spat out a mouthful of blood. He could breathe again. *I was almost killed by these Haji bastards!* he thought, using the all-purpose Army slang for Middle Easterners. All he wanted to do was go home to Texas and crawl into bed the way he had when he was a little kid, with the comfortable feeling of newly laundered sheets and a fluffy pillow.

Then Valdez heard the voice again, the same one that had told him he was not destined to die that day. "Whatever you do now," the voice said, "in this moment, will define you."

Valdez was almost annoyed to hear this, to be called on to do anything, but the voice was right. His eyes and ears weren't working right, and he went through a mental checklist. *I probably have a concussion,* he realized. He took off his helmet and started to check himself for injuries. Suddenly he came to his senses. *Whoever just tried to kill me is probably still close; they could be watching,* he realized. He reached for the pistol strapped to his leg.

By now Sergeant Wright and the rest of his crew had jumped out of their Humvee, leaving only their gunner behind to guard them. Wright ran toward Todd's truck, where Valdez and Bundy were stumbling about in a daze.

A barrage of gunfire erupted.

"Get down!" Wright yelled.

Bundy jumped into the ditch. Another soldier knelt next to him and fired south across the river. Bundy looked at Valdez, who still seemed out of it. As Bundy watched, Valdez stood straight up, cutting his pants leg with angled scissors to expose his wounds, completely oblivious to the firefight.

"Deezy! Get down!" It was Specialist Nania, now crouched behind the blasted Humvee. Valdez crawled over; only when he reached Bundy and Nania did he seem to realize there was a battle going on.

"Cease fire!" a voice boomed, and the shooting was over.

TODD WAS STILL STUCK inside the Humvee, and by the time Nania got back to him, two other soldiers were trying to pull him out. His head and arms slumped toward the driver's side; he was still unconscious and still stuck under the radio mount. His helmet was gone; his rifle was destroyed. He had a cut above his right eye, but otherwise his face seemed fine. Nania, six feet tall and 205 pounds, grabbed hold of Todd's flak vest and pulled with all his might. Finally, Todd's torso broke free, and Nania saw to his horror that Todd's lower legs were still pinned. He began to drag Todd up the embankment and toward the road.

"Oh my God! His legs are gone!" another soldier yelled.

Todd was completely unconscious, bloody stumps where his legs had been. Nania tore off his belt and started tying a makeshift tourniquet on one of the stumps. Sergeant Wright quickly joined him, tying a tourniquet on Todd's other leg. Valdez stumbled up the hill behind him, barely able to see and with blood streaming down his leg. He pushed his way in.

"You're wounded," Wright told Valdez. "We'll handle the lieutenant. You go worry about yourself."

Valdez wouldn't hear of it. He went to work fast, cutting Todd's clothes open and scanning him, trying to find what was killing him. Both legs were gone, both arms were broken, but, since the tourniquets were holding, none of the wounds were currently life-threatening. Then he noticed a small hole in Todd's upper cheek. Head trauma, he realized. Another medic reached them from the rear of the convoy, took one look at Todd's legless torso, and froze.

"Go get the oxygen!" Valdez yelled at him. The medic spun on his heel.

Just as he ran off, Todd began slipping away, his pulse fading to nothing. Valdez started CPR, pounding Todd's chest and breathing air into his mouth, trying desperately to bring him back.

WHEN THE IED EXPLODED, Captain Taylor had been in the fifth Humvee in the convoy, three vehicles behind Todd. He hadn't seen the explosion, but as soon as he heard it he'd looked up to see the big smoke cloud. Now, Sergeant Wright ran up and reached him at his Humvee.

We've got five casualties, he said. Five in the truck; one serious. "The lieutenant lost both his legs and he's just barely there. We're working. We're trying to get him revived."

Wright saw the shocked look on Taylor's face. "What?" the new company commander said.

Wright repeated his report, then ran back to check on Todd.

"He's gone," a medic told him. "We're not getting anywhere but we're going to continue to try."

"Keep trying," Wright ordered.

LIEUTENANT JIM MODLIN, a West Point classmate who had seen Todd briefly in Kuwait, happened to be leading another platoon on the opposite side of the Euphrates River when the bomb went off. His platoon raced across the river toward the stricken convoy, calling the battalion on the radio and trying to get a bead on where the friendly forces were. All they heard was Sergeant Wright's report that a vehicle had been hit and that they were calling in a medevac.

Modlin recognized the markings on Todd's Humvee as soon as he reached them. He jumped out and ran over.

"The LT," one of the sergeants told him as he approached. "He's dead."

Modlin had seen quite a few dead bodies in the month he'd been in Iraq, but this was the first time he'd seen someone he knew. He watched as Valdez worked, pushing himself to exhaustion trying to bring Todd back. It was clearly futile. The crater the bomb had made in the road was several feet deep and several feet across, probably the result of a couple of artillery or tank rounds. Whoever had done it had hidden it well.

The company first sergeant ran up, and pushed his way between Sergeant Bundy and Todd.

"You don't need to watch this," he told Bundy, who was bleeding from the head. But Bundy stood fast, trying to help. Valdez wanted him to stick an IV in Todd's arm, but it was broken in so many places that it flopped like spaghetti. Todd made a gurgling little last gasp. Valdez kept trying to do CPR, but eventually McCarroll told him it was too late.

Later, years later, Valdez still remembered every second vividly. He wanted to think that Todd had died painlessly. Most likely, he was brain dead on the spot. He had probably been unconscious from nearly the moment of the blast, when his head had slammed into the radio mount and hit a metal ammunition box.

Valdez knelt over Todd and said a silent prayer, asking God to take him. Then he placed his hand on the lieutenant's forehead, trying to comfort Todd as his own mother had done for him as a child when he was sick.

Todd J. Bryant, twenty-three years old, was dead. Valdez and the others covered him with a silver blanket in the middle of the dusty road.

10

It was very late, but Jen Bryant lay awake in bed, rereading Todd's letters. She had practically memorized them. She needed to hear his voice, craved even a few moments of connection over the phone. Finally she dozed off, and though she went to school the next morning, she didn't have the energy to do much with her students. She was so down, thinking about Matt and Jen Homa, and worried about her husband. And even her mother was leaving that weekend, which meant she'd be alone in Kansas again.

The morning dragged on. After lunch, the assistant principal walked into her classroom.

"You're needed down in the office," he told her.

Jen's chest caught as she walked down the stairs.

No, she thought. *Don't think the worst. This has nothing to do with Todd. It's probably just some parent angry about report cards.*

She reached the principal's office and felt an immediate sense of relief as she looked around—no Army officers. The only person she saw was one of her students.

"Oh," the student said, pointing to the principal's big office in the back. "They're in there."

Jen walked in and looked to her right. There they were, four military officers in green class A uniforms standing next to the school principal. She recognized one of the officers, a general from Fort Riley. An Army chaplain was there, too, along with Vanessa Swisher.

Jen fell to the floor.

"No!" she shrieked. "No! No! No!" The general knelt next to her, taking her hand. Whatever he said, Jen couldn't hear. "Don't tell me! Don't tell me! Don't tell me!" she said over and over. "No! No! No! No!"

"We need to take you home," somebody said. Jen couldn't stand. She had no interest in ever getting off the floor. Somehow they got her up and guided her outside, and a soldier went to her classroom to get her purse and car keys. They got into a plain government van, and then she really started crying. The Army officers began a barrage of questions.

"Where are his parents?"

"Are they in good health?"

"Is anybody at your house with you?"

Jen managed to say that her mother was at the house.

"Your mom's in the house," the officer parroted back. "How's her health? How's your mom's health?"

The question seemed like a total non sequitur. Why did it matter?

"I don't understand what you're getting at," Jen said through her tears. Finally she figured out that they were trying to ensure that nobody would have a heart attack when they heard the news.

Vanessa Swisher really liked Todd and Jen; they were young and sweet and obviously in love. Todd's death was tragic, but Vanessa had a strong respect for Army procedure. An official Army regulation spelled out exactly how a grieving widow should be notified of her husband's death, who should do it, and what their role should be. Jen was the "PNOK," as the regulation and Vanessa herself referred to her—the "primary next of kin" and under the regulation they had four hours to find her and notify her of Todd's death once they received the official, verified word. His parents were the "SNOK," the "secondary next of kin." Only after Jen had been notified would another Army team in another region of the country begin the grim, methodical process of notifying them of their son's death.

· ✻ ·

THE RIDE BACK to Fort Riley took half an hour or more. Through her tears Jen kept asking, "What happened? What happened?" But they couldn't tell her. All Vanessa and the soldiers knew was the brief message they'd received on the official certificate confirming Todd's death. In fact, the Army regulation suggested that the officer who told a dead soldier's spouse the news should leave immediately, to stave off more questions, and so the general had left in a different car.

One of the officers and the chaplain got out of the van first when they reached the Bryants' redbrick townhouse on post. Jen and Todd's next-door neighbor, whose husband was also deployed, was watching through the kitchen window. Assuming the soldiers were there for her, she immediately broke down in tears and ran out the front door screaming. Jen's mother watched out the window, and for years afterward she would swear that the first soldier she saw walking toward the house was Todd, handsome in his green dress uniform. *How wonderful,* she thought. She came outside beaming. "I don't get it. What's going on?"

The Army officers ushered Jen inside, past her shrieking neighbor and her smiling mother. As soon as they helped her onto the couch, the whirl-wind of official Army activity resumed. One of the soldiers identified himself as her casualty assistance officer.

"This is the process that's going to happen from here," he said, and started explaining.

Vanessa Swisher interrupted. "Pick two ladies from the FRG that you want to come over." It was Halloween, she reminded them. "We need to have somebody man the doors so we don't have trick-or-treaters."

Jen couldn't speak. Her mother was in shock as well. It was all so re-markable, so businesslike, so surreal. Vanessa called two of the other lieu-tenants' wives, saying simply that they were needed at Jen's house. As each new person arrived, Jen watched numbly from the couch. Vanessa met them at the door, one at a time, trying discreetly to tell them what had happened. The looks of horror and shock were burned indelibly in Jen's memory. She didn't want to look at them, didn't want to watch as they learned the terrible news.

KARA POND WAS PROBABLY the first of the D-1 Ducks to learn what had happened. She came home from work at Fort Hood that day to find her husband, an aide to the III Corps chief of staff, standing there.

"Kara, I'm so sorry," he said, handing her a printout of an e-mail that had been sent to the chief of staff, reporting in a single line that Todd had been killed. Kara immediately became hysterical. She ran to the phone and called Tim Moshier, but got his voicemail. She dialed her parents and tried to call Todd's father in California. Finally, she sat down at the computer and e-mailed Tricia LeRoux Birdsell in Germany. The subject line was just one word: "Todd."

TIFFANY BRYANT HAD BEEN ON SICK leave all day, recovering from laser eye surgery. She was looking forward to a Halloween party, happy that for once she could wear a costume that didn't have to accommodate her glasses.

Around seven-thirty P.M., her phone rang. It was Jen.

"Are you alone?" Jen asked. She could barely bring herself to utter the words: "Todd's dead."

Linda Bryant had seen a brief mention on TV—in the running scroll at the bottom of one of the cable news channels—that a soldier from the 82nd Airborne had been killed and four wounded in Iraq. Although Todd was in the 1st Infantry Division, they were attached to the 82nd, and Linda was immediately certain that her son was dead. She'd never gotten over her dread at the thought of Todd being deployed without tanks.

She pulled into the driveway. Her neighbor stood there, crying.

"It's Todd," Linda said, before anyone told her.

Within hours, Linda started calling Todd's friends to let them know. Tim Moshier wanted to call his parents when he heard. "No," Katie told him. "We call Jen." Then, she added, "I'm getting on a plane tomorrow."

She would go and be with Jen. She might lose her teaching job over it, but she didn't care.

Tim Bryant, the Marine major, had flown out for the weekend to Indiana, where he was going to meet some college friends for a football game. Around nine P.M. Friday, he pulled his rental car into the parking lot of a Buffalo Wild Wings restaurant to grab a late dinner. He'd had his cell phone off during the flight and he turned it back on as he was walking into the restaurant.

There were three voicemails. Tiffany. Linda. Tiffany again. "Really need to talk to you," Tiffany said the second time she called. "Don't care what time it is. If it's two in the morning, call me back."

He turned back to the car and dialed Tiffany's number.

"Poco's dead," Tiffany said flatly. The signal cut out, and Tim called his father in California. Then he dialed Jen in Kansas, but he was almost unable to say anything. He sat in the car in the parking lot outside the restaurant for hours, crying, making phone calls, and trying to take in the news.

Eric Huss's mother called Will Tucker as he was going out to a party in Savannah, Georgia. Will was immediately racked with guilt—he and his unit should have stayed in Iraq and done more. People like Todd and Eric were still over there handling it, while he was back in Georgia. Will had survived so many close calls; it was inconceivable to him that Todd could go to Iraq and be killed so soon after his arrival. The next morning it took him an hour to summon up the courage to call Jen. All Will could do was say, "I'm sorry, I'm sorry, I'm sorry," over and over.

MATT HOMA was in Ward 46 at Walter Reed Army Medical Center, the cardiac ward. He'd had a pretty decent Saturday. His wife had come out to Washington to be with him, and though she was officially living in a nearby hotel, she spent most nights in his hospital room. She walked into the room late in the afternoon, crying.

"Todd's dead," Jen Homa said bluntly.

Matt started bawling. There were so many bandages and tubes sticking out of him that Jen could hardly get close enough for them to comfort each other. He just had to lie there and take it, alone. In the moment, he thought to himself that it was brave of his wife just to blurt it out like that, no cushioning, no "Matt, I have some bad news . . ."

"I wish I could trade with him," he told his wife.

Tricia LeRoux Birdsell was training with her unit for deployment to Iraq in a few months. She was on an extended field exercise in the German countryside. Germany was exactly like Iraq, the joke went, except that it was only thirty degrees outside.

Tricia had been thinking about going to law school. Toby Birdsell loved the infantry and really wanted to stay in the Army beyond the five years for which he was committed, so, for her, practicing law would probably mean transferring to the Army Judge Advocate General's Corps. She planned to apply for a program in which the military would cover three years of civilian legal education in exchange for more time on active duty. Because the deadlines would all come while she was in Iraq, she wanted to get everything taken care of before she left. That meant taking the law school admissions test, which in turn had meant bringing her prep books with her into the field. At the end of every long day's training, she would huddle in her shared tent in the dark, making her way through the LSAT study guide by flashlight.

Tricia hadn't been able to call anyone or check e-mail for several days, and she finally got to use a computer and check her e-mail at around midnight on November 2. The message from Kara was there with its single-word subject: "Todd." Tricia sat in the dark tent reading and crying, and the next day she had to finish the training exercise. Of all things, she was acting as a platoon leader in an IED attack, simulating exactly how her friend had died. Somehow she pulled it together, and at the end of the day her commander let her leave early to call Kara. They barely talked—just cried together on the phone, grieving the loss of their brother.

ERIC HUSS'S BATTALION was still on the gunnery range in Iraq, out of action for a bit and feeling content, totally out of contact with the rest of the world. After a few days, he got his hands on a satellite phone and called

Julie. Their breakup before he left now seemed like a mistake, and they wrote to each other often. He was upbeat and happy when he heard her answer the phone.

"You didn't hear, did you?" Julie said, crying. She'd been told there was a Red Cross message on its way to him.

"What?" he said, the single syllable traveling six thousand miles.

"Eric, Todd's dead."

Eric couldn't even ask her what had happened. "I have to let you go," he said, and hung up.

He was utterly crushed. Todd was like his brother, and he could think of hardly anyone outside his immediate family who'd had a more profound impact on him. He called Tim Moshier in Alabama. Katie Moshier was with Tim when he took the call, and he broke down as she'd never seen him do before, completely inconsolable.

IN THE DAYS after Todd's death, Jen Bryant learned to hate the sound of the ringing telephone. The media started calling. Friends, family, and colleagues learned what had happened. Everybody wanted to comfort her, to ask what had happened, to share her grief. But Jen didn't want to talk to anyone. She couldn't talk. Everyone meant well, but she could only hear "I'm sorry" so many times.

The Army had been so clinical. *Here's this form that you need to fill out. Here's the death gratuity check. Let's talk about the life insurance and the burial.* Someone held a form for her to sign confirming that she understood that parts of Todd's body hadn't been recovered, and agreeing as his next of kin to have his funeral anyway.

Vanessa Swisher tried to find out how Todd had died and explain it to Jen, but the details never quite made sense. When her casualty assistance officer tried to tell Jen what had happened, more discrepancies turned up and only added to the confusion. Letters poured in, some from Todd's commanders in Iraq, and even a four-sentence condolence note from President Bush, scrawled in black marker. But none seemed to agree on exactly how Todd had been killed. Captain Taylor's letter said, "Todd's platoon was ambushed with a detonation of an improvised explosive device," and that he had died at the scene. But then Jen got a letter from Todd's brigade commander, who wrote that Todd had "died en route to the hospital." And on a West Point website, Jim Modlin's wife, Kelly, also a West Point classmate, had posted a line saying that Modlin had led his platoon and ended up killing the Iraqis "who fired the RPG at Todd's vehicle."

Which was it? An IED or an RPG? Jen wanted to know.

The discrepancies, coupled with what Jen had learned about the Army in the past two years, were enough to make her think that there was at least a remote possibility that the whole thing was a massive screw-up. Maybe Todd was only wounded. Maybe they'd misidentified him, and notified the wrong wife. She knew it almost certainly wasn't true, but some tiny part of her clung to that hope.

Larry and Linda Bryant drove from California to Kansas. Tiffany and Tim flew in from the East Coast. The Friday after Todd's death, Fort Riley held a memorial service in the post chapel. Tim did a double-take when he saw the display at the front of the chapel—an inverted rifle with a helmet hanging on top, dog tags, and boots. He'd been at quite a few memorial services for Marines at Camp Pendleton, where they'd had similar displays, but he wasn't prepared to see the familiar symbol standing for his brother. Sergeant Wyma and another 1-34 Armor soldier who had come home injured gave eulogies. One of the senior officers read the citations awarding Todd the Bronze Star, Purple Heart, and Meritorious Service Medal, and he gave the medals to Jen. Tim listened intently, surprised to learn only then that his little brother had been patrolling outside the wire almost every single day he'd been in Iraq.

Toward the end of the ceremony, the top sergeant assigned to Todd's unit who was still at Fort Riley stood at the front of the chapel. In alphabetical order, he called out the names of the soldiers in attendance. As he called each name, the soldier would stand and call out a response.

"Here, First Sergeant!"

He got through the As and into the Bs.

"Lieutenant Bryant," he called out.

There was silence.

"Lieutenant Bryant!" the sergeant called again, in a strong, military voice.

Still nothing. Slowly, he repeated a third time: "Lieutenant Todd J. Bryant!"

The silence was complete until a bugler broke into the slow, sad notes of the military dirge "Taps."

Jen hadn't known about the roll call, and she was overcome in the front pew. She fell backward, sobbing.

JEN, TIFFANY, AND TIM decided that Todd should be buried at Arlington National Cemetery, but there was a sudden rush on funerals there. In the days after Todd was killed, three military helicopters were shot down, and twenty-one more soldiers lost their lives. The first available date for Todd's services was in mid-November.

Meanwhile, Todd's body would be sent to Dover Air Force Base. Tim Bryant wanted to be there when it arrived.

"You can't go alone," Tim's girlfriend insisted, and so he asked a friend, a Marine chief warrant officer named Jeff Pcola, to go along. Jeff had never met Todd, which made him even better suited for the mission. Tim and Jeff drove north in a rental car from Virginia to Delaware on a clear, warm late-autumn morning, talking about everything in the world they had in common—hunting, fishing, cars, the Marine Corps—everything except where they were going.

They arrived a bit early, went to the Air Force Exchange for a cup of coffee, and changed into their dark blue Marine Corps dress uniforms in a men's room. Then they drove to the Charles C. Carson Center for Mortuary Affairs, a well-lit, seven-thousand-square-foot building that had opened only a few days before. One wall in the entryway was dedicated to the memories of the deceased who had passed through. A vaulted glass ceiling, plants, and a mock stone well made the place seem serene.

An Army sergeant offered them a tour. They walked through the area where the bodies arrived after they were taken off the plane, and passed a room in which they were checked to ensure that there were no explosives or booby traps somehow embedded in them. There were DNA and dental records testing areas, and a station where the staff prepped bodies and ensured that they were dressed in the right uniform, with ranks and ribbons lined up correctly. Through a window Tim could see that they were preparing a dead soldier at exactly that moment.

Another sergeant brought out Todd's file. They went through the forms with Tim, line by line, cataloging Todd's injuries and strongly recommending that the casket remain closed. Tim found it very tough to read the form. His eyes fell on a note about identifying marks, including a mention of the tattoo on Todd's left upper arm: "S.P.Q.R."

How many kids have that tattoo? Tim asked himself. *How many people even know what it means?* Until that moment, he realized, some small part of him had hoped they would learn the Army had been wrong, that it hadn't been Todd, that he'd been misidentified, maybe only wounded. Now he finally knew for sure. His brother was dead.

Tim finished the forms and signed his name, taking possession of Todd's body. They gave him Todd's dog tags and the Claddagh ring Jen had given Todd for Christmas two years before. Tim and Jeff went outside to the large circular driveway, where the flag-draped casket was set behind a hearse. An announcement came over the building's public address system: "All personnel not attending to duties, please form out front."

Soldiers, sailors, airmen, and Marines poured outside. They put on their caps and stood along the driveway. As Todd's coffin was loaded into the hearse and the door closed, they all saluted. No music, no words, no bugle playing "Taps," just a line of service members who had never known Todd and might not even have learned his name, offering their respect.

Tim got into the passenger seat of the rental car. Jeff would drive this time. They led the hearse back to Virginia, reaching the funeral home in late afternoon.

JEN AND TODD's parents had very different ideas about how to plan the funeral. What would the programs say? Who would print them? What kind of music should be played at the funeral and reception? Linda Bryant wanted them to play the West Point alma mater and other military music, but Jen objected.

"Todd was more than just West Point and the Army," Jen insisted. The funeral was the last thing she could ever do for him, she felt, and she wanted it to be done correctly, personally, uniquely. She didn't want him to be just Iraq War Casualty No. 364.

There was also the question of religion. Todd had definitely become more spiritual since he'd been with Jen. But growing up the Bryant kids had been Christmas-and-Easter Protestants. His family didn't want to be hypocritical at the funeral, so they hoped to strike a balance between a religious and a military ceremony. Other practical considerations came up as well: the sequence of events; when and for how long to have visitation; the arrangement of limousines and cars. There were so many people coming in from out of town, some looking for hotels and wanting to stay with friends and family, others staying at Tim's house near the Marine Corps base at Quantico. How would they accommodate everyone? Somehow Jen, Tiffany, Tim, and Todd's parents settled the issues, one by one.

"Todd truly loved our country," Jen wrote in an e-mail to the minister who would be overseeing the services, and who had wanted to know a little bit about the young man she was burying. Jen listed his character traits: kind, generous, sarcastic, and funny. He loved and looked up to his sister and brother, and even hoped to have a son someday whom he could name after Tim. "He was as patriotic in the idealistic or theoretical sense as a person could get," Jen wrote. "But he was not as crazy about the army or military itself. He was proud to serve his country. But there was also much more to him than a military career."

A FEW DAYS before Todd's funeral, Eric Huss landed at Baltimore/Washington International Airport. As he got off the plane, still transitioning from war zone to the civilian world, a sergeant briefed him and handed him a leave form saying he had fifteen days before he had to return to Baltimore and catch a flight back to Iraq. Eric immediately got on another plane for Cleveland, where Julie picked him up. She was thrilled to see him after eight months of war, and it was easy to forget for a while that he was home to bury his best friend. He flew back to Kansas to get his dress uniforms, returned to Cleveland, and then he and Julie flew to Virginia together.

By now, word of Todd's death had spread throughout the West Point 2002 community. He was the first member of the class to be killed in action, and scores of people promised to make it to the funeral. The core group of D-1 friends descended. Will flew in from Georgia, Tricia from Germany; Tim and Katie Moshier and Pat Killoran came up from Alabama.

The casket would have to be closed at the funeral, the Army's casualty assistance officer now told Jen, but she had the right to see Todd's remains. When Jen, Tiffany, and Tim Bryant arrived at the funeral home, though, the woman in charge said that it wasn't possible.

"What do you mean, I can't see him?" Jen said.

No, the funeral director explained, in a calm, measured voice better suited to dealing with a child throwing a tantrum than with a war widow, Todd's body had arrived wrapped in plastic and gauze and couldn't be opened up. No one at the funeral home had seen his body.

Jen was choking on her words now, pleading. "Please let me see him," she said, trying hard not to lose her composure. She had been clinging to the idea that the moment she'd watched him walk away to board the bus at Fort Riley would not be the last time she would ever lay eyes on him. If she could not see him now, how could she truly believe he was gone? How could she stop trying to bargain with God, praying constantly for this all just to be a bad dream? *Keep it together,* she told herself. *If you cry, they'll think you're irrational. They'll simply usher you away in some misguided attempt to help.*

The funeral director asked Jen to describe what had happened to him, and what would have caused the Army to wrap him as they did. Jen explained what little she knew. She didn't know the actual cause of death, she said. But they'd told her his face was fine. That was all she wanted, to see his face—that, and to put his wedding ring back on his finger where it belonged. He'd left it with her in Kansas, for safekeeping.

The funeral director said she would look at the wrapping, but couldn't promise anything. By now, Jen was beside herself with grief and anger;

she went to the restroom and sat on the floor, sobbing, feeling that she had failed Todd once again.

A day or two later, Tiffany called Jen to say that she'd talked with the funeral director, who was now willing to make some sort of accommodation. Jen stayed up all night writing Todd a letter that she hoped could be placed in the casket with him, trying to express every thought and feeling she had. She apologized for not getting pregnant before he left, and for having been so emotional. She wanted him to know she wasn't mad at him for dying, even though everyone said she had that right. If there had been any chance of him coming back home, she knew he would have done so. In the past few days, a lot of people had told her that at their wedding, they'd had a feeling that Todd wouldn't be coming home. How dare they!

Jen finished the letter and put it together with Todd's wedding ring and his West Point ring. They would never have kids to pass the West Point ring along to, and Todd had only worn the wedding ring for ten days before he left. Now she wanted him to have it forever, proof that their love and commitment had been real.

Jen and Tiffany got to the funeral home, and the director explained to Jen that Todd's body was wrapped in several layers of gauzelike cotton and plastic. All they could uncover were his hands. She wouldn't be able to see his face. The casket was in the basement, and Jen went downstairs with the director, leaving Tiffany behind. It looked and smelled very much like any basement—gray concrete walls and mustiness.

Todd's casket was just to their left as she walked in. As she'd been warned, his entire body was wrapped, but his hands were free, and they seemed to float there oddly on the gauze and plastic. Jen began to cry, recognizing the hands she knew as she knew no others, thinking of the countless times she had held them, and how it had felt for him to touch her face. She wanted so badly just to throw herself over Todd's body, to let him hold her. Instead, she stood there, quietly stroking his hands for several minutes as she cried, with the funeral director's hand on her shoulder. Finally, she placed the letter inside the casket. She lifted Todd's right hand to put the West Point ring on him, but his fingers were swollen and she could barely get the ring past his first knuckle. Her own hands shook as she slipped the wedding ring onto the third finger of his left hand, thinking about how she had done the same thing in church on their wedding day just two months before. Then she stood there, as long as she could bear, with her hand on top of his.

AT THE WAKE, a few hours later, Eric Huss found a quiet moment, opened the casket, and slipped an old Soviet-made flask inside, just like one Todd had had at school. They'd shared that flask many times, sipping Jack Daniel's covertly in the giant assemblies that West Point held, when it seemed every third retired general would come in to talk with them about leadership, or about how special they were.

Later that night, most of Todd's West Point friends sat in the lobby of their hotel together, eating pizza and talking. Tricia and her husband, Toby, would both be going to Iraq soon; she was nervous and full of dread, and she felt as if everyone who heard about their upcoming deployments now looked at her with undisguised pity, as if they didn't expect to see her alive again.

Eric was irritable, and he grew angry when the topic of conversation turned from reminiscing about Todd to talking about the war. Tricia and he talked about where she was going in Iraq, and she asked Eric if he knew how it compared to Anbar Province, where both he and Todd had been. But after a while, he became annoyed. Julie was sitting right next to him. He didn't want her to hear all this talk of war, nor did he want to focus on the fact that he'd be leaving again so soon. Granted, they were all in the Army; granted, many of them would be going to war eventually. But Eric's situation was different; he would be back in combat in just a few days.

"Nobody knows what it's really like over there," Eric told Julie later when they were alone, adding with disdain, "They're all looking forward to their *tours.*"

THE WEATHER WAS DECENT for November, a little cold but dry, and the funeral services at the First Presbyterian Church in Arlington were crowded.

Many of Todd's friends, especially those from West Point, drove together in a large van. Kara sang "On Eagle's Wings," and Tricia did a reading. Katie Moshier was struck by how terrible it was to watch her husband and Todd's other friends escorting the casket inside.

"Promise me you'll never put me through that," Katie said to Tim when he sat down with her.

"I can't promise," he said.

One of Todd's high school friends gave a eulogy, and then it was Tim Moshier's turn. Tim remembered his West Point roommate as a friend on a constant mission for fun, eager to ensure that everyone joined in the party. He had kept a blender in his car at all times, Tim recalled, "just in case someone wanted margaritas." Todd was intensely loyal. "When upperclassmen from other companies would try to haze the plebes of D-1, Todd would borrow a line from the movie *Animal House:* 'They can't do that to our plebes! Only we can do that to our plebes!'"

Todd was introspective, "aware of his failings and always working to surpass them." He loved to debate. Tim could remember many late nights in the unkempt room they had shared, arguing with Todd about all manner of controversial subjects. And Todd was deeply in love with Jen. He had talked freely with friends about how he much he cared for her from the earliest days of their relationship.

Inevitably, though, Tim would remember Todd as the fun-loving Tralfamadorian he had aspired to be. "I have never met someone so eager to make others laugh," Tim said. "He was, I think, one of the happiest people I have ever known."

MATT HOMA COULD NOW WALK, but the doctors at Walter Reed would let him attend Todd's funeral only if he promised to use a wheelchair the whole time. And he had to ride in the backseat, because in an accident an inflating air bag would kill him. Jen Homa drove. They got lost on the byzantine streets of Arlington, finally finding the church and going in just as Tim Moshier was finishing his eulogy. Matt felt like a complete jerk for coming in late, and he felt even worse when he was ushered forward to the only pew with a wheelchair cutout, directly in front of Jen Bryant. He was called up to the altar almost immediately.

Matt stared at his eulogy, but could not speak. After a minute, he handed it to the pastor.

"Todd Bryant was and always will be my best friend," she began reading, as Matt sat in his wheelchair, head in his hands the entire time.

A bagpiper started playing "Amazing Grace," and the Bryants followed Todd's casket as it was taken out the door. Tim Bryant walked down the aisle somberly. It struck him how many people he recognized from distant parts of his life—Marines he'd served with years before, guys he hadn't seen since Naval ROTC at Purdue University, fellow officers he barely knew but who were attending the same Marine Corps class as he was. Two of his Marine friends held the doors open. Outside, Jen Homa was virtually besieged with offers of help as she tried to collapse Matt's wheelchair and fit it in the trunk of their car.

The motorcade was very long, and it snaked its way through the streets to Arlington National Cemetery. The Bryants rode up front. The whole town seemed to be holding its hat in its hand, quiet and still. People stood in place on the sidewalks, and police officers saluted. They reached Fort Myer, where an honor guard of about two dozen soldiers stood at attention.

Matt Homa's car was mobbed. Everyone knew who he was now—the lieutenant in the wheelchair with the Purple Heart ribbon on his uniform jacket, the soldier who had been in Iraq with Todd and who had been wounded so recently that he hadn't had time to sew a combat patch on his right sleeve. An Air Force major rushed over to push his wheelchair. When they reached some steps, four senior officers gripped it by the corners and carried Matt to the top. They waited for the burial inside the mausoleum, where the acting secretary of the Army offered Matt his condolences and gave him a ceremonial coin.

Matt was embarrassed. He didn't think of himself as any kind of hero, and it bothered him that people were treating him like one, especially since this was Todd's funeral. He'd never met Todd's parents or his brother and sister before, and he felt awkward and unworthy sitting there, wounded but alive. Still, they smiled and greeted him warmly.

THE GRAVESIDE SERVICES at Section 60, Plot No. 8128 were relatively brief. A military chaplain read from a prayer book, sounding as if he'd performed the same service many times before. The honor guard fired off a salute, and a bugler played "Taps."

Tears streamed down Tim Bryant's face. He really didn't want to cry, didn't think it was appropriate for a Marine officer in dress blues to show that kind of emotion, even at his little brother's funeral. Someone made an announcement about a reception at the home of a family friend not far away. As the final notes of "Taps" sounded, people started to drift off.

Jen, Tiffany, Tim, Linda, and Larry stayed behind in the front row. Everyone was crying, especially Jen. A handful of Fort Myer soldiers stood at parade rest, escorts for the casket. After a long while, Jen stood, and Tiffany and Tim followed her to the car.

Later, after they were gone, the burial detail lowered Todd into the ground.

11

Todd Bryant's eulogy page on the West Point website now brimmed with entries. Eric Huss's parents told a story about the time he had challenged Eric's brother to an eating contest at a restaurant that offered all-you-can-eat prime rib. "A draw was declared at fourteen slices each," they recalled, "but Todd woke the next morning with what he described as a 'meat hangover.'"

"The Ducks gang will never be the same without Todd to liven up the group," wrote Reeves Garnett, whose wedding Todd and Jen had gone to after Christmas 2002. Tim Moshier wrote that he'd laughed more as Todd's roommate than at any time in his life.

As the days and weeks passed, more and more people signed on, wrote eulogies, sent letters.

But inevitably, the flow of new entries diminished. And life, for the living, continued.

ERIC HUSS'S LEAVE SLIP said he had four days left after Todd's funeral, and he planned to burn every minute with Julie and his parents. He was pretty sure now that the only way he would come home from Iraq again was in a box with a flag on top. His predecessor as platoon leader had been killed, Todd was dead, Matt Homa had barely survived, and it was impossible not to conclude that the life expectancy of a lieutenant wasn't very long. But Eric never entertained the thought of refusing to go back. He'd long ago given up his freedom for the greater glory of the state, and if he ever forgot his obligation, a vivid reminder—the initials "S.P.Q.R."—was indelibly inked on his left arm. Eric believed that Todd was the good friend who had died in the graphic nightmare he'd had. Now, the night before he went back, he dreamed his own death.

His leave over, Eric retraced his steps, flying back to Iraq through the Baltimore airport. That night around midnight, Julie's phone rang.

"Where's Lieutenant Huss?" a voice demanded. It was Eric's company commander in Iraq.

Julie told him that Eric was on his way, but it was only the first sign of trouble. Leave slip or not, his battalion commander wasn't pleased that Eric had taken the extra days rather than go straight from the funeral to the airport, and as punishment he delayed Eric's promotion to first lieutenant for a month. Eric didn't particularly care anymore; he showed the colonel the least respect he could get away with. If there truly was a choice between being the brass's representative to his platoon or his platoon's representative to the brass, Eric threw in wholeheartedly with his platoon. Get above the rank of lieutenant, he thought, and not many soldiers were spending days and nights outside the wire, getting shot at and risking their lives. The colonels and majors did what their jobs required, but that meant they mostly would drive out in their Humvees, check on the troops, and then drive back to the guarded compounds.

After his talk with the colonel, Eric apologized to his troops, the only people whose opinions he cared about. They understood. If it had been their friend who had died, and they'd had a chance to spend a few days back in the States, they would have done the same.

DREW SLOAN HADN'T KNOWN Todd Bryant, and although he thought often of some of his own close friends facing danger in Iraq—Brian Oman was a prime example—the truth was that he was having an awfully good time. Back from visiting his father in Rome, he realized now he had one of the best assignments in the Army, and he could hardly imagine why he had once thought that asking to be stationed in Texas would be a good idea. The weather was always gorgeous, and he had two dozen or more good friends, all living near one another. Drew and three West Point classmates, all infantry officers, rented a huge place together overlooking a beach on the northwest shore of Oahu, a gorgeous house that everyone came to call the Sunset House. There was always somebody to have fun with. They went out to the bars and clubs of Honolulu almost every Friday and Saturday night, and they spent their days off on the beach.

Drew had been hanging out in a bar on the North Shore one day when he ran into a West Point classmate he had known only in passing. They got to talking, and it quickly emerged that Lieutenant Greg Londo was assigned to one of Drew's unit's sister brigades. He had only just arrived on the island, and yet he already had an aunt and uncle coming out to visit, and he invited Drew to come along for a day of golf, followed by drinks and dinner. Drew didn't play golf, but he met them all afterward for dinner at a new resort called the Ko Olina, which was just being developed as a hotel and condominium complex.

You know, Greg's uncle suggested, the two of you should think about buying something here.

It wasn't the craziest idea; real estate seemed like a great investment, and they both had steady jobs with a decent income. A week later, on a Sunday afternoon, Drew and Greg went back to the Ko Olina and walked into the development office. They weren't actually selling units yet, the woman behind the desk explained, but she'd be happy to take their names and other information. They left feeling quite savvy and financially astute.

Word came down that the brigade Drew was assigned to would be going to Afghanistan earlier than planned, and would stay for an entire year now, in order to free up another unit for Iraq. The training schedule grew more intense. In November, their unit prepared to go to the Pohakuloa Training Area on the Big Island, Hawaii, where there was enough room for giant military exercises.

The day before they were supposed to leave, Drew's troubled platoon sergeant, Sergeant Seaver, didn't show up for work. It wasn't as though Seaver had never been late before, and Drew had so little professional use for the man that he didn't feel any need to look for him.

"Sir, you've got to try and find him," the company first sergeant told Drew a few hours later when he realized Seaver was still missing. Drew promised to send someone to Seaver's house.

Two or three hours later, the first sergeant came back. "Sir, you sent someone to look for Sergeant Seaver, right?"

"No," Drew admitted. "I didn't get around to it."

"Really? Because I told the commander that we were going to do it. I really need you to go do that."

The last thing Drew wanted to do was go roust his platoon sergeant out of bed in the afternoon. But he realized he couldn't send anyone else. He grabbed Staff Sergeant Rob Felts, and they drove to Seaver's house.

The sergeant's car was in the driveway but his house was quiet, and Drew and Felts knocked on all the doors. Nothing. They could see inside. The place was a mess, and both soldiers noticed a white piece of paper in the front room. Drew and Felts looked at each other, thinking the same thing: suicide.

"Sir, do you want to go in there?" Felts asked.

Drew pulled out his cell phone. The battery was dying, but he quickly called his company commander, Captain Ducote, and described the situation.

"What do you want us to do, sir?" Drew asked.

"If you can get in the house," Ducote told him, "get in the house."

Drew watched Felts pick the lock using nothing but a credit card, and was pretty impressed. Drew walked toward the bedroom; Felts made for the couch. Beer cans littered the place, and Drew heard an odd noise from the bathroom. He followed it and pushed open the door. At first he saw nothing, but then—

"Holy shit!" Drew yelled. There was Sergeant First Class Seaver, leader of men, standing nearly naked in a corner of the shower, very much alive and wearing nothing but a pair of smiley-face boxer shorts. He was a little guy, early forties, wiry and taut, with skin like sun-dried leather. His physique, laid bare, suggested that Seaver's nutritional intake included little more than Budweiser, Mountain Dew, and Marlboros.

Drew spun on his heel and stalked out of the bathroom.

"Sir, did I scare you?" Seaver said, slurring his words.

"Fuck yeah, you did!" Drew yelled. Sergeant Felts came running up, and the three of them stood there staring at one another. Seaver's eyes were droopy, as if he'd been drinking all day. Drew hadn't known before this that his platoon sergeant's two front teeth were fake; he apparently hadn't put them in yet today. He looked like a hockey goalie or a guy who'd just been in a bar fight. But he was holding an unopened beer.

"Sergeant," Felts began, "what are you doing?"

Seaver popped open his can of Budweiser and took a sip. He looked up at Drew and Felts. "I'm getting fucked up," he said, slurring again. "What are you doing?"

"Working," Drew responded. He looked over at Felts in disbelief. "Well, Sergeant," he said to Seaver. "We deploy out of a formation at three o'clock tomorrow morning. I hope we see you there."

His platoon sergeant nodded drunkenly. But the next morning, Seaver didn't show. When some other soldiers went back to his house again, he was gone.

A FEW WEEKS LATER, Drew was back on Oahu, sitting on his couch with something on his mind. He thought back to when he and Shannon had broken up for good at the end of the summer. A question she asked him then had nagged at him ever since.

So, she had said in a tone somewhere between anger and resignation, *are you going to call Chloe now?*

Wow, Drew had thought. *Chloe Hayes.*

He barely recalled mentioning her to Shannon, and yet obviously her name had made an impression. He dug through his old phone numbers and called Chicago.

Chloe was quite surprised: More than a year had gone by since she'd last heard from him. He'd been thinking of her, Drew explained, and then he told her about going through Ranger School, just as her Old Grad father had done thirty years before. Now he was back in Hawaii, and he admitted he'd broken up with a pretty serious girlfriend.

Chloe figured as much. She, too, had been dating someone else, a high school boyfriend whom she'd never quite lost touch with. But now she was on the road, driving back to college after a weekend at home, and she was happy to hear from Drew. They talked about the war for a bit, and about friends of Drew's whom Chloe had known who were now fighting in Iraq.

No, Drew told her, he hadn't been over yet, although he was going to Afghanistan early in 2004. He told her about what he'd done over the summer, working back at West Point—

"Oh my gosh!" Chloe interrupted. "We were both in New York!"

It turned out they'd spent the months of June, July, and August barely more than an hour away from each other. Chloe had done an internship for a television news program in New York City, and she'd even been up near West Point a couple of times, working on a freelance magazine article about hiking trails north of the city.

It was a six-and-a-half-hour drive back to Missouri, where Chloe went to college, and while she felt a little guilty—she had that boyfriend, after all—she welcomed the conversation. She didn't think there was much chance that this could ever develop into more than a flirtatious long-distance friendship, so what was the harm?

Drew leaned back on the couch at the Sunset House; Chloe drove south on Interstate 55 toward St. Louis. They picked up right where they had left off two years earlier, and they talked for a very long time.

REYNA PELAEZ, A PRETTY, dark-haired first-grade teacher, was out with her cousin at a bar in Austin called Speakeasy on a Saturday night in December 2003. They'd picked the place so Reyna's cousin's boyfriend, a 1995 West Point graduate, could watch the Army-Navy football game on television. Reyna was twenty-five, the single mother of a six-year-old girl, and she had immigrated to the United States from Peru when she was just a little older than her daughter. She had no military background and no interest in football, but she was happy just to be out for the evening. A bald-headed guy who seemed to know her cousin's boyfriend—or clearly, at least, had something in common with him—struck up a conversation with her, and before she knew it, they'd been talking for three hours in the noisy bar.

I really want this guy to call me, Reyna thought as they traded numbers. She programmed his name—as she believed she'd heard it—into her cell phone: "Gabe."

The following Monday, the guy Reyna had met—not Gabe, but Dave Swanson, West Point class of 2002, still proud of his dubious distinction of having the lowest SAT scores in the history of West Point Prep—called her at eleven in the morning. Reyna stared at the blinking cell phone and didn't answer, suddenly nervous. But that night he called a second time, and again they talked for hours.

Dave was stationed at Fort Hood now, about sixty miles from Austin. He'd reported to the 1st Cavalry Division after washing out of the first day of Ranger School, endured the classic left-shoulder-peek treatment, and spent most of 2003 learning to lead a platoon. He'd just returned from a month at the National Training Center in the California desert, and his unit had orders to leave for Iraq in a few months.

On their first official date, Dave and Reyna went to her cousin's office Christmas party, and again they clicked right away. Reyna hadn't really thought that much about the war in Iraq or been exposed to the Army before, and she was amazed the first time Dave took her to Fort Hood. To her, the idea of an Army base was something out of history—she expected to see a fort like the Alamo.

"Wow," she exclaimed as he drove her around, past the gas stations, the convenience stores, the Wal-Mart-like post exchange, and the thousands of apartment-style barracks, townhouses, and family residences. "This is like a city."

When Dave invited her to a party with his soldiers at his two-bedroom townhouse one Thursday evening, Reyna was amazed. Many of his troops didn't look old enough to shave. They called her new boyfriend "sir," and they really seemed to look up to him. That caught her off guard. There was a keg of beer and a lot of food; some of Dave's soldiers had brought their wives and little kids. There were even a couple of pregnant girl-friends. Reyna knew firsthand how hard that could be.

It's a different type of woman who decides she's going to do this for the rest of her life, she thought.

Dave and Reyna spent a lot of time together over the next month, but, as it is for so many military couples, the calendar was their enemy. Soon Dave would be leaving for Iraq, gone for an entire year.

"What do you want to do?" he asked Reyna one night at a restaurant.

"I want to get to know you," she said, "but I'm not the type of girl who's going to be standing there with five other girls saying good-bye." If Dave was just looking for a fling, if he wanted to fool around with as many girls as he could before he went to war, he had every right, Reyna told him, but she wouldn't stick around. "If you want to do that, I'm not going to hate you. But I'm just not going to be there."

Dave said he wasn't sure what he wanted. Everything was moving so quickly. And, he added, with more clinical bluntness than romanticism, there was an opportunity cost to dating Reyna exclusively: It might pre-clude finding someone else he liked even more. Just then his cell phone rang. It was another girl.

Reyna was taken aback. *Wow,* she thought as Dave quickly got rid of the call. *This guy is something else.*

They both left the restaurant feeling totally unsettled, but as soon as Reyna got home, Dave was on the phone again. He'd thought things over.

"Let's do it," he said.

"Okay," Reyna said, not knowing exactly what he meant or how to re-spond. It was as if they were in a football huddle and he was calling a play. "So you want to date exclusively?" she asked cautiously.

"Yeah."

Despite this unsteady beginning, Dave and Reyna grew close quickly. A few weeks before Dave was due to leave for Iraq, he took Reyna up to Nashville, where his parents now lived. At the end of the visit, they were saying good-bye at the airport. Reyna watched Dave's mother hug him, and she saw the unmistakable look of a woman who didn't know whether she'd ever see her son again. Reyna suddenly realized that would be her in a month, saying good-bye. And, at the same moment, she realized she was in love with Dave Swanson.

She held her tongue for the whole ride back to Texas, and went home to the apartment she shared with her daughter and her cousin. But after she'd played with her daughter for a while and put her to bed, Reyna broke down.

"It is so my luck," she complained to her cousin. "This is my life. This is the way it always works out." She'd been in Texas for a long time, and never met anyone she could care about. Now, she'd fallen in love with a guy who was heading off to war in a matter of weeks. She had to tell him how she felt.

They had a long conversation on the phone later that night. "I have something to tell you," Reyna said, and then paused, wondering if she really wanted to go through with saying it. But she had no choice; her feelings were too strong. She told Dave she loved him, and that even though he hadn't asked her to, she would wait for him while he was in Iraq. Dave told her he loved her, too.

In the weeks before his deployment, Dave and Reyna were inseparable. Dave was leaving on a Tuesday, and Reyna spent the weekend with him and took Monday off from work. That last visit wasn't particularly romantic—Dave had had last-minute dental work done and was all doped up on pain medication—but she helped him pack and felt closer to him than ever. The night before he left for Iraq, when it was finally time to say good-bye, she hugged him and told him she loved him again. Then she walked briskly to her car, never looking back. She was crying but didn't want him to see, holding on to one last bit of pride, knowing he might never come home and might break her heart even if he did.

Dave watched her go, hardly able to believe their good-bye had gone so quickly.

TRICIA LEROUX BIRDSELL and Toby had been separated for most of their marriage. They had trained at different bases—Tricia in Texas, Toby in

Georgia—and then she had arrived in Germany six months before Toby, since he had to finish Ranger School first. Now they were both going to Iraq. They would be stationed only about fifteen or twenty miles apart—Tricia's medical unit would be assigned to Toby's infantry brigade, and she would be helping to run an aid station at a base near the city of Baqubah, north of Baghdad—but Tricia was beginning to realize they would probably have very little opportunity to see each other or talk.

Though they were both in the military and both going to war, they still had to face some of the same questions deploying soldiers faced with civilian spouses. What if the worst happened to either of them?

Toby had refused to talk about it, but Tricia had a single request. "If anything happens," she told him, "bury me near Todd. I want to be near my friend."

Toby left for Kuwait in early February 2004; Tricia's unit followed a few weeks later, flying in the back of a dark, noisy, windowless Air Force C-17 cargo jet. They landed in the middle of the night in Kuwait City, then boarded buses for the same desert base Todd Bryant had set out from the previous September. Toby was there to meet her when the bus arrived before dawn. Their reunion was short, as his battalion quickly moved up into Iraq while Tricia's support unit was stuck in Kuwait for a full month, surrounded for miles by nothing but desert. The place looked like a minimum-security prison, and it was soon clear that the Army had vastly underestimated how many soldiers would be coming through. It was hot. Sometimes the wind kicked up and created fierce sandstorms. Just getting food was a challenge each day, and Tricia's entire company slept in giant tents, crammed so tight that they nearly rolled onto one another at night. The place was so uncomfortable that the soldiers agreed it must be a ploy to make them actually look forward to reaching Iraq.

At last, they saddled up for the drive north. Tricia and three male soldiers drove in a temperamental soft-skinned Humvee they'd nicknamed the Death Trap during training in Germany. The truck was unarmored, so they packed it with sandbags against IEDs, which made it awfully cramped. Tricia's six-foot-three driver, a 1990s-era Marine and ex–police officer named Brock McNabb, had enlisted in the Army after 9/11. With all the sandbags under his feet, his knees were flush against the bottom of the steering wheel.

As they watched each "chalk," or group of thirty or so vehicles, leave the camp ahead of them, driving off into who knew what, they'd honk the horn in salute. Tricia passed the time for the first few hours by leading her camouflaged quartet in sing-alongs, though it was a bit strange to go to war singing "Under the Boardwalk." She enforced a strict no-smoking rule, so McNabb pacified himself by chewing tobacco constantly. They drove through the desert toward the border, watching camels and the occasional crazy Kuwaiti driver drifting into the oncoming lane, and the singing stopped for a while when they crossed into Iraq. On and on they drove, for hours and hours, stopping only when other vehicles in the convoy broke down or when they spotted suspected IEDs and had to call for bomb disposal units.

As a woman traveling with three men in a packed Humvee for days at a time in a combat zone, Tricia now had a problem. The guys could pee in a bottle on the move, or just open the door and face outboard when the convoy briefly stopped. But things were a little more difficult for female soldiers. The temperature was upward of ninety degrees, and the military's mantra in desert climates was to drink water constantly, which only made matters worse. Enter the Army-issue Female Urinary Device, the FUD, a funnel-like cup with a short hose. Someone in Army R&D or acquisitions clearly had a sense of humor, because Tricia's FUD was made of pink molded plastic. In theory, the FUD was simple—you held one end up to your groin and stuck the other end in a bottle or out the door. But in practice, the FUD was a dud. With the other guys in the truck, sitting right there, Tricia just couldn't go no matter how much her bladder ached. She kept a vigilant eye out for port-a-potties and IEDs, and coveted the quasi-secluded spots between Army trucks and their trailers whenever they stopped.

After two days of driving, they reached an Army base just north of Baghdad where they could sleep for a few hours in the Death Trap. Then they linked up with a convoy from the unit they were replacing in the 4th Infantry Division. They had a hard time keeping up, not yet understanding that the prime defense against IEDs was simply to haul ass everywhere. They stopped near the Tigris River while their escorts recovered a trailer that another unit had abandoned before them. Tricia stood by her Humvee, besieged by little kids who seemed to presume that because she was female she'd be a pushover.

"Give me candy!"

"Water!"

"Give me food!"

Older kids tried to sell them bootleg DVDs, knives, and porn magazines. Tricia tried to smile and say no politely at first, but that only seemed to encourage them, and she pushed a few away with her rifle.

"No!" she barked.

McNabb came to her rescue, spitting long, nasty streams of tobacco juice in the kids' direction. It was a creative, nonlethal use of force, and the kids mostly scampered away.

They finally reached Forward Operating Base Warhorse in Baqubah, a city of about 300,000 people, thirty miles north of Baghdad. Tricia was delighted to find she'd be living in an air-conditioned trailer, with only one roommate—a big improvement, she knew, from the living conditions in Iraq just a few months before. The dining facility was amazing, considering where they were: It offered everything from a short-order grill to fried chicken, pasta, beef, and other entrees. There were trailers with hot showers and, perhaps most important, flushing toilets. After a month in Kuwait and three days on the road, Tricia stood there in the bathroom trailer, flushing the toilets over and over, just to reassure herself that they were real.

LIFE IN IRAQ for Eric Huss had picked up much as it had left off before Todd's funeral: He drove around getting shot at, tried to keep his troops motivated and safe, and waited for the IED big enough to send him home in a coffin. But near the end of December, word had come down that his battalion, 2-70 Armor, would be going home in early 2004. Eric felt like he'd used up eight and a half of his nine lives, but he had begun to let himself believe he might see home again.

The change in outlook meant he had to address other issues. He still owed the Army more than three years, and the way the war was going, it seemed likely he'd wind up back in Iraq for a second tour. He had no desire ever to return, and if he could find an honorable way to fulfill his five-year military obligation without setting foot in the country again, he wanted to do it. The normal career path for an armor officer would leave Eric in 2-70 Armor for several more years, perhaps even for the rest of the time he owed the Army. He could think of only two real options. One, he could volunteer for a year in Korea. But when the year was up, he figured, he would risk simply being sent to the next unit in line to deploy to Iraq, so that wasn't much of a solution. Or, two, he could apply to be a staff officer or instructor back at Fort Knox, where he, Will, and Todd had gone to armor school just a year before. The job wouldn't be that bad and, besides, Fort Knox was a heck of a lot closer to Cleveland—to Julie—than Fort Riley, Kansas, was.

Ah yes, Julie. Eric realized now how much he loved her and how committed he was to her. They wrote to each other every day now, and he called when he could, usually once a week or so. The only question in the back of his mind was whether they would still have the same chemistry when he got home, the same thing Todd and Jen had worried about. Eric knew he'd changed after nearly a year of combat. How could Julie possibly understand?

He had to try. As a Christmas present to himself, he had filled out the paperwork for Fort Knox and turned it in to his battalion. And then, a few weeks later, he had sat down at a computer, logged on to the website of the Blue Nile jewelry store, and ordered a diamond engagement ring.

The battalion turned in its tanks and headed for Kuwait in February. At the last minute, there was talk that they might be extended, issued Humvees like the one Todd had been killed in, and reassigned to another area of the country. But the next day—February 29, 2004—they left on the first leg of their journey to the States. As thrilled as they were, they grumbled that, after weeks of waiting, they had been rushed out of the theater to keep them from staying one day into March, which would have entitled them to tax-free combat pay for the entire month. Also, since they'd been overseas for 360 days, the Army could include them in its bureaucratic category of units "deployed for less than a year." But still, they were coming home. And they'd lived to tell about it all.

✷ 12 ✷

Dave Swanson reached Camp Marlboro, an old cigarette factory in the middle of the Baghdad slum of Sadr City, on March 3, part of a small group of soldiers traveling in advance of the rest of their unit. Sadr City was 100 percent Shiite, and since Shiites had been the Iraqi underclass under Saddam, they had the most to gain from the U.S.-led invasion. Instead of fighting insurgents, Dave's troops had been told, they would be on a Bosnia-style peacekeeping mission, winning hearts and minds by delivering sewer, water, electricity, and trash-collection services to the people. "SWET" was the Army acronym.

Camp Marlboro could have used a little SWET itself. The place was infested with rats, and there was no electricity. But Sadr City seemed quiet, and during a briefing an intelligence officer from the outgoing unit reported that they hadn't fired a shot in nearly six months.

"If we left the city right now, what would happen?" asked an officer in Dave's unit.

"Nothing," said the intelligence officer. "Nothing's going to happen here. The city is fine."

It took a while before Dave could get in touch with Reyna back in Texas, for there were no phones and little access to e-mail, but when he finally found a computer he sent her a quick message. Overall, he said, things were good, and he was happy to be in Iraq. The people seemed to like Americans, and though Dave had been on only a few patrols, they'd been greeted with waves and smiles.

Reyna, meanwhile, was anything but happy.

How could we have been so stupid? she'd thought, as she checked the results of a home pregnancy test and saw that it was positive. Though her relationship with Dave was intense, they'd known each other for only three months, and now he would be gone for a year. She debated whether to tell him. What could he do from eight thousand miles away? But Dave's upbeat e-mail made her mad. She wrote back heatedly, telling him the news. He was gone, and she was left to deal with the consequences of their romance. She saw no point in pretending she wasn't angry.

WILL TUCKER HAD ALMOST been afraid to call Jen Bryant during the first weeks after Todd's funeral. He was back at Fort Stewart now, still in charge of his tank platoon, and had already started hearing that they would probably be heading back to Iraq for a second tour at the end of 2004. Though he had once promised Todd that he would take care of Jen if anything ever happened, the idea of one of them dying had seemed at the time like a far-fetched joke. Now, Will felt terribly guilty, as if he should never have played along, as if by joking about death they had tempted fate—as if, had he told Todd to drop the idea, Todd might still be alive.

He finally telephoned Jen a few weeks after the funeral; they started talking regularly after that. The soldiers of Todd's battalion, 1-34 Armor, were still deployed, and Jen quit her teaching job, unable to bear returning to the school where she had learned of Todd's death. She spent Christmas in California with Todd's parents, but Will was worried afterward, not wanting her to be alone on the dates that might be especially hard to endure. In January, when Todd would have turned twenty-four, he invited Jen to visit him in Georgia; in February, before Valentine's Day, he flew out to see her at Fort Riley.

But things had grown a bit awkward. Life wasn't a movie—they were friends, not romantic partners—and as much as Will wanted to help Jen, he couldn't step in like Todd's understudy, playing Jen's dead husband's role in her life. Their calls back and forth came less frequently, and their conversations ran shorter. And when Will finally confided in Jen that Todd had asked him to look out for her, she told him no.

It's okay, Jen said. "You don't have to worry about that."

IN THE NEXT MONTH, March, Fort Riley became a virtual ghost town: The schools were on spring vacation, and the spouses and children who had stayed on post to await the return of their soldiers fanned out across the country for a week to visit their families.

Jen sat in her brick townhouse one evening, alone and depressed, drinking Maker's Mark and Coke, and holding a small white envelope in her hands.

"To My Jen, My Everything," read the inscription on the front, in perhaps the neatest handwriting Todd had ever used. Matt Homa had told her about the letter at the funeral, but since Matt had left everything behind in Iraq when he was injured, she hadn't received the letter until Captain Chavez came home in December.

It had sat unopened for more than three months, after Jen held it up to the light once and made out one word inside: "Farewell." That was just a fancy word for good-bye, she had thought, and she didn't want to know anything more. She couldn't bear the idea of such finality. But now, reading Todd's letter was part of her plan. She opened the envelope.

My Soulmate,

If you are reading this, then I fear the worst has happened, and I will not be coming back home. I debated not writing this but I did not think it would be right to leave this world without telling the most important [person] in it goodbye. I want you to know that I love you, I always have, and I always will. There are two things I am sure of. First, my last thoughts were of you and how you made life worth living. Second, our souls will be reunited in heaven when the time comes. I will wait for you there, my love.

The Army had told Jen she could stay at Fort Riley for six months after Todd's death, but now, nearly five months later, she felt she had nowhere to go. Her hometown in Pennsylvania was a dying industrial city. Her friends and family urged her to go to Boston, where she had gone to college and where she and Todd had once talked about living, but now that city seemed full of mocking memories of the wonderful times they had enjoyed. By default, Jen had stayed in Kansas, the only place she and Todd had truly lived together. The inertia of her grief made it impossible to leave.

Do not rush to me. When the time comes our spirits will meet again. You are the strongest person I've ever met and I know you can make it through this. My last wish is that you do just that for me. Live your life to the fullest, do the great things you are capable of. Teach future generations, stand up for what you believe in and be you. You are amazing and can do anything your heart desires. We will spend eternity together, so please Jen, live your life to the fullest. I will always be with you, looking down on you and protecting you. I can't imagine what you are going through, but please do not do anything foolish.

"Foolish." What was foolish? Jen had been planning this night since the day she'd learned of Todd's death. She'd held on for his sake, for his funeral, and then for the holidays. She'd dealt with all the practical little details. The life insurance proceeds had been several hundred thousand dollars, and she didn't want that money just to be wasted, so she'd waited for the payment and had a will drawn up. Jen had seen her friends and family one last time, though of course they didn't realize she was saying good-bye.

I thank God that I married you and trust in his judgment. Do not hate him, but rather look to him for guidance and strength. I don't know if there is any good way to conclude this letter. As I said before, know that my love for you is constant and will not end with my life. Bury me somewhere nice, and save a plot for that day, years and years from now, when you can join me. You are the best wife a man could ever have and I know you would have been a perfect mother. All I can say is that I will see you on the other side. There we will be reunited in the presence of God when the time is right. Never forget me, remember my love for you. You are the best thing that ever happened to me. I am sorry for all the pain I caused you in life. I hope in time you will remember all the good times we had.

Jen had been praying, begging for Todd to visit her, to bridge the gap between the afterworld she was sure he was in and the earth where she had been left behind. She needed him to hold her hand and walk her through her grief. She'd had a dream once, the night after the funeral, where he'd come to see her, one she was sure was real. But where was he now?

August 30, 2003 was the best day of my life. You were so beautiful and shined like a star on that day. Thank you for everything you were to me, all you brought into my life, and giving me your heart. You showed me a whole new world of happiness and love that I am eternally grateful for. Farewell my love, stay safe. I am yours forever.

Until we meet again.
Always,
Your Todd

But Jen could not wait for that day "years and years from now." As she closed the letter, she opened the three boxes of sleeping pills she had bought. She was very drunk now, and each pill was individually wrapped, so it took time to open all of them. She took as many as she could, washed them down with Maker's Mark, and lay down to die.

A DAY LATER, maybe two, Jen woke up, groggy and confused: Why was she still alive? She had vomited in her sleep, and later she could only conclude that she had thrown up all the pills. At the moment, though, she was just delirious. She stumbled out into the parklike backyard her townhouse shared with the others. A neighbor found her there, talking nonsense, and rushed her to the on-post hospital.

"My friend here tried to commit suicide, so we need to get her some help," the neighbor said, as Jen stood silently at the admitting station. They gave her a plastic bracelet and sat her in the waiting room with everyone else.

DAVE SWANSON'S BATTALION moved to a newer base in Sadr City called Camp War Eagle; the rest of their soldiers caught up with them in the first few days of April. On Sunday, April 4, 2004, Dave's platoon was assigned to escort a civil affairs officer to Baghdad's heavily fortified Green Zone for an early afternoon meeting. The unit they were both assigned to, 2-5 Cavalry, would officially take over responsibility for Sadr City at six P.M.

They drove to the Green Zone without incident, and since they had a few hours until the civil affairs officer was ready to head back, Dave and his soldiers decided to kill time in a nearby dining hall. A captain sitting next to them at one of the large tables wore the collar insignia of an engineer and had a 1st Infantry Division patch on his arm.

"Do you know Matt Baideme?" Dave asked the captain, realizing it was a long shot. Matt was a West Point classmate and a former H-2 cadet, but he was also an engineer in 1st ID. Though he and Dave hadn't seen each other since graduation, they had been trading e-mails since Dave got his orders for Iraq.

"That's my XO!" the captain said, meaning his executive officer, the second-in-command of his company. He led Dave to his unit's living trailers, where Matt was packing to go back to Germany in a matter of days.

"What are you going to be doing in Sadr City?" Matt asked. They were walking around the trailers now, gathering Matt's leftover food and office supplies in a big cardboard box for Dave and his guys.

"Man, we're not going to be doing anything," Dave said without enthusiasm. "Humanitarian missions. Sucking up the sewers."

A few days before, four American contractors from the Blackwater security firm had been ambushed, killed, and strung up on a bridge in Fallujah, Matt told Dave. But this was Baghdad, not one of the unsettled areas of Iraq like Anbar Province and the Sunni Triangle. Fallujah was only forty miles away, but it might as well have been on the other side of the world.

Someone else might have considered this good news, but not Dave. He wanted to keep busy. He had called Reyna a day or two after she sent him the e-mail about being pregnant, and tried to be as supportive as he could manage from so far away. But a couple of weeks later, Reyna miscarried while on a visit to her parents' house. The whole experience felt like a dream, and it bothered him greatly. He loved Reyna and missed her, but the best way he could deal with the separation was to dedicate himself totally to the well-being of his troops and to their missions. He would find that a lot harder to do if there wasn't much going on.

Around four in the afternoon, the civil affairs soldier was ready to go back to Camp War Eagle. As Dave and his troops left the Green Zone, he started picking up traffic on his battalion's radio network.

"Lancer Fourteen, this is Comanche Red One!" came the transmission, almost drowned out by static and gunfire. "We are in contact! We are in contact!"

The call sign identified the speaker as the leader of another platoon from Camp War Eagle. His transmissions grew more frantic. "Urgent casualty . . . Vehicles that won't move . . . What's the guidance?!"

It was a quick drive back to War Eagle, and when Dave reached the camp a few minutes later, his company commander, Captain George Lewis, quickly filled him in. The platoon Dave had been listening to had been ambushed. They'd abandoned their vehicles and were now pinned down somewhere in Sadr City. Other platoons were already lined up near the main gate, forming a rescue team.

"Get ready to go," Lewis ordered.

Dave and his soldiers ditched their soft-skinned vehicles for their platoon's armored Humvees and Bradley Fighting Vehicles. The scene was mad chaos and a jumble of vehicles, exacerbated by the fact that Dave's unit was still an hour shy of officially taking over responsibility for Sadr City. Nobody even seemed to know where the ambushed platoon was.

Just follow the vehicles in front of us wherever they go, Dave said to his driver, a sergeant named Tranquilino Pineda. The battery in the laser sight on Dave's rifle died as they moved out; he scrounged around the Humvee for a fresh one amid gunfire and explosions. He looked at the other vehicles in the convoy, most of which lacked any armor, and felt chills. Today, Dave realized, could be his last day on earth. He was suddenly afraid of death.

Just as quickly, he forced the fear from his mind. He had his whole platoon to lead, and if he showed fear it would spread like wildfire.

The impoverished but apparently tranquil façade of Sadr City, Dave soon understood, had masked a community filled with suspicion and rage. The week before, the American administrator of Iraq, Paul Bremer, had ordered that a newspaper controlled by the radical Shiite cleric Moqtada al-Sadr (Sadr City was named after his father) be closed. Though Dave and his fellow soldiers were unaware of it, Sadr had given a speech in response on Friday, April 2, in which he called on his thousands of followers to "terrorize" the occupying army. On Saturday, U.S. forces had arrested Sadr's top aide. Now it was Sunday, and the city was erupting.

"Contact right!" someone in Dave's Humvee yelled, and the bullets really started flying. The convoy raced south from the base toward the city, taking fire as they drove on a border road alongside a soccer field. As they turned right onto one of the main streets, lined on each side by two- and three-story buildings, Dave felt he was living the sequel to *Black Hawk Down*. There were hundreds of fighters, shooting at them with AK-47 rifles from the roofs, the alleys, and from in and behind cars. Dave's truck was hit dozens of times.

"Sir, I got hit!" yelled Pineda, who had been driving with one hand and shooting his M-4 rifle out the open window with the other.

"You all right?" Swanson yelled back.

Pineda shook his head, and his Kevlar helmet fell off. The bullet had come through the open window and hit the helmet at just the right angle, splitting it in two. Actually, yeah, he was okay.

"You're fuckin' lucky, man!" Swanson shouted in disbelief. "Keep driving!"

The road was blocked now with concrete barriers, scrap iron, old cars, and trash. Dave ordered Pineda to move into a military formation called a herringbone, and the other trucks followed, getting out of the way so the Bradleys behind them could crush the barriers. But in the ninety seconds or so it took for the Bradleys to move up and blow through, the Humvees were riddled with bullets. Out the window, Dave spotted one of the men shooting at them, a scruffy guy in his thirties or early forties in a long dishdasha, or "man dress," as the U.S. soldiers called them. Quickly, Dave moved his M-4 rifle and lined the red dot of the laser sight directly on the man. He fired several times, and the man fell backward, dead. For a split second, it hit Dave: He had just killed someone. Then he refocused his attention on his platoon. His Humvee had four flat tires by the time they were moving again. The Bradleys and intact Humvees from the other platoons took off, but with the flat tires, he couldn't keep up. Captain Lewis's truck pulled away.

"Floor it!" Dave yelled at Pineda as they crept along at no more than ten miles an hour, bullets ringing off the sides of the vehicle.

"It is floored!" Pineda yelled back. The noise was deafening—the yelling, the impotent strain of the engine and the *crack-crack-crack* of their M-4s as they shot out the open windows. Every few seconds the gunner above their heads would fire the .50-caliber machine gun, jarring and ugly. Whenever the shooting died down for an instant, the ringing silence seemed loud.

The other platoons in the convoy were long gone now, and Dave ordered Pineda to get off the main road and out of the line of fire. His new Humvee didn't even have a radio installed yet, and he was leading five limping vehicles through a profoundly hostile city. They went up a block, down a street parallel to the road where they'd been nearly ripped to shreds, and then turned back toward the first street. As they made the last turn, they saw the remains of Captain Lewis's Humvee, wrecked and engulfed in flames, with no sign of Lewis or the other soldiers who had been with him. Insurgents swarmed, firing at the dead Humvee and at Dave's slow-moving convoy.

With no way to contact anyone else, and no idea where the ambushed platoon was hiding, Dave's only option was to head back to Camp War Eagle to regroup. They retraced their route through a hail of gunfire. When they'd almost made it out of the city, the firing died down, but there was a soft sound, a lonesome little "dink-dink," as two bullets ricocheted above. Dave's machine gunner, a private named Riley Soden, had been hit.

Man, what the hell happened? Soden thought as his legs flew out from under him. He toppled into the truck, staring in pain at the hole in his foot.

Camp War Eagle was completely chaotic now. There were four dead soldiers from 2-5 Cavalry, and more than forty wounded. There was no electricity at the aid station, and so soldiers raced their damaged Humvees and trucks there so the doctors could work outside by the glow of their headlights.

One of Dave's soldiers ran up. "Hey, sir," he called out, "one of our Bradleys is broken down!" Its crew was stranded in Sadr City, alone and immobile.

Rescuing the guys in the Bradley was now Dave's number one priority. He sent one of his able-bodied soldiers to escort Private Soden to the aid station, and he ran to the motor pool to find any kind of working vehicle. On the way, he spotted Captain Lewis, who was alive after all, though covered in blood, and looking a little dazed.

Lewis's Humvee hadn't had any armor—hadn't even had doors, for that matter. His driver had been shot and killed just after they passed the barricades where Dave had lost them; his machine gunner had been badly wounded, and another passenger was hit as well. Then the Humvee's fuel tank had ruptured and the truck had stumbled to a halt. They'd almost been stranded in the city like the platoon they were trying to save, but a Bradley rescued them at the last second. Lewis and the others had made it back to the base cramped in the troop compartment, with his driver's dead body sprawled on the floor.

"Sir," Dave said, grabbing his captain and talking as calmly as he could. "One of my Bradleys is down."

Lewis stayed quiet.

"Sir, I'm going to get my Bradley."

Lewis still didn't say anything. Dave and his soldiers ran to the only two Humvees that were left—both unarmored—jumped in, and headed back toward the gate.

The Bradley recovery went more smoothly than anything else so far. The insurgents apparently hadn't found it yet, and Dave and his men hooked up a working Bradley to the dead one and towed it back to War Eagle. When they returned, around nine P.M., they saw troops lining up to head out into the city yet again.

By now a tank unit from a neighboring base had rescued the original stranded platoon. But with insurgents running wild throughout the city they had just taken responsibility for, 2-5 Cavalry had to establish control. Captain Lewis was back in charge, and although the unit had fewer than forty able-bodied troops now, they were the only soldiers available.

They rolled back out in the darkness, with the Bradley Fighting Vehicles leading the way, hauling ass to their first objective, an Iraqi police station that had been overrun by insurgents, taking rifle fire most of the way. Dave watched through the unarmored windshield of his Humvee as one of the Bradleys was hit with more than a dozen RPGs but kept going. One of Dave's soldiers fired back with a grenade launcher through the open window as they moved, killing two fighters. It was a hell of a shot.

Dave was down to ten men now, since they'd reorganized to make up for all the casualties in other platoons. They cleared the police station, going room to room in the dark, never knowing what was on the other side of any door. His troops then hunkered inside, defending the place against rifle and RPG attacks, until they got an order around two A.M. to move on and clear yet another police station. With only six guys now, they found that place deserted as well, and all the weapons had been looted.

Night wore on. Every hour or two, they fended off attacks by men with rifles and RPGs. After a while it was clear that nobody was going to be able to overrun them, but the attackers kept coming, only to be lined up in Dave's soldiers' sights and cut down. It was eerie and uncomfortable. Often the sounds of gunfire and battle would die down, only to give way to the moans of the wounded and dying who lay in the street.

By morning a dozen more soldiers had joined them, and Dave found himself thinking about West Point. Enduring the academy, he realized, had prepared him to take more shit than most people. He reflected with detachment that he was able to go without food or rest in times of great stress, compartmentalizing his fears and getting the job done. Two of the senior sergeants who were with him now were dead tired, and he ordered them to go downstairs into the comparatively comfortable office of the police chief to get some sleep. They came up four or five hours later.

"Hey sir, it's your turn," said one of them, a sergeant named Matt Mercado.

"Yeah, whatever," Dave replied. It was now late Monday afternoon, more than twenty-four hours after he'd seen Matt Baideme in the Green Zone, fully thirty-six hours since he'd had any sleep. But he didn't feel he could leave his troops until either the fighting was over or he collapsed.

Another night passed, then another day. Enemy fighters kept charging the building, wave after wave. Twice a day, it seemed, the mosques would broadcast a call to arms. It was crazy, suicidal.

Finally, Dave stumbled and fell to the floor.

"Yeah," he said to the soldiers he was talking with. "I can't do this right now. I think I have to go sleep." It was now Tuesday night, more than two days after Dave's first trip into Sadr City, sixty hours since he'd last slept. Dave went down to the police chief's office and slept for five hours.

Wednesday continued much the same, but by Thursday night the attacks died down, and on Friday nobody attacked them at all. Finally, exhausted after a week at the police station, Dave and his soldiers were called back to War Eagle. Dave got a shower, some food, and a long sleep.

The phones and Internet were shut off at War Eagle until the Army could be sure that all the wives and mothers—the PNOKs and SNOKs—were officially notified of their loved ones' deaths. It took several days because so many families had scattered around the country for the deployment. When Dave finally got access to e-mail, it was the first time in more than a week that he'd had any contact with the outside world.

"I saw your name in the Wash Post and I was very impressed of course," Reyna had written. A reporter had interviewed Dave in the middle of the battle. "I had to show it to the whole school. So now the school is aware that I have a boyfriend." She had closed the e-mail with "con todo mi amor"—with all my love.

TIM AND KATIE MOSHIER reached Fort Hood in early spring 2004, where Tim's new unit, 1-6 Cavalry, would spend a year transitioning to new, upgraded Apache Longbow helicopters, which used state-of-the art computer equipment. The unit was a shell when they arrived, since it made more sense to bring in new personnel than to retrain people who were already experts on a different type of helicopter. The few soldiers there when Tim and Katie arrived were working on administrative and formal matters, such as preparing for the ceremonies inaugurating what was essentially a new command.

Upon arriving at the base, Tim introduced himself to the first higher-ranking officer he saw, a burly captain named Erik Kober. Kober didn't let on, but he recognized Tim's name right away from a list of lieutenants who would be assigned to his troop.

"Let's sit down and talk about invitations," he said after a few pleasantries. Kober and another officer had been overwhelmed with paper: They had about four hundred envelopes to address for the "uncasing ceremony" that would officially assign 1-6 Cavalry to Fort Hood. Now they were happy to have an extra set of hands. Tim smiled and sat down. If he was disappointed that his first assignment in the new attack helicopter squadron smacked more of Emily Post than of search-and-destroy, he didn't say so.

In the days and weeks that followed, the unit filled out. Five more Apache pilots from Tim's flight school class joined them, including Holly Harris and another member of the West Point class of 2002, Jim Reynolds. They were organized into companies and platoons, and Tim and Holly wound up as brother and sister platoon leaders under Captain Kober. The majority of their soldiers were warrant officers, pilots with college degrees and ten or more years in the Army. Most important, they had many thousands of hours of flight time under their belts. Although he'd been out of West Point for almost two years, this was Tim's first real opportunity to lead other soldiers, and he got off to a rough start. One day early on, they went to the rifle range for an annual qualification on M-16 rifles. Tim was nervous. He started checking his soldiers' canteens to make sure they were full, as if he were still a West Point firstie looking out for a platoon of clueless plebes. He reached out to grab the canteen belonging to one of the most experienced aviators, a chief warrant officer with eighteen years in the Army. The chief turned away with his mouth open, shocked that some brand-new lieutenant had the gall to touch him.

Another of his pilots realized that Tim was making a classic new lieutenant's mistake, letting his anxiousness get the best of him.

"Your enlisted soldiers need leadership," the pilot told Tim. "Your warrant officers need information." Tim didn't need to be told twice.

Katie Moshier adapted well to the role of military wife. Among the D-1 veterans, she became known as the "Mother Duck," the woman who kept the small group in touch, mainly via e-mail, as its members served all over the world. Come fall, she would be teaching high school Spanish in Belton, about twenty miles away from Fort Hood, but for now she threw herself into setting up their new home and took over as the leader of the company's Family Readiness Group. The job usually fell to the company commander's wife, but Erik Kober was proudly single. Katie made it a point to greet all of the unit's soldiers as they arrived, and to drop in on their spouses. Maria Williams, whose husband, John Paul, was a mechanic in Tim's platoon, was amazed when Katie came by. In three years in the Army, Maria had never heard anything from the FRG before. She was very happy to have the company, especially since she was spending her days alone at home with their two-year-old son, Arthur.

Katie sat at Maria's kitchen table, rattling off the names of the other members of the unit, taking care to note which ones had kids around the same age as Arthur.

"I'm never going to remember these people," Maria said, on which Katie drew a little flowchart, filling in the names of nearly three dozen soldiers in the company from memory, along with their spouses and children.

The two women started seeing each other at all kinds of lightly formal military functions—battalion runs at six-thirty A.M. on the first Friday of every month, baby showers, and the parties and other events that made up the mandatory fun of the helicopter unit. In time, they grew very close. Arthur took to Katie almost instantly, clinging to her leg after meeting her only a few times. Maria could barely get him to call his relatives Aunt or Uncle, but Lieutenant Moshier's wife quickly became Aunt Katie.

★ 13 ★

At night, Forward Operating Base Warhorse seemed like the darkest place in the world, Tricia LeRoux Birdsell thought. As one of the most heavily mortared bases in Iraq, Warhorse was under strict "light discipline," and the only lights allowed were tiny blue-tinted beams no stronger than what one might find on a keychain, the only thing separating the soldiers at Warhorse from unadulterated blindness once the sun went down.

Tricia was in charge of the medical company's treatment platoon, which included about thirty soldiers, mostly enlisted medics, plus a few doctors, physician assistants, X-ray technicians, and other medical professionals. In her first two months, they had treated more than seventy trauma cases, mostly Iraqi civilians and prisoners captured by the U.S. forces. All the injuries were beginning to take a toll on her, and the fact that she had little news from Toby, whose infantry platoon was fighting about half an hour to the north, didn't help. Every once in a while, Toby would find out that a convoy was on its way to Warhorse, he'd hop on, and they'd get an hour or so together. But otherwise, she barely talked to him. She had access to e-mail and phones, but he did not, and so they relied on old-fashioned snail mail. Weeks into the deployment she already had a stack of letters from her husband.

Tricia woke one morning in early April to a knock at the door of her trailer. Her company commander, Captain Rassmusen, and the company first sergeant were standing there.

"You need to sit down," Rassmusen told her. "It's Toby."

Tricia started shaking. "Don't freak out," the captain continued. "He's okay, but he's been shot."

"How can I not freak out?"

Tricia started asking all sorts of questions, but they didn't have any answers.

"Don't worry, he's fine. But we just wanted to let you know."

The captain and first sergeant left. Tricia burst into tears briefly, then pulled herself together and ran to the aid station. Rumors flowed in about a huge firefight near Toby's base camp, but there was no news about Toby. If he'd been shot, but not brought to Warhorse, it might mean his wounds were superficial. It could also mean he had been rushed straight to one of the more sophisticated combat surgical hospitals in Baghdad or at Balad Air Base.

Tricia was frantic with worry, but a few hours later, Toby walked right into the aid station himself. He hadn't been wounded at all; one of his soldiers had been shot, and not even that badly—a stray round from an AK-47 had hit him during one of the raucous Iraqi wedding celebrations. Tricia ran to him, feeling him all over and looking for the wound, not quite believing that he wasn't hiding the wound from her so she wouldn't worry.

Toby couldn't stay long, and soon after he left, mortar rounds started falling on the base. An Iraqi civilian with gunshot wounds to the head and pelvis was rushed in to the aid station. The doctors worked frantically, but to no avail. That was the first time Tricia actually watched someone die.

The day's events left her terribly concerned, not just for herself and her soldiers but also for her husband. "I am so afraid of losing him in this war," she wrote in her diary that night. "I just pray that we all make it out of here."

ALTHOUGH SHE WAS IN CHARGE of a medical platoon, Tricia had no medical training, so one of her biggest challenges was to remain useful while staying out of the way. One day not long after the scare involving Toby, she led a convoy taking the body of a dead soldier to Balad so it could be sent home to the United States. It was heartbreaking to watch as the body was carried from the truck to a big refrigerator, and to think that a few months ago this was probably exactly what had happened to Todd. The next day, a Bradley Fighting Vehicle from another platoon in Toby's company raced to the aid station and dropped its back ramp quickly. A twenty-year-old soldier from Ohio named Allen "A.J." Vandayburg had been trapped, unconscious, inside the gun turret after an RPG hit it. It took a while to get him out, and Tricia stood outside with his squad while the medics worked. Through Toby, she knew many of Vandayburg's fellow soldiers.

We have a great surgical team, she assured them. They'll do everything possible to save him.

The medics finally got Vandayburg free and rushed him inside. Tricia climbed into the Bradley and washed out the blood as well as she could. Her first sergeant came out soon after, took her aside, and told her Vandayburg had been dead on arrival. Tricia couldn't stay near the Bradley—definitely not within view of the soldiers she'd just been talking to. She went to her office and broke down.

Then things got crazier: Over the next five hours, seventy-five trauma patients came in to the small aid station, U.S. soldiers and Iraqi civilians alike. The next day they lost another soldier, a reserve engineer sergeant from Ohio named Gary Eckert. Tricia found it painful to see all that death and destruction, to have it brought to her doorstep almost every time there was a loud explosion off in the distance.

A few days later, mortar rounds fell on the area where many of Tricia's own medics lived, destroying two of her soldiers' trailers. The soldiers had been working at the time, but a third medic who had happened to be walking in the area was rushed to the aid station with a broken leg and a hand that looked like it had been through a meat grinder.

He was upbeat: "I've got a million-dollar wound," he told Tricia. "I'm going home."

But Tricia was shaken. "Nowhere is safe. Not even where you lay your head at night," she wrote in her daily journal. "But in the end, we cannot let the fear run our lives."

FOR MONTHS, Drew Sloan and Greg Londo hadn't done anything about their idea of investing in Hawaiian real estate. Back in December, though, they'd noticed that condominiums in Ko Olina were already selling for thousands more than in September, even though construction hadn't started and the units wouldn't be finished for close to another year. They drove over to the sales office, only to find that there was now a waiting list sixty-five investors deep, with only twenty units scheduled to be built.

"That's a bummer," Drew told the sales representative. "We were here in September." He said he didn't remember that he and Greg had signed up for the waiting list, but supposed it was possible they might have.

"Londo/Sloan . . ." she said, looking through the names on the list. "Sloan/Londo."

Sure enough, "Sloan/Londo" was number 14 on the list. The two lieutenants raised the money for their deposit quickly, and signed the papers in January, one day before Greg Londo's unit left for Iraq.

IN LATE MARCH, Drew got some sad news. A West Point classmate named Mike Adams, who had been Drew's roommate during Beast Barracks, the first summer of basic training–style indoctrination at West Point, had been killed on the last day of his yearlong assignment in Iraq. Mike had been a very squared-away cadet, Drew recalled. He'd gone on to be assigned to another company once West Point started in earnest, and after graduation he had became an armor officer like Todd Bryant and Will Tucker.

He had been killed in a bizarre accident as his unit traveled in a convoy heading south toward Kuwait. A passing vehicle had clipped the .50-caliber machine gun on the tank Mike was riding in, whipping it around and hitting him in the head. He had died instantly. When Mike was buried at West Point, the soldiers he had led in Iraq served as his funeral honor guard, the first time anyone could remember that rank-and-file sergeants and privates had rendered such an honor at the academy cemetery for a fallen officer.

Brian Oman, who had been in Mike's unit in Iraq, called Drew from New York. Brian had recently proposed to his girlfriend, and with his just-completed deployment and Drew's upcoming departure, the two friends had much to be excited about and talk over. But the fact of Mike's death cast a pall over the conversation, and reminded them both of how fragile life could be.

MORE 2002 GRADUATES FROM H-2 arrived in Hawaii. Among them were Christine Ray, a military intelligence officer who had spent her first year in the Army in Korea, and Emily Wnuk, who had been the last cadet to get her diploma on graduation day. As their social group expanded, Drew stayed single, and he enjoyed himself immensely. He went out nonstop in Honolulu and enjoyed a wild, fleeting weekend with a woman he met in Las Vegas.

But he kept thinking about Chloe Hayes. They e-mailed and called each other as regularly as possible. As the deployment date grew closer, though, his workdays stretched longer, and it was often well past midnight on the mainland by the time he was done. Drew still held out hope for a relationship with Chloe, but she seemed to be slipping away, a small sacrifice to his chosen profession.

Drew's father came out to Hawaii to visit in April 2004. His semester in Rome complete, David Sloan was anxious now about the prospect of his son going to war. Yet he believed wholeheartedly in the American mission in Afghanistan; and it bothered him that he didn't think most Americans shared his passion. What about the Taliban's persecution of women, and the fact that they had punished men for having homosexual affairs by crushing them to death? Why weren't feminist and gay rights groups in the United States strongly voicing their support?

Now Drew's departure date was fast approaching, and he wrote "death letters" to his parents, just in case, mailing them to the law firm where he'd worked in high school for safekeeping. He liked to say that he was "a big fan of a wrap-up," but in his mind the letters were just a far-fetched precaution. Drew had virtually no idea what he'd really be doing in Afghanistan. His battalion had practiced air assaults, urban combat, and "soft power" exercises in which they pretended to negotiate with leaders of primitive villages, but Afghanistan just didn't seem as dangerous as Iraq; it was like a forgotten junior varsity war. The month before he left, *Time* magazine ran a cover story on the conflict, with headlines like REMEMBER AFGHANISTAN? The Taliban had been toppled, the magazine reported, but Afghanistan's warlords and militias—funded in large part by the opium trade—had risen to fill the vacuum. There were only about thirty thousand coalition troops in the country, less than a sixth of the force in Iraq, and the interim government controlled almost nothing outside of the capital city of Kabul.

There was no point in paying rent when they would be gone for a year, so Drew and his housemates gave up the Sunset House. Ryan Beltramini's wife, Alisha, was going to head back to the mainland for graduate school while her husband was deployed, and Drew and Ryan stayed for a few days with another friend and classmate who wasn't going with them to Afghanistan. The night before they were set to leave, they popped a movie into the DVD player—the Hugh Grant romantic comedy *Love Actually*—and opened a bottle of Pinot Noir. It struck Drew that this was not the most manly way to spend his last night in civilization before going to war, but he and his friends were the ones going overseas, they liked the movie, and they'd spend their time any way they pleased. They drained the first bottle and then a couple more before realizing they had nothing left but white wine. They made the switch—it was either that, or quit drinking.

Drew had been thinking a lot about Chloe Hayes lately and had talked with her that afternoon. With the taste of the wine on his lips and the romantic themes of the movie still in his head, he went upstairs and wrote her a letter, working his way through several drafts on the computer before copying the whole thing over longhand.

He had screwed things up with her three times, he wrote, and he listed them, "without hope or agenda," stealing a line from the end of the movie.

First, he'd failed to keep in touch with her after Ring Weekend at West Point. He could make excuses—9/11, for example, and the distance between New York and the Midwest—but he now regretted it.

Second, he'd run into her briefly once at a Cubs game, when he was out in Chicago for the bachelor party and wedding of one of his friends. He should have changed his plans, stayed in town an extra day, and gotten together with her however he could. Lunch would have worked fine, but he'd blown it.

And finally, he wrote, he should have called her in July 2003, after he and Shannon McCartan had officially broken up. It still bothered him to realize that Chloe had been so nearby, in New York City, while he'd been at West Point—but he hadn't known.

Alas, opportunities lost. Drew could do little about them now, but when he got back, he wrote, he didn't plan on making the same mistakes. The next day, before he left, he ordered flowers for her, arranging for them to be delivered at her college graduation a few weeks later. He liked the idea that she'd have a reason to think of him after he'd already left for Afghanistan.

He stopped at the post office in Haleiwa, on the northwest shore of Oahu. Besides the letter, he had two other things for Chloe: a copy of the formal picture they'd had taken together at the Ring Weekend dance, and a music CD he'd burned, starting with an obscure Chicago rock band they both knew, and ending with a slow ballad called "The Scientist" by the English band Coldplay. If Chloe listened to the mix the whole way through, the last lyrics she'd hear would be about separation and second chances.

A couple of hours later, Drew and Ryan settled into the first-class cabin on the World Air jet their unit had chartered. At long last, they were heading to war.

THE BATTLE ON APRIL 4 was only the beginning of eighty-two straight days of combat in Sadr City for Dave Swanson and his unit, 2-5 Cavalry.

In that first week alone, Dave himself had gone through about ten magazines of 5.56-mm ammunition, which meant he'd lined up the red dot on a target, squeezed the trigger, and fired as many as three hundred times. Every day, their patrols would be ambushed, or they would be assigned to defend buildings that came under fire. Dave went out mostly in a Bradley Fighting Vehicle now, and he lost count of how many IEDs he had run over and how many RPGs were fired at them. On one day alone—it happened to be Mother's Day—he hit ten IEDs before his Bradley started sputtering oil. He went back to War Eagle to switch vehicles and had to leave several of his troops behind there—they were shell-shocked, crying, unable to head back out into the fight.

He thought of a line from the miniseries *Band of Brothers*, in which another U.S. Army lieutenant, in another war, observed: "The only hope you have is to accept the fact that you're already dead. The sooner you accept that, the sooner you'll be able to function as a soldier is supposed to function: without mercy, without compassion, without remorse. All war depends on it."

They'd be standing outside, or in a building talking to locals, and the streets would suddenly empty, portending an attack. One day, Dave watched with amusement and awe as pigeons flew over the American positions and he realized that insurgents had trained the birds to mark their location for ambushes. Again he thought of a movie; he recognized the tactic from the Denzel Washington film *Training Day*.

Before long, the fighting and killing simply became normal. On one mission, Dave and Sergeant Pineda, the driver whose helmet had been split in two during their first battle, ran into a school building only to find a man aiming an AK-47 at them. Two red dots instantly appeared on the man's chest, Dave and Pineda both fired, and the man fell backward over a ledge.

"Who gets that one?" Dave said to Pineda. "Is that yours or mine?"

"I don't know," the sergeant responded.

"We'll call it a half," Dave said.

Another night, around two or three in the morning, Dave was sitting inside the turret of a Bradley on yet another "movement to contact" mission, going out to look for the enemy so they could defeat him. Dave's stomach had been bothering him all day—God only knew what nasty diseases you could pick up by drinking local water or somehow coming into contact with the unwashed masses of Sadr City. Suddenly, he had to go to the bathroom. Now.

His gunner could see his discomfort, and he started poking Dave in the stomach, teasing him but making things much worse.

"Seriously, don't," Dave said, now in severe distress. No way was he going to get out of the Bradley in the middle of the night in Sadr City, but this was fast becoming a real emergency. "I have to go."

Fortunately there were no soldiers in the troop compartment in the back of the Bradley. Dave got down from his seat and unzipped the flame-retardant jumpsuit he was wearing. He ripped open the plastic bag from an MRE and used that, crouching in the still-moving Bradley. With no toilet paper, he pulled off his T-shirt, preparing to sacrifice it as a casualty of war.

Bang!

They hit an IED, and Dave went flying, holding onto the nasty MRE bag. The whole Bradley filled with dust and dirt.

"Oh my God!" Dave yelled. He stood there, naked, jumpsuit down around his ankles, one hand clutching the bag and the other feeling around his body in the dark, making sure everything was where it was supposed to be.

"Sir, are you all right?" his gunner called. "Are you all right?"

Dave fumbled with his jumpsuit and climbed back into his seat, covered with soot, still holding on to the MRE bag so it didn't spill all over him. He popped the hatch slightly and threw the bag out onto the street. Sadr City was practically one big overflowing sewer main anyway, he figured.

As the days of fighting went on, it became clear to Dave that there were two kinds of soldiers at Cap War Eagle: those who did the fighting and those who stayed on the base. Sometimes that wasn't a matter of choice. One day the battalion personnel officer, a lieutenant with just a few years more in the Army than Dave, came up to him before a mission and asked to come along.

"I want to go out there," he told Dave. "I want to get in a fight."

"You honestly want to get into a firefight?" Dave replied, almost in disbelief. By now, Dave had a reputation as an RPG magnet; as a result, reporters or other visitors to War Eagle who wanted to see combat were often sent out with him. When this happened, one benefit from Dave's perspective was that he had to free a seat in one of his vehicles, which in turn meant that he could let one of his soldiers stay behind on the base.

Dave agreed to take the personnel officer with him. They headed to a Sadr City police station, where Dave had to try to persuade the chief to get more of his officers to show up for work each day. The police were scared, Dave knew, but, as he told the chief through a translator, "I don't quit my job, and they're shooting at me too."

Within minutes, the police station was under full-fledged attack from insurgents with rocket-propelled grenades and a Russian-made machine gun. An intense battle raged, with Dave's troops laying down a massive stream of fire. At one point, the personnel lieutenant burst into the building. "I got an RPG near me, about fifteen to twenty feet away! That was pretty sweet. This is what I wanted to see."

On the way back to Camp War Eagle, they were ambushed several times. "I killed one!" the lieutenant exclaimed as he fired out the window of the armored Humvee. He was thrilled with his accomplishment.

NOT WANTING HER DAUGHTER, Isabel, to get attached to Dave, in case things didn't work out, Reyna had never let him meet her before he left. Now she began talking about Mommy's special friend who had had to go away, and showing Isabel the picture of herself with Dave that she kept on the nightstand next to her bed. Reyna carried her cell phone with her everywhere these days, too, not wanting to risk missing one of Dave's infrequent calls from Iraq. She and Dave's mother, though they had met in person only once, called each other weekly to check in. Reyna worried constantly. She would hear a report on the local news—"Five soldiers from Fort Hood died yesterday in Iraq"—but then all communication would go down. She knew that without official standing with the Army, she wouldn't be notified if something happened to him. Whenever Dave's mother called after Dave hadn't been able to call or e-mail for a few days or weeks, Reyna's heart would sink with fear that she was about to learn her love was dead.

When she did get to talk with Dave, their conversations rarely lasted more than ten or fifteen minutes, and Dave wasn't eager to talk about all that he'd seen and been doing. The phone calls with Reyna were his chance for a quarter hour away from the war, so she tried to focus on whatever had been going on at home, both good and bad. It meant a lot to her that despite all the death and destruction Dave had seen, he clearly still thought about the unborn child he and Reyna had lost.

"Have you told anyone?" Reyna asked him during one call.

"No," Dave said. "I'm not going to."

"You have to tell somebody," Reyna insisted. "Please, promise me you'll share it with at least one person this week."

She would read his e-mails and realize she was misconstruing things he wrote simply because she didn't know very much about the Army. Dave would mention a mission he'd been on, but to her untrained ears the word "mission" had little meaning. She'd think about the *Mission: Impossible* movies, with Tom Cruise as a super-secret spy, and that would confuse her more. As the months went on, though, she learned more and more about Dave from his mother. They began e-mailing each other every day, and each would call the other immediately after talking with Dave, comparing notes and asking, "How did he sound to you?"

THE FOB WARHORSE aid station was no place for the squeamish or the emotional. Often enough now, Tricia and her troops knew the American soldiers coming in to the station—people they'd seen at the post exchange, at the gym, in the dining facility, or just walking around the base. The doctors did great work on a wounded soldier named Holmes, who came in after an IED attack with terrible wounds to his legs, groin, chest, arms, and lungs, and then sent him on to the bigger hospital in Baghdad. But a few days later, they learned that he'd died there. Four more soldiers were doomed on May 3, after they'd been trapped in a vehicle that rolled into a canal. Tricia remembered one of them, Lieutenant Chris Kenny, especially well. Just a few days before, she'd been joking that she didn't want her husband to join his unit because they were among the aid station's biggest customers. Now he was dead, along with three of his soldiers.

On May 21, one of Tricia's good friends, Matt Caldwell, a West Point 2002 graduate and a platoon leader in another unit, raced into the aid station. His troops were right behind. They'd brought with them an eight-year-old Iraqi girl who had been hit by a civilian car. He'd watched it happen, Matt told Tricia; the girl had been thrown twenty feet in the air by the impact. It had taken some time to convince the girl's uncle to let Matt's soldiers take her to the military hospital, but eventually he'd acquiesced, and the girl, her uncle, and her mother had all arrived in an M113. Tricia knew immediately that the girl's chances weren't good, for more than thirty minutes had passed since the accident.

While the doctors worked, Tricia ran to get a chair for the girl's mother. She grabbed Tricia, talking frantically in Arabic. Tricia sat next to her and they both prayed for a miracle, the woman presumably praying as a Muslim, Tricia praying as a Christian. But the girl couldn't be saved. The doctors called the death, and one of Tricia's soldiers who spoke some Arabic explained the situation as well as possible to the uncle. The girl's mother kept trying to get close enough to hear, but the uncle would push her away. Finally, he turned and told her that her daughter was dead.

The mother wailed and cried and collapsed. Unable to bear it, Tricia left the room as quickly as she could.

ON JUNE 8, a huge explosion shook FOB Warhorse, and a giant cloud of dust filled the air just a few hundred yards from where Tricia was driving a Humvee. She hurried back to the aid station, expecting the now familiar routine of a formation in which they made sure that everyone assigned to the company was accounted for after blasts like this one. As she arrived, however, a frantic call came over the radio from one of the soldiers at the gate. He was so upset, she couldn't even understand what he was saying.

Soon a Humvee came racing up to the aid station with two injured soldiers, followed by more and more vehicles with more wounded. Tricia ran among the wounded, organizing teams of litter carriers, and even offering rudimentary treatment she'd picked up on the job—irrigating wounds and bandaging patients who would be heading to medevac helicopters. In all, there were seventeen wounded soldiers.

Slowly a picture of what had happened began to emerge. A "vehicle-borne improvised explosive device," or VBIED—Armyspeak for a car bomb—had hit the front gate of FOB Warhorse. One of the company's sergeants came up to Tricia and said she needed to take her across the street to tell her what had happened: A good friend of Tricia's, a captain named Humyan Khan, had been killed.

Tricia somehow managed to maintain her composure. She and Khan had been buddies back in Germany and had studied for the Law School Admissions Test at the same time. Later, she learned that he'd been a real hero: Deciding that the car looked suspicious, he'd confronted the driver and warned a number of other soldiers to stay away. If he hadn't been so proactive, others would have been killed as well.

As hard as it was to lose people she knew, Tricia had to move on; she did so in large part with the help of friends she'd made among the other female lieutenants in the battalion. Tricia spent so much time with three women in particular—two physician assistants and another medical service corps officer—that some of the other officers referred to them as the Sewing Circle. After a while they adopted the nickname themselves. They ate dinner together in the dining facility and spent a lot of down time together in their trailers, watching movies and television shows from back home. Sometimes they sat outside Tricia's trailer, eating microwave popcorn, drinking near beer, and playing "Name That TV Theme Song" over the battalion radio with the company first sergeant. It was nice to enjoy a bit of normalcy whenever they could, though occasionally their get-togethers were interrupted by mortar and rocket attacks; then they'd grab their gear and run to the aid station.

Throughout the spring of 2004, the casualties kept coming, and the aid station was a busy place. In the third week of June, another soldier died in the aid station, an artilleryman who had grown up in the U.S. Virgin Islands. He had been shot in the back.

"His name was PFC Jason Lynch," Tricia recorded in her war diary. "He was 21."

WILL TUCKER HAD more or less dropped off the face of the earth as far as the rest of the D-1 Ducks were concerned. Though he still traded the odd phone call with Tim Moshier and Eric Huss, they were at slightly different stages of life. Tim had Katie and his life in Texas; Eric was engaged to Julie and was in Kansas, waiting for the transfer to Fort Knox that would keep him from having to deploy to Iraq again. Will called Jen Bryant occasionally, but nowhere near as often as he had before. Being stationed at Fort Stewart, near Savannah, Georgia, put him physically far from his small group of close West Point friends, and he was extremely busy. By summer 2004, he'd spent eighteen months as a platoon leader, and his unit, 3-7 Cavalry, would be going back to Iraq for a second tour beginning sometime in late 2004 or early 2005.

Two years in the Army had aged Will greatly. He kept his head shaved—a practice he'd started in Iraq for the sake of convenience and hygiene—and he'd gained weight. He'd turn twenty-four in August, but he could easily pass for someone ten years older. He was still reeling from Todd Bryant's death, and he carried a heavy burden of guilt. When he went home to visit his parents and sister in Alabama, his father had a few friends over, and his mother asked him to show the men the medals he'd been awarded for his Iraq service. Reluctantly, he complied.

"I didn't deserve the Purple Heart," Will said as he passed the medals around, choking back tears. He'd been awarded the medal because of some small cuts and scratches he'd suffered on his arm after a mortar attack in the very first days of the invasion. (He never would have even reported the incident, except that the shrapnel had also torn the protective suit he was wearing that was supposed to safeguard him from chemical attacks. Later, however, it had occurred to him that if he had not shielded himself with his arm, the arteries in his neck might well have been severed, and he could easily have died.) Now, he said, he was almost ashamed to have the medal, since it was the same award the Army had given to Todd Bryant for sacrificing his life.

"I was never in the Army," one of his father's friends said, "but I don't think they give them to you if you don't deserve them."

In July, one of Will's soldiers came to him asking a favor. The soldier had been dating a seventeen-year-old girl from back home in Tennessee, he explained, and the relationship was getting pretty serious. The girlfriend was planning her next visit, and her parents were sending a family friend to check him out. The soldier's girlfriend had told him that this chaperone was supposed to be all right, and she was older, probably about Will's age. The soldier wanted to know if Will would come along when they went out to dinner, kind of like a double date.

Will agreed. He sometimes wondered whether he allowed himself to get too close to his soldiers, but he liked the kid and worried that he might be in over his head. What harm could it do to go with him for a meal at the local Ruby Tuesday?

The chaperone turned out to be a blond psychiatric nurse practitioner from Knoxville named Sallie, and Will's attention shifted from the soldier to the attractive, appealing woman. They clicked immediately. Over dinner, the normally taciturn Will unleashed a torrent of detail, talking about his tour in Iraq. Soon he was telling Sallie stories he'd never told anyone else—what it had been like to feel the ground rumble as B-52 bombers dropped their thousand-pound explosives on the enemy, and what he had felt as he'd watched men die. He'd never had the chance to tell Todd or Eric Huss about most of what he'd seen, and he'd never wanted to tell his family. He certainly wasn't going to unload the details on Jen Bryant. But from that first night, Sallie was somehow different. She had a rare capacity to listen to him with her whole being, and he could barely help himself.

Back at West Point, Todd and Tim Moshier had sometimes teased Will, saying they couldn't imagine what the woman made for him would be like. But soon he and Sallie were commuting between Fort Stewart and Knoxville almost every weekend.

AMONG DAVE SWANSON's favorite soldiers was a short, skinny, twenty-one-year-old Puerto Rican named Jacob Martir. At Fort Hood, Martir had been a problem soldier, always late for formation and usually in one kind of trouble or another. But here in Iraq, he seemed to have found his niche. He was like a utility infielder on a baseball team, Dave found, a soldier he could put in any job in the platoon. If he needed a gunner, Martir was a gunner; if he needed a driver, Martir was a driver. He tried to act tough, but he was clearly just a kid. Dave was reminded a bit of himself as a young, enlisted trooper, and he nicknamed Martir "Puss in Boots," after the character in *Shrek 2.*

Martir had been on some of the platoon's worst patrols, so Dave pushed him to the front of the line for two weeks of home leave. Martir called his mother, telling her she needed to pick up a package at the airport in Miami on a certain day in June. Of course, he was the package. When Martir came back, he couldn't stop talking about how much fun he'd had—seeing his family, meeting girls, hanging out at the beach.

In late June 2004, the United States transferred sovereignty over Iraq from the American-led Coalition Provisional Authority to the Iraqi government itself; at the same time, Moqtada al-Sadr called for a cease-fire in Sadr City. The cease-fire held for a month, but on August 5, all hell broke loose again. Martir was on a patrol that day, driving Dave's Humvee. Suddenly, the city seemed to clear out, just as it had in April, May, and June when they were about to be ambushed. They heard small-arms fire and an RPG somewhere. Dave and Martir turned together to see a man standing no more than thirty or forty feet away, aiming an RPG right at them. He squeezed the trigger before they could react, but then nothing happened.

Both Dave and Martir watched in disbelief as the man turned the weapon sideways, looking at it as if trying to figure out what he had done wrong. In that moment of hesitation, the machine gunner in the Humvee's turret spun around and blew the RPG man away. Over the next few days, Dave and Martir had several more close calls—IEDs exploding nearby, bullets shot right over their heads. Dave had been shot at so many times now that it was sometimes hard to distinguish one near miss from the next, but Martir couldn't get used to it.

"There's something with you, sir, that doesn't allow anything to happen to you," Martir told him. "I don't know what it is."

The whole of 2-5 Cavalry went out in force in August, trying to rout insurgents out of Sadr City in a major sweep called Operation Iron Fury. It was really a "movement to contact" on foot, meaning the U.S. forces would methodically march through the city until they found the insurgents. Martir nearly bought it the first morning, when a mortar round hit the roof of a building he was standing on. He walked away from that episode, and he was with Dave later in the day when a half dozen or so insurgents in an alley ambushed them.

Dave's soldiers hugged the walls of the alley, looking for cover and firing back. One of the soldiers closest to the insurgents ran out of ammunition, and he and Martir ran to switch places so that the other soldier could reload. Martir turned sideways; in doing so, he exposed a small area on his torso where his body armor didn't extend. A shot rang out. Martir fell back quickly into Dave's arms.

"Medic!" Dave screamed.

The medic began working on Martir immediately, and Dave called one of his Bradleys right up to the alley, as close as it could fit. They loaded Martir in the back within a minute after he'd been shot, and rushed him to Camp War Eagle, crushing cars and anything else that got in their way.

Dave had to stay behind to direct his platoon, but he kept checking in on the radio. Soon he got good news. One of the staff officers back at War Eagle told him that Martir had survived and was on his way to the hospital.

Operation Iron Fury continued for several more days. When it was finally over, Dave walked into a government building in the center of Sadr City where the top American officers had set up a command post. It was quite a scene: the commanders and staff officers, standing around smoking cigars and congratulating one another on how many insurgents they'd killed, celebrating as if they'd won the Super Bowl. Their behavior irked Dave, especially since he felt they never faced much personal danger.

"It's too bad what happened to that kid," one of the staff officers, a major, said to Dave, his manner offhand. "Martin? Maytor? Something—"

"Martir, sir?"

"Yeah," the major said. "You know him?"

"Yes, he was my fucking soldier. What happened to him?"

He'd been dead within an hour of making it back to Camp War Eagle, the major told Dave.

Dave was incensed. He didn't believe the earlier miscommunication had been a mistake. He was convinced his chain of command hadn't told him the truth about Martir because the officers were worried he would refuse to lead his men back into the city if he knew. Dave had been through so much with his troops, and he truly believed he would give up his life for them if necessary, to say nothing of his military career. But he'd already had a talking-to for taking too many risks, during which his commander had pointed out that a lieutenant was harder to replace than a private.

As he stood there smelling the officers' cigar smoke, Dave's love for the Army simply dissolved. As difficult as Iraq had been until this point, he hadn't really minded the hardships. He had loved being a leader, loved his soldiers, and loved the fact that his nation's army had given him the chance to grow, go to college, learn, and become a better person than he might otherwise have been. But now, in that stark moment, he understood that the Army was just a ruthless bureaucracy. He and his soldiers were merely "assets," replaceable cogs in the military machine.

Just then, Dave's battalion commander came over, questioning Dave about the circumstances when Martir had been hit.

"Why wasn't he in the prone position?" the commander wanted to know, meaning lying down in the alley to return fire, rather than standing up. Dave took the question as a not-so-subtle jab, an attempt to put the burden of Martir's death onto Dave's shoulders.

"In the prone position, sir?" Dave said. The suggestion struck him as an outlandish tactic, suggesting that the commander had no idea what it was like to actually be under fire. But Dave held his tongue, knowing he was vastly outranked.

FORTUNATELY, DAVE WAS SCHEDULED to go on leave from Iraq just two days after Martir's death. He didn't tell Reyna when he was coming home, but instead went straight from the airport to the school where she taught. He was skinny, unshaven, and still wearing his desert camouflage uniform. But she was ecstatic to see him, and the short time they had together reconfirmed everything they'd felt before he left. They visited Dave's extended family in Ohio. People couldn't believe they'd known each other for less than a year and been separated by war for five months.

"When you know you're with the right person, you just know," Dave's uncle told them, adding that he'd only been involved with Dave's aunt for six weeks before he proposed. "When you know, there's no need to keep looking around."

Reyna finally introduced Dave to her daughter. With them all together, Reyna felt, for the first time in her adult life, that she had a family of her own. But hanging over them the entire time was the fact that Dave would soon be going back to war. He was hurting badly inside—Reyna could see that; she had majored in psychology in college, and she was sure he was suffering from post-traumatic stress disorder. He either had nightmares or couldn't sleep, every night. Reyna found the change in him hard to articulate, but something *had* changed. Dave wasn't quite the same happy person he'd been before he left.

"I tried," he told her as he attempted to explain what had happened to Jacob Martir. It was amazing that after all the combat he'd seen, only one soldier in his platoon had been killed, but he took the death very personally. "I did everything I could."

The days and hours slipped away. Of all things, Dave was supposed to testify in a court-martial at Fort Hood sometime in September or October, and he and Reyna held on to the hope that the Army would order him to stick around until then. To Dave, that made a lot more sense than spending a week traveling back to Iraq, maybe a week or two in country, and then another week traveling back to the United States for the trial.

But then, fifteen days into his leave, Dave had to call Reyna at school in the middle of the day.

"You're not going to believe where I am right now," he told her. "I'm on my way to the airport."

Reyna had answered her cell phone in the middle of class, and she had to turn away from her kids and face the wall so they couldn't see her expression. Dave called her several more times that day, as he waited in different airports to change planes again and again between Texas and Kuwait. Reyna would cry, and Dave would get mad at the Army, and then, a few hours later, when he landed again and waited for a plane to take him on the next leg of his journey, they'd go through the same process once more.

Reyna was beside herself with worry and grief. At home, she found the civilian clothes Dave had bought on leave, and she cried some more. *Six more months, and I'll be able to breathe,* she told herself. *Six more months, and it will be okay.*

★ 14 ★

Calling Afghanistan a war seemed like a stretch—by the end of June 2004, Drew Sloan had seen virtually no fighting. But he lived in an austere base camp in the central province of Ghazni, carried his M-4 rifle wherever he went, and led his platoon on missions to nearby Afghan villages. He'd talk with their leaders through an interpreter, trying to figure out what he and his troops could do to make their lives better. He thought of himself as the head of a traveling, proactive complaints department, dealing with a society that seemed to have been forgotten by time.

"The utter, abject poverty of these people is amazing," Drew wrote to his father after just a few days in the country. "Nothing, and I mean nothing, compares to this back in America. But still, most of the people seem happy with their lot in life—or maybe they simply don't know any better."

They would visit three or four villages a day, talking for an hour or two with the leaders, and it wasn't long before Drew could tell how things would go even before he entered the village. Each conversation took a long time, because every sentence had to be translated.

"Do you have a well?"

Sometimes the answer was yes; more often, no.

"Do you have schools?"

Always, no.

"Do you have a medical clinic? How far is it to the nearest medical clinic?"

No, and the closest was always many miles away.

And finally, "Do you know where the Taliban are?"

The answer was either no, or vague and virtually useless. "The people out riding motorcycles at night are the Taliban," was the reply one time.

The idea was that Drew and his men would write reports, and the information on which villages needed what would be compiled in a central database. The battalion's engineers could go out and start building whatever it was, and if all went well, they'd build up goodwill toward America in the process. But there were immense problems. For one thing, Drew's unit knew almost nothing about the history of U.S. forces in the area, and thus didn't know which villages had been happy to see the Taliban go, and which ones felt they'd been mistreated by the Americans since the invasion. (*The New York Times* would later report on a secret Pentagon study that said that in March 2004, American troops had made prisoners of the entire population of one village in retaliation for the death of a U.S. soldier. Just a few months later, troops from Drew's battalion visited that same village, looking for information on the Taliban.) Even more comically, the Americans assigned code names to all of the villages, naming them after U.S. cities. So even if lieutenants like Drew could get the village elders to say which of their neighbors harbored Taliban fighters, they then had to figure out whether the suspected Taliban village was "Miami" or "Topeka" on their maps.

After about a month, Drew's unit was ordered to pack up and relocate to an area near a small city called Tarin Kowt, in the central Afghan province of Uruzgan. In November 2001, Tarin Kowt's people had risen up against the Taliban, and a U.S. Army Special Forces team of eleven soldiers, along with a few dozen untrained guerrillas, had moved in. Directing airstrikes, they had defended the town against a major Taliban counterattack involving perhaps as many as a thousand soldiers. But now, two and a half years later, the American military seemed to have lost interest in the area, raiding the nearby settlements only when intelligence suggested Taliban leaders were present. Most of the military's recent focus in Afghanistan had been on securing the capital and the border region with Pakistan, where Osama bin Laden was thought to be hiding. Militias now controlled much of the rest of country, and the opportunity for the Taliban to rise again seemed very real.

Drew knew none of this, only that he was heading to a base called FOB Ripley that had been established by Marines. The first stop was Bagram Air Base, a former Soviet airfield about twenty-five miles north of Kabul. He and his soldiers were waiting in one of the dusty, gravel-floored transient tents for their flight out to Ripley when the door flap opened and his friend Christine Ray, from H-2 and Hawaii, strode inside and gave him a big hug.

Drew's troops yelled out catcalls and laughs.

Drew and Christine had a few minutes to talk before she had to go back to work. He and his soldiers were looking forward to going to Ripley, he told Christine. A bigger base, they figured, would probably mean better facilities.

"Oh," she said when she heard that he was heading to Ripley. "Yeah. That's not a nice place you're going to."

Very early the next morning, Drew and his soldiers boarded a C-130 cargo plane; as it landed at FOB Ripley an hour or so later in the predawn darkness, they saw exactly what Christine had meant.

"Oh fuck," Drew muttered.

There was nothing anywhere as far as Drew could see, nothing but a vast desert wasteland. They were inside the wire at Ripley, they were assured, but they couldn't see the outer border of the base, and they had no idea where they were. For a minute he thought about simply not getting off the plane. They marched a half mile in the dust and ankle-deep sand, finally making out their destination: a lonely row of pup tents, the only visible evidence that one of Drew's sergeants had flown out a day earlier with a couple of their soldiers.

For now, they had no orders to do anything, so Drew set up his tent and climbed inside. He hadn't slept at all the night before, and he passed out immediately on his inflatable mattress pad. By the time he woke up about three hours later, the temperature had risen to well over 100 degrees, and he was lying in a puddle of his own sweat. He crawled outside onto the desert floor, feeling as if he'd shed every bit of moisture from his body and clamoring for water. The bottle he found was nearly as hot as his tent, but it would do.

Finally, they got some orders. Two platoons were assigned to the base, and each would spend three days out on village assessments, followed by three days securing and defending their base camp. Drew was very busy on the three days outside the wire; his platoon's main job was to keep him safe when he went out to talk with the village elders. But there was very little for him to do during the three days of defense. His friend Ryan Beltramini, who was now a company executive officer, joined him at Ripley for a few weeks, and they sat up at night smoking cigars together. Though they were at different stages of life, since Ryan was married and Drew was quite single, they had been tight from West Point, through the infantry officer basic course, and in Hawaii.

"Going to war with your best friend is not such a bad deal," Drew wrote his father. Just three months into the deployment, he had read thirteen books, everything from John Irving's *A Son of the Circus* to Mark Haddon's *The Curious Incident of the Dog in the Night-time*. In his replies to Drew's letters, his dad had all sorts of questions and also passed along things his grandmother wanted to know about. "I don't wear underwear," Drew volunteered in answer to her question about how he washed his clothes in the field. In fact, he'd worn the same uniform for the duration of one ten-day mission. "The same T-shirt as well. I changed my socks once. Cleanliness is no longer a huge concern."

But even in that remote area of the world, cut off from everything, Drew still thought about Chloe Hayes. He carried two things with him wherever he went—a tiny American flag, and his Ring Weekend photo with Chloe—and he chose the words in his letters to her very carefully. Drew was perfectly content to be leading his platoon, but Tarin Kowt was still like living on the moon. When he sent out his letters he was dreaming of Chloe and the real world of America.

EVERY TIME TRICIA LeRoux Birdsell left FOB Warhorse now, she carried a picture of Todd Bryant in her rucksack. He was her guardian angel, she was sure, looking over her and keeping her alive. She faced death constantly, she worried about Toby, and she deeply missed Todd.

"He was the one person that I could talk to about anything at all and I knew that I would not be judged. Mocked relentlessly, but not judged," she wrote in her journal. "He had the most amazing ability to make me laugh no matter how mad, sad, or frustrated I was with the world."

In summer 2004, a soldier on Tricia's base was caught while high on some narcotic. Under the military's General Order No. 1, U.S. forces throughout the Middle East were strictly prohibited from using alcohol or other drugs, and the Army came down hard, launching a full-scale investigation. Like every other officer in her battalion, Tricia was called in for questioning, read her rights, and required to give a sworn statement.

"What do you know about alcohol usage in the unit?" the investigating officer asked her straight off.

Tricia's heart sank. She knew that several friends on the base had family and friends back home who sent them alcohol, much as Linda Bryant had done for Todd. A few of her closest friends had offered her drinks, and although she'd turned them down, she'd heard about at least one night when some of them had gotten quite drunk. Now she was torn: She didn't want to turn in her friends, but she also didn't want to risk being caught in a lie. The West Point honor code rang in her ears: "A cadet will not lie, cheat, or steal, or tolerate those who do." She danced around the investigating officer's questions at first but eventually came clean, naming names and passing along what she knew.

A few days later, Tricia's captain and company first sergeant called her and one of the unit's sergeants in for a talk. Though neither the captain nor the first sergeant had been accused of drinking themselves, they had been in charge, and they were both being relieved. Tricia and her sergeant were the only people available to take command immediately. "You guys are in charge."

That was it—no small talk, no further explanation; suddenly, Tricia was the acting commander of an entire company of soldiers. It was a great shock. Because doctors and nurses generally were under the command of medical services officers, Tricia was now responsible for professionals who were several years older than she and of higher rank—captains and majors. Her company even included friends who were now the targets of an official investigation as a result of the information that Tricia and others had given. One member of the so-called Sewing Circle whose career had been dealt a possibly fatal blow now reported to Tricia.

But another friend who had been drinking got off scot-free. She'd learned as an enlisted soldier before she was commissioned that telling the truth in the Army doesn't pay, the friend explained to Tricia. "Sometimes you have to do what you have to do for your career."

"If you can live with yourself, that's great," Tricia said. She was unhappy about being put in this position to begin with, and now she felt that her friend was asking her to endorse the deception. "I can't live with lying," Tricia said.

With so many more soldiers and medical personnel under her command now, Tricia was nearly consumed by work. She was dealing with issues she'd barely thought about before. One of her soldiers announced that she was gay. The Army operated under the "Don't ask, don't tell" policy, and its regulations on the matter ran many pages; Tricia and her acting first sergeant visited the battalion's legal office for advice. Another soldier tried to kill herself, taking pills and slitting her wrists, after she learned that her husband had been cheating on her back home. A third soldier had to go home on emergency leave to Germany, after her thirteen-year-old daughter wrote to say that her father was molesting her while the mother was in Iraq.

And then there was the medical part of the job. The aid station remained busy, as the insurgency intensified. One day in mid-July, mortar rounds started falling on the base, and news arrived that insurgents in the city of Baqubah had taken over several government buildings and inflicted many civilian casualties. Humvees began arriving at the aid station, carrying wounded soldiers; as the acting company commander, Tricia would have to report to the colonels above her how many casualties there were, what each of their wounds were, and what was being done for them. She grabbed a big dry-erase board and got to work, trying to keep track of who was where and in what condition, and longing for her old job, when she had been simply an extra pair of hands. A Bradley Fighting Vehicle roared in and its crew jumped outside, carrying a captain from the North Carolina National Guard. Another soldier from his unit was rushed in behind him. The doctors did all they could, but there was little that could be done for either man.

IN EARLY AUGUST 2004, barely a month after reaching FOB Ripley, Drew Sloan learned that he would soon have to relinquish his platoon. He had been expecting the move, but he didn't welcome it. His battalion had a large group of brand-new lieutenants who were just transferring in and would join them on the ground in Afghanistan. He would probably be reassigned as a battalion staff officer or a company executive officer like Ryan Beltramini, but he didn't want to give up leading men, even after sixteen months in command.

"I love being a rifle platoon leader," Drew wrote his father. "I don't think there is a better job out there and I'm not simply talking about just the military."

But then he caught a lucky break. His battalion had one heavily armed mobile platoon, outfitted much as a regular infantry platoon in Iraq would be, with armored Humvees, .50-caliber machine guns, and MK-19 automatic grenade launchers, and Drew was put in charge. Technically, the new unit was categorized as an antitank platoon, although Drew would have bet his monthly base pay that there hadn't been a working enemy tank in Afghanistan since the Soviet retreat a decade and a half before. As commander of one of the more heavily armed platoons in the country, Drew's unit's new job was to defend supply convoys and come to the rescue of other forces if they got into trouble they couldn't handle. The job also meant venturing farther from the protection of the rest of his battalion, on missions in more remote areas where he was likelier to get into firefights.

Just a week into his new command, Drew's platoon escorted a convoy of ten vehicles far out into the countryside; they were to participate in a raid on a village where top local Taliban leaders were thought to be hiding. They drove for two days, passing the burned-out remains of previous convoys that had been attacked by Taliban and militia fighters. When they reached the village that was the target of the attack, Drew's platoon and its convoy wound up stranded and alone. They ran low on food and water as they waited for weather at the U.S. airbase back at Kandahar to clear, so that the helicopter-borne force they were supposed to link up with could try to take off.

Over the battalion radio, Drew listened as another unit that was part of the attack reported its dwindling supplies, saying that their water reserves were now at "black"; they'd have to drink whatever water they could find and hope their purification tablets did their job. His own convoy had to keep its vehicles shut off to conserve fuel; they couldn't patrol the area since if they did they might not have enough fuel to make it back to the base. A day went by, and then a night, and then another day, and with each passing hour their luck in not being attacked seemed more and more unbelievable—and less and less likely to hold.

Finally, the mission was postponed. "The Taliban missed quite an opportunity," Drew wrote to his father with undisguised relief. With machine guns and automatic grenade launchers, they might have been able to fight their way out if they'd had to. But he was glad they hadn't had to try.

BY THE TIME A NEW, permanent commander was assigned to take over her medical company in September 2004, Tricia LeRoux Birdsell had decided that she had no desire ever to be a high-level commander. She was even having second thoughts about the Funded Legal Education Program. She wanted out of the military; she wanted never to return to a place like Iraq. But she also had a husband who was eager to stay in the Army. She talked it over on the phone with her mother, who was shocked by her stories of close calls with mortar and rocket attacks on the camp.

"You're in a medical unit!" her mother exclaimed. "You're far from the fighting!"

Okay, Mom, Tricia thought. *If you want to believe that.*

Her brother wrote to her, asking how she was able to cope with all that she'd seen. The answer was simple, she realized. She was working as hard as she could, and somehow she was putting off any notion of dealing with the experiences until she came home. She'd lost Captain Khan, she'd lost Todd, and she saw the ravages of war every day at the aid station. She'd never imagined having to deal with these issues at the age of twenty-four, she wrote her brother, and she surmised that maybe it would all flood her mind at an odd moment, triggered by something unexpected and seemingly unrelated. Tricia also wondered what it would be like to visit a war memorial in the United States someday and realize that it had been built in honor of her friends. Most especially, she imagined going to Arlington to visit Todd's grave.

She worried constantly about Toby. Whenever her mind wasn't completely occupied with work, she was filled with thoughts of what he was doing, of whether he was safe, of all the terrible things that could happen to him. Though she was still no more than twenty or thirty miles away from him most of the time, and she could track the broad outlines of his unit's activities by listening in on his battalion's radio network, she rarely had a real sense of where he was or what kind of danger he was in.

"I think about him all day and wonder what he is doing, if he is safe, and when he is coming back," she wrote in her diary. "The thing I hate to admit though is that I also worry that he won't come back. After losing Todd, the reality of war became so real."

IN MID-AUGUST, Drew was ordered to take half of his platoon, along with a small unit of local U.S.-allied fighters who were part of the Afghan National Army, on a patrol through an even more remote area of the province. Their small convoy drove out into the middle of nowhere, passing ancient, abandoned mud-walled compounds that looked as if they'd been built God knew when in case some invading army might one day need them. The area seemed totally deserted.

A few weeks later, his battalion commander decided to set up a firebase in the same area where Drew had just been, and one of Drew's soldiers, a specialist named Hutchinson, urged Drew to choose one of the

West Point cadets are assigned to companies, and the members of the class of 2002 remained in the same units all four years. The men and women of Company D, 1st Regiment—known as "the Ducks"—were especially close. Clowning around in spring 2002 are (left to right) Eric Huss, Reeves Garnett, Tim Moshier, Todd Bryant, and Will Tucker.

Company H, 2nd Regiment—"the Highlanders"—was an easygoing unit whose cadets benefited from the fact that upperclassmen from other companies had to climb six flights of stairs to harass them. First row: Brian Oman, Drew Sloan, Dave Swanson. Back row: Colin Kielick, Andrew Decker, George Prate.

By their senior, or "firstie," year, both Todd Bryant (left) and Will Tucker knew they were going to be leading armor platoons. They were eager for the chance to fight in giant tank battles like the ones the Army had won in Operation Desert Storm.

Todd Bryant lived directly above two of his close friends and classmates, Tricia LeRoux (center) and Kara Pond, during their freshman, or "plebe," year. Once, when Tricia had a layover in Los Angeles on the way home to Hawaii, Todd drove nearly 140 miles from his hometown east of Los Angeles just to take her to In-N-Out for a hamburger—and to prove that in his beloved California, even the fast food was better.

Eric Huss (left) and Todd Bryant got matching tattoos: "SPQR," the mark that Roman legionnaires had worn two millennia before. It was perfect, Todd said: "We, too, are the poor saps who have given up our freedom for the glory of the state."

Drew Sloan (left) was destined for the infantry; Brian Oman would be a tanker. They were both sworn into the Army on graduation day by Brian's father, a colonel in the air defense artillery.

Jen Reardon's college roommate was suspicious of Todd Bryant's motives. "Those West Pointers," the roommate said. "Their goal their firstie year is to find a wife that will follow them around the Army and cook and clean for them." But in spring 2002, when Todd asked Jen to marry him, she said yes immediately.

President Bush gave the commencement speech at the class of 2002's graduation, and he used the occasion to make the case for preemptive war. Afterward, brand-new Second Lieutenant Joe DaSilva, president of the class, presented Bush with a ceremonial West Point saber. "God bless you for what you do," Bush said as he shook Joe's hand. "Be ready."

Drew Sloan had three things going for him in Ranger School: He could keep his mouth shut; he could carry a lot of weight; and he had good friends from West Point who were going through the ordeal with him. His father beamed with pride on the day Drew was awarded his black-and-gold Ranger tab.

With so many of their close friends deployed to Iraq by the time of their wedding in July 2003, Katie McKee Moshier (center, standing) and Tim Moshier (right, standing) attached enlarged copies of some of their classmates' yearbook photos to sticks, so they could be represented in the wedding photos. Front row, left to right: Ryan Cryer, Pat Killoran, Nick Suhr, Todd Bryant, Kara Pond. Photos-on-sticks, left to right: Reeves Garnett, Eric Huss, Will Tucker.

Joe DaSilva was the lieutenant with perfect timing. He reached the 101st Airborne Division on the day the division got its deployment orders for Iraq, took over his platoon days before the invasion, and was among the first soldiers in his brigade to see real combat.

Todd Bryant's unit was ordered to Iraq in summer 2003, less than two weeks after he and Jen Reardon were married. On the day Todd left for war, Jen smiled only once—when one of Todd's soldiers insisted that the couple let him take a keepsake photograph.

Lieutenant Matt Homa (left) had been one of Todd Bryant's closest friends at Fort Riley. Minutes into their first joint patrol in Iraq, they came under fire, and one of Todd's soldiers was wounded. Badly shaken, Todd wrote to Jen that night and told her what happened. He added: "I promised I would tell you everything. Like coming home, that is a promise I intend to keep."

Dave Swanson (right) reached Sadr City, Iraq, in 2004, and was embroiled in combat for eighty-two straight days. Among his favorite soldiers was Specialist Jacob Martir (second from left), who was shot and killed during Operation Iron Fury in August, just hours after this photograph was taken.

After a life-changing experience in combat in 2004, Drew Sloan was determined to return to the battlefield. Here, on patrol in Iraq in 2007, he stands with pride again as a modern American soldier at war.

In its first two months at Forward Operating Base Warhorse, near Baqubah, in Iraq, Lieutenant Tricia LeRoux Birdsell's medical platoon treated more than seventy trauma cases. As her year-long tour in Iraq wore on, Tricia (right) wrote her brother that she had put off any attempt to deal with the death and destruction she had seen until she came home.

After a year in Iraq, and after nearly three years of marriage during which they'd rarely lived together, Tricia LeRoux Birdsell and her husband—classmate Toby Birdsell—longed for a chance to spend more time with each other. In October 2004, they flew home on two weeks' leave and tried to figure out how they could stay in the Army without having to be separated again.

After West Point, Tim Moshier spent more than a year in flight school learning to fly Apache helicopters. By the time his unit, 4-4 Aviation Battalion, left for Iraq in December 2005, he and Katie had a baby daughter, Natalie.

Quiet and tough, a man who saw as much combat as any member of his West Point class, Will Tucker was stop-lossed by the Army and served a third tour in Iraq as part of the "surge" strategy. While on leave in early 2008, he and his wife, Sallie, christened their young daughter, Savannah.

compounds they had seen as their new home. They drove back out and found a suitable one, about half the size of a football field, surrounded by twelve- and fourteen-foot walls of hardened dirt and set in a valley surrounded by brown hills rising several hundred feet. Captain Ducote led his company out, one hundred men strong, and they met up with Drew and his half platoon. Among them they had a single small tent, a tiny gasoline generator to power their radio and a lamp, and five camouflage nets. They set up the tent and the generator, and Ducote tried to convey to the Afghan National Army soldiers where they needed to be on the surrounding hills in order to give early warning of attacks. With that, Forward Operating Base Cobra was born.

The first night, Drew and the rest of the soldiers slept on the ground in the open within the four walls of the compound; he woke to the sound of fireworks and the sight of pretty little red flashes. The sound was familiar and reassuring—*Saturn missiles,* Drew thought sleepily. He'd played with the little bottle rockets as a kid in Arkansas, and he recognized the whistle they made before they exploded a hundred or more feet off the ground.

Then Drew came fully awake. He wasn't seeing fireworks—he was seeing red tracer rounds, and they were coming into the camp. Somebody was shooting at them. After four months in Afghanistan, these were the first shots he'd seen fired. Jumping up, he grabbed his rifle and fumbled around in the dark for his helmet and body armor. He ran into the center of the compound, yelling at his soldiers to wake up. The firing grew more intense, and he could see that it was coming from the hill where the Afghan soldiers were supposed to have set up. Either they had been overrun, or they were simply in the wrong place. Fortunately, the angle was such that whoever was shooting at them could not fire directly into the compound, and most of the rounds were flying by a little too high to hurt them.

Just then, a round cracked no more than a few feet over Drew's head.

All right, he thought to himself. *Not that high.*

Feeling protected by the mud walls, he had been walking around upright as he organized his troops. Now he ducked. As he did so, he turned to look where the rounds were coming from and saw a glowing red ball of fire speeding right at him. It missed him by no more than a foot and streaked across the compound into the wall on the far side, where it exploded with a tremendous boom. Later they discovered that it had smashed into their gasoline generator.

Captain Ducote's mortar team fired a few rounds, to no great effect. They didn't know where the Afghan National Army platoon was and didn't want to hit them by mistake. Before long, the Taliban fighters ran off, and the battle was over almost before it had begun.

JEN BRYANT'S TIME at Fort Riley was finally over. She had worked out a deal to pay rent and stay a little longer, but by summer the Army was pushing her to move on. After her suicide attempt, she had spent less than twenty-four hours in the military hospital; they had sent her on to a military psychologist and a grief counselor in Junction City, but she had gone to only one session. A few weeks later, as the number of casualties in Iraq increased, Fort Riley had started a grief and support network for widows; this was the first thing Jen had found truly helpful. Only three other widows lived on post, but the counselor who led the group, and who also saw Jen in private sessions, was excellent.

In August, Jen moved in with her sister Erin, a twenty-year-old college student in their hometown in Pennsylvania, but the situation was less than ideal for someone in Jen's depressed condition. Erin often left for school as early as six in the morning, and also worked at a nearby Italian restaurant. She frequently came home at ten P.M. to find Jen sitting in the same spot on the couch in her pajamas. The empty pizza boxes piled on the floor provided the only indication that time had passed. Jen reread Todd's letters and watched TV, going through the entire ten-season DVD collection of the sitcom *Friends* and feeling totally alone.

Jen hadn't known Todd's siblings all that well before his death, but now Tiffany dragged her out of the house, taking her on a Mediterranean cruise. In Rome, Jen explained to a puzzled Tiffany that the reason she was taking photograph after photograph of the street was that the Italians still used the letters "SPQR" on municipal fixtures like manhole covers. Taking pictures of them made her feel almost like Todd was walking there beside her.

But Jen was fixated on September 9, 2004, the first anniversary of Todd's departure from Fort Riley for Iraq. She couldn't bear the thought that she'd have passed a whole year without her Todd. *I'm not going to do it*, she decided. *I'm not going to go a whole year.*

Because sleeping pills hadn't worked, she decided on a more drastic method. She figured that with an out-of-state driver's license she wouldn't be able to buy a gun, so she got a Pennsylvania license and drove thirty miles to a gun shop in another town where no one would recognize her. She had rehearsed an elaborate story about moving to a big city and wanting a gun for protection, but the saleswoman asked no hard questions. She sold Jen a small revolver and was happy to teach her right there at the counter how to load and shoot it.

Jen waited until a late summer evening when Erin had to work at the restaurant. She sat on her bed with the pistol and a note of explanation and apology, trying to work up the nerve. She'd debated whether to kill herself in the apartment or in the relatively new Subaru she'd inherited from Todd. Erin's car was an old piece of junk, she reasoned, so she was doing her sister a favor by shooting herself in the apartment. Erin could always find a new apartment, but this way she could keep the car.

Well, Jen thought. *This is it. If there's a reason not to do this, then somebody's got to tell me now and I won't go through with it. Otherwise—*

Just then she heard the door opening downstairs: Erin had come home from work early. Jen quickly put the gun back in the paper bag it had come in, and shoved it under her bed.

With no job, and no place to live permanently, Jen started talking about joining the Army. What she really wanted was to find a way to go to Iraq. Todd had never had the chance to fulfill his promise to tell her everything; in fact, he'd died just hours after he'd written her pledging once again to do so. Now Jen felt that the six weeks he'd spent in Iraq were the one part of his life she knew very little about. She wanted to know what the country felt like, smelled like, sounded like. She started watching every TV show she could about Iraq and the war, and reading every first-person account by soldiers who had been in combat.

Jen knew that she wasn't making any real effort to move on, that she was clinging to her pain. But pain was all she had to connect her with the only man she'd ever loved; when the pain was gone, she feared the connection would be gone as well. His last letter, unfortunately, hadn't helped. While he'd told her to continue to live her life, he hadn't said the magic words: Find someone else who will make you happy. Instead, he'd told her to plan on being buried next to him one day. But Jen refused to be angry with Todd, and felt both guilty and cursed that she was still alive when he was gone.

Whenever she was asked to give an interview about Todd or be involved with a memorial to him, she agreed. Even before she'd left Fort Riley, Todd's parents had called her to say that *The New York Times* wanted to publish excerpts from the letters of dead soldiers. Since Todd had died before he'd written a single letter to his parents, it was up to her to decide whether to cooperate. She did. Todd's letters were so visceral and descriptive that the *Times* gave more space to his letters than to those of any other soldier.

BY LATE SEPTEMBER, Todd's old battalion, 1-34 Armor, was back at Fort Riley. Though Jen was only dimly aware of it, the battalion was being studied now as an example of a unit that had gradually learned how to fight a counterinsurgency campaign. Several months earlier, *The New York Times Magazine* had run a feature about how Major John Nagl, the 1-34 Armor operations officer who had written a book on counterinsurgency tactics before the war, had found its practice much more difficult than he'd expected. "Even when I was writing that insurgency was messy and slow, the full enormity of that did not sink in on me," Nagl was quoted as saying. "I am seeing appreciable progress, but I am starting to understand in the pit of my stomach how hard, how long, how slow counterinsurgency really is. There is no prospect it's going to end anytime soon."

In the months following Todd's death, Captain Taylor, Todd's second company commander, had earned the respect of his men and grown into a strong combat leader. But the battalion had been bloodied. In December 2003, a sergeant named Uday Singh, who had been in Todd's platoon and was a gunner in one of the armored Humvees, was killed by an IED. In mid-February, Specialist Roger Ling, the soldier who had driven the blown-apart Humvee back to base to save Matt Homa's life, was killed by a roadside bomb. A lieutenant named Jeff Graham, who had planned Todd's memorial service at Fort Riley and later taken over Matt Homa's platoon, was also killed, again the victim of an IED. And in August, Lieutenant Neil Santoriello, from Alpha Company, was killed. He and his wife, Lisa, had been part of the small group of young married officers and wives who had been friends with Todd and Jen during the summer of 2003; now he lay not far from Todd at Arlington. Over the course of 1-34 Armor's deployment, a total of twenty-two soldiers had been killed, and more than one hundred had been awarded Purple Hearts.

A few weeks after the battalion came home, Jen flew down to Fort Riley for a visit. She had dinner with Verle Wright, Todd's old platoon sergeant. Wright could see that she was suffering; he watched her closely, hoping in vain for the barest glimmer of a smile.

Jen begged him to tell her exactly what had happened to Todd. For the better part of a year, she'd been hearing bits and pieces of the story; no one had ever resolved the conflicting details provided by the letters she'd received. But Wright had been with Todd. He'd seen the whole thing happen. She begged him to tell her, and not to spare her any details.

They moved into the backyard, and he started at the beginning. Telling Jen Bryant what had happened to her husband was the last and best thing Verle Wright could do for Todd. He told her everything he knew.

∗ 15 ∗

In late September, Drew Sloan led his platoon on more missions, taking his armored gun trucks deep into the Afghan desert, a tapestry of tan and brown. Though he kept hearing that Taliban fighters knew where they were, and though he saw the aftermath of attacks on Afghan National Army forces and the burned-out hulks of vehicles that had been victims of Taliban ambushes, he had yet to encounter the enemy up close. He hadn't even fired his own weapon.

Many of his missions now involved following the same twenty-mile route, escorting Afghan trucks carrying supplies to FOB Cobra from a more established Special Forces base to the north called Tyz. If they'd been traveling on their own, Drew's trucks could have made the trip in a couple of hours, but the elaborately decorated Afghan vehicles, known as jinga trucks, had a much harder time getting through the rough terrain. Often the trip took twenty-four hours or more, with a tense overnight stop along the way. Once his troops were stuck for three days, trying to tow an Afghan supply truck that had been caught in a riverbed. Eventually, they abandoned it, intending to return with a more powerful vehicle. That night, they heard massive explosions as Taliban fighters blew up the truck. The enemy was out there, and Drew was certain he had talked with Taliban leaders blending in with the people he met on his village assessments. But for now, the Taliban fighters remained a shadow.

On another mission, Drew wound up stuck at Tyz for just over a week, waiting for help with another crippled vehicle, and for the arrival of more civilian vehicles that they were to escort to Cobra. After sleeping in the dirt for weeks, Drew's soldiers were glad for the respite. The Special Forces troops knew how to live, even in the middle of nowhere. They had set up their base with cots and air-conditioning. They'd built a gym and a mess hall with a roof.

Best of all, the base had Internet access and a satellite phone. Drew's first thought was to call Chloe Hayes. The connection wasn't great, and it took Chloe a few minutes to believe he was really calling from Afghanistan, primarily because the Pentagon routed his call through Virginia and the display on her caller ID showed a 703 area code. But talking with her was like being thrown a lifeline to the civilized world.

Drew already had planned his two weeks of leave. In December, he would fly to New York, where he'd attend Brian Oman's wedding. And now, encouraged by Chloe's warm reaction when he called, he e-mailed her: "Meet me in Manhattan while I'm home."

Drew spent the day getting his convoy ready to roll back to Cobra, a mission that was shaping up to be one of the riskiest yet. He had only two Humvees, and a very small unit—ten soldiers, an interpreter, and about half a dozen fighters from the Afghan National Army. With that modest force, he had to escort six jinga trucks carrying giant CONEX shipping containers full of supplies, another huge truck with a crane mounted on it, and two more brand-new *unarmed* Humvees—all this through some of the most rugged and dangerous terrain in central Afghanistan. The containers would stay at Cobra, so that the soldiers could use them as shelter and a platform from which to observe and shoot at anyone threatening the base. They needed the crane in order to be able to move the giant containers around.

.They would be moving especially slowly—at a walking or jogging pace—at some points, because the Afghan trucks couldn't go any faster. With so few forces, the convoy would be unusually vulnerable.

Just before he left, Drew checked his e-mail one last time. He found a message from Chloe, and it carried good news: She'd love to meet him in New York.

Drew was headed out with far too few troops to be comfortable into some of the most rugged and dangerous terrain in Afghanistan. But he found himself breaking into a smile, over and over again.

THE ROUTE from the Special Forces base back to Cobra led across a river, through a valley, and up narrow mountain switchbacks. Drew rolled out in the last Humvee in his convoy, watching to make sure that none of the jinga trucks fell behind or were picked off by Taliban forces in a sneak attack. A couple of hours into the journey, the crane truck broke down, and Drew's troops fanned out to defend the convoy while its owner and the other drivers and mechanics got it running again. As Drew watched the truck driver jury-rig a replacement for a broken fan belt using nothing but a bit of old rope, he decided that if he ever were to open a garage, he'd hire all Afghans. Soon after the crane truck was repaired, they reached the river, only to watch as the same truck got stuck trying to ford. After they finally towed it out, it broke down again.

The journey went on like that all day and into the evening. They moved to higher, safer ground and set up camp for the night. A squad from the Special Forces base hustled out to join them so they would have enough troops to fend off a Taliban attack. It was a long night, but quiet. In the morning, Drew decided that the balky crane truck made them too vulnerable; they left it behind.

They crossed the mile-long valley floor. Drew was uneasy, because they were completely exposed to anyone observing from above; it didn't help that they were still moving only ten miles an hour. Finally, they reached the mountain; Drew had to presume that the Taliban knew they were coming and would mine the road, ambush them, or both. He sent one of his two gun trucks slowly up the mountain, assigning a soldier to walk point to check for mines and watch for a possible ambush. It took three hours to get all the trucks up, since most of the jinga trucks didn't have enough power and had to be towed by the Humvees. Meanwhile, a group of about a dozen polite, extraordinarily patient Afghan men crammed into a white Toyota Hylux pickup truck were stuck behind the convoy the entire way.

Finally they started down the hill, and soon reached a fork in the path. The forks would reunite farther along; Drew took the path to the right, and the Afghans in the Toyota, finally able to pass the convoy, took the path to the left.

Not ten seconds later, there was a huge explosion. Drew looked at his driver, a specialist from Guam named Todd Lanke. "Is that what I think it was?"

"Yes sir," Lanke said. "The Afghan car!"

They backtracked and raced down the fork the Afghans had taken, fully expecting to see a smoldering hulk and bodies everywhere. But the men all seemed fine; they were sitting by the side of the road, and their truck was only slightly damaged. The explosion must have just missed them, and whoever had set it was long gone.

"Are you all right?" Drew yelled as he ran up to them, his interpreter in tow.

Several of the men spoke excitedly. "Bomb blew up," his interpreter translated.

Drew could see that. "Why are you guys still here?"

His interpreter listened to the answer. "They're waiting to know if they can leave."

Drew let them go and called on the radio to Cobra. This was the first IED he'd encountered or even heard about in Afghanistan; he reported what had happened and said he was going to push forward, trying to make it the rest of the way to Cobra before nightfall. He took photographs of the aftermath of the explosion, and they moved out.

Five minutes later, Captain Ducote called back from Cobra, relaying a message from their battalion commander.

"Hunter Six," Ducote said, using Drew's radio code name, "I need you to go get the IED."

Drew couldn't believe it. "Cobra Six: What?"

Ducote repeated the order: Their battalion commander wanted him to go back and get the IED.

"We've got to go back," Drew said to Specialist Lanke.

"Are you kidding me?"

Drew raced back to the site of the explosion, angry as hell. He jumped out of his Humvee and ordered the rest of his troops to stay far back. As he walked up to the crater where the IED had detonated, he was fully aware that whoever had laid this bomb might also have planted a second explosive, or that perhaps only part of the original bomb had blown up, and that he was now about to get himself killed. It pissed him off to no end that he was taking a huge risk in order to retrieve a bomb fragment that would most likely be stuffed in some storage locker and forgotten.

But Drew was the ranking officer and the West Point graduate, and he realized that his commander's order wasn't illegal or immoral—it was simply stupid, in Drew's estimation—and he decided that the absurdity would end with him. The book answer in this kind of situation would have been for Drew to order one of his men to retrieve the fragments, since a platoon leader was supposedly more important to the mission than an ordinary infantryman. But he was slightly more fearful of going through life with the death of one of his soldiers on his conscience because of something like this than he was afraid of his own death.

He found a wire leading from the site of the explosion and yanked it, kicking up dirt and rock and walking the wire back until he found the trigger. *Good enough,* he thought, cutting the wire with a Leatherman knife and retrieving the trigger.

As the day went on, there were no further explosions, but there was more trouble. Cobra 6 radioed once more to report that the main road to the base was now mined. With nightfall approaching, Drew urged the convoy along, trying to find another way through the rugged terrain. He found a little path, not much more than a goat trail, leading up over another mountain, but the jinga truck drivers refused to try it.

"We can't get up there," one of the drivers said through Drew's interpreter. "We'll take the mines."

"Yeah, well, that's not your choice," Drew snapped back. But the drivers' response convinced him to keep looking, and finally he found one of the best dirt roads he'd seen in Afghanistan, a route that wasn't marked on any of the maps but that clearly led directly where they needed to go. When they made it to the base ninety minutes later, he christened it Route Razorback, in homage to his Arkansas roots.

They still had one more problem. With the crane truck abandoned at the riverbank, they had no way to remove the containers from the jinga trucks and move them to their proper locations within FOB Cobra.

"You're just going to have to go back and get another crane," said a first sergeant who had remained at the base. Drew hoped he was joking; he could hardly imagine trying to navigate that route with a similar convoy again. Besides, it wasn't as if there were dozens more crane trucks in the Afghan wilderness, with drivers just waiting to be hired.

Give us a minute to figure this out, First Sergeant, Drew said.

His platoon quickly improvised a clever solution, backing the jinga trucks into a dried riverbed and using its banks as a natural loading dock. Then they roped the containers to their Humvees, dragged them across the dirt into the compound, and rammed and shoved them into position.

It wasn't pretty, but it worked.

AT FORT HOOD, Tim and Katie Moshier had settled into a routine by October. Katie had started her new teaching job, and she still volunteered for projects with the Family Readiness Group. The only hitch was that Tim was now out in the field on exercises for days and weeks at a time. He would leave for Korea sometime in 2005, and it was an open question whether Katie would be allowed to go with him. They held out hope.

Tim was quiet and difficult to get to know, but he was developing a reputation as a very competent pilot. The Unit Fielding and Training Program that now occupied 1-6 Cavalry offered a wide variety of challenging field problems and exercises; for the new pilots, like Tim Moshier and Holly Harris, it was almost like an extra year of flight school. The Apache Longbow was the Army's most advanced tank-killer helicopter, and the $18 million machines—they cost three times as much as a Black Hawk—were both a marvel and a challenge to fly.

As always, Tim was extremely competitive. In one exercise, the entire company, with five helicopters up and running, was due to simulate an attack in a nearly sixteen-thousand-square-mile training area west of Fort Hood. The 21st Cavalry instructors playing the role of the opposition force would be arrayed on the ground with vehicles that fired laser beams, which the helicopters' computers interpreted as different types of weapons. The odds were deliberately stacked against the students, for there was no point in wasting training time on an underwhelming enemy.

Before the exercise began, Tim told Captain Kober that he and his instructor pilot, Chief Warrant Officer Tom Nowlin, had come up with a plan. Instead of attacking all together, as the instructors in the 21st Cavalry would expect them to do, they wanted to fly far out ahead, loop around, and attack the target from the other side. They'd act as a diversion while the rest of the company came in full force from the south.

"We're going to kick butt," Tim said excitedly.

Kober agreed to the plan. Tim and Tom followed their roundabout route and approached the training area about five minutes ahead of everyone else, flying 120 knots at treetop level, between one hundred and two hundred feet off the ground. Suddenly they encountered a torrent of simulated antiaircraft fire, and the computer informed them that they'd been hit by a Soviet-style missile launcher called a 2S6. The mission was technically a success, in that Kober and the other pilots came in completely undetected from the south. But Tim was embarrassed afterward at having been shot down so quickly.

"I can't believe we got up there and got it handed to us, sir," he fumed when he saw Captain Kober again.

"Don't worry about it, man," Kober said. "We did all right. It was a good training mission. Learn anything?"

"Yeah, we did. Not to do that again."

THE LONGBOW HAD incorporated the Army's most advanced computerized targeting systems, and software updates and upgrades were common. Instead of lights and dials, the Longbow had a glass cockpit with multipurpose display units and a computerized female voice nicknamed Bitching Betty that warned when things weren't going well.

Early one morning, before sunrise, Tim and Holly and their instructor pilots were waiting for their turn on a helicopter gunnery range. In the distance they could see the anticollision lights on one of the helicopters that was already on the range. Every so often there would be a brilliant flash as the helicopter fired its rockets.

Holly was quite impressed, and her instructor pilot, Chief Warrant Officer Matt Stauffer, told her to zoom in on Fort Hood on the moving map, a high-resolution satellite map system that was one of the helicopter's newest updates.

"You can watch them fire the rockets from there, too," Stauffer told her. This was a joke: The satellite pictures they were looking at had been taken days or weeks before. But Holly didn't understand, and Stauffer let her keep searching and searching until he couldn't stand it anymore.

"Attention Blackjack Flight," Matt called out over the radio. "Just want you guys to know that LT Harris is upset because she can't find the Apache firing on the range on the sat map."

Tim and Tom Nowlin thought this was hilarious. A few minutes later, they flew out to do the training mission, which involved nearly twelve hours of flying, landing, waiting, and shooting on the gunnery range. At the end of the day, as they flew back to the airfield, Tim called out to Holly on the radio.

"Blackjack Two-Six, Blackjack One-Six."

"Blackjack Two-Six, go ahead," Holly replied.

"Hey, Holly, why don't you check the sat map and see if you can find a parking space for us?"

Holly walked over to Tim once they landed. She was used to being the butt of jokes, and she didn't mind that—she wanted to be accepted as one of the guys, and being made fun of came with the territory. But she was also proud of Tim in an odd way. Slowly, he was breaking out of his shell.

"That was some cold stuff!" she said, laughing.

"Yeah," Tim said. "Tom told me I didn't have a hair on my butt if I didn't do it."

AFGHANISTAN'S FIRST PRESIDENTIAL election since the U.S. invasion was scheduled for early October 2004, and Drew's platoon would help monitor the voting. It was a tricky assignment: They had to make their presence known to the Taliban and so discourage them from disrupting the voting, but they couldn't leave the impression that they were part of an American effort to run the election or rig the outcome. The night before the ballots were cast, Drew's platoon hit the road, driving from village to village trying to cover as much of their territory as possible. His small unit split up; Drew rendezvoused with Captain Ducote in a valley not far from several of the villages. They had just two vehicles and were so isolated from the rest of their battalion that their normal radios didn't work. They had to rely on satellite communications instead.

They spent the night of October 9 on a mountaintop, watching the settlements below. All seemed quiet and peaceful. The next day, they would drive down into several villages, gather boxes of ballots, and head back to Cobra. A helicopter would come through and bring the ballots to Kandahar, then on to Kabul, where they would be counted.

They rolled into the first village, Saraw, where they met with an elder named Haji Wazir. Captain Ducote had been dealing with Wazir for months and thought of him as excitable but generally trustworthy. Today Wazir seemed especially fidgety and couldn't sit still. Ducote's interpreter translated for them: "Taliban nearby, coming to get us."

Warnings that the Taliban were in the vicinity weren't at all uncommon, but Drew and Captain Ducote had no desire to stick around any longer than necessary.

"Which way should we go back?" Ducote asked Drew.

They had two choices. One route went straight down to a dry riverbed, which they could follow back toward Cobra. The other, much slower route—the way they had come in—would take them back up into the mountains.

Drew picked the riverbed. A basic military tactic in a situation like this was not to return the way you came. But he also thought that if the Taliban were nearby, the U.S. group was likely to be ambushed no matter which way they went. Although they had weapons mounted on their armored Humvees—a .50-caliber machine gun on Captain Ducote's truck, and a MK-19 automatic grenade launcher on Drew's—they weren't well equipped for a lengthy firefight. The riverbed was more exposed, but if they were attacked they could just go like hell and hope to bust through.

Specialist Lanke drove Drew's armored Humvee. A section sergeant named Brian Hobbs, who had just returned from two weeks of leave visiting his wife and children in Arizona, sat in the front passenger seat. Specialist Joey Banegas, from New Mexico, was in the turret, manning the automatic grenade launcher. Drew sat in the backseat behind Sergeant Hobbs, and another soldier sat behind Lanke.

They had driven about six or seven miles when they realized that Ducote's Humvee had fallen behind enough to be out of sight in the rearview mirrors on either side of the truck. Lanke slowed down to let the captain catch up. Minutes later, they started taking rifle fire from somewhere in the fields on either side of the riverbed. The rounds bounced off the Humvee's armor.

They could barely hear one another over the gunfire and engine noise, and from the backseat Drew had a good view of little more than Sergeant Hobbs's head. But as their Humvee turned a corner on the path through the riverbed, Hobbs saw two men standing in the middle of the road. They were holding rocket-propelled grenade launchers.

"Blow through!" Hobbs yelled. "Blow through!"

THE EXPLOSION WAS JARRING and disorienting. The RPG had struck right on the front of the Humvee, but Lanke and Hobbs realized to their amazement that they were unhurt. Even up in the turret, half exposed, Banegas was simply shaken up.

Lanke floored the gas, but the truck didn't respond, and in the next second flames began to shoot from the engine compartment. The Humvee rolled impotently to a stop, and the fire grew bigger. Fighters emerged from the surrounding weeds, opening up on them with AK-47 rifles.

Banegas swung in the turret. He fired one round from his grenade launcher, and it landed with a bang, but then the launcher jammed. Bullets bounced off the stricken Humvee, and more and more fighters emerged, from nowhere, it seemed—too many to count. Surrounded now, Drew's men had no way to maneuver and a limited supply of ammunition; it seemed only a matter of time before they were all captured or killed.

Banegas ducked down in the Humvee, trying to shield himself from the bullets and fix his weapon. He looked down into the backseat and only now saw what had happened to his lieutenant, Drew. He sat drooped over, unconscious, with blood spurting from his mouth and the left side of his jaw hanging unnaturally.

CAPTAIN DUCOTE'S GUNNER fired round after round from the .50-caliber machine gun mounted on their Humvee. Ducote had been only a couple of minutes behind Drew's truck, but it had seemed like an eternity. The enemy fighters were completely exposed, having assumed that Drew's truck was traveling alone. Now they pulled back a bit as Ducote reached the scene, though they didn't break off the attack completely, and the soldiers in both Humvees fanned out, setting up a defensive perimeter. Ducote's driver pulled up alongside Drew's stricken truck.

"Sir," one of the soldiers from Drew's Humvee yelled, "the lieutenant is injured!"

Banegas had jumped down from the turret and was trying to pull Drew out, even as bullets rained down on them. Drew was now semiconscious and more or less capable of moving under his own power. But he obviously had no awareness of his surroundings; Banegas had to guide him away from the burning vehicle and toward Ducote's Humvee.

The Taliban fighters—or whoever they were—pressed a second attack. As the shooting grew intense, Ducote realized that there were mortar rounds inside the burning Humvee, which would very likely cook off within the next few minutes. When that happened, whoever was nearby would be in big trouble.

Sergeant Hobbs ran to the stricken Humvee to grab the radio and several other sensitive items they didn't want falling into enemy hands, and Ducote ordered everyone into the working Humvee. They pulled away, ten troops crammed in or hanging on to a vehicle built for five.

None of the three radios in Ducote's truck worked in the deep valley. They drove about four miles away to higher ground, and soon reached a small village where he thought the locals were trustworthy. From there, Ducote got through on the radio to the battalion firebase and called in a medevac helicopter.

Drew was in rough shape now. Their small group did not include a real medic, but some of the soldiers who had taken a course in combat first aid held Drew down, trying to keep him still so his airway would stay open. Drew was semiconscious and combative, fighting back when the soldiers swept the broken teeth of out his mouth and pulling out the IV every time they stuck it in. Fortunately, the helicopter arrived within ten minutes.

"Don't drop me, Banegas," Drew somehow managed to say as Joey Banegas carried him to the bird. But no sooner was he on board than he went into respiratory distress. A medic on the Black Hawk performed an emergency tracheotomy and forced a tube into his throat to keep at least a small airway open.

They raced toward Kandahar.

EMILY WNUK, Drew's H-2 friend, had arrived in Afghanistan only about three weeks before. She was in the adjutant general's corps, a purely administrative branch, and her working conditions were radically different from those of soldiers like Drew. Emily was in an air-conditioned office most days and had a telephone and constant Internet access at her desk. She was even able to call home to Long Island once a week, and in fact she was talking with her mother, telling her how well Afghanistan's presidential election had gone, as she signed into the classified military version of the Internet.

There was a single reported casualty: Sloan, Andrew.

"Oh my God!" Emily gasped into the phone. "I need to go!"

She hung up the phone and dialed yet another H-2 veteran, Christine Ray, who had last seen Drew at the transient tent at Kandahar in June. As an intelligence officer, Christine had access to a more detailed report than did Emily. She pulled it up on her computer. "VSI" was the notation next to Drew's name: very seriously injured.

★ 16 ★

It was after midnight in Arkansas, but Drew Sloan's mother, Vicky, was still up, reading a website devoted to soldiers wounded in the forgotten war in Afghanistan. Finally she went to bed, but at 4:45 A.M. the ringing phone woke her. A colonel in Hawaii was on the line: Drew had been wounded in combat and was in "very serious" condition.

What does that mean? Vicky asked, instantly wide awake. How bad was "very serious"?

"There's only one step worse, ma'am."

"Death?"

"Yes, ma'am."

The colonel provided Vicky with some sketchy information, not all of which turned out to be accurate. "Fragmentation of the chest," he told her. "Gunshot wound to the head." Drew's platoon had been ambushed, he reported, and he rattled off the names of weapons involved: RPGs, AK-47s, and some kind of pistol Vicky had never heard of before. If you can wait forty-five minutes, he promised, we'll get you more details.

Vicky hung up the phone and screamed at the top of her lungs. It was the worst hour of her life. Finally, the phone rang again; this time the caller was a lieutenant colonel in Kandahar. He described a thirty-minute firefight and a quick medevac, and then told Vicky that Drew would be coming home to a military hospital, most likely San Antonio or Walter Reed. He tried to be reassuring, saying he had a report that the doctors had upgraded Drew's status to "serious," meaning his wounds were bad but not immediately life-threatening.

"I don't want any of those phony euphemisms," Vicky interrupted. A retired high school history teacher, she had taught an A.P. course about the Vietnam War, and she believed the government hadn't been straight with the American people during that war. She sure as hell wasn't going to let the military give her the run-around now, not when the subject was her son.

All right, the colonel said. He acknowledged that he hadn't seen Drew himself. But he had heard that half his jaw had been blown clean off.

Vicky Sloan sat in her house in Arkansas, envisioning her son with only half a face.

CHRISTINE RAY HAD E-MAILED many of her West Point friends saying that Drew had been wounded. The e-mail was quickly forwarded to others in the class, including Matt Baideme, the engineer who had seen Dave Swanson in the Green Zone on the first day of what had turned out to be the Sadr City uprising in April. Matt's tour in Iraq had been extended for several months because of the deteoriating security situation, but he was now back at his home base in Germany. He knew that most casualties from Iraq and Afghanistan came through Germany, and after making a few phone calls he learned that Drew was already at Landstuhl Regional Medical Center. Christine's e-mail hadn't conveyed the gravity of Drew's injuries, so when Matt picked up another H-2 veteran and friend named Christian Bowen on his way to visit, they stopped off to get Drew a sandwich and milkshake. They imagined it had probably been a few days since he had eaten anything other than hospital food.

Drew's condition came as a complete shock. He was unconscious and hooked up to a respirator, IV tubes, and all sorts of wires and monitors. Half his face was black and blue and hugely swollen. He was virtually unrecognizable.

You're going to be okay, Matt told Drew, hoping he could hear. You're going home.

Drew showed no sign that he was aware of their presence.

One of the doctors tried to reassure them. I know it looks horrible, she said, but he's going to make it.

Matt went home and hit "Reply All" on Christine's e-mail, trying not to sound as discouraged as he felt. He had witnessed some terrible things during his year in Iraq, he wrote, but seeing Drew lying there like that was very hard to take. "It's definitely different when this stuff happens to a friend."

A COUPLE OF DAYS after learning about Drew's injury, Vicky Sloan got a phone call from a group called Wounded in Action, a liaison and advocacy group for soldiers. The volunteer was calling to say that they had located Drew's hospital room in Germany and wanted to patch her through to him. At Drew's bedside, a nurse held the phone up to his ear. He gave no sign that he recognized his mother's voice, the nurse said, but at least Vicky could talk to her son and tell him that he would be all right.

About a day later, Wounded in Action called again: They knew the Army would be flying Drew to Washington, D.C., and they'd figured out what flight he would be on. Vicky called Walter Reed as he was being brought in, and just as her call was put through, a doctor was deciding whether Drew should continue to be classified as "seriously" wounded.

Vicky had been warned about this issue. You want him classified as "serious," Wounded in Action had told her, because otherwise the Army won't pay for his family to visit him in Washington. From her battles against cancer when Drew was a child, Vicky had a lot of experience advocating to doctors. Wounded in Action faxed Walter Reed the right forms, and the doctor checked the appropriate box.

Vicky and Drew's father, who also still lived in Arkansas, both arrived at Walter Reed later that evening, four days after the attack. They were brought in to see Drew right away. He looked better than they'd expected—his face was badly bruised and swollen, but it was whole. Still, he was unable to talk and only semiconscious, and he didn't really look like their son, with all the tubes sticking out of him and the tracheotomy hole in his neck. He looked very thin, too: He'd lost seventeen pounds in four days.

Two of Drew's West Point friends had driven all night from Fort Stewart, Georgia, to visit. John Dorffeld and Jon Barton, artillery officers in the 3rd Infantry Division, had been in H-2 with him back at the academy. Both had done a year in Iraq and would soon be returning for a second tour.

"Look, Drew," Vicky said, bringing them over to her son's bed. "It's your friend John Dorffeld."

Drew reached out and Dorffeld clasped his right hand. But then Drew quickly passed out again.

The doctors took his parents aside to explain that they needed to start operating almost immediately. First, and easiest, they needed to implant a feeding tube in his stomach. Second, a few days later, would come the real challenge: surgical reassembly of the inside of his face. X-rays and a CT scan showed that almost every bone above his neck had been broken. Imagine a shatterproof window that has been hit with a baseball bat, one of the doctors said.

"Don't worry about the little white ones," the doctor added, meaning the hundreds of tiny fractures that Drew's parents could see on the films. "Those will heal by themselves."

Drew's wounds had not, in fact, been caused by shrapnel. Instead, he had suffered a "blast pressure" injury, caused by the violent rush of air flowing backward in the Humvee after the RPG hit. Vicky had never heard of such a thing, but the doctors explained that with troops traveling in armored vehicles, they were seeing more and more of this kind of wound.

A few hours later, Drew's doctors took him into the operating room for the feeding tube surgery. He awoke afterward, but he was delirious and panicky; he grabbed a nurse who was trying to treat him and pushed her across the room. He did recognize his parents at his bedside—a fairly remarkable feat considering that he didn't have his glasses and was nearly blind without them—but he was convinced he was in a prisoner-of-war or reeducation camp, and that his mother had betrayed him and turned him over to al Qaeda sympathizers.

"Sloan!" Drew screamed, somehow getting the word out despite the tracheotomy tube in his throat. He yelled as loud as he could, repeating his last name several times and rattling off his social security number. In his panic, he thought that if he could identify himself to the doctors, they would realize who he was and stop his mother from giving him to the enemy. Vicky leaned close to try to comfort him, but Drew grabbed at her throat with his left hand. He was full of adrenaline and very strong; for a moment she was terrified.

One of the nurses raced over and injected a sedative. Drew passed out again.

WHEN HE WOKE the next morning, Drew was no longer hallucinating. He couldn't talk, because of the trache, but he could scribble on a notepad. It was a huge relief to his parents that he could now communicate, even in this clumsy fashion.

Though the war in Afghanistan had been nearly forgotten in the United States, casualties were piling up. Just days after Drew arrived at Walter Reed, Joey Banegas was admitted, with a stump where his right leg had been. And Sergeant Hobbs was dead. They'd been out on another mission and had been ambushed again, not far from where Drew had been hit. Their driver had been killed instantly, and another trooper from their company had been blinded.

By the time he got this rash of bad news, Drew was well enough to feel terrible. His face and skull surgery would be a grueling marathon: His doctors would remove several teeth that had been driven into his skull like spikes in a railroad tie, set the shattered bones in his sinus cavity, reconstruct part of his skull, and rebuild his jaw, which had been broken in several places and was now a full inch out of alignment. Drew had endured nine years of braces as a kid, and all that orthodontic work had been wiped out in a second.

The surgery took eighteen hours; Drew looked a lot worse afterward, bad enough to make his father cry. Drew's head now seemed to be held together by staples, and his face was once again swollen and bruised. He still couldn't talk, but he was writing notes to his mother again. They made no sense.

"Don't answer the phone," Drew wrote. There was no phone. "Don't eat the food." There wasn't any food. Once again he seemed to think he was a prisoner of war. A hospital chaplain came in to visit, and Drew was convinced he was an evil imposter. But at least he wasn't violent this time.

By now, Vicky Sloan was having a very difficult time with the situation. Drew was in a shared room, separated only by curtains from the moans and screams of other patients on the floor. The soldier one bed over cried constantly. Twice, other patients' hearts stopped, and the room suddenly filled with chaos as doctors and nurses rushed in. Vicky wanted to get Drew out of the shared space and into a private room upstairs, but Walter Reed was extremely overcrowded. The doctors and nurses worked hard and seemed to truly care, but there simply wasn't enough staff to take care of everyone. The building was clean, but it was old, and some of its shortcomings could never be fixed.

Vicky pushed Drew's doctors to sedate him. She insisted that the impact of the long operation and his surroundings were wearing him down.

"I appreciate your input," one doctor told her in a condescending tone. But Vicky wouldn't take no for an answer. She called in the hospital's psychiatric team on her own.

It had become increasingly clear to Vicky that her son needed her to be his advocate. Drew's father would have to travel back and forth between Washington and his professorship in Arkansas, but Vicky was retired now, and fortunately she could afford to move into Walter Reed with him. Nurses would inevitably forget things, or fall behind, and without his glasses and with a trache in his throat, Drew was effectively blind and mute. Getting her son a private room became Vicky's first major advocacy project. By noon the day after his marathon surgery, she'd succeeded.

A WEEK OR SO LATER, a one-star general came through the hospital, handing out Purple Hearts.

Should I stand? Drew wrote to a nurse on his notepad.

Whatever you want to do, she replied. He remained in his bed, someone took his picture, and the ceremony was over in seconds. Drew was struck by how unremarkable it felt to be awarded his nation's oldest military honor.

But soon he got something better. In Afghanistan, Ryan Beltramini had endured a few days of great anxiety after he heard about his friend's injury, and he was hugely relieved when he learned that Drew would be okay. And he also did Drew a big favor. Ryan had never met Chloe Hayes, but he had heard Drew talk about her often, and it had occurred to him that she might not have heard what had happened. He had dug around on his computer, looking through the group e-mails he'd received from Drew over the years. Finally he found Chloe's address and sent her a message.

Chloe was just a few hours into her first day at a new job in Chicago when she opened Ryan's e-mail. She ran outside immediately, not wanting her new coworkers to see her crying. When she had had a chance to compose herself, she came back inside and called his parents to find out where he was and how he was doing. She sent him balloons, as flowers weren't allowed in his section of the hospital. They perked Drew up considerably.

Chloe asked Drew's parents whether she could come visit, but Drew refused. He hadn't looked in a mirror yet, but he had seen the photograph taken of him as he was receiving the Purple Heart. He had looked terrible, he thought, and he couldn't bear for Chloe to see him like that.

Chloe e-mailed him a recent photograph of herself, taken at a party just the month before, and Drew had it printed and placed on the table next to his bed. When a doctor asked who she was, Drew told the story of how they'd met and how he had turned down her offer to come visit him.

"Mistake," the doctor said. "Women are much better in situations like this than you give them credit for."

But Drew had made up his mind. Chloe was special, and when he saw her again, he wanted to look his best.

ON NOVEMBER 9, about two weeks after Drew's eighteen-hour surgery, and a week after President Bush won reelection over Senator John Kerry of Massachusetts, Drew was picked to be among the patients the president would meet on a tour of the hospital. Drew's condition had improved—he could talk now, and he was able to walk again—and he and his mother were escorted down two floors and taken into a room with three other wounded soldiers. While they waited for the president, Secret Service agents and junior staffers from the White House kept coming in, filling out forms, getting their social security numbers, and asking questions.

"Okay," one woman said to Drew, reading to him from her clipboard, trying to keep him straight among all the soldiers Bush would visit. "You're a lieutenant from Afghanistan."

Hours went by with no sign of Bush. They weren't allowed to leave the room, although none of the patients had eaten anything since breakfast. Finally, Bush swept in, with the First Lady right behind him. Drew, the only one of the four wounded who could stand, got to his feet as quickly as he could. Vicky was surprised at how small Bush looked in person, yet how, even so, he managed to fill the room. The president went straight for the wounded soldiers, greeting them before talking with the relatives.

"Well, it looks like you lost a leg, but you've still got another one," Vicky overheard Bush say to a wounded Marine. "Hopefully you'll keep that one and things will get better. I'm proud of your service. We really appreciate what you've done." He moved on to greet an Army captain from Puerto Rico, and then walked over to Drew and his mother.

"Sir, you spoke at my commencement," Drew said.

"I thought I might have," Bush replied. "Well, son, it looks like you've been through a whole lot, but it looks like you're going to make it."

"Yes sir," Drew said.

"What happened?"

"Sir, I was wounded the day after the elections in Afghanistan."

"Oh, so you were the one!" Bush said. Drew had been told he was the only American casualty during the course of the Afghan election, and now Bush seemed to confirm it.

"Yes, sir, I guess I was."

"Are you going to stay in the Army?" Bush asked.

How do I answer that one? Drew wondered.

Drew's doctors had told him he would qualify for a medical discharge, but he knew he didn't want one. He thought about the visits he'd witnessed from generals and other dignitaries. They would ask the wounded soldiers what they could do for them, and usually the soldiers said the same things: *Send me back to my unit. Send me back to the war.* Later politicians would cite the requests in speeches, suggesting that they proved the troops supported the president and his foreign policy. But for Drew the reason was deeper, and more basic. One minute, he had been what he'd wanted to be for years—an infantry officer, leading men on the battlefield; the next minute, he'd been reinvented as a hospital patient. He would fully recover, Drew concluded, only if he went back to war. And that meant staying in the Army, at least for now.

But Drew said none of this to the president. Instead, he simply answered, "I don't know about that, sir."

"Well," Bush replied before moving on to visit with the next soldier, "you've earned it either way."

IN THE DAYS that followed, Walter Reed was flooded with still more wounded. War casualties had dropped significantly in the months leading up to the presidential election, but in mid-November, the U.S. military began a major assault on the Iraqi city of Fallujah, an insurgent stronghold about ten miles from where Todd Bryant had been killed a little more than a year before.

Tricia LeRoux Birdsell had almost been sent to Fallujah as a logistics liaison officer to the units involved in the assault, but she begged her battalion commander to let her serve anywhere in Iraq but Anbar Province. She did not want to be so close to where Todd had died.

"Suck it up," her commander told her: Sometimes soldiers just had to do what the Army wanted them to. But in the end, Tricia wasn't needed. Nor was Toby; most of his unit was sent to Fallujah, but at the last minute his company was left behind in Diyala. Tricia sighed in relief.

The day after the U.S. offensive began, the phones and Internet at FOB Warhorse were shut off—this condition was called a Duke Blackout— because a soldier from Toby's battalion had been killed and his family had not yet been notified. The next morning they learned that the dead soldier was the command sergeant major, Steven Faulkenburg, the highest-ranking enlisted soldier in his unit. A few days later, there was another Duke Blackout, this one for Lieutenant Ed Iwan, twenty-eight, of Nebraska, executive officer of Alpha Company in Toby's battalion, who had been hit with an RPG. Tricia knew Iwan; he had preceded Toby as leader of Toby's old platoon. Then, just as that Duke Blackout was lifted, another came down: Captain Sean P. Sims, thirty-two, from Texas, commander of the same company that Lieutenant Iwan had been in. Tricia and Toby had sat with Sims, his wife, and their new baby at a Christmas party just before the deployment. He'd been shot in the head and had bled to death on a dirty tile floor in a house in Fallujah. By month's end, 137 U.S. troops were dead, and 1,431 wounded, more than twice as many as in the month before Bush's reelection.

BY VETERANS' DAY, Drew no longer needed twenty-four-hour care, but although he could leave Walter Reed, he had to stay nearby for follow-up appointments so that the wires holding his face together could be removed as the bones began to heal. The biggest risk he faced now had nothing to do with his medical condition, but with the possibility of being assigned to the medical holding company at Walter Reed. Drew had heard stories of wounded troops stuck in medical hold for a year or more, reporting for formation in the morning and then doing nothing all day, just waiting for the Army to decide what to do with them.

"Drew," his mother said simply when she heard about it, "you are not going to medical hold."

She got them a room in Mologne House, a redbrick motel on the hospital campus that had originally been built so the families of wounded soldiers would have a convenient place to stay. The facility was nice enough—it had daily maid service, and even a bar in the lobby—and Vicky and Drew moved into room 410. That first night, they each lay on one of the room's two full-size beds, and as Drew closed his eyes and began to drift toward sleep, his mom turned on the TV and began watching soap operas on the WB network.

"This is never going to work," Drew told her over the sound of the television.

But they made do. Drew would not be able to eat solid food again for weeks, so Vicky got a blender and found a ride to a grocery store. After each meal, she would wash the blender out in the bathtub. Compared to many of their fellow residents, Vicky thought, she and her son were fortunate. Staying with Drew did not present a financial hardship, and her experience as a cancer patient and a teacher at a public high school had left her adept at battling bureaucracy. But she still had to advocate for her son. For one thing, the Army cut off Drew's combat pay, even though military regulations said he was entitled to continue receiving it for three months after being injured. Vicky marched over to the finance office, made them print out sixty pages of regulations and records, and convinced them to reinstate his pay.

She also heard that in order to clear out Mologne House faster, the Army was going to stop paying a daily expense allowance to the visiting families. Vicky was incensed. The change didn't really burden her—she was collecting her pension just as if she had been living at home—but some people had been forced to leave jobs and were trying to make their mortgage payments and feed their kids on the $48 daily allowance while they cared for their soldiers. On paper, the Army offered all sorts of assistance and programs for the families of the wounded. But in practice, Vicky saw, not enough people were being helped. She came to suspect that the failure to provide assistance to many of these families was intentional: If people didn't take advantage of programs they were entitled to, the government saved money.

It broke Vicky's heart to see the struggles of families who weren't as sophisticated as she was, or who had money problems. Whenever she ate in the hotel dining room, she saw at least one wife or mother of a wounded soldier crying—not only because of his injuries but also because of the stress of caring for him.

BY THE FIRST WEEK of December, Drew was ready to be released from Walter Reed. He looked forward to leaving Mologne House as well. He and his mother were close, but Drew was pretty sure that any twenty-five-year-old man sharing a motel room with his mom for a month would experience at least a few frustrating moments. He was pleased that his recovery was going so well: Though he had a long road ahead—his jaw was still tightly wired, and his eyes weren't lining up symmetrically—the rest of his surgeries and rehab could apparently be handled at Tripler Army Medical Center in Honolulu. The prospect of returning to his division's home base left him in very good spirits. Drew planned to stay on the mainland until after Christmas, visiting family in Arkansas; and, he figured, he could make it to Brian Oman's wedding near West Point before heading back to Hawaii.

Two days before he was due to leave, Drew had a follow-up appointment with an eye doctor. The muscles controlling the movement of his eyes had been damaged, and as a consequence he was somewhat cross-eyed; his doctors didn't plan to correct the problem for a few more months. The ophthalmologist numbed Drew's right eye with drops, and then tapped the eyeball lightly with a pair of forceps. The eyeball swiveled quickly, almost as if it weren't attached to anything.

Clearly worried, the doctor ordered a battery of additional tests. By six P.M., Drew and his mother were sitting with a new doctor, a neurosurgeon named Rocco Armonda.

You've got a brain aneurysm, Armonda announced. Drew's doctors had completely missed it during the past month of treatment. "The good thing," Armonda said, "is that I'm one of the only specialists in the Army who can do a noninvasive aneurysm surgery."

The surgery, called a coiling procedure, was truly cutting-edge, Armonda told them. He would puncture Drew's femoral artery, insert a flexible tube, and run the tube up the length of the torso, through Drew's neck, directly to the site of the aneurysm. Then he would fill the aneurysm with platinum coils so that blood would clot inside and create a seal. The alternative, much messier and more dangerous, would involve cutting Drew's skull open and operating around his brain matter.

Though the surgeon seemed confident, Drew felt as if he'd been punched in the gut. Thus far he'd been on a steady trajectory toward recovery; this was clearly a major setback.

"I'm not quite sure if this aneurysm is in a place where I can get to it," Armonda continued. So, he explained, he would bring Drew into surgery the following morning, and figure out while he was unconscious whether he and his team could perform the coiling procedure. "If we can't, we'll wake you up and talk about what we're going to have to do."

At eight o'clock, a resident removed the wires keeping Drew's jaw together, so that they wouldn't interfere with the surgery. By midnight, Drew had been moved to Bethesda Naval Hospital for the operation. He settled into a new hospital bed, and his mother, exhausted, slumped in a nearby chair.

Events had moved so quickly that until now Drew hadn't had time to think clearly about how close he'd come to death without knowing it. He was still in great danger: If the aneurysm burst before the surgery, he would quickly bleed to death. Oddly, he felt at peace with the notion. Perhaps he wouldn't be given the chances he'd hoped for—to become the military officer he'd wanted to be; to see whether he had a real shot at a relationship with Chloe Hayes; to offer the "lifetime of selfless service to the nation" that West Point had prepared him for. But now, in the hours before the operation, there was absolutely nothing he could do to improve his odds. If the aneurysm was going to burst, it would burst. He'd lived life as fully as he could. If this was the end, so be it.

As Drew often said, he was "a big fan of a wrap-up," so, before going to sleep, he told his mom he wanted to plan his funeral. This was the last topic Vicky Sloan wanted to discuss, but she obliged, writing down everything her son wanted. Drew considered himself agnostic, or at least non-denominational, despite having been raised as a casual Methodist. He remembered Zac Miller's funeral two years before—it had been a religious ceremony, held in a church—and he decided he didn't want a sober, pious memorial service that would suggest he had believed in things he truly hadn't. Drew wanted people to remember him as he really was, not as a caricature of a Christian soldier.

He didn't want a long series of hymns or military music played, he told his mom. The one song he wanted someone to play was by the rock band Weezer: " 'The World Has Turned and Left Me Here,' " he said. "It's the third song off the blue album." As for prayers, the only one that he wanted read or spoken aloud was the Twenty-third Psalm—"The Lord is my shepherd; I shall not want . . ." He'd memorized it as a kid and still found it comforting.

By now, both Drew and his mother were crying.

"Mom," Drew continued after a while, "you're going to have a temptation to bury me in Arkansas close to you, but that's not where I want to be. My home is West Point. That's where I want to go."

With that, Vicky folded the paper on which she'd been taking notes.

"That's it," she said. "No more tears, because you are going to wake up tomorrow. There isn't going to be a funeral. You're going to be just fine."

Finally, Drew dozed fitfully. Vicky sat quietly in the chair, awake and afraid, the entire night.

A few hours later, the chief surgical resident came by with a question. "If Dr. Armonda cannot do the noninvasive [procedure], Drew, do you want your mom to make the call whether he cuts your head open and does it right there?"

"My mom," Drew said, nodding. Then they led him to prep for the surgery, with his mother watching the whole time. It took an hour and a half just to deaden Drew's mouth enough to insert a breathing tube. Just before the nurses wheeled him into the operating room, Drew squeezed his mother's hand.

THE OPERATION WENT EXACTLY according to plan, and Drew was told that within days he could leave the hospital. The only significant side effect was that his eyes no longer seemed to focus properly: Each worked fine independently, but they sent conflicting signals to his brain that threw off his depth perception and made it very difficult for him to keep his balance. The doctors gave him an eye patch and told him they'd wait to see if his body learned to compensate on its own.

David Sloan came to stay with his son at Bethesda, giving Vicky a break. A few days later, they got another visit from President Bush, who happened to be at the hospital for his annual physical. They went through the same drill that Drew and his mother had endured at Walter Reed, except for the long wait.

Bush walked into the room, and showed no sign that he recognized Drew from a few weeks before, although, Drew realized, the eye patch could have thrown him off.

"What, did we lose an eye?" the president asked him.

We? Drew thought. *"We" didn't lose shit.*

But that wasn't the kind of thing you could say to the commander-in-chief. Instead, Drew briefly described the surgery, explaining that his eye would be fine.

"Well, that's good." Bush turned to Drew's father. "You're a historian. You teach history at Arkansas"—clearly he had been briefed before he entered the room. They spoke briefly about the elections in Afghanistan and the upcoming elections in Iraq, as well as Bush's recent electoral victory.

"History will show that what we're doing here is the right thing, and an extremely significant thing," the president said.

Bush turned to talk with another wounded soldier, but then he stopped to tell Drew and his father one more thing.

He'd gained ten pounds on the campaign trail, he said. "I'll have to stop drinking milkshakes."

✶ 17 ✶

Dave Swanson's war was nearly over. The fighting in Sadr City had quieted down to a whimper in the early fall of 2004, and by November Dave's time as a platoon leader was done. A new generation of lieutenants was coming up right behind him; after nearly a year and a half in charge, it was finally his turn to step aside.

His first new assignment was as an assistant public affairs officer; he would follow the battalion commander around and write feel-good press releases about how many frozen chickens they were handing out to the poverty-stricken people who'd been trying to kill them a few months earlier. He held a few other staff jobs as well, and finally he joined half a dozen other lieutenants and became one of the battalion's assistant operations officers. In part because there were so many new officers coming into the battalion, Dave seemed to slip through the bureaucratic cracks. Most days he had no assignments or duties; he worked out in the base gym and played marathon games of Risk with a couple of other senior lieutenants whose careers had followed a similar pattern.

He called Reyna in Texas more often now. She didn't quite grasp why Dave was now safer, but she was happy that she didn't hear a lot of stress in his voice and that he had stopped talking about "missions" that she didn't really comprehend. Gradually, they began making plans, talking about what life would be like when Dave came home in March.

But although his life was suddenly much easier and safer, Dave was sad, down, and low. With no real job or assignment, he felt little sense of purpose. He missed his soldiers. And, though he hated to admit it, he was livid when he learned that he'd be awarded the same medal for his Iraq tour that virtually all of the officers in the battalion were getting: the Bronze Star for merit. There was a world of difference between the Bronze Star for valor, indicated by a tiny "V" on the ribbon, and the much more common Bronze Star without the "V." It was bad form to acknowledge, but it burned Dave up that he—a lieutenant who had led his platoon on hundreds of combat missions—would receive the same award as some staff officer captain or major who had almost never left the base.

AFTER A YEAR IN IRAQ, and after nearly three years of marriage during which they'd rarely lived together, Tricia LeRoux Birdsell and Toby Birdsell longed for the chance to spend a little time with each other. They had gone home on two weeks' leave together in October 2004, and while it wasn't the most relaxing vacation—Tricia's parents had been reassigned to the Army hospital in San Antonio, and Toby's still lived in Washington State, so they spent the entire time traveling—at least they'd been together and safe for fifteen days. Now, in December, with both their tours in Iraq almost over and their return to Germany on the horizon, the plan was that Tricia would apply to law schools in the Washington, D.C., area, and Toby would put in for a transfer to the 3rd U.S. Infantry Regiment, the ceremonial unit at Arlington National Cemetery.

Gnawing at Tricia, however, was the worry that their plan might be derailed by the alcohol episode. She hadn't been implicated in the drinking, but she had been admonished for not immediately reporting her friends to their commander. She traveled to FOB Speicher, an Army base near Saddam Hussein's hometown of Tikrit, for an interview with northern Iraq's highest-ranking colonel in the judge advocate general's corps. The whole time, she half expected the colonel to break off the interview and say, Wait a second! How dare you think we'd take you as an Army lawyer? But the conversation went well enough, and soon Tricia was putting together her law school applications. Because the Army would only pay tuition at public law schools, she applied to all those within driving distance of Washington, including the University of Maryland and George Mason University, in Virginia.

Focusing on the future improved Tricia's morale greatly, but even better was that she was finally able to give up her temporary company command and take on a much less stressful staff job. She had a new group of friends and colleagues to replace the Sewing Circle; she ate with them and hung out with them during her off hours. Slowly, she began to relax. She allowed herself the luxury of believing that she and Toby would soon be home.

But one evening, with only a few weeks to go in her tour, Tricia and several friends were eating in the Warhorse dining facility when the base came under attack. A rocket exploded just a couple of hundred yards from the building. All around them, soldiers grabbed their helmets and flak vests and hit the floor, while Tricia and her friends, callused veterans now, just kept eating. But then, as Tricia walked back to her office, she heard another loud explosion, and a minute or two later she heard over the radio that the rocket had hit the group of trailers where she lived. Although nobody was hurt, the trailer just two doors down from her own had taken a direct hit.

Instantly, Tricia was once again holding on for dear life, waiting anxiously for mid-February, when she and Toby would fly home and she could finally exhale. Each day now brought another "last time you'll ever do this" milestone, and she rejoiced at the arrival of the first soldiers from the unit that would replace hers.

In one of the last entries in her war journal, Tricia wrote: "It is such a great feeling to see an end in sight. There are very few things that I will miss about his place, but there are several things I can't wait for once we leave.

I can't wait to . . .
  Fall asleep at night and not wonder if I'll make it through the night
  Go through an entire day and not worry about whether or not my
  husband is safe

Hear a door slam and not jump because it sounds like an explosion

Not have a radio next to me at night

Fall asleep in my husband's arms and know it is not a dream and that
we really are at home

Not have nightmares about what I've seen here

Grieve for those we've lost

Celebrate our return

Not be afraid anymore

Carry a purse instead of my machine gun

Wear anything other than desert colored uniforms

Be truly happy away from here with my husband for the rest of my life.

WILL TUCKER WAS headed the other way; he would soon be going back to Iraq with 3-7 Cavalry. Although he and his girlfriend, Sallie, had been dating for less than six months, they decided to get married in December 2004, just a few weeks before he left. Sallie had come home to Haleyville with Will to meet his parents at Thanksgiving, but now she and Will told no one of their wedding plans, so it almost felt like an elopement. They arranged for a small, simple ceremony at the Chatham County courthouse in Savannah, paying the justice of the peace a little extra so they could have the wedding on a Saturday afternoon. Sallie picked out a dress, and Will would wear his dress blue uniform.

But the Friday before the wedding, Will's unit was locked down because a piece of equipment was missing; nobody was allowed to leave Fort Stewart. He and Sallie decided that she would wait at the courthouse for him, in the hope that the equipment would be found, and Will might be dismissed in time for the ceremony. She wore everyday clothes instead of the cream-colored dress so if Will couldn't get there she wouldn't be mistaken for a jilted bride.

Will was crazed with impatience as the day dragged on. *To hell with this*, he finally said to himself. He told his troop commander there was somewhere he just *had* to be, promised he'd be back in an hour, raced to Savannah still wearing his desert camouflage fatigues, and found Sallie and the justice of the peace waiting by a fountain outside the courthouse. The ceremony was over in ten minutes.

Will told Sallie he loved her and left immediately for the base. "Please don't hate me," he told her on his cell phone as he drove back. He didn't know when the lockdown would be lifted, or when he might be able to see her again. "I'll make it up to you when I return from Iraq."

They kept the wedding a secret for a few days—Will played it off when he returned to Fort Stewart as if he'd had to do something urgent but inconsequential, like renew his driver's license or pay an overdue electric bill. The newlyweds weren't even able to move in together full-time. Sallie had a house and a psychiatric nursing practice back in Knoxville, and she couldn't just abandon that life for Georgia, especially when Will would be leaving for Iraq in just a few weeks.

But in the final weeks of December, they were able to spend time together, and they told their friends and family the news. It came as a complete shock to Will's parents, who had no idea he and Sallie were so serious. And at military bases around the world, former D-1 Ducks read their e-mail in disbelief; most of Will's West Pont friends had no idea he'd even had a girlfriend. Will's commander even called him in for a professional counseling session. Army posts were crawling with opportunistic women who married soldiers just before deployment, looking for an easy paycheck and a ticket in the "SGLI lottery," the possibility that their new husbands might be killed in combat and that as widows they would get the $250,000 in Servicemembers' Group Life Insurance benefits. But it was usually the nineteen-year-old privates who fell for those women, not West Point graduates.

First Sergeant Tony Broadhead, who had been through hell with Will in Iraq, was especially skeptical. Not long afterward, he met Sallie for the first time, at the wedding of one of Will's soldiers, a sergeant named Curtis Anthony Mitchell.

"By the way, Tony," Sallie said to Sergeant Broadhead after Will introduced them to each other, "I don't need his money. I'm not going to treat him bad. I just want to love him."

Broadhead didn't smile. "Where is your family from?" he asked.

"Atlanta."

"Good," Broadhead said. "Because if you do him wrong, I know where to find you."

DREW SLOAN was very nearly the perfect patient, willing to endure almost anything to hasten his return to duty. He'd recovered quickly after the aneurysm surgery, and was well enough by the end of December to travel to Poughkeepsie for Brian Oman's wedding. He was released from Walter Reed a few days before Christmas, then spent nearly a month in Arkansas on convalescent leave.

In late January, he came back to Washington for several days of check-ups before the doctors would clear him to return to his unit in Hawaii and continue his treatment there. He called Alisha Beltramini, who was now living in New York City while studying for her master's degree in social work at Columbia University, and asked if he could visit for the weekend.

For Alisha, New York had turned out be the perfect place to wait out Ryan's deployment to Afghanistan. The city was exciting, the program kept her busy, and when she grew depressed or anxious, she had more than seven hundred classmates, all training to be counselors and ready to listen. A few women in the class even had husbands who had been in the Army, so they understood what it was like to be a military wife.

Drew took the train out of Union Station in Washington on a snowy Friday evening, and he buzzed the door at Alisha's building on the Upper West Side of Manhattan about five hours later. Alisha was shocked when she came down to let him in. Drew had been a good-looking guy back at West Point and in Hawaii, and the change in his appearance was painful. Though he was obviously vibrant and mobile, he was now cross-eyed, with thick glasses and missing teeth. The scars on his face were vivid, and his blond hair was grayer and thinner. He was pale, and seemed much skinnier than she'd remembered.

"I know I look different," Drew said, staring at his feet.

Alisha hugged him quickly, hoping her anguish wasn't too obvious. She grabbed one of his bags and led him up the stairs, forcing herself to keep moving because if she stopped to think for a second, she would start to cry.

"It's good to have you here," she said. "Let's go out. Let's have fun."

But when they reached the apartment, Alisha sent a text message on her cell phone to the friends they were going out with: Drew is here. He looks completely different. Please be kind.

The evening was a great time, and not a bad substitute at all for hanging out with Chloe Hayes in New York as Drew had planned many months before. Another lieutenant from his battalion was home on mid-tour leave. Mike Baskin had also been in Drew's class at West Point; they'd become friends in Hawaii, part of the group of young officers who had spent Friday and Saturday nights in Honolulu together before they'd left for the war. Mike couldn't help but cry, overwhelmed with relief, as soon as he saw Drew—but he shut off the tears quickly, and they focused on the fact that they were together, in one of the world's greatest cities, with a group of good-looking women.

The next morning, Drew and Alisha went to brunch, and then they spent the afternoon sitting in the Barnes & Noble at the corner of Broadway and Sixty-sixth Street, watching through the floor-to-ceiling windows as the snow fell. It was beautiful, and America's wars could not have seemed farther away.

DREW GOT BACK to Washington in time for his follow-up appointments at Walter Reed the next day. For all the outward signs of his injury, he was truly making remarkable progress. When he left the hospital for convalescent leave in December, he hadn't been able to open his mouth more than a quarter inch, so his maxillofacial surgeon had given him a viselike tool called a jaw spreader. Three times a day, all month long, Drew had used the tool to pry open his mouth as wide as he could stand.

"Did you see any improvement?" the surgeon asked when Drew came in for his checkup. She started to describe the surgeries that would improve his odds of one day being able to open his mouth completely.

"Well," Drew said, his mouth opening to almost its full range, "what do you think?"

He was that kind of patient—show him the path to a goal, and he'd work hard and endure pain to achieve it. While the coiling in his brain continued to take hold and heal, he was forbidden to do any strenuous exercise, and he found he was soon going crazy for lack of it. But he had calculated that his unit would probably be going back to war—in Iraq this time—sometime in 2006. That gave him a year to get better if he wanted to go with them; he was determined to do so.

On February 1, 2005, Drew flew back to Hawaii, where he became the executive officer of his battalion's rear detachment—second in command of all the soldiers who, for whatever reason, weren't deployed. The job gave him little to do, but salvation from boredom came quickly, in March, when he volunteered to be the temporary aide-de-camp for a new general assigned as one of the two assistant commanders of the entire 25th Infantry Division. The job would only last three months, and it didn't seem to be hugely challenging: Drew would run the general's daily calendar and be his all-around assistant. But he'd heard good things about the new one-star general, John M. "Mick" Bednarek, who was coming to Schofield Barracks after a stint as a commander at one of the Army's giant training areas. Drew, looking every bit the wounded war hero, met the general at the airport. He liked his new boss immediately.

Sergeant First Class Seaver, the sergeant with the serious drinking problem who had deserted from Drew's platoon in 2003, had turned himself in. He'd been restricted to the base for more than six months, waiting for the officers of 2-5 Infantry to come home so he could be court-martialed. A platoon sergeant who had walked out on his unit just before it went to war would almost certainly be sentenced to prison, and Drew was called to testify against him.

The prosecutors really wanted to make an example of Seaver, saying that his platoon had suffered in war because he hadn't been around to train and lead them. But Drew didn't think a long prison sentence was warranted. He didn't respect the sergeant by any means, but neither did he think Seaver deserved to be drawn and quartered. He was a drunk, no more and no less, and as Drew had the story, there was a high-drama love affair involved in his sudden disappearance. Not that his behavior was in any way excusable, but the truth—and in court, that was Drew's duty, to tell the truth—was that Seaver's soldiers were better off without him.

The prosecutor wasn't happy with Drew's testimony, but Seaver was convicted and sentenced to two years in a military prison and a bad-conduct discharge. He also lost his entire military pension, a severe penalty in its own right. But when the trial ended, he looked like a man who was glad that the uncertainty about his future was finally over.

"Thank you, sir," he said to Drew, and then the military police led him away.

THE REST OF 2-5 Infantry started coming home in April. Drew met Captain Ducote as he got off the plane, and he was thrilled to see Ryan Beltramini. Soon, however, Ryan was packing again, getting ready to leave Hawaii for good. Alisha was finishing her degree at Columbia, and she had pretty much had it with the Army and the war. She was tired of the constant fear for her husband, and anxious that Ryan might come home from Afghanistan only to find some other overseas deployment—most likely to Iraq—on the horizon. Like Toby Birdsell, Ryan had put in for a PCS, a permanent change of station, to the Military District of Washington. The transfer was approved; he planned to finish his five years in the Army assigned to the Old Guard at Arlington Cemetery.

Greg Londo, Drew's investment partner in Hawaiian real estate, came home from Iraq in early spring as well, and the two officers moved together into the condominium they'd bought. Somehow, they'd completed the paperwork for the purchase when Drew was in Afghanistan and Greg was in Iraq. Greg had actually sent the condo documents to Drew for his signature at Camp Cobra just before Drew was injured.

The place was gorgeous, right on the northwestern coast, about twenty miles from Schofield Barracks, with beautiful beaches and a perpetual island breeze. But after just a year with the 25th Infantry Division, Greg was about to be reassigned, and Drew wasn't thrilled at prospect of keeping up the condo on his own. Besides, the real estate market was hot. The condo was snapped up almost immediately; on a nine-month investment, the two young officers split a quarter-million-dollar profit. They had each made far more on the sale of a two-bedroom condo than they had for fighting wars in Afghanistan and Iraq.

DAVE SWANSON HAD SLOGGED through the final months of his year in Iraq, and finally, in early March, his tour was over. Almost as soon as he got home, he bought himself a present: a silver Ford Mustang GT convertible. He and Reyna had decided to move in together, which meant that Dave would in effect become stepfather to Reyna's daughter, Isabel; he understood the magnitude of the risk Reyna was taking. They found a place in Georgetown, Texas, roughly halfway between Fort Hood and Austin, where Reyna taught school. Within days of moving in, they both felt like they'd been living together forever. A couple of weeks later, Isabel came home from school with a picture she'd drawn of her family. She'd included three people, not two, and Reyna knew she was happy.

About two months after Dave's return from Iraq, he and Reyna drove to Baylor University, where one of Dave's friends was getting married. Reyna had never seen Dave look nervous before, but he was quiet and uneasy the whole way. They parked outside the church, and there, sipping bottled water in the Mustang in the late spring Texas heat, Dave asked Reyna to marry him. He was falling all over his words, barely able to articulate the question. They'd never talked about marriage before; she had a practical, even jaded idea of the institution, in part because her own parents hadn't tied the knot until several years after she and her sister were born. But it was like Dave's uncle had said: Sometimes you just knew. Reyna said yes immediately.

She was stunned by the size of the ring Dave had bought her: two and a half carats. Reyna had grown up without money, and she taught in a low-income school. Spending thousands of dollars on a diamond ring made little sense to her. She was even nervous about wearing it to work, in case she was perceived as a showoff. But she understood why giving it to her was important to Dave. He had spent a year in Iraq, and for most of that time he had salted away his tax-free salary. The ring his savings had paid for symbolized not only what they would share in the future, but also what they'd already gone through.

But life wasn't perfect. Dave tried to put the war completely behind him, but he couldn't simply choose not to be affected by what he had gone through, especially those first five months. He had trouble sleeping. He seemed impetuous—the Mustang, the ring; he even went to Las Vegas to learn to jump out of an airplane. (He'd been through the Army's paratrooper school, but basic military jumps didn't involve a freefall. He wanted the feeling of hurtling toward the earth for a full 120 seconds before pulling the chute.)

One night, as he and Reyna lay in bed asleep, Isabel crept into the room. She'd had a bad dream and wanted to be near her mother. Dave thrust out his hand, instinctively defending himself and Reyna against a threat. "Isabel!" he snapped as he awoke fully and realized what had happened. "Don't do that again!"

Dave had a strong, deep voice to begin with, and when he used his Army command presence, even Reyna found it intimidating. But she had rarely heard him speak so harshly. Isabel just looked at her mother, eyes wide. Reyna jumped up and carried her daughter back to her bedroom, and stayed with her until they both calmed down.

Yet both Dave and Reyna grew to feel that in many ways Army life wasn't so bad now that Dave's unit was in garrison rather than deployed. He would almost certainly deploy again, but he assured Reyna that his next assignment wouldn't be anything like the drawn-out combat he'd seen. He was a signal corps officer and his temporary detail to the infantry was reaching its end. Moreover, he was just a few months shy of promotion to captain. While there were no guarantees in the military, higher-ranking officers in the combat support branches simply didn't get shot at anywhere near as often as lieutenants in the infantry.

Besides, Dave had been in the Army for nearly a decade now, if you counted his enlisted time and the years he'd spent at West Point. He knew the system, and the Combat Infantryman Badge on his chest and the 1st Cavalry Division combat patch on his right shoulder gave him a certain status. By the time 2007 came around and his five-year commitment following West Point was up, he would have nearly eight years in the Army that would be credited toward retirement (the four years at the academy didn't count). It was easy to imagine he could make it to lieutenant colonel, and retire at twenty years with half his base salary. He'd be forty-two.

But one evening he and Reyna got together for dinner with a group of Dave's fellow officers and their wives, some of whom had been married for many years. At one point, the dinner conversation turned to deployment and how hard it was to be separated. But some of the women seemed remarkably jaded.

"You see these young girls crying for their soldiers, their husbands or boyfriends," one of the wives said to Reyna. "And here I am saying, 'Take them. Take them. Go right ahead.'"

Reyna understood that the woman wasn't being entirely serious, that she and the others loved their husbands. But the comment included a grain of truth, Reyna saw: The women were so used to separation that they just accepted it. Separation was a part of life, when marriage to a soldier was the life you chose.

Later, Reyna told Dave she didn't think she could ever get used to being apart from him. Nor could she get used to a strange irony. Dave and his fellow soldiers fought for freedom; that was what they all told themselves. But in some ways, this military life was imprisoning—more restricted, and less free than any Reyna had ever imagined.

* 18 *

The funny-'cause-it's-true joke about Pittston, Pennsylvania, self-proclaimed Quality Tomato Capital of the World, was that there were only two seasons: blizzard and construction. Jen Bryant had shivered through the winter of 2004–05 without her cold-weather clothing, all of which was stored in an Army warehouse in Kansas. She didn't want to stay in Pennsylvania with her sister for the long term, but a military widow was only entitled to have her things shipped to her once. If Jen wanted her sweaters and coats back, she had to pick a place to live.

In early 2005, Jen decided on northern Virginia. Though she hadn't been able to bring herself to visit Todd's grave since the funeral, the thought of being near Arlington Cemetery comforted her. Even more important, Tim Bryant was stationed at the Marine Corps base in Quantico, Virginia, and Tiffany was still at Fort Bragg. Jen was driving down to visit both of them pretty regularly now; they'd become her surrogate family. Even if she remarried, Tiffany told her, Jen would always be their sister. "You're stuck with us," she said, with an ironic laugh.

Jen wanted to teach again, but it was tough to find a job in the middle of the school year. Fortunately, between the life insurance money and her savings, she could afford to go a few more months without working. But when she looked for apartments in Virginia, she couldn't bring herself to explain to potential landlords how a single, twenty-four-year-old woman with no job could be counted on to pay the rent each month. Telling people about Todd's death was a conversation-killer, and she could no longer bear the look it reliably induced, the mixture of shock and horror. Consequently it took her a few weeks to find the place she moved into, in Fairfax, about twenty miles outside Washington. Here she began trying to make a life.

Jen recognized that she needed to talk again with a therapist or psychologist about her grief. She no longer thought directly about suicide, but she worried about what was going on in her subconscious. She'd be driving her car, for example, and notice that she hadn't put on her seatbelt. The Veterans Administration sent her to a military counselor, a major in the Army medical corps at Fort Myer, but Jen found her conversations with him frustrating. He only wanted to talk about her relationship with her parents and her childhood, and when they finally discussed Todd, all she got was practical military-style advice: You're gaining weight, so we need to put you on a diet; you need to start exercising; you haven't been to see your husband's grave yet? By May 30, then, you have got to go!

It felt more like a pep talk than a counseling session: Take that hill! Heal that grief!

She stopped going to sessions. Jen couldn't be some kind of latter-day Jacqueline Kennedy Onassis, majestically dignified in widowhood. She wasn't sure of much, but she understood that she had to grieve her own way. If that meant sitting on her couch for six months and crying all the time, then so be it.

THIRTY-FIVE MONTHS HAD PASSED since Drew Sloan had last seen Chloe Hayes in person, but still he held out hope that they might someday have a relationship. Morning in Hawaii coincided with the middle of the workday in Chicago, and soon after he arrived at Schofield Barracks, they fell into a pattern of sending half a dozen or more e-mails back and forth every day, punctuated by occasional phone calls. An ocean, both literal and metaphoric, separated them, and by late spring, he decided he'd waited long enough. He bought a plane ticket to Chicago.

Chloe was still with her high school boyfriend, some guy named Peter who worked in pharmaceutical sales or something. But in five months of daily e-mails, Chloe had barely mentioned him, which Drew took as a good sign. Chloe was a smart, gorgeous girl; of course there would be guys lined up to take her out. Whatever her arrangement with Peter, at least she was still free to go out with Drew while he was in town.

That first night, they went with a group of her friends to see the band Coldplay, the same group Drew had chosen to anchor the CD he'd sent her just before he left for Afghanistan. But Drew was tentative, nervous, and awkward. He wasn't ready for a deeper involvement with Chloe, he realized during the visit; all he really wanted to do was maintain the status quo. It didn't help that he was deeply self-conscious about his facial scars and crossed eyes. And when they talked, their timing just seemed perpetually off.

On the last morning of his visit, though, he finally saw a glimmer of hope. Four hours before his flight, he and Chloe went to breakfast. The feeling was faint at first, but as the minutes ticked by, their old connection grew. This was what Drew had been dreaming of in remote places like Ghazni and Tarin Kowt, what he'd thought about during his darkest moments at Walter Reed. Finally alone with Chloe after all he'd been through, he found that his nondescript spinach and tomato omelet tasted better than any meal he'd ever had in his life. He had miles to go before he was done rebuilding himself, but Chloe was right here, holding out the promise of a larger, freer, civilian world. In that moment, a life with her seemed a least a possibility, and that was enough for now.

They held hands the rest of the way to the airport. When it was time to go, Drew hugged Chloe fiercely, and said good-bye softly, his mouth against the side of her head. He pulled back, kissed her forehead, and flashed as confident a smile as he could manage. And then he walked away.

BACK IN HAWAII NOW, Drew had a fresh sense of purpose. He and General Bednarek got along well, and what had originally been a three-month detail soon became Drew's official job. Though Bednarek worked Drew hard, and though Drew had limited motive or opportunity for a real social life, the general was also very good about pushing him to put his physical recovery first. Drew arrived at work before the general did most days, and stayed until after he left. And now that he was finally allowed to exercise again, he spent hours and hours at the gym.

With surgeries virtually every month, Drew tried to schedule as many operations as he could for Fridays, so that he could recover on the weekend and be back in the office on Monday, or Tuesday at the latest. A piece of bone from his hip was grafted into his mouth to replace bone in his palate that had died. In June, he had an outpatient surgery to realign his eyes, shortening and reattaching the muscles that controlled the movement of his eyeballs. A second or two after a doctor jabbed him with a needle, Drew faded off into a deep sleep.

In a dream, he heard someone ask: "Has anyone read *Love in the Time of Cholera*?"

"I have," he heard himself say. Gabriel García Márquez's novel about a hopeless and pathetic romantic's lifelong pursuit of the woman he truly loves was one of Drew's favorite books. In his more quixotic moments, he could identify with it—in fact, he planned to send Chloe a copy for her birthday later in the summer. Maybe he'd ask the general's administrative aide, who spoke Spanish fluently, to help him translate a line from the book—"without an instant of encouragement"—as an inscription. It would be transparently obvious, and she'd recognize the phrase when she read it later in the story. He had a feeling that just maybe, if he ever got back to Chicago—

"Oh," one of the doctors said. "You're awake."

"Yeah," Drew said, groggy and a little nervous. He had no idea how long he'd been under, but slowly he realized they were still operating on his eye. "Uh, I kind of feel this," he said.

"Can you hang in there just a few more seconds?" the surgeon asked. "We're almost done."

Drew recovered from that surgery, and the next one, and the next one. For now, his focus had to be on healing physically, emotionally, and spiritually. Though the surgeries and therapy were difficult, they were oddly comforting. This was the pattern of his life: Identify a goal, figure out the path to achieve it, and work methodically toward it, step by step. He began to think about what life would be like if he decided to leave the Army. Maybe business school; he started studying for the GMATs every night. Maybe politics. He didn't know, but the idea of having the option to choose whatever future he saw for himself excited him.

One night in July, he and Ryan Beltramini had a long talk on the phone about just what they were doing with their lives. Ryan's departure for the Old Guard had marked the first time in eight years that he and Drew weren't living near each other, starting with West Point, going through Fort Benning and Ranger School, and then Hawaii and Afghanistan. Ryan was almost certainly getting out of the Army in summer 2007; he had Alisha to think about, and she did not want to be an Army wife for another decade and a half.

But Drew was conflicted. He understood the desire for a more stable life, but West Point was a big part of him, and the idea of an able-bodied officer leaving the Army while the nation was at war—especially a war that seemed to him to be going poorly—didn't sit well. Another good friend, Brian Oman, was back in Iraq for his second tour. Drew had recently learned that in June, Brian had seen intense combat in the northern Iraqi city of Tal Afar. In less than two weeks, five soldiers in Brian's scout platoon had been killed or seriously wounded.

How much was enough? Drew wondered. *How much could he or any soldier be expected to give?* He'd deployed, been wounded, and would carry some of the scars for the rest of his life. If he stayed in the Army for a full twenty years or more, and if the American military remained involved in Iraq and Afghanistan for the indefinite future, he could expect to see combat every other year for the next dozen years or so.

Another of Drew's friends, Mike Baskin, who had visited him at the bar in New York City with Alisha, was back in Hawaii. Mike was an avid distance runner, and he was passionate about rediscovering his family's Jewish roots. When an Army personnel officer had asked him what he wanted to do next, he'd answered honestly: I want to run seventy miles a week for a year and see how fast I can get. I want to be a company commander. I want to live in Israel for a year. And I want to go to grad school.

The personnel officer's answer was pretty much what was to be expected: *Are you crazy?* It was a vivid illustration of how inflexible the Army could be. Drew loved his country, and a life of service to the nation appealed to him. But the idea of making a twenty-year professional commitment to a large, bureaucratic organization—even one with as honorable and important a role as the U.S. Army—was foreign to most people of his generation, Drew included.

Of his West Point classmates, he could hardly think of any who were talking about staying in past five years. But they were all worried about the stop-loss policy, which could keep soldiers on active duty even after their service obligations were up if the military needed the manpower. They might all decide they wanted to leave, but would the Army let them go?

BECAUSE OF THE EXTRA TIME he owed for flight school, Tim Moshier's commitment ran well into 2009. Tim didn't particularly mind, and he could easily imagine making the Army his career. He loved flying, and he and Katie were comfortable in the military life. Though the war in Iraq had gone on far longer than anyone had expected, his unit had spent a year training for an upcoming mission in Korea, and the fighting in the Middle East seemed far away. But toward the end of 2004, two things had happened that dramatically changed his plans and his outlook.

First, Katie was pregnant. For days after he learned about his impending fatherhood, Tim had walked around looking dazed. Katie thought his response was silly. Having babies was what married people did; most of their friends and colleagues were already doing so. But she knew her husband well enough to understand that, as with everything else good in their life, he just needed time to get comfortable with the idea. Sure enough, by the time they got the first prenatal ultrasound, Tim was ecstatic.

Second, Tim's unit, 1-6 Cavalry, was reassigned. Instead of going to Korea, they were going to be assigned to the 4th Infantry Division, right there at Fort Hood. The base was divided down the middle, with 4th ID on one side of the post and 1st Cavalry Division on the other, and the rivalry between the two units was intense. The 4th ID had history and traditions—not to mention that a unit of the division had captured Saddam Hussein just a year and a half before—but the cavalry had the swagger, with their Stetson hats and spurs. And now, with Korea off the itinerary, the newly designated 4-4 Combat Aviation Battalion was near the front of the line for a year's deployment in Iraq.

A few of the more experienced warrant officer pilots in the battalion had been involved in the invasion, as had several of the instructors in the training course that Tim and his fellow pilots were taking. The news that they would be going to Iraq raised a number of questions, one of which was: Exactly what kind of missions would a tank-killer attack helicopter designed during the Cold War *do* in a counterinsurgency campaign? Most of the unit's training in Texas involved company-sized exercises at a minimum, meaning eight helicopters working together in the air. That seemed the very definition of overkill when the target was a few guys on the ground with rifles, a shovel, and a few mortar rounds they'd stolen from an unguarded weapons dump. You might as well hunt rabbits with a machine gun.

The question went largely unanswered. One plausible speculation, however, was that they'd borrow the concept of hunter-killer teams from armored units, flying in teams of two Apaches, one responsible for finding the enemy and the other in charge of destroying him. Improvisation would be the key.

KATIE MOSHIER and Maria Williams were getting to be better and better friends, and of course, Katie planned to attend the third birthday party for Maria's son, Arthur. But at the last minute she called to apologize: "Maria, I'm sorry, I'm not going to be able to make it. I'm so sick. But I sent Tim."

He showed up a few minutes later, holding Arthur's birthday gift and looking about as awkward as he felt.

Maria had more or less presumed Tim would stay for five minutes, since she didn't really know him that well—he was gone on field exercises for days and weeks at a time—and it was pretty clear this was not his comfort zone. She cut him a piece of birthday cake, saying she could wrap it for him if he had to leave. But Tim stood there for nearly ninety minutes, holding the plate in his hand and never leaving the same square of concrete on the patio right outside the back door.

The enlisted soldiers couldn't quite get over it.

"Dude, what's Lieutenant Moshier doing here?" they said to Sergeant Williams. "He's at your house!"

It was funny in a very awkward way, but Maria felt bad for him. As outgoing and gregarious as Katie Moshier was, there was just something that kept Tim buttoned up.

THE 4-4 COMBAT AVIATION BATTALION got a new commander. Lieutenant Colonel John Novalis was a 1987 West Point graduate who'd been working as the 4th ID's assistant chief of staff. Fast-talking and intense, Novalis was in some ways Tim's emotional opposite, but he took an instant liking to his fellow academy graduate, fifteen years his junior. Unfortunately for Tim, Novalis also took away his platoon and gave it to a younger officer. It was nothing personal—Tim had had more than a year in the job, and there were others who needed a shot at leading pilots and troops—but Tim was now assigned as one of the battalion's staff officers, which meant he would fly far less often.

The battalion continued training intensively throughout the spring. In May, Katie's younger sister, Ali, a photojournalism student, came down for the summer for an internship with the Fort Hood newspaper and to be there when Katie had their baby. The following month, Natalie Moshier, seven pounds, two ounces, was born. Tim was giddy, but shaky and scared at the idea of holding his tiny daughter. At Katie's bedside, he clutched little Natalie tightly, as if she were a fragile piece of porcelain that might slip out of his hands if he wasn't careful.

Within days, he was back in the field with the rest of 4-4 Aviation, ramping up for his year away. No one knew for sure exactly when they would be sent to Iraq, but they could make a strong educated guess that they wouldn't be spending Christmas at home.

JEN BRYANT FINALLY PAID her first visit to Arlington National Cemetery since Todd's funeral on Memorial Day weekend in 2005. Jen; her sister, Erin; and Tiffany Bryant were among hundreds of guests at an event sponsored by the nonprofit group Tragedy Assistance Program for Survivors (TAPS). President Bush and the chairman of the Joint Chiefs of Staff attended the event, and Jen watched from about fifty yards away as the president spoke in the cemetery's amphitheater, reading from the letters of soldiers killed in Iraq and beseeching their families' support to continue the war.

"As we look across these acres, we begin to tally the cost of our freedom, and we count it a privilege to be citizens of the country served by so many brave men and women," Bush said. "And we must honor them by completing the mission for which they gave their lives, by defeating the terrorists, advancing the cause of liberty, and building a safer world."

But when Erin, Tiffany, and most of the other guests walked over to Section 60 after the speeches, Jen couldn't bring herself to go with them. She still wasn't ready, and when she did finally visit Todd's grave, she wanted to go by herself.

On television the next day, Vice President Cheney declared that the insurgency in Iraq was "in its last throes"; he added later that the United States would "succeed in Iraq, just like we did in Afghanistan." But as much as Jen wanted to believe that Todd had given his life for a greater purpose, and that he'd died doing what he loved, she couldn't believe any cause could justify the loss of her husband: He'd loved his country and she was proud of him, but he would have been able to give so much more had he lived. Jen wasn't one to protest in the streets, carry signs, or make speeches, but she was angry—angry at the war, and angry at President Bush for sending her husband to Iraq.

The muggy Virginia summer dragged on. Jen started looking for a teaching job for the fall; psychologically, she was making slow, steady progress, although mostly she still felt miserable. In early August, she had a particularly bad day, alone in her apartment while it poured rain outside. She sat on the couch in her sweat pants until almost six P.M., rereading Todd's letters once again, looking at their wedding pictures, and doing whatever she could to rekindle her memories of Todd and remind herself of how much she had once been loved.

And then something came over her, something external, a force that seemed to pull her up off the couch. She heard a voice. No, she felt the voice: *You're going. You're going to Arlington right now.*

The last visitors for the day had to be inside the cemetery gates before seven P.M. Jen raced around her apartment getting ready, the lethargy of her day giving way now with equal force to frenetic energy. Since this would be her first visit to Todd's grave, she wanted to look nice. She rummaged through her closet, got dressed, and ran to the Subaru she'd inherited from Todd, with its In-N-Out Burger license plate frame. Jen pulled onto Interstate 66, the heavy rain still falling, and drove northeast toward the District of Columbia. Luckily, she was traveling against the evening rush hour traffic. The rain began letting up as she got closer to the cemetery. Because she was a war widow, she had a pass that let her drive right through the gate and straight down the access road to Section 60. Just as she parked, the rain stopped completely.

The sun started to break through the clouds, and the summer evening heat hit her hard as she got out of the air-conditioned car. The grass was muddy, so she pulled a blanket from the trunk.

Slowly, Jen walked to Todd's grave and stood before it, reading the granite marker for the first time:

TODD J

BRYANT

1LT

US ARMY

JAN 14 1980

OCT 31 2003

BSM PH

OPERATION IRAQI

FREEDOM

Standing in front of her husband's grave, with her back to the marker, Jen could look through the trees and see the dome of the U.S. Capitol, where Todd had once hoped his career might lead. She spread the blanket in front of his headstone and sat down, directly above where his body was buried. Her tears came immediately and she cried unabashedly for a full forty-five minutes as the sun sank lower in the sky. She couldn't think what to say to Todd, but slowly she began to feel as if she were crying on his shoulder, and, in so doing, allowing some small bit of the sadness to leave her soul.

Feeling foolish now, she apologized to him silently. *People come here, and they're supposed to be able to talk out loud and feel better,* she said without speaking.

It's okay, she heard Todd reply—or maybe, again, it was more that she *felt* him say it. The body in the coffin, the headstone: Those weren't her husband. They were memorials, symbols, physical things that she could latch on to if it helped, but he was somewhere else. Todd was in her head, in her heart.

It's okay, his voice continued. *It's okay to come here.*

IN THE SUMMER OF 2005, Dave Swanson faced the quintessential modern American soldier's dilemma: Find a new home in the Army, or steel himself to head back to Iraq within the year. He'd had to attend a big assembly where the top general in charge of personnel had railed against rumors that the Army was hemorrhaging captains. The general had claimed that young officers were leaving the Army at a rate no higher than before September 11, 2001.

Dave had laughed to himself: *Yeah, that's because there's a stop-loss. If you took the stop-loss off, the numbers would double or even triple.*

His first priority was to make sure that he didn't get caught up in an involuntary deployment. A human resources officer told him he had three choices, all of which would eventually lead to the Middle East. He could stay with his unit, or he could go to Korea for a year, or he could ask for a transfer to Fort Bragg and the 82nd Airborne Division. But Dave was holding a trump card. As a signal corps officer on loan to the infantry, he could apply to go to the signal advanced course at Fort Gordon, Georgia. He'd need the course if he wanted to make a career of the Army; more important, he couldn't be sent to Iraq while he was a student.

"I can't live like this," Reyna told Dave when she learned of his plan to apply for the course. For one thing, it meant that Dave was volunteering to spend nine months in Georgia so he wouldn't have to spend twelve more months in Iraq. Was this all there was to Army life, an endless flow-chart of unattractive choices, of always picking the least-bad option? Fine, she decided. They would take matters into their own hands. Though she'd never lived outside Texas and was extremely close to her family, she and Isabel would go to Georgia with Dave. And she didn't want to do what so many other military couples had done, rushing to the courthouse to get their marriage papers so that the Army would treat their relationship as legitimate. Reyna wanted them to enjoy their engagement, plan a wedding, and live life on their own time, not Army time.

One of the officers Dave worked for learned about his plans and called him in. Was this just a ploy? the higher-ranking officer asked, his tone unfriendly. What were Dave's long-term plans?

"I think I'm getting out, sir," Dave said. "It's because of family."

"I've been in twenty-two years, and I still have a family," the officer snapped back.

Dave had long since learned to keep his mouth shut, but his unspoken response was "Yes, you do. And look how messed up it is."

Besides, today's field-grade officers had had it easy when they were Dave's age. You could walk around Fort Hood and see plenty of majors and lieutenant colonels without a combat patch on the right sleeve, meaning that in ten or fifteen years in the Army they hadn't once deployed to war. What right did they have to judge him and his cohort?

As the move to Georgia approached, Dave found himself thinking often about his future. He vacillated constantly, weighing the difficulties of service against the fact that the Army was the only career he'd ever known. He had no idea what he'd want to do if he got out. But how many more tours in Iraq or Afghanistan would he have to endure if he stayed in? And that didn't even count the twelve- and fourteen-hour days in garrison, the weeklong field problems, and the monthlong rotations at the National Training Center in the California desert, or the Joint Readiness Training Center in the swamps of Louisiana. He loved his country and was proud to be serving it, but he also loved Reyna. How much could he reasonably ask her to sacrifice?

With only two weeks before the officer course began, he and Reyna were so busy packing that they barely paid attention to the world around them for several days. As they began their thousand-mile trek across Texas, Louisiana, Mississippi, Alabama, and Georgia just before Labor Day 2005, they were only dimly aware of the Category 5 hurricane that had slammed into New Orleans that very morning.

Soon, however, they could tell something was amiss. Even though Interstate 20 was two hundred miles north of the Gulf of Mexico, traffic was very heavy, and the weather was hot and sticky, well over a hundred degrees. As they drove east into Louisiana, they began to see debris and storm detritus all over the place. They kept going without a break for hours, Dave in his Mustang and Reyna in a Honda CR-V. They hoped to make it to Meridian, Mississippi, by nightfall, where there was a Navy base and a plethora of cheap motels. Dave kept letting his speed get away from him, and Reyna would phone him to tell him to slow down and let her catch up.

About seven hours into the drive, the appalling aftermath of the hurricane was everywhere—fallen trees, lots of damaged houses, motels with full parking lots and "No Vacancy" signs. Most gas stations were closed; those that were open had lines hundreds of cars long. By the time Dave finally pulled up in front of a pump, the display on his dashboard read "1 Miles to Empty." He tried to call Reyna, but all the circuits were busy. They wound up relaying messages through her mother in Texas.

Giving up on the idea of spending the night in Mississippi, they drove on to Tuscaloosa, Alabama, only to learn after eighteen hours on the road that the University of Alabama was playing its first football game of the season the following afternoon. Every hotel and motel was mobbed with football fans—and with Katrina refugees who had fled with their pets and whatever else they could carry.

Dave told Reyna they were just going to have to drive into Georgia. But finally, around ten P.M., they found a Hampton Inn, with perhaps the last vacancy in Tuscaloosa.

✷ **19** ✷

In the fall of 2005, a year and a half after Eric Huss came home from Iraq, he was finally feeling like himself again. He and Julie were engaged, and he was training young armor officers at Fort Knox, the same base where he, Todd, and Will Tucker had attended their basic officer course in the summer and early fall of 2002.

It had been a very hard road to travel, going from combat to an almost civilian-style life. Eric had been a menace behind the wheel when he first returned. It was tough transitioning from a sixty-ton Abrams tank to a car; he'd become accustomed to having everyone who wasn't trying to kill him race to get out of his way, and now he had to share the road politely and worry about traffic laws. He instinctively looked for IEDs and snipers rather than other cars, and after one close call too many, Julie refused to let him drive.

For more than a year, he had memory trouble—he and Julie might have a conversation on Tuesday, but if she mentioned the same subject on Wednesday he'd have no idea they'd talked about it before. At first, she hoped he was just being a stereotypical guy who didn't pay attention, but soon she knew the problem was serious. Eric was different in other ways, as well. She began urging him to see a counselor—somebody, anybody—to talk about what he'd seen and experienced.

But Eric was reluctant to see a psychologist who was on the Army's payroll. He figured they'd just want to pump him up with drugs. Moreover, he didn't want visits with a shrink on his official military record: Entries like that could kill a career. By now, he was pretty sure he wanted to get out of the Army at the first opportunity, but it was always possible he'd choose to work elsewhere in government someday. Or he might need a security clearance for a job in the private sector. Potential employers were always asking intrusive questions about whether you'd ever sought help for psychological or emotional difficulties.

Besides, Eric figured, no counselor in a comfortable office could relate to what he'd seen and experienced. It seemed almost belittling to suggest otherwise. Finally, though, he agreed to talk with a military chaplain who had been in Iraq but had come home early after a soldier in the chaplain's vehicle accidentally fired his rifle, blowing the head off a third soldier. Eric wouldn't wish such a terrible experience on anyone, but at least it might enable the man to comprehend the difficulties he was having.

Talking did help, Eric discovered, as did realizing that he wasn't alone. Another veteran officer at Fort Knox took him aside.

"Hey, if your short-term memory is kind of screwy right now," he told Eric, "don't worry too much. It took me about a year to get it back."

The lieutenant was right; by mid-2005 Eric was close to his old self. And now, with the benefit of hindsight, he'd developed a theory. In Iraq, he'd been doing a difficult, dangerous, crappy job, fourteen or more hours a day without a break. He never knew when something horrible or disgusting or terrifying would happen. And yet no matter what happened on any particular day, no matter what he saw or how he felt, he had to get up the next day and do the same thing all over again. Was it Einstein who had said the definition of insanity was doing the same thing over and over, expecting different results? Maybe that was the brain's defense mechanism, learning to forget. He had coped by living almost entirely in the present. Things became automatic. He would go on patrol, check rooftops and overpasses and streets, get shot at and blown up, and then purge the memories. And then he'd do it again. Act, react, forget. Repeat as needed.

WILL TUCKER HADN'T had the opportunity to introduce Sallie to any of his West Point friends before he went overseas again, but he'd talked so much about Todd Bryant that Sallie wanted to reach out to Jen, if only to let her know that Will and she still cared. Jen opened up on the phone almost at once, telling Sallie how difficult things had been. She'd gone back to Todd's grave again on what would have been their second anniversary and had sat on the blanket for two solid hours, flipping through the wedding album he'd never had a chance to see.

"I perfectly understand, Jen," Sallie said. "Grief is different for everybody."

Sallie could only imagine what it was like. Will had been home on leave in July 2005, and Sallie couldn't believe how quick to anger he was, how wound up; he seemed to be on a constant adrenaline high. She offered to help Jen in any way she could.

Well, Jen replied, there was one thing: *Would you go to Eric Huss's wedding with me?*

Sallie had received an invitation, but she was certain it was just a courtesy. She dreaded the idea of going, not having met a single soul beforehand. But now she couldn't say no.

In October, she and Jen met up in St. Louis and checked into the Sheraton where everyone was staying. The lobby was the site of a spontaneous D-1 reunion—this was the first time so many Ducks and their families had been together since Todd's funeral. Jen listened with sadness as some of the Ducks' parents congratulated them all on being promoted to captain; Todd would be a lieutenant forever. And at the reception after the wedding, Sallie, Jen, and Katie Moshier sat at a table with an Army officer from Texas and his wife, along with several other guests. The dinner conversation turned to Iraq, and the talk grew heated and political.

"I am sick and tired of the American public not understanding the price that is paid for all of this," Sallie declared. "Some people pay the *ultimate* price."

Jen stood up, burst into tears, and rushed from the table. Katie Moshier ran after her.

"What just happened?" the other Army officer asked.

"Her husband died on October thirty-first, two years ago," Sallie said matter-of-factly.

"Oh my God!" the soldier exclaimed. "Why didn't you tell me?"

But to Sallie's mind, nobody was doing Jen any favors by pretending to ignore the fact that Todd was gone. She'd watched as Jen had signed both her name and Todd's in the register as they walked in for the ceremony. It wasn't healthy. And why was Jen still wearing her wedding and engagement rings nearly two years after Todd had been killed? Where were her friends and family? Who was supporting her in her grief? Sallie worried about all this, but she didn't feel comfortable enough among Will's friends to say anything.

Tim Moshier, sitting at the head table with Eric and Julie, sensed Sallie's discomfort. Tim had lived so much of his life wanting to find a way to fit in that he intuitively recognized anyone who was ill at ease or feeling excluded. In only a month, he would be heading to Iraq, and soon it would be his wife trying to manage everything on her own. He walked over to Sallie, much as he had walked up to Holly Harris that day at flight school.

"We've been wanting to meet you," he said, giving Sallie a big hug. "We're glad you make Will so happy."

Later, he and Katie talked about Will and his surprise marriage.

"I didn't know if there was a woman in the world for Will Tucker," Tim said. "But she's perfect for him."

IN THE MIND of Joe DaSilva, there were no such things as problems, only "challenges." But if anything could chip away at his optimistic attitude, the Iraqi army might just be up to the task.

Joe had gone back to Ranger School at Fort Benning after his first tour in Iraq. Ironically, he was far more nervous going through the Ranger Assessment Program again than he'd been in a real shooting war, but he gutted it out and finally won the right to wear his tab, thereby putting his career as an infantry officer back on track.

Afterward, it had been almost right back to war. He was still in 1-327 Infantry, still part of the 101st Airborne Division, but he'd been promoted to captain and had had to give up his platoon in order to get his second shot at Ranger. For months after he deployed, he spent twelve-hour days as a staff officer in the tactical operations center at Forward Operating Base McHenry near the northern Iraqi city of Kirkuk, listening to radios, watching computer screens, and managing a little corner of the war. Though Joe could repeat platitudes to himself all day long about how his job was important and everyone played a crucial role, the truth was that he hated the prospect of spending his deployment behind a desk. Finally, in October 2005, his commanders took pity on him, and assigned him to be the battalion's liaison with the newly formed Iraqi army.

His new job required no self-delusion. Two and a half years into the war, it was clear that building up the Iraqi security forces was an absolute prerequisite to any scenario of success for the United States in Iraq. Joe knew that the problems—strike that; the "challenges"—were myriad. The language and cultural barriers were dauntingly high. He pushed to ensure that every time American platoons went outside the wire, they took at least a few Iraqi soldiers with them, but the Iraqis often seemed less than committed to building their own strong army. One day, for instance, Joe met with the Iraqi commander of a hundred-soldier company, only to find that half the troops had left.

"Where did everybody go?" he asked through his interpreter.

"Vacation," the Iraqi commander said.

"What do you mean, they're on vacation?"

"They had to go pay their families."

With no functioning central bank, the Iraqi army paid its troops in cash, and the only way the troops could deliver money to their families was to bring it to them in person. But as soon as Joe started working on that problem, the American lieutenants began resisting the idea of bringing the Iraqis with them on patrols. They couldn't trust them, the Americans would complain. All it would take was one traitor in the lot to put

American soldiers' lives at risk. And even if the Iraqi soldiers weren't enemies in disguise, the U.S. lieutenants complained, they were lazy.

"Sir, they won't go," one platoon leader told him.

"You don't seem to understand this, Lieutenant," Joe snapped back. "You're taking these Iraqi army guys or you're not going on patrol. And if you're not going on patrol, you're explaining it to the S-3"—meaning the major in charge of the battalion's operations—"and the colonel."

It sounded impressive to say that the United States was fighting a new kind of war, a twenty-first-century counterinsurgency campaign, but it was often difficult to actually believe that. So much of the Army's leadership clung to the notion that you measured your success in a conflict by how much land you occupied. After nearly two years in Iraq, Joe was sure that was wrong. What mattered in a counterinsurgency were the people. A Western, English-speaking army could never completely win over the Iraqi people on its own. They needed Iraqi partners. And if the Iraqi institutions weren't competent, the Americans would have to build them for them.

"You guys have got to make this work," he told another lieutenant who balked at his direction. "And if you're not making it work, you're failing, just as if you didn't take that building, or take that hill. Not getting them to go out on patrol is a failure on your mission."

Joe was proud of his role, but sick of the destruction, sick of hearing about the deaths of soldiers in his battalion and of his West Point classmates. He'd sat wretchedly in the tactical operations center one day calling in medevac missions after an IED had killed four soldiers. And it had fallen to him one morning to wake up a good friend of his in the battalion, Clint Olearnick, with the news that Clint's West Point roommate, a transportation officer named Jim Gurbisz, had been killed in Baghdad. A month later, another 2002 graduate, a soccer player named Kevin Smith, was gone, yet again the victim of an IED. By the end of 2005, 2,383 American soldiers had been killed in Iraq, and while the number of casualties was tiny by the standards of previous American wars, that was no comfort to the families of the fallen.

The war would continue, Joe knew, until the American military ramped up the Iraqi security forces to the point where they could take responsibility for their own country. Why did every new generation, every society, have to learn the same lessons all over again?

THE MOSHIER FAMILY—Tim, Katie, and five-month-old Natalie—was flying up to New York for Thanksgiving and Tim's last few days in the United States before he would deploy to the Middle East. Maria Williams drove them from Fort Hood to the airport in Austin at five A.M., laughing as Tim crammed his huge frame into the backseat of her Chevy Blazer, squeezed between Natalie's car seat on one side and three-year-old Arthur's on the other. She was touched when he bear-hugged her good-bye. Tim was not a hugger by inclination, but after getting to know Maria for the past year and a half, he was clearly, finally, comfortable around her.

A week later, Tim was on another plane, this time heading to Germany on the first leg of his trip to Iraq; he was part of the battalion's advance party. The change of planes in Frankfurt, he wrote home with amusement, marked the first time he'd ever set foot in another country. "I am not counting Canada," he added, "because, well, it's Canada."

After another full day of delays and travel, Tim finally reached the base in the northern Kuwaiti desert where they'd be training for a week or two. Camp Buehring, as it was called, had been named for an Army lieutenant colonel who had been killed in Baghdad just five days before Todd Bryant. The camp was vast and stark; white, domed tents dotted the sand and gravel that extended for miles in every direction.

The temporary posting had a silver lining: Tim was unexpectedly reunited with Pat Killoran. His fellow D-1 Duck, who had been with him at Fort Rucker but then had trained to fly Black Hawks, had been in Kuwait for nearly a year, part of a unit that flew VIPs all over the Middle East. For days, Pat had been asking every chief warrant officer he could find at Buehring whether they knew a tall pilot from the 4th ID named Moshier. Finally, one of the warrants pointed him toward a tent. Pat popped open the door, and sure enough, there was good old Tim Moshier, smiling, sitting on his cot with his gear strewn all around him. All that was missing was an empty B-52 pizza box and a tub of Ben & Jerry's.

Tim's days at Camp Buehring were filled with welcome-to-the-war classes, and he and Pat made sure to link up for dinner each evening. He talked nonstop about Natalie, how cute she was and how amazed and excited he was to be a father. But he and Pat also griped about their lot in life. As junior captains in aviation units, they had both been shoehorned into staff jobs that gave them much less time in the air. Tim had spent two years learning how to fly attack helicopters, and he couldn't believe he had been sent to Iraq only to sit behind a desk.

"I managed to contract the upper respiratory infection known colloquially as the Kuwaiti Crud," Tim wrote home a few days later in an e-mail. "Basically it's a sore throat, combined with a nasty sinus infection, sometimes accompanied by explosive diarrhea. I managed to avoid the latter, but I had both of the former in spades." After a week, he was relieved to be assigned as one of five officers to head directly up to their base in Iraq. The unit would be flying missions out of Taji, a former Iraqi air force base near Baghdad that had once been the home of Saddam Hussein's air defense artillery units. Tim was very happy to be leaving Kuwait.

"Camp Buehring's primary purpose is to be so miserable that you can't wait to get to Iraq," he wrote. "And I have to say, mission accomplished."

WILL TUCKER HAD STARTED his second tour in Iraq in charge of a scout platoon of Bradley Fighting Vehicles, but in late fall of 2005 he was reassigned as the executive officer of his old troop. He'd probably seen as much combat and led troops on as many patrols as any of his peers in the West Point class of 2002. By any objective standard, he needed the break, and in his new position he went out on fewer missions. Yet it was hard for him to get used to a less hands-on role.

In mid-December, one of his soldiers came running up to him, urging Will to rush to the tactical operations center. A tank driver and a platoon leader were yelling excitedly over the radio. Somebody had been badly injured, but it wasn't clear who or how.

First Sergeant Broadhead, Will's old platoon sergeant, raced to the aid station. Will stayed by the radio for another minute or two, until he heard the name of the wounded trooper: Staff Sergeant Tony Mitchell, the soldier whose wedding Will and Sallie had attended just before 3-7 Cavalry left for Iraq, where Sallie and Broadhead had met for the first time. Tony's little brother, Jimmy, was also in the unit.

When Will reached the aid station, Tony's M1 Abrams had just roared in and Sergeant Broadhead was already atop it. He gestured silently to Will—Tony Mitchell was dead—and lowered himself inside. Will climbed on top of the tank, and together he and Broadhead pulled Tony's body out and zipped him into a bag.

Sergeant Broadhead left to find Jimmy Mitchell, and the rest was up to Will: For the next hour or so, working alone, he pulled out the weapons and equipment and cleaned away the blood and flesh. It was, he later said, the hardest day of his life.

The phones and Internet were shut down for a few days after Mitchell's death. When Will was finally able to call Sallie a few days later and acknowledged he'd been right there when his friend's body arrived, she pushed him to talk about it. She sensed that he needed to say what he'd seen and done, to describe to her how terrible it had been. When he was finished talking, she asked him to visualize returning to her safe and sound. So many things were out of their control, she told him, but they could choose to hope and believe. And then Sallie insisted that he perform the ritual they followed each time they talked on the phone.

"I'm coming home," she made him say.

"Who you coming home to, baby?"

"I'm coming home to you."

Jimmy Mitchell returned to Fort Stewart a few days later, escorted by another soldier from the unit. "Ms. Tucker, you should have seen Will," the other soldier told Sallie when she visited. "He was covered in blood from head to toe. It was awful."

He paused, as if asking permission to tell her more. This was what a psychiatric nurse did for a living, counsel people; but never did Sallie's work get this personal. That little detail—her husband, covered in someone else's blood—hadn't been part of her mental picture before. And as hard as it was to hear the details, she wanted to know. She needed the connection, needed as much understanding as she could get about what her Will and his soldiers were going through.

She let the soldier go on, taking in the whole account, even though every instinct of self-preservation told her to cover her ears and run from the room.

No, she told herself. Listen to the story.

THE DAY TIM MOSHIER left Kuwait for Iraq, Pat Killoran came by to say so long, but he had missed him by just a couple of hours: Tim was already in the back of a C-130 headed for Balad air base, north of Baghdad. The pilots flew directly over the airfield at fourteen thousand feet, then dove nearly straight down in a tight, quick corkscrew designed to protect them from rockets and shoulder-fired missiles. Tim's Kuwaiti crud had pretty much declared war on his sinuses, and he hunched forward through the entire descent in intense pain, feeling as if his eyeballs might pop out of his face.

Tim slept for thirteen hours at Balad—"on a real mattress," he wrote home—and the next day, he caught a ride to Taji in a Chinook helicopter. "This was clearly a combat operation," he wrote. "The back door was lowered, and a machine gunner sat there manning his weapon and dangling his legs off the back. We were flying low level, lights blacked out, racing across central Iraq. I didn't like not being in control of where we were going and what we were doing."

On the ground at Taji, he looked to the sky toward Baghdad, where hundreds of red tracer rounds lit up the night sky. For each red flash he saw, he knew, there were four unilluminated bullets.

I was out there flying around in that? he thought.

A brigade of ten thousand Iraqi soldiers lived on half the base at Taji, subsisting on spoiled food, sleeping in decrepit, eighty-year-old barracks, and rationing the fuel they used to power their lights. But for the Americans, the base wasn't too bad as war zones went. Segregated from the Iraqis by massive concrete barriers, ten thousand U.S. soldiers lived in air-conditioned trailers. The PX was the size of a Wal-Mart, and American contractors had built a first-rate dining facility, complete with Baskin-Robbins ice cream and cheesecake desserts at each of the day's four all-you-can eat meals. "I don't know how the Army expects to keep people fit," Tim wrote after just a few days. He'd decided to eat just two meals a day.

Adam Sabourin, another 2002 West Point and flight school buddy, tracked Tim down at Taji. Adam was a Black Hawk pilot and, like Pat Killoran, he spent his time ferrying VIPs around the country. In his year based at Taji, he'd counted the president and prime minister of Iraq among his passengers, along with U.S. congressmen and generals.

Tim and Adam would overlap for a couple of weeks, and since Tim's days weren't all that busy yet—he was mainly acting as liaison with the unit they were replacing—they spent a lot of time together. Adam had set up his living trailer comfortably, almost like a college dorm room; they watched DVDs and hit the chow hall together each night. When Adam's tour was over, he passed along most of his creature comforts to Tim, including his television and his little refrigerator. They weren't quite worth the cost of shipping home, but they were like treasure in the war zone.

"Don't worry about me," Tim wrote home. "I'm not roughing it by any stretch of the imagination. I mean, who ever heard of an Army base with a Cinnabon?"

"MERRY CHRISTMAS, SIR!"

Until one of the radio operators in the tactical operations center where he worked greeted him, Tim had barely noticed the date. It bothered him that Christmas seemed like just another day, even though it had fallen on a Sunday. By now, the rest of his unit had arrived and he had a routine. His alarm went off at five thirty each morning, and as he walked to the showers in the predawn stillness, he could sometimes hear the call to prayer broadcast from the local mosques. He liked to think it might be a live person singing, not just a recording.

By five minutes to six, he would head over to the tactical operations center, the TOC, for his twelve-hour shift. The air was so dry that he could barely talk most days until he'd had his morning coffee. Tim's job title was battle captain, which meant that when Colonel Novalis wasn't in the TOC, he was in charge, coordinating the helicopters in the air, responding to requests for help on the ground, overseeing the radio operators and an intelligence analyst, and planning future operations.

The base was mortared regularly, but Tim felt pretty safe. There were concrete and sandbag bunkers every hundred yards or so, and his trailer was well protected. He missed flying, though, and he was thrilled on New Year's Eve when he was able to get up in the air for a few hours, flying over the base. His skills were a little rusty, he wrote home, and he was still a staff officer, so soon he was right back in the TOC. On January 4, 2006, he watched on television as USC and Texas played for the national collegiate football championship, calling in regular updates to the pilots in the air. "Longbow 41, this is Gambler X-ray," he announced when Texas went ahead late in the game. "New slant: Tango 41, Uniform Sierra Charlie, 38. One-niner seconds remaining. Over."

The pilots who flew missions every day were frustrated. Apaches simply weren't designed for the kind of patrolling they were doing; their sophisticated surveillance systems and powerful ordnance were intended for intense combat situations, not deterrence. The pilots were often simply not allowed to fire their weapons, for fear of killing civilians. Apache pilots were aggressive, forward-leaning soldiers who found it difficult to watch as insurgents set up checkpoints or planted IEDs when they sometimes had to restrain themselves from doing anything about it. Still, the Apache was one of the few weapons systems that the insurgents truly feared, so if flying over convoys lessened the chance that they would be attacked, that was something. But when the desired outcome of every mission was peace and quiet, the pilots might fly forty or fifty missions without enemy contact. Inevitably, many of them felt they weren't contributing enough.

Tim heard these complaints, but he still wished he were flying. His desk job began wearing on him. Because he worked long hours, he had little opportunity to develop camaraderie with the other pilots. And he was surprised how hard it was to find the time to stay in touch with Katie even though he had Internet access in his trailer. He wasn't allowed to leave the

TOC during the day, so unless someone brought him breakfast or lunch, dinner was his only chance to eat. If he wanted to do laundry, go to the gym, or get a haircut when he needed one, he had only those few hours between the end of his twelve-plus-hour day in the TOC and whenever it was that he collapsed. When they talked over a video connection, Katie could see he was exhausted; his eyes were sunken and his comments were punctuated by yawns. He was having a hard time, he told her; knowing that he'd be doing the same things—day in and day out, without a break for an entire year—was really getting to him.

Will Tucker was finally home again. By the end of January 2006, he and Sallie had two homes, one right outside the gates at Fort Stewart, and one up in Knoxville where they planned to move for good once Will was out of the Army in mid-2007. They commuted back and forth, and tried to enjoy a life together as newlyweds, one year delayed.

His tour had been easier the second time, he told Sallie. It had helped to know he had someone to come home to. But Sallie wasn't sure the Army would take the same view. For all the lip service the Army paid to family, she was convinced it would prefer its soldiers were single. Families cost a lot of money and took a lot of time. For her part, Sallie often reflected that if it were not for her professional training as a psychiatric nurse practitioner, she would be much less equipped to deal with Will. When he was angry, she was less likely than the typical new Army spouse to think it was because he was angry at *her*. Will had spent more time on the ground in Iraq than he had in the United States in the last three years. He had killed and nearly been killed, and he'd lost some of the best friends he'd ever known. It didn't surprise her at all that he sometimes became angry for no apparent reason.

They were cooking dinner together one evening—instant rice in the microwave, the rest of their dinner on the stove—enjoying an unremarkable evening together in their house near Fort Stewart. Sallie had forgotten to cut a hole in the rice package, and it burst with a loud bang inside the microwave.

Will dove to the floor, hands instinctively covering his head. They laughed as he stood up again.

Once, Will was showing Sallie some pictures from his deployments; mixed in with the photos of his troops and the candid shots of him posing in a captured Iraqi army helmet were some truly grotesque images. One photo showed a man lying by the side of the road who seemed to have lost his toupee; on further inspection, Sallie saw that the man's scalp had been peeled off his head. Will had seen this kind of thing often in Iraq, she realized—blood, guts, body parts, burning flesh. She could only imagine what such horrors did to the human mind, but she knew he had to talk about it.

IN MID-JANUARY 2006, Tim Moshier had his first opportunity to fly a real mission when some of the line pilots needed to take a day off. The day was hazy, the sky full of smoke, fog, and pollution. Once in the air, Tim looked down on rows of one-story houses stretching toward Baghdad. He saw a mash of shantytowns, markets, and landfills, poverty everywhere; even areas that had clearly once been more affluent now bore the scars of war. One home in particular caught his eye: its second story had been blown apart by an explosion, and the swimming pool was filled with green algae.

Jim Reynolds, a West Point classmate from Rhode Island, rode in the front seat of the other Apache in the hunter-killer team. Not long into the mission, Tim and Jim noticed a car driving aimlessly on the back roads below them. This was the first potential target for both pilots since they'd been in Iraq, and the car's erratic progress made them suspect that the driver might be carrying a bomb and looking for a promising place to attack. The two Apaches followed ostentatiously for nearly an hour as the car drove down deserted roads, stopping, starting, making what seemed to be halfhearted attempts to lose them. Tim could only imagine how nervous the car's occupants must be with two heavily armed helicopter gunships overhead. Finally, the car pulled up at a house and the driver and his passengers emerged, looking up at them and gesturing fearfully. Tim saw a woman holding a baby, and soon another woman came running out of the house, seeming upset.

"It looks like they're catching hell from their mom," Tim said to Jim Reynolds over the radio. He felt bad about scaring what now appeared to be nothing more than an Iraqi family. But what could he do?

"Well," Jim said, "at least we escorted them home safely."

KATIE MOSHIER HAD given up teaching when Natalie was born, but she kept extremely busy with the baby, the company FRG, and other volunteer activities. A classmate of Tim's, Kara Pond, was stationed at Fort Hood now—an intelligence officer, she had come back from a year in Iraq the day after Tim shipped out–and Katie picked her up at the airport. When Kara discovered that while she was gone her landlord had torn up the floors in her apartment to replace the tile, she moved in with Katie for three weeks.

In late January, Katie and Maria Williams went through training together to be part of a "go team," a group of women who would drop everything to be with the families of Fort Hood soldiers who had been killed or wounded, so that someone could answer the phones, cook, and take care of the kids in that moment of need. Though neither Tim nor John Paul, Maria's husband, held a particularly risky job—Tim rarely flew, and John Paul, a helicopter crew chief, never left the base—the training was sobering.

"I don't want a go team," Maria said as they were leaving.

"I know. I don't think I do, either," Katie said.

"I don't want anybody in my house, because my house is going to be a mess."

"Don't worry," Katie said. "I'll come clean your house before anybody else comes."

ONCE DREW SLOAN got past the fact that he had nearly been killed by a rocket-propelled grenade, he considered himself a lucky man. For having suffered a traumatic injury in combat, he'd even gotten a $25,000 insurance payment, all of which he poured into his stock and bond portfolio. Hawaii, meanwhile, was as beautiful as ever, and he was making a steady recovery. He compared himself to a sports team rebuilding after a bad season—he wasn't trying to make a lot of progress in the win-loss column, but was shoring up his fundamentals for the future. Surgery, recovery, a week or two of normalcy, then another surgery—on it had gone, month after month, for more than a year. Drew noted with bemusement that he didn't even seem to suffer from post-traumatic stress disorder. The injury had happened so quickly and been so catastrophic that he had no memory of it whatsoever; in fact, he remembered nothing after they had left the village of Saraw with their Humvee full of ballots. Once every few weeks, a counselor from Walter Reed would call to ask whether he was having nightmares or experiencing other symptoms of stress. His answer was always no. By October 2005, the first anniversary of when he was wounded, the counselor stopped calling.

When Drew looked back on the attack, what he felt more than anything else was curiosity. *Could I have acted differently?* he wondered. What had the events really looked like and felt like? It was the only time he'd actually taken direct fire from an enemy close enough to see, and yet he couldn't remember it. Even the question of who had tried to kill him was a mystery. It was easiest to answer with Armyspeak—he'd been attacked by terrorists, insurgents, or Taliban fighters. But he had a gut feeling that the men with the RPGs had just been the Afghan equivalent of street punks, paid by some opium lord to attack the Americans.

Working for General Bednarek took more time now, but as he'd learned how to do the job efficiently, it was less demanding. Drew knew the general well enough to anticipate what he'd want done most days. People had trouble pronouncing Bednarek's name, so Drew had come up with a handy mnemonic that he shared repeatedly: "*Bed*, like the kind you sleep in; *Nair*, like the hair removal product; and *Ek*, as in, well, Ek."

Because he worked for the general, Drew was among the first to get a look at the deployment schedule for the 25th Infantry Division. By the fall of 2005, he knew that his old unit was scheduled to deploy to Iraq in the summer of 2006, just as he had predicted back at Walter Reed. Bednarek would be going, too, as the number two general overseeing Drew's old brigade, along with four others.

Drew always had to have a plan, and his current one had two parts. First, after thinking about it for a long time, he had decided that he would definitely get out of the Army at five years. He'd done well enough on the GMATs, and he had his sights set on either the Kellogg School of Management at Northwestern University or Harvard Business School. Second, he desperately wanted to go with his unit on the Iraq tour. He had long ago realized that the only way he would truly feel whole again was to return to combat, and this was his one chance.

Though Drew knew what he wanted, he wasn't ready to talk about it. Whenever Bednarek asked about his plans, Drew deflected the question by saying, quite reasonably, that he hoped to stay in his current job in Hawaii until his surgeries were complete. But he put off the conversation he knew would eventually come, the moment when he'd have to admit that he was rejecting his boss's career path in favor of something else. Other senior officers took offense when captains and lieutenants talked about leaving the military. Furthermore, Drew worried that the general might decide to replace him right away: Service as a general's aide was considered a stepping-stone for fast movers and high risers, and Bednarek might decide he wanted someone who was fully committed to a career in the Army.

In January 2006, Bednarek visited some of the units training at the National Training Center; as usual, Drew traveled with him. While they waited for their flight out of Las Vegas, the most convenient airport for travel to Hawaii, he and Bednarek ate dinner at the MGM Grand.

"So, Drew, what do you want to do next?" the general asked.

Drew took a deep breath and plunged in. "Sir, I want to get out of the Army." After briefly explaining his plans for business school, he hastened to add: "But I want to go to Iraq with you."

"Okay," Bednarek replied simply. "I understand what you're asking. And don't worry about getting back in time for grad school."

Drew was enormously relieved. After weeks of concern, it had been so easy.

IN MARCH, BEDNAREK and Drew flew to Iraq, where the general and his closest subordinates spent several weeks meeting with the leaders of the units they'd be replacing later in the year. Contingency Operating Base Speicher, where they would be headquartered, was a huge, sprawling base near Tikrit. Compared to Drew's minimalist accommodations in Afghanistan, Speicher was a small city. He would never be in command of anything here, Drew realized; his job would be to follow the general around for a year with a notebook and pen at the ready. But he would get a bird's-eye view of the war in Iraq, a view he never could have had as a lieutenant or even a company commander. On the way to Iraq, Drew had wondered what it would feel like, flying in a helicopter over enemy territory again, walking on the ground, inhaling the Third World. But it felt like nothing special at all; truth be told, it felt flat-out normal.

The brigades Bednarek would help to command covered all of northern Iraq, including cities familiar from newspaper datelines: Baqubah, Kirkuk, Mosul, Samarra, Tal Afar, Tikrit. Knowing Bednarek as well as he did, Drew figured they'd be traveling around the country and going out on patrols with soldiers fairly often. But he also knew the Army would take the utmost care to ensure that no general ever got hurt on a mission.

TIM MOSHIER'S BOSS, Colonel Novalis, was also planning for the future, even though it was still early in Tim's deployment. When they got back from Iraq next year, Tim would be on schedule to return to Fort Rucker for the aviation officer career course. The colonel wanted to know whether Tim would want to come back to the battalion afterward. One day in early March, he pressed for an answer on the spot, and Tim told him he'd like to transfer to Fort Bragg and the 82nd Airborne Division.

"What do you think of that?" he asked Katie in an e-mail that evening. "I hear good things about the 82nd. I don't know why he was asking, so I don't know whether my answer means good or bad things for us. Time will tell, I suppose."

Novalis did tell Tim that he planned to rotate him through other staff jobs, and ultimately make him his adjutant. Tim was glad to know that eventually the monotony of his work would be broken; meanwhile, the phone calls home and e-mails with Katie kept him going. The calls were sometimes difficult, in part because they could rarely talk at length. Maria Williams passed on some wisdom that she and John Paul had garnered the hard way: Make sure you say you love and miss each other right at the start, because calls were likely to get cut off in the middle.

One day, Katie got Natalie on video saying "da-da" and e-mailed it to Tim.

"I watch that video over and over :-)," he e-mailed back. "Really, I just love her. I miss you too, though. If you were here, I would rub your feet, and make cookies with you (don't ask me where, though). Mostly, I just want to snuggle you, and forget about being away, and just feel normal again."

In late March, Tim was scheduled to fly a few more missions, both to give some of the line pilots a break and to ensure that his flight skills didn't suffer too much from lack of use. After an uneventful patrol on the last day of March, paired up in the Apache with a chief warrant officer named Santiago Torres, he called home. He was thrilled, he told Katie, because Torres—an older pilot who had been flying for many years—had allowed Tim to sit in the higher, rear seat of the helicopter, which normally went to the more experienced aviator. This was a bit of an honor, because it meant Torres respected Tim's flying ability. Even better, he told Katie, he was on the schedule to fly two more missions that week.

Tim's sister, Lauren, had stopped by on a cross-country drive to see her niece and sister-in-law, so when Natalie needed her mother's attention during the call, Katie put Lauren on the phone. By the time Katie got back, there were only a few minutes left in the call. Knowing how much Tim loved to fly, she told him she was happy for him. And she also teased him about how when he switched staff jobs in a couple of months, one of his duties would be to deliver birthday cards from the FRG to all of the battalion's soldiers.

She laughed at the thought: It was awfully hard to imagine her shy husband as the cheerful bearer of birthday cards.

THE SECOND OF TIM's three scheduled patrols was set for April 1, the evening after his phone call home. Tim would be flying now with Mike Hartwick, a top-notch chief warrant officer pilot. A captain named Kim Mitchell and another chief warrant officer named Matt Stauffer would be flying behind, as the second half of their hunter-killer team. In late afternoon, the four of them went in for their preflight briefing. They learned that the weather was lousy and that, owing to humidity, haze, and dust storms, visibility was low. But in terms of enemy activity, it had been a very calm day. More than twenty-four hours had passed without a shot fired.

The briefers listed the ground targets they wanted the pilots to investigate, everything from roads to buildings and fields. As the designated air mission commander, Tim ended the briefing by reiterating their route, one that the pilots who flew every day knew quite well. For the most part, they would be traveling along Highway 1, known to the military as Route Tampa, the main road leading from Baghdad to the airport.

The route was becoming a bit of an issue with the pilots, to whom it seemed that they were checking out the same targets day after day.

"We're kind of setting patterns where we're going," one of the CWOs griped. This early in the deployment, they probably didn't have to worry too much, but if they continued flying over the same places at roughly the same times of day, they'd be setting themselves up for an ambush. Apaches were durable aircraft, but insurgents had still managed to shoot several of them down over the past three years of war in Iraq. Besides, the pilots would just as soon avoid getting shot at.

John Paul Williams, Maria's husband, was the noncommissioned officer in charge of preparing the helicopters before they took off.

"Be sure you keep your finger on the button," he told Tim, meaning the button that fired chaff flares, little bursts of metal and plastic that were designed to confuse the homing systems of guided surface-to-air missiles. Tim chuckled and walked off to pick up his flight gear.

This is Longbow Six-One, Tim announced over the radio as they took off at about five P.M. *We're off at this time.*

It took about five minutes to reach the first location of their planned patrol. Stauffer and Mitchell followed, a little less than half a mile behind Tim and Hartwick.

Gambler Mike, this is Longbow Six-One, Tim called out again, speaking to the base at Taji. He'd been on the other end of these radio transmissions so many times, tracking helicopter teams as they relieved each other in the air, trading reports in the process known as a battle handover. *Ready for BHO,* Tim said.

Longbow Six-One, this is Gambler Six, Colonel Novalis chimed in. He and his wingman were just finishing up the previous mission; Tim and the others were flying in to take over for him. *Ready for battle handover.*

Tim acknowledged the transmission. Colonel Novalis then rattled off a description of the situation: where unmanned aerial vehicles were flying and what friendly forces he knew of on the ground. Today's report was brief; in five hours Colonel Novalis had come into contact with exactly nothing. Tim acknowledged that they were taking over the patrol, and Novalis's two Apaches headed back to the base at Taji.

This is Gambler Six, Novalis said as he flew back toward Taji. *Be safe out there.*

Gambler Mike, Tim said over the radio, talking now to the base at Taji. *We've got the fight.*

Their first objective on the mission was Zone 309, one of the areas that had recently been most active. Below was the town of Yusufiyah, where American units had been trying to capture or kill a twenty-nine-year-old insurgent leader named Abu Musab al-Zarqawi, the head of a terrorist organization that had taken the name Al Qaeda in Iraq. Soon, they arrived in Zone 309; though Tim and his fellow pilots didn't realize it, they were over almost exactly the place that Colonel Novalis and his wingman had been covering for nearly an hour.

They were flying roughly four hundred feet off the ground as they patrolled. In the second helicopter, Matt Stauffer noticed a man standing next to a small Opel truck with a tiny cab and a flatbed—a bongo truck, as the pilots called them. The truck was parked by the side of a road cutting through marshy swamps and walls of ten-foot-tall reeds. A person, or even a vehicle, could hide in the reeds, Stauffer thought, and you'd never see them unless you flew directly overhead.

White truck, Stauffer radioed to Tim and Mike. *He's stopped on the side of the road. It doesn't look like he's doing anything suspicious, but maybe if we back off and come back and take a look at him . . .*

Captain Mitchell trained their Apache's video camera on the man, who seemed to be watching them calmly. They sent the image and its exact location from their onboard computer to Tim's.

Did you get that target? Stauffer asked.

Yeah, I got it, Tim replied. The guy wasn't doing anything menacing, although from four hundred feet and with the deafening whine of the Apache's engines, he could have been cursing them at the top of his lungs and they'd never know.

Matt Stauffer glanced up from the video display to make sure he was following Tim and Mike Hartwick correctly. They were right where they were supposed to be, straight ahead about half a mile away, flying casually from left to right. Stauffer glanced back at the video display; when he looked outside the aircraft again, there was a huge fireball on the ground, and black smoke rising.

Hey Mike, did you see that car bomb? he called out to Hartwick over the radio. *I think it's right in front of you.*

There was no answer.

Mike, are you there? Stauffer tried again. He and Captain Mitchell spun frantically in their seats, looking for the lead Apache. Tim and Mike Hartwick had simply disappeared.

Oh my God! Stauffer called out to Mitchell. *It's Mike! Oh my God! It's Mike!* He called out to the tactical operations center at Taji: *Gambler Mike! We have a Fallen Angel!*

They raced to the spot, banking to get a better view of the ground. Except for an immense plume of fire and smoke, they saw little—Stauffer could just make out a couple of rotor blades. On the radio, Kim Mitchell was urging ground units to hurry to the scene. They hadn't seen even a single tracer round, and Tim and Mike had never radioed to say they were taking fire. It had to have been some kind of catastrophic mechanical failure, Stauffer thought.

They turned and flew right over the boiling black smoke. Tim and Mike had taken off with three thousand pounds of jet fuel, twenty rockets, and five hundred rounds of 30-millimeter high-explosive ammunition, and now it was all on fire. Stauffer and Mitchell turned and made yet another pass, this time at a different angle and banking the Apache for a closer look. There was nothing to see except an inferno right in the middle of the field.

Taking fire from the left! Captain Mitchell called out. *Break right! Break right!*

The sky was suddenly awash with tracer rounds, and with no idea where the attack was coming from, Stauffer dove for the ground, at the same time trying to put distance between them and whoever was shooting at them. They picked up speed, moving about nine hundred yards away from the crash site and then banking and coming back toward it. They could see the bullets were coming from men behind them on the ground, hiding behind a second white bongo truck. The men realized that they had been spotted and ran toward a ditch. Stauffer opened fire with the Apache's 30-millimeter cannon and watched as they fell to the ground.

Once the immediate danger had passed, Stauffer and Mitchell kept their eyes glued to the crash site. *It's just nothing but a fireball,* Stauffer radioed back to Taji. *There's no way they could have survived.*

THE SHOT THAT KILLED Tim Moshier and Mike Hartwick was one in a million, the Army later concluded. A shoulder-fired missile had hit the helicopter's main rotor at a freak angle, destroying it. Hartwick, especially, had been an extraordinary pilot. Back at Fort Hood, Holly Harris was 4-4 Aviation's rear detachment commander, and she vividly recalled an occasion when his superb flying had saved their lives in terrible weather and zero visibility. If there had been any way to control that Apache in Yusufiyah after it was hit, Hartwick would have done it, but with the rotor gone, the stick in his hand simply wasn't attached to anything.

A convoy raced to the scene immediately, hitting several IEDs en route. When the rescuers arrived, the fire was still raging, and not until nine-thirty P.M. were they able to get close to the wreckage. Colonel Novalis and the brigade commander flew in on a Black Hawk at around ten. The Apache, they saw, was essentially incinerated, after being consumed by metal-melting heat for nearly three hours. Even now it was impossible to approach the wreckage, since live ammunition was scattered on the ground all around the destroyed helicopter. At about one thirty in the morning, when the site was finally safe enough to get close, Novalis saw that the entire transmission assembly had crashed through the front of the helicopter, plowing straight through Tim's seat and out the bottom of the aircraft. Even had there been no fire, the damage was catastrophic. The only consolation was that death for Tim and Mike had come almost instantaneously.

NEWS OF THE CRASH of a two-seater Army helicopter in Iraq leaked quickly; in Texas, nine hours behind Baghdad, Maria Williams heard about it on the radio before the day was out. She called Katie immediately. A two-seater could only be an Apache or a Kiowa scout, as she and every other spouse from their battalion well knew. Katie's phone would soon be ringing off the hook, and Maria wanted her to be ready.

"I haven't heard anything, but I'll look," Katie said, and hung up the phone.

She flipped on CNN, and called Maria back. Yes, she said, a helicopter had been shot down, but that was about all the news. "Here we go."

If another unit had been involved, Mary Novalis would have known right away and would have called to tell Katie that the spouses of 4-4 Aviation had nothing to worry about. But the colonel's wife didn't call. Finally, Katie called Mary herself, but Mary could give her no useful information. Normally Katie was the rock, the solid one in the unit who could always help other spouses calm down, but this time she had a terrible feeling. She called her mother and father, and Tim's parents in New York.

"You're going to see it on the news," she told Tim's father. "An aircraft is down, and it's in Tim's area."

Soon the trickle of phone calls coming in became a flood. Do you know anything? Have you heard anything? Have you heard something but you're not allowed to tell us?

Katie prayed, begging God: Don't let it be Tim. Don't let it be anyone else in our battalion.

THE MILITARY'S PUBLIC affairs office in Baghdad released a brief statement the day of the attack, confirming that a helicopter had been shot down and declaring that the status of the crew was unknown. When *The New York Times* went to press that night, it carried a two-paragraph mention of the crash, buried at the bottom of an article about the Iraqi prime minister.

In Georgia, Sallie Tucker saw a brief mention on television and ran to tell Will.

"No," Will said. "No. It wasn't Tim. Don't worry."

By nightfall, Katie Moshier had still heard nothing of substance and was feeling completely helpless. She felt she had no choice but to try to go on with her weekend as planned until she heard either way. The next morning she was supposed to take Natalie to a children's Easter party sponsored by the battalion. But her daughter wasn't feeling well, so Katie wasn't sure they'd go to the party after all.

Meanwhile, she stayed out of the living room. If the soldiers in their green uniforms appeared at her door, the living room was where they'd deliver their terrible news; if she didn't go in there, the soldiers couldn't tell her, and it wouldn't be Tim who was dead.

At ten P.M., she breathed a sign of relief. Army regulations prohibited notifying next of kin between ten P.M. and six A.M. Katie went to bed and did her best to believe that everything would be okay.

★ 21 ★

The phones started ringing at Katie Moshier's house again early Sunday morning, but nobody had any new information. Overnight, Natalie had developed a horrible infection in both of her ears; before going to the supermarket to buy Motrin, Katie called Maria so her friend would know where she was, and to tell her that she definitely wasn't taking Natalie to the battalion's Easter party. She also called her parents again in New York.

Just as she reached the supermarket, Matt Stauffer's wife, Summer, called on her cell phone.

"Do you have somebody to watch Natalie?" Summer asked.

"What do you mean?"

"In case something happens and you need to go be with somebody."

"I have people to watch her," Katie said. "But what do you know?"

"Nothing."

"Okay," Katie said. "Who do you feel like it is?"

"I don't know."

Katie got home just before noon and put Natalie down for a nap. She walked back into the living room and saw a van parked in front of the house. She opened the door. Officers in green uniforms were coming up the walk.

"You have the wrong house," Katie called out before they could say anything.

"Are you Katherine Moshier?" one of them asked.

She nodded, and opened the door all the way. As stepped back, she motioned to them to follow her inside.

"Your husband is presumed dead," one of the officers told her. "We're not sure one hundred percent," he added, saying that they were waiting for a DNA test. "We'll come back later today."

You'll come back later? Katie thought. *How odd.* But when they started taking down her information, her social security number and the like, she knew from her FRG training that there was no hope. Tim was dead.

She walked calmly to the phone.

"Maria," she said when her friend picked up. Katie's voice was barely a whisper.

"What?"

"It's Tim."

"How do you know?" Maria asked, her heart pounding.

"Because they're sitting in my living room."

"I'll be there in ten minutes." Maria grabbed Arthur's hand and ran out the door. The drive to Katie's normally took ten or fifteen minutes; she made it in eight. Then, in front of the duplex at 4211 Thunder Creek Drive, Maria turned to her four-year-old son.

"Honey," she said, "there's some grown-up stuff happening right now, and Aunt Katie is probably going to be sad. She might be crying, and Mommy might be crying some, too. And I just need you to be a big boy."

"Okay, Mom," Arthur said simply.

"I assume you're Maria," one of the Army officers said as she entered. "Thank you for coming." To Maria, this was as if she had been thanked for breathing. Where else would she be at a time like this?

Natalie was still napping. Katie wasn't really crying, just sitting on her couch in a state of shock. She called her parents; they would fly to Texas that afternoon. But she couldn't yet call Tim's mother and father in New York: The Army wanted to make sure they were notified officially first, so that there would be a casualty assistance team on hand when they heard the news.

Maria sat down next to Katie and wrapped her arms around her shoulders.

"It's okay," Maria told her. "You can do what you've got to do."

Katie finally broke down crying. "It's not supposed to be Tim. This wasn't supposed to happen," Katie said through her tears. "I didn't even know, Maria. I should have felt it. I didn't know. How did I not know?"

"Katie, you couldn't have."

Katie cried for a while longer, and then turned her attention to Arthur, sitting nearby. He watched her silently.

"Have you told him yet?" she asked Maria.

Maria called Arthur over, and he stood in front of them.

"Arthur," Maria began, "do you see how Aunt Katie and I are sad?"

"Yes," Arthur replied.

"I'm going to tell you why. But you need to be brave. And it's okay if you cry, and it's okay if you're upset. We just need you to be brave."

"Okay."

"Uncle Timmy was in his helicopter. Uncle Timmy was in Iraq. And Uncle Timmy died. He's going to heaven and he's going to be with God."

"But I didn't want him to die," Arthur said, and broke down.

Katie turned to Maria. "I don't know what to do with Natalie."

"What do you mean?" Maria said.

"She's not old enough. How do I tell her? She's not going to understand. But I feel like I need to tell her."

"Then, Katie," Maria said, "you go in there and you tell her."

Maria watched as Katie walked into Natalie's room, where the ten-month-old baby lay sleeping. She picked her up, sat in a rocking chair, and held her in her lap.

"Baby," Katie began, her tears starting again, "Daddy's helicopter crashed."

TIM'S MOTHER HAD been repainting his childhood room that morning, going through some of his things, wondering what she was going to do with his old Star Wars books. The doorbell rang; outside she found a po-lice officer and a soldier in his green class A uniform.

"No," she said. "Oh, no. No. Go away."

Tim's father was out with a friend after church; the police tracked him down on the friend's cell phone, saying only that they had to get home. Jim Moshier pulled into the driveway and felt a flicker of hope when he saw an Army sergeant in camouflage. They'd be wearing dress greens, he thought, if they were here to tell him his son was dead. Maybe Tim was only wounded.

"No sir," the sergeant said when Tim's father approached. "I'm not the one you want to speak with. He's inside."

AN FRG "GO TEAM" ARRIVED; the phone rang constantly. Some of the other women in the battalion, frantic because they did not yet know whether their husbands were alive, called because Katie was a leader in the FRG. But Katie had promised the Army officers that she would not reveal her terrible news until Mike Hartwick's widow had been notified, so Maria played press secretary, taking the calls so that Katie wouldn't have to talk.

The two friends sat at Katie's kitchen table as the afternoon wore on. Tim had been not only Katie's husband but also her best friend; the loss was so huge and horrible that it would take time to absorb. She did not hold out hope that the Army had simply made some grotesque bureau-cratic error—that Tim was alive, and they had notified the wrong soldier's family. Rather, she seemed to understand that his death was just too much to consider all at once. Katie was naturally a strong person, and she did not have the luxury of allowing herself to be overwhelmed: She had her daughter to care for. She kept herself mostly composed, not letting herself focus on the incomprehensible fact that Tim would never come home, but instead attending to the immediate details, the first small steps that she would have to take on a long and lonely road.

Mike Hartwick's wife hadn't been home when the casualty notification officers went to her house. Katie sat at the kitchen table, scrolling methodically through her cell phone contacts list and reading off numbers to Maria, who would call Katie and Tim's friends and family as soon as Kerri Hartwick had been officially notified. Later, Katie scratched notes on a sheet of paper, wanting to preserve memories of Tim for their daughter.

Once Kerri Hartwick had been located—she had taken her children to the battalion Easter party—Katie called Eric Huss.

Eric hadn't seen any of the reports about the downed Apache, and the news of Tim's death was a terrible shock. Katie asked him to let the rest of the D-1 Ducks around the country know what had happened. One after another, he made the calls: Will Tucker. Reeves Garnett. He tried to reach Pat Killoran, now stationed in Alaska, but Pat was away on a mission. He would not hear the news for several days.

When Eric reached Kara Pond on her cell phone, she had just pulled into the parking lot outside her little apartment after going to church. They cried together for a minute or two, and then she raced over to Katie Moshier's house. One of the women from the FRG met her as she walked inside.

"I lost my brother today," Kara said, breaking down. "I'm losing them one at a time."

COLONEL NOVALIS CALLED TIM and Mike's wives and parents from Iraq within hours after they had been notified. He'd wanted to wait until they could absolutely confirm to the division commanding general that the two men were dead. This was the first time anyone under his command had died, and he found the conversations very difficult. But Katie, Tim's parents, and Kerri Hartwick all responded by comforting *him*.

"I can tell you're hurting," they would say, "but you'd better take care of those guys. Don't give up." Novalis was amazed by their courage.

That night Katie was putting Natalie to bed, and as she walked out of the room she heard her daughter say two simple words: "Bye-bye, Da-da."

She stopped short and walked back to Natalie's crib.

"Do you see Daddy?" Katie asked.

Natalie just smiled.

KATIE ASKED ADAM SABOURIN, the flight school friend with whom Tim had spent time when he first arrived at Taji, to meet Tim's remains at Dover. Adam sat in the same room at the Air Force base where Tim Bryant had waited for Todd's body two and a half years before. He struck up a conversation with a colonel who was also waiting there. The colonel had been home for two weeks of leave from Iraq, he explained, and meanwhile, his driver had been killed in action. Now the colonel was bringing the kid home to his family.

A hearse pulled up outside. As always, the "Attention all personnel" announcement came over the loudspeakers; as always, strangers lined the driveway to salute the fallen soldier. Adam rode behind the hearse on their way to the airport in Philadelphia. There was a flight to Albany that evening, the biggest city near Tim's hometown, and Adam sat in the terminal in his class A uniform, waiting for the moment when Tim's body would be loaded onto the plane.

"Oh my God! Adam!" a voice called out. Another West Point classmate and his wife—Bill and Jerilyn White, who, like Adam, had been part of the Moshiers' group of friends at Fort Rucker—were waiting in the terminal.

Jerilyn gave Adam a huge smile, but it quickly disappeared. "Does this mean—"

Adam finished the sentence: "Tim's on our flight."

As the coffin was loaded, Adam and Bill stood by and saluted, just as Tim had done on funeral detail back at Fort Rucker. And when the plane landed in Albany, at around ten P.M., another honor guard was waiting on the tarmac. Tim's sister and her husband served in the New York Army National Guard, and the local soldiers considered Tim one of their own. Parked near the honor guard were the airport fire trucks, their flashing red lights illuminating the early spring night.

· ✮ ·

FIVE DAYS AFTER THE CRASH, 4-4 Aviation held a memorial service on the base at Taji, with more than three hundred soldiers in attendance. Two pilot's helmets sat atop rifles at the front of the room, behind two pairs of boots, two sets of medals, and two photos of Tim and Mike. Jim Reynolds eulogized Tim, and another chief warrant officer who was close friends with Mike Hartwick spoke for him. The most poignant moment came when Colonel Novalis read a letter that Katie Moshier had sent to the battalion. She had convinced herself it couldn't be true, she acknowledged in the letter.

> I was heartbroken. And then, I thought of you. . . .
>
> I know that a lot of you are worried about us, especially me and Nat. Please know that I feel blessed to have such a wonderful extended family in 4-4 Aviation. The best way you can honor Tim is by soldiering on, doing what's right, and not slacking off. Tim always expected 100 percent effort from all of you. In the days and weeks and months to come our hearts will continue to mourn the loss of our friend. Please remember Nat and me in your prayers, and send me your thoughts in e-mails and letters. You have no idea how much your words mean to me, because they demonstrate your deep admiration for a man who I call my best friend. Tim is here with us now, and will continue to be with us for eternity. Next time you are in the sky, wave your wings at him, because he will be watching.

ONE MORNING, a week after Tim's death, Katie logged into her Yahoo e-mail account, which displayed the top five news stories of the moment. The first news photo was a grainy image of the Yusufiyah crash site. The headline read, "U.S. Military Doubts Burning Pilot Video."

Insurgents had posted on the Internet a grainy video of a crashed helicopter, along with footage of a burning body being dragged through a field. A group affiliated with Al Qaeda in Iraq claimed that the dead man was one of the Apache pilots. The news article named Tim Moshier and

Mike Hartwick and speculated whether the body in the video might be one of them. Until now, the media had more or less ignored Tim's and Mike's deaths; Katie was infuriated that the video had made the crash into a hot story.

The military suspected, but couldn't confirm, that the video was a fake. For one thing, partial remains of both men had been recovered at the scene, so although it was hard to be certain, owing to the video's low quality, the burning corpse was unlikely to be one of them. And the body in the video seemed to be dressed in the digital camouflage that ground soldiers wore; Army flight suits in Iraq were mostly solid tan.

Besides, Matt Stauffer and Kim Mitchell had stayed overhead after the crash as long as they could, trading fire with insurgents on the ground. When their helicopter had been hit so many times that they had to pull away, others rushed to the scene to replace them. There might have been a few brief intervals when no helicopters were overhead, but the coverage had been almost complete and nobody had seen anyone on the ground pulling a body from the wreckage. In any case, it was nearly impossible to imagine that such a person could have gotten near the Apache, given the intense fire and the exploding ammunition.

For Katie, no logic could make the video less hurtful, and the military could never say for sure that it was simply a propaganda trick.

"It's not even so much sadness," Katie told Maria when they talked about the video. "It's fury."

THE DAY BEFORE THE FUNERAL, the Ducks descended on Delmar, New York. For the first time since the invasion three years earlier, none of their close-knit group of friends was in Iraq. That Todd and Tim—roommates, buddies, and the Abbott and Costello of the D-1 Ducks in the West Point class of 2002—were both dead was utterly devastating: Where was the justice? Where was God?

"I have no faith anymore," Will Tucker said to Eric and Julie Huss when he saw them. Tricia LeRoux Birdsell called her husband shortly after she arrived. She was in law school now on the Army's dime, and she was obligated to serve for nearly another decade. "I've got to get out," she told Toby on the phone. "I've got to find a way not to have to do this anymore."

Katie was still on autopilot, focusing on details to ensure she could make it through each day. She had insisted that her sister, Ali, who had studied photojournalism in college, keep her camera with her at all times, documenting everything. Ali had a friend and colleague take pictures as well, especially at moments that were too emotionally draining for her. And Katie asked all of Tim's Army friends to donate unit patches from their uniforms, so they could be sewn on a quilt. It meant a great deal to her to preserve such memories, not just for herself but so that Natalie might one day have them and could learn more about her father.

Tim's community was tight-knit; the local newspaper, the *Albany Times-Union,* had run stories every day leading up to the funeral. Nearly sixteen hundred people attended Tim's wake. The next day, eight hundred packed St. Thomas Church in Delmar, the same church where Tim had been an altar boy, where he and Katie had been married, where Natalie had been baptized. Many of Tim's pallbearers had been Todd's, as well: Will Tucker, Eric Huss, Pat Killoran, and Reeves Garnett. Also carrying Tim's coffin were Adam Sabourin and Bill White.

They just shouldn't have to do this, Katie thought. Tim's friends tried to look stoic as they escorted the casket slowly down the church's center aisle. But as they drew near, Katie realized they were all crying, and the edge of the casket was anointed with their tears.

Not again, she thought. *It's not fair to them.*

AFTER THE FUNERAL, Sallie Tucker convinced Will to take her to West Point. It was about a two-hour drive, and Sallie had never been there. They drove to the academy the next day.

"The last time I was here," Will said to her as they drove onto the campus, "I had more friends."

"I know," Sallie said. "I'm sorry."

She asked him to show her around and to tell her about his life as a cadet. They spent most of the day walking. The day was dreary and rainy,

and Will had a laugh about that—with the gray weather, the place was ex-
actly as he'd remembered it. They went to the D-1 company area, where
West Point had dedicated a conference room in memory of Todd Bryant.
Most of the cadets were at class, but Will introduced himself to a second-
year cadet who was on duty in the company area, and they talked a bit.
Will pointed out the room he'd lived in when he was a firstie.

The cadet had come to the academy in 2004—which, Will realized,
meant that from the start his class had fully expected to go to war when
they graduated. Will thanked the cadet and wished him good luck; but
once they were out of earshot, he turned to Sallie.

"I wonder if he will make it," Will said as they walked away.

★ 22 ★

By the spring of 2006, three years into the Iraq war, the morale of the West Point class of 2002 was as low as it had ever been. The young officers understood duty and honor. But many of them admitted among friends that they had a rough time seeing any true strategy in Iraq. Heading into their second tours there—or, in some cases, just back and wondering whether they would be sent for a third time—they were simply exhausted. There were exceptions, but the dominant mood was one of frustration.

They weren't alone. Retired generals were speaking out against the management of the war. And the e-mail in-boxes of Old Grads from the class of 2002 filled with forwarded newspaper articles: here, a *New York Times* article reporting that one-third of the West Point class of 2000 had left active duty in 2005, "the earliest possible moment, after completing their five-year obligation"; there, a *Washington Post* report that the Army calculated it would be running 3,500 short on captains and majors by 2007, when the so-called Golden Children would normally be eligible to leave active duty.

The sister of one West Point 2002 graduate sent an account of a speech she attended in Los Angeles by Colin Powell, who had served as President

Bush's secretary of state. Her widely forwarded e-mail quoted the retired four-star general as saying:

> What we're worried the most about is our best and brightest young officers—I'm speaking of our West Point graduates—who are resigning at extremely high rates when their duty is done. Now let me emphasize that their duty is indeed done. In fact, it is done and then some, so I don't blame them. . . . We have to recognize that we have a group of young officers in particular who are carrying the lion's share of the hardship with this war and an unsustainable deployment schedule. For good reason, they're say-ing, "Okay. I signed up to serve my country and have made enormous per-sonal sacrifices, but other people need to step up to the plate as well."

Of course, there was an inevitable backlash, and what stung was criti-cism aimed by previous generations directly at officers like those in the class of 2002. The March–April 2006 edition of *Military Review* featured an article by a 1951 West Point graduate, a retired general named William R. Richardson, entitled "Getting West Point Back on Mission." In 2005, General Richardson explained, the academy had subtly changed its mis-sion statement. No longer did it exist to prepare the cadet "for a lifetime of selfless service to the nation"; instead, its mission was now to prepare him or her for a career "as an officer in the United States Army." The previous, more generic description of service, Richardson argued, had become, "lit-erally, an escape clause for those wanting to go to the Academy, get a fine free education, and then leave the Army. Countless cadets and junior offi-cers felt it was perfectly acceptable to perform selfless service to the Nation on Wall Street or Main Street."

No, Richardson argued, there was only one acceptable path for a West Point graduate to follow: his. Richardson had retired in 1986; he was a decorated soldier who had served in combat in Korea and Vietnam. But he was of a different era. Granted, he acknowledged, many fine potential applicants would go elsewhere if West Point's emphasis were on commit-ting oneself at a young age to a full career in the Army. "So be it," he wrote.

"Better then that they go elsewhere than consume a first-rate education and then leave before contributing significantly to the quality of the Army's officer corps."

It was a flat-out insult. The twentysomething soldiers of the early twenty-first century felt they were shouldering the entire burden of the war. For the rest of the country—and even for the top military brass—life went on as it had before. You could see cynicism in the graffiti that troops scribbled in latrines on bases in Iraq (in one case, not far from a sign posted by a sergeant major warning that anyone who wrote on the walls risked retribution): "The Army is at war. The country is at the mall."

"I want to strangle that guy," said one 2002 West Point alumnus who read Richardson's article, an active duty captain who had served two Iraq combat tours in his four years in the Army.

MOVING TO GEORGIA together had turned out to be one of the best things Dave and Reyna Swanson could have done. They were married now; they had gone to the Bahamas over Christmas and had a small, private ceremony, because it didn't seem right to Reyna to spend tens of thousands of dollars on a wedding. Dave did fine in his course at Fort Gordon, and while he had originally applied to go to Georgia as a way to avoid being sent right back to Iraq, he started thinking again about staying in the Army. With so many officers getting out, the path for promotion looked clear, and the notion of serving just twelve more years until he was eligible to retire was appealing. Most important, as a captain, part of Dave's role in school was to mentor lieutenants; he found these younger officers enthusiastic and excited to serve in the Army, and their passion rubbed off on him. Much as Specialist Martir had reminded Dave of himself when he was a young enlisted soldier, the lieutenants now reminded him what he had been excited about in the Army in the first months after he graduated from West Point.

Still, he leaned hard toward getting out. One of his old sergeants from Fort Hood and Sadr City came to visit. Matt Mercado was still with 2-5 Cavalry; he and Dave had been through a lot together and could talk freely.

Mercado rode Dave up and down about his plan to get out of the Army. Dave found it funny that though every other word out of Mercado's mouth during these tirades was an obscenity, he still started every sentence with "Sir."

"Why don't you just stay in?" Mercado pleaded. He thought Dave was one of the best officers he'd ever known, a guy who put his soldiers first and would never ask any of them to do anything he wasn't prepared to do five times first. "How are you going to leave me and not be my company commander one day?"

"Look, I can't do it anymore," Dave replied.

Reyna was teaching Spanish in a high school for juvenile delinquents. It was a hard job, but she grew to enjoy it. Though it seemed odd to Dave that he was a stepfather—at twenty-eight, he still thought of himself as too young to have kids—he had grown to love Isabel. Most important, the three of them were together. Much of the pressure of Army life had been lifted, and simply living in a place new to both him and Reyna was exciting.

But in May, Dave finished the course at Fort Gordon and was reassigned to Fort Sill, Oklahoma. Dave could hardly count how many times he'd moved since he first enlisted in the Army—eleven, he thought, if you counted going to Iraq and back as two moves. On the way, he and Reyna stopped to visit family in Nashville, where Dave's sister implored him to wear his dress uniform and all his ribbons to church with them. The pastor recognized Dave and a few other service members who were present; he was slightly embarrassed by the enthusiastic applause that followed.

DREW SLOAN FLEW to Boston to visit Harvard Business School in May, staying with John Kelly, the retired Air Force officer who had been a mentor at West Point. He also checked out the Kellogg School at Northwestern. He hadn't seen Chloe Hayes in a full year, but since he had an excuse to be in Chicago, he asked her to dinner. She brought her parents, which seemed less than promising, but Drew took comfort in two facts. First, he had met Chloe through her father to begin with—and he liked the man—

so perhaps, he told himself, it made sense that she would bring her folks along. He could imagine them wanting to see whether he was all right, and to wish him well before he left for Iraq. Second, and more important, he didn't hear a word about Chloe's supposed boyfriend, Peter. If they didn't bring him up, certainly Drew wasn't going to. Besides, even if Chloe had dramatically professed her love for Drew over dessert, it couldn't change the fact that he would soon be leaving for another year. No, the status quo was fine—when he came home from Iraq, that would be the time to really think about taking his shot at a relationship with her.

In the last week of June, Drew had his last significant operation: dental surgery, implanting new, permanent artificial teeth to replace the ones that had been destroyed in the RPG attack.

"After 21 months, 12 surgeries, and more appointments than I could ever count," he wrote to family and friends, "I've finally pulled myself out of that riverbed in Pir Jawad, Afghanistan. It feels pretty good."

VICKY SLOAN HAD moved to South Carolina; when she came out to visit Drew in Hawaii during the summer of 2006, she left no doubt about how she felt about his going to Iraq. And she found it especially upsetting that he'd volunteered for the tour. Drew's father felt the same way. Before his son's first deployment, he'd assumed Drew would be okay; that naïveté had been crushed. But Drew's parents understood that returning to combat was something he had to do. They didn't like it, but they knew it was his choice to make.

And, though he understood the frustration of his fellow soldiers, Drew had come to believe that the war in Iraq was winnable. He wondered whether he wasn't heading over at exactly the right time, for he had concluded after his brief visit in March (and from picking up on bits of the intelligence reports General Bednarek received) that the Army had finally seen the light: Get the Iraqi army and police up and running. Get them to start taking the lead. Teach them to secure their own country. He was quick to admit that he got much of his news from Fox News, which played in the base dining hall and could always be counted on to cheerlead for the war. Even so, Drew was convinced that victory was possible.

He flew over with General Bednarek in August, and they settled in for the long term at Contingency Operating Base Speicher. Drew shared a double-sized trailer with the general's interpreter, a Lebanese-born American named George who had come to Iraq for the tax-free salary that would help put his daughter through college. Drew had a number of friends in the division, including some from West Point, and Saturday night quickly became movie night, with everyone coming to his trailer since he had the most space and the best TV. He got along well with the general's enlisted aide and de facto bodyguard, Sergeant Ryan Abbott, a redheaded, twenty-five-year-old military police officer who had served a previous tour in Iraq with the 101st Airborne Division. General Bednarek had two Black Hawk helicopters from the Pennsylvania National Guard at his disposal, so Drew didn't even have to scrounge for transportation, as aides to other officers often had to do.

Soon they began touring northern Iraq. Usually the four of them—the general, Drew, Sergeant Abbott, and George—would simply fly to the various bases and promptly head out as observers on infantry patrols. To his amusement, Drew found he was a minor celebrity; soldiers who had been in the division back in 2004 were surprised to learn that he'd recovered and was still on active duty.

"You went on a mission?" a female sergeant asked him after one early patrol, as they waited for the general to come out of a briefing.

"Yeah," Drew said.

"Weren't you pretty badly hurt in Afghanistan?" She said she'd been thinking about him on the flight on the way over to Iraq. If he wasn't worried about what might happen, she had thought, how could she possibly be?

AT SPEICHER, Drew shared a small office with the general's third aide, a twenty-one-year-old sergeant from Los Angeles. A small couch sat against one wall, and a television stood in a corner, piled high with DVDs—the movie *Jarhead*, the television shows *Smallville* and *Gray's Anatomy*, and the HBO series *Entourage*, which Drew found amusing because he spent his days following a general around. Their M-4 rifles were secured in a small wooden rack against the wall. Tacked to other walls were maps of Iraq and programs from memorial services for fallen soldiers. One of the general's duties was to attend every such service.

One morning in early September, Drew sat at his desk and checked his e-mail. He found a message from Chloe Hayes.

Drew,

I've got some news that you're not going to like and I've dreaded telling you, but I don't know what else to do. Over this past weekend, Peter proposed to me, and I said yes. I know this isn't what you want to hear, but I'm young and in love and happy. I know this means we probably won't be able to be friends, but I really hope I'm wrong.

Chloe

Drew stared at the screen in disbelief. As far as he was concerned, the engagement came from out of nowhere. Granted, he had never quite laid his feelings out explicitly—but clearly Chloe knew; otherwise, why would she write that she dreaded telling him? What kind of love story was this, where the girl he'd spent years pining for wound up with Peter the Pharmaceutical Salesman?

Later, Drew concluded that perhaps he'd never actually been in love with Chloe; perhaps he'd been more in love with the *idea* of her. Viewed from a distance, it seemed possible that she had represented the life he had sacrificed by serving in the military, going to Afghanistan, getting wounded, and deciding to return to war. The image of Chloe standing next to him on the banks of the Hudson River on Ring Weekend in 2001, beautiful in her black dress, had always served as a wistful reminder of life before the deployments, before the injuries and the deaths, before the larger, civilian world had moved on without him.

The choices had been his to make and Drew did not regret them—not West Point, not Ranger School, not Afghanistan, not Walter Reed, not Iraq. He wouldn't have forgone even his injuries and the long recovery. His experiences in those places had made him the man he was, and he was proud of his service and the roles he had played. Still, Chloe's news stung, and even the surety of his belief that he had chosen the right path was no inoculation to the pain. He was deeply saddened.

With a heavy heart, Drew sat at his keyboard wondering how to respond. Part of him wanted to lash out; part of him wanted to plead with her. But after a few moments of contemplation, he realized that neither tactic would accomplish much. Enough was enough. He started to type:

Chloe,

All I really wanted for you was to be happy, and while I wanted to be the one to provide a lot of that happiness, I guess you had other ideas. If this is what you want, and it sounds like it is, then I wish you and Peter all the best.

Always,
Drew

They exchanged a few more brief e-mails in the weeks that followed, but slowly tapered off. Whatever Chloe had been—a love, a reminder of what might have been—she, and it, were gone.

TRICIA LEROUX BIRDSELL spent the summer of 2006 working for the Army as a legal intern in Arlington, Virginia. She'd been tempted to try to get out of the military's funded legal education program after Tim Moshier's death; it hadn't helped that she and Toby were living on opposite ends of the continent. Originally, Tricia had hoped to attend law school in Washington while Toby served with the Old Guard at Arlington. But she'd studied for the LSATs by flashlight, and then taken the test right after Todd Bryant was killed. It showed in her scores; she'd been turned down at George Mason, wait-listed at the University of Maryland, and wound up at the University of Washington, in Seattle. Despite her misgivings, though, as her first year there came to an end, she decided to continue.

Now her summer internship, just outside the District of Columbia, had brought her and Toby back together. Tricia worked in an office that argued the government's side of appeals, trying to uphold the convictions and sentences of soldiers who had been found guilty in courts-martial. Though Tricia couldn't argue in court until she graduated and passed the bar exam, she was assigned to write the government's briefs in several cases, including a couple involving involuntary manslaughter, and a rape case in which the defendant claimed he should have been allowed to bring up the victim's sexual history at trial. The amount of material she had to assimilate was challenging, but Tricia was excited to be doing real legal work.

She owed so much time to the Army now that her official military record listed the date on which she would be eligible to leave active duty as a series of black X's. But summer ended on a happy note: Toby would be coming back to Seattle with her. He had accepted the Army's offer to pay for grad school in exchange for more time on active duty. Since Tricia was now committed to many years of service, and since he wanted to continue on active duty anyway, Toby didn't find the decision very difficult. That fall, he started taking classes in urban planning, trying to squeeze a twenty-four-month master's degree program into the eighteen months that the Army would allow. He and Tricia rented an apartment and wore civilian clothes. For the time being, they lived much like other married couples going to graduate school together, except that they ate better than average on their salaries as Army captains.

In October, Tricia came back to West Point for the first time since graduation. She and some of the D-1 Ducks—the women, mostly—had agreed that the next time they got together, it would be for a happy occasion. They picked the West Point homecoming football game against Virginia Military Institute. Katie Moshier and Tim's parents agreed to come, along with a few other Ducks. They'd tailgate and go to the game. It would be like old times.

As she landed in New York and drove to the campus, Tricia felt the same butterflies that she used to get when returning from vacations. Soon after arriving, she met up with Kara Pond, who had done two tours, one in

Kuwait during the invasion and a more recent one in Iraq. Now Kara was the rear detachment commander for her battalion at Fort Hood. She was stop-lossed until the unit returned home from its most recent deployment, but planned to leave the Army then.

Tiffany Bryant came to the mini-reunion too. Though she'd been assigned to another company at West Point, Tiffany was almost an honorary Duck because she'd used her upper-class status to look out for Todd and his friends during their first two years. Like many from the West Point class of 2000, Tiffany had left the Army; she was now living in Maryland and working for a defense contractor. But Tiffany hadn't found her niche in civilian life; she admitted to Tricia and Kara that she had a hard time motivating herself to work hard just so her shareholders could see the value of their portfolios rise.

As Tricia, Kara, and Tiffany strolled around the campus together in civilian clothes, they were amused by the thought that anyone who saw them would almost certainly assume that they were the girlfriends or wives of Old Grads, rather than West Point alumnae and war veterans themselves. Kara spotted a female lieutenant colonel talking with two women in civilian clothes.

"That's us in ten years," she said to Tricia and Tiffany.

The three women were happy to be together again, but at a wreath-laying ceremony before the game the moment that Tricia had envisioned in Iraq suddenly became real. The prayers, the solemn words, and the promises never to forget the sacrifices of the departed members of West Point's Long Gray Line—these were for their friends, for Todd and Tim and the others, for men they had known and loved.

It was too soon for that, they thought. God knew it was far too soon.

JOE DASILVA had returned from his second tour in Iraq in September 2006 and he planned to leave the Army when his five years were up in June. He was exactly the type of experienced combat leader that the Army desperately wanted to keep, and he loved being an officer; but if he stayed in, he'd probably be sent straight back to Iraq for a third tour in 2007, or else be assigned to Fort Benning for the career course, only to be reassigned six months later to whatever unit was next in line to deploy. Joe was proud to have served overseas, but he needed a break.

He went on leave in September. Visiting his family in Boston, he felt he was forever defending his choices: going to West Point, serving in the Army, fighting in Iraq. Civilians didn't always understand why the military mattered to him so much. He, his classmates, and his fellow soldiers had given their all for the nation. He didn't think that the sacrifices he himself had made were at all unusual, but he was in awe of some of his brothers in arms. There were Rhodes scholars who had extended their Army service, even though had they left they could have made a heck of a lot more money and stayed home with their families. And there were young kids who had joined up right out of high school, hoping to earn money for college, then discovered along the way that they were capable of immense courage. Joe understood that a majority of his countrymen no longer thought the war in Iraq was worth fighting, but he shared Drew Sloan's conclusion: America had learned from its mistakes and was now following a viable strategy. Joe thought Winston Churchill had it about right when he observed that Americans could be counted on to do the right thing, but only after exhausting all other options.

As Joe saw it, the biggest drawback of leaving the Army was that he'd never have the chance to command a company. But he could map out his career with considerable confidence, and he was unlikely to get a command until his fourth tour in Iraq. The military kept officers' career progression on a strict schedule, never mind that repeated deployments made it hard to punch all the tickets required for the next step up the ladder.

Besides leading soldiers, practicing law was the only other work Joe had ever thought he might be interested in; ideally, he wanted to put himself on a path that would lead to a job as a federal prosecutor. When he returned from leave, he enrolled in a crash course to prepare for the Law School Admissions Test. But he wound up canceling his scores even before he left the testing room, feeling like he hadn't quite nailed the exam the way he wanted to.

With time running out before he had to make a final decision, Joe came up with what seemed to be a good compromise. The Army offered him the chance to move to Texas and serve as an ROTC instructor. He'd have a little stability and a break from the deployments; maybe he'd get a master's degree while he was there. The job as an instructor would be like sticking his toe in the water and learning whether the civilian world was as inviting as it sometimes seemed.

"TODAY IS THE SECOND ANNIVERSARY of my last day in Afghanistan," Drew Sloan wrote in an e-mail update on October 9, 2006. "The anniversary of so significant a moment cannot help but to bring pause, and during my reflections, I came to one very simple conclusion: I am very lucky. I was lucky to have survived and I was lucky to have healed, but more than anything, I am lucky to be where I am today."

He'd been on patrol on October 8, he wrote, out in the streets of Samarra, an ancient city seventy-five miles north of Baghdad. One of his favorite things to do in Iraq was to go on missions where he got to hand out toys to little children. He liked to think that years from now, they would associate the idea of America with a dirty-blond soldier in thick glasses, far from home, who had given them a stuffed animal or a soccer ball.

He offered a teddy bear to a cute, barefoot little girl. No more than five years old, she had long brown hair and wore a green print dress. "When she tenderly reached out for the bear and then flashed me the most glorious of smiles, I knew exactly why I was lucky. I was lucky because here I was, standing in a Samarran neighborhood, actually looking at hope."

Not all of Drew's missions were so peaceful. Diyala Province, where Tricia LeRoux Birdsell had been stationed two years earlier, was the most volatile part of the area for which the 25th Infantry Division task force was responsible. On Thanksgiving Day, insurgents overran all but one of the police stations in Baqubah, the province's capital city. Just before the attacks, a platoon of American soldiers from the 1st Cavalry Division had been paying a visit to the headquarters for the local police Emergency Reaction Force (ERF), in theory the Iraqi equivalent of a SWAT team. When the attacks came, the Iraqi police ran away; the Americans had held the headquarters in a fierce three-day firefight. Afterward, a CNN reporter checked the local morgue and hospital and calculated that 150 Iraqis had died in the battle.

In the weeks following the attack, two platoons of U.S. soldiers alternated defending the ERF headquarters, with each platoon serving three days on and three days off. Slowly the Iraqi police came back to work, although they were chronically short of weapons and equipment, and claimed they went weeks or even months without pay. The Americans stationed a soldier at the top of the stairs of their living quarters with a Squad Automatic Weapon, ready to shoot to kill any Iraqi—police or otherwise—who tried to come upstairs without authorization. Though the soldiers were there to protect the Iraqis, they didn't trust them. They built a sandbag bunker on the roof of the ERF headquarters, working at night because snipers regularly targeted the place.

General Bednarek and his three-man entourage—Drew, Sergeant Abbott, and George the interpreter—flew to FOB Warhorse, where they accompanied a patrol so they could inspect the ERF headquarters four days before Christmas. On the roof, two U.S. soldiers hid inside the sandbag bunker, trying to locate and kill two snipers who were in turn targeting them. A few days before, one soldier had been shot in the head, and the lieutenant in charge of another platoon had taken a rifle round in the back of his bulletproof vest. He'd been fine, but the mood among the soldiers was very tense.

General Bednarek jogged from the top of the stairs and across the roof to the bunker, blithely ignoring the snipers, and Drew and Sergeant Abbott chased after him. The bunker had barely enough room for Drew, and he crammed Abbott inside, trying not to push the general, but also to keep as much of his body covered as possible.

"Is there anything we can do for you at all?" General Bednarek asked the men inside the bunker. "Anything you need?"

"Some clean underwear," one of them replied—meaning, Drew surmised, that he was so afraid that he'd already shit his pants. Or maybe the guy was joking; Drew couldn't tell. Either way, it was hilarious that he'd say that to a general.

They stayed a few more minutes, then raced back across the roof, down the stairs, and out to the convoy of four armored Humvees in which they'd arrived. General Bednarek climbed into the third of the four vehicles. Drew sat in the left rear passenger seat of the Humvee behind Bednarek's truck. Sergeant Abbott climbed inside the same truck as Drew, sitting in the front passenger's seat. A soldier from the unit they were visiting was behind the wheel, and other soldiers sat in the backseat with Drew and manned the machine gun in the turret.

They drove out of the ERF headquarters compound and through the streets of Diyala. They passed a building with the five-ring symbol of the Olympics painted on the side.

Somebody started shooting at them. At least one round hit the Humvee's turret.

A minute later, a huge explosion rocked Drew's Humvee.

Instantly, the air was thick with dust and smoke. Drew had seen the bomb go off out of the corner of his eye; he was pretty sure it had exploded right between their Humvee and General Bednarek's Humvee directly ahead. The driver hit the gas, hoping to get out of there before another bomb exploded. He couldn't see a thing, and for the moment the greatest danger was of crashing into the crater created by the IED. A second passed, then two, and the Humvee raced forward. They had escaped. They were all okay.

Sergeant Abbott spun around. In the backseat, Drew was smiling broadly; fired up, he reached out to pound fists with Abbott. A little more than two years and a thousand miles from where he'd been wounded in Afghanistan, Drew had experienced the same scene, all over again. He'd been riding in the backseat of a Humvee, and once more an unseen enemy had tried to kill him. But this time it had played out differently. He had escaped unscathed. Drew was alive, so very alive. And now, finally, he felt healed in full.

∗ 23 ∗

By the end of 2006, most of the soldiers Will Tucker had served with in Iraq had left the Army or moved on to other assignments, but he was still an officer in the same cavalry squadron that had participated in the invasion of Iraq nearly four years earlier. It was clear that 3-7 Cavalry would deploy to Iraq again soon, probably in summer 2007, and Will was determined to avoid a third tour. Sallie was pregnant; after being away from home for so long, Will wanted nothing more than to start a civilian career, settle down somewhere with his wife, and raise a family.

He and Sallie spent a lot of time trying to figure out the surest way of getting out of the Army without going overseas. He could ask to transfer to a unit that wasn't on the deployment schedule. Or he could apply to the armored officers' career course at Fort Knox, and hope to run out the clock by preparing on paper for a career in the Army. But neither option was without risk. He would incur a commitment of an additional year on active duty if he moved to another Army post, and twelve months from now he might find himself facing the same situation.

Most of the West Point class of 2002 was entitled to leave the Army on June 1, 2007, the fifth anniversary of their graduation. But as a practical matter, Will could get off active duty by the end of March if he saved up all his leave. Troops in 3-7 Cavalry would most likely be stop-lossed as of April or early May, ahead of a summer 2007 deployment. So if he sat tight as a staff officer in 3-7 Cavalry, Will reasoned, and didn't take any time off, he could be on terminal leave—and out of the Army's grasp—just before the stop-loss order came down. He'd be cutting it pretty close, but of all the options, this seemed the safest bet.

He and Sallie still lived apart for most of the week, separated by a six- or seven-hour drive. Sallie had her psychiatric nursing practice in Knoxville; Will planned to move there with her when he was out of the military for good. (He was an Alabama football fan, but he could deal with living in Tennessee; at least it was still the South.) And though maintaining two households was difficult, as long as Sallie kept her practice, they could afford to live on her earnings for a few months. That would be her gift to Will when he got out of the Army: time to decide on a new career.

Hoarding his leave, Will spent Christmas Day with Sallie, but on December 26 he was right back at work, even while most of Fort Stewart was shut down. Sallie stayed with him through New Year's, then drove back to Knoxville. Ten days later, alone at home, she settled in to watch President Bush address the nation and outline what he called the "New Way Forward" in Iraq. The killing was out of control, and for weeks news reports had suggested that the administration was thinking about sending a "surge" of additional troops. The idea was that a significant number of new soldiers would provide the Iraqi government a respite from violence and thereby allow it to achieve some political milestones.

"I've committed more than twenty thousand additional American troops to Iraq," the president now said. "The vast majority of them—five brigades—will be deployed to Baghdad. These troops will work alongside Iraqi units and be embedded in their formations."

"Oh my God," Sallie said, out loud. *Five brigades.* Her husband's unit was one of the most deployed in the Army. Their motto was "Send Me," for goodness' sake. She instantly realized that Will would be swept up in the surge.

Sallie and Will had a long talk on the phone that night. He was as distressed as she, but no one had any solid information, so there was nothing to be done. The next day, Sallie saw patients until a little after noon, then immediately began the long drive down to Fort Stewart. At about five P.M., she reached a small town northwest of Atlanta near where her parents lived; she often stopped at their house to break up the trip. Her cell phone rang.

"Hey baby," Will said. "Where are you?"

"I'm coming through the square in Marietta," Sallie replied. "About ten or fifteen minutes away from Mom and Dad's. What's up?"

Will said nothing.

"Go ahead and tell me," Sallie said.

"No. I don't want to talk to you now. You're driving. I don't want you to be upset."

"I'm already there," Sallie said, her heart pounding. "I'm already upset. Just tell me, because I already know."

"I'm so sorry," Will said. "I'm going back to Iraq."

DAVE SWANSON FORMED a plan for the first few months after he got out of the Army. Reyna had told him she wanted to live in Texas, although she didn't care where. Her parents lived in Beaumont, east of Houston and near the Louisiana border, and she just wanted to be in the same state. Dave was flexible, and they agreed to go to Austin. Before he joined the civilian workforce, though, he wanted to do something different, epic, and useful. He hatched a plan to bike across America, raising money for St. Jude Children's Research Hospital in Tennessee.

At Fort Sill, the unit he was assigned to—1-17 Field Artillery—was deployed in Iraq until the end of 2006, so he'd had few responsibilities and plenty of time to work out and get in great shape for the trip. He ran a marathon, and rode his bike constantly.

Dave knew firsthand how easy it could be for a soldier to slip through the cracks, and he could envision being days away from leaving the Army before his bosses realized he was going. It just seemed like common courtesy to ensure they knew. Because his battalion commander was still in Iraq, Dave decided to go one step above, and let his brigade commander, Colonel Samuel Johnson, know that he was planning to get out.

When he went in to see Colonel Johnson, though, he began to have second thoughts. Johnson had presence, and Dave's few dealings with the man had persuaded him that Johnson cared as much about those under his command as Dave had tried to. The colonel was not only a West Pointer; he was a prepster, as Dave had been. And he was a triathlete. When Dave had described his plan to bike across America, Johnson had sounded almost envious.

His overall reaction now sealed Dave's impression. The colonel told Dave to take a week, think things through, and come back. If he still felt that getting out was the best thing for him and his family, the colonel said, he wouldn't hold it against him.

Reyna was teaching kindergarten now in a school nearby, and she was still leery of the idea of Dave staying in the Army. If he truly wanted to stay, she would make it work, but she was occasionally reminded of how difficult being a military wife could be. One of the teacher's aides in her school was married to a private military contractor who was in Iraq, and Reyna had noticed that the woman kept her cell phone in her pocket at all times.

"That breaks my heart," Reyna said to another military wife who had become a friend, and whose husband had been deployed to Afghanistan. Reyna thought of how much she had clung to Dave's phone calls from Iraq, and how she had carried her phone with her everywhere for fear she might miss him. "I know what that's like."

They both stuck with their conclusion: It was too much. Dave submitted his paperwork to get out of the Army.

AT ABOUT TEN THIRTY one January evening, Drew Sloan logged on to his computer at COB Speicher and went straight to the website for the admissions office at Harvard Business School. He found the news he was looking for quickly: He was in.

He felt a rush of adrenaline, then sat silently for a minute. Drew hadn't spoken with General Bednarek for a while about his post-Army plans; he hadn't wanted to make a big deal about them with his boss. The general had taken good care of him—not only had he brought Drew to Iraq and written recommendations for him, but he'd also promised to find a way to get him home in time for business school if he got in. Now, when Drew went to Bednarek's office and gave him the news, the general was almost more excited than Drew was.

"We've got a Harvard man!" Bednarek yelled with glee into the giant open-bay division headquarters just outside his office, where scores of soldiers were working.

For Drew, the end of his Army career was in sight. General Bednarek was heading home on mid-tour leave for two weeks in February, and Drew scheduled his leave for the same time. Instead of going home, though, Drew would travel to Africa, where he would meet up with a cousin who lived in London, and one of his cousin's friends. The three of them shared an ambitious goal: to climb Mount Kilimanjaro. For weeks, Drew had been ordering cold-weather clothing and hiking gear online. He even bought a solar charger and speakers for his iPod, so he and the others could listen to music as they climbed.

Soon, on a clear day in early February, Drew found himself at the base of Africa's highest mountain. A couple of other Americans were also on the trip, but most of their fellow hikers were Europeans and New Zealanders. Drew had long hair for a soldier—he told people the hair covered his surgical scars, which was true, but he also just didn't like the military buzz-cut look—and his appearance did not immediately betray that he served in the military. But when people asked about his profession, he answered honestly. Before long, he had become the de facto ambassador for and defender of American foreign policy. Naturally, everyone on the trip wanted to know how he felt about Iraq.

He did his best to explain. The U.S. invasion had been launched with the best intentions, he told them, and by liberating the country from Saddam, America had intended to bring prosperity to the Iraqi people. Obviously things haven't gone as well as we hoped, Drew said, but he was convinced that if the United States pulled out now, the result would be utter chaos. Having created a power vacuum, he reasoned, America had an obligation to stay until it was certain that whatever emerged in the wake of the U.S. military would bring positive change to the country.

They reached the top of Kilimanjaro on a cloudy, snowy day; after the descent, they went on safari in Kenya. Drew, his cousin, and her friend spent the last few days of the vacation on a beautiful stretch of Kenya's Indian Ocean coast. One morning, he went scuba diving.

Drew liked to say that nobody came home from a war without scars, but his own were now uncovered as he stripped down to his bathing suit and readied his gear—the gashes on his hip and stomach from multiple surgeries, the shallow dimple in his throat from the trache. The South African dive instructor kept checking him out.

"You look like you've been in the wars," she said, in a tone of voice that suggested armed conflict was the last place she thought he might really have been injured. "What was it, a car wreck?"

"No," Drew replied. "You were right the first time. It was war."

WILL TUCKER HAD never been particularly gregarious, but now when he and Sallie were out shopping or having dinner, and they saw a mother or a couple with an infant, Will would always ask, "How old is your child?" He and Sallie now knew they were having a daughter; he'd look carefully at the stranger's baby, as if committing to memory what a six- or nine- or twelve-month-old looked like, figuring out how far along he'd be in his Iraq deployment when their little girl was that age. Would she be walking or talking before he came home? Would she know her father?

His situation was now simply absurd. Will had already done two tours in Iraq and seen as much combat as anyone in his class; now his wife was seven months pregnant and he'd been caught in a stop-loss. One day he hurled a chair across their garage in frustration, only to burst out laughing when it stuck in the wall, its legs embedded in the plaster. At times, the stress became so intense that Sallie would just break down sobbing. They both knew that this wasn't good for the baby; Will did what he could to comfort his wife.

And then, in early February, they turned an emotional corner. Will's third deployment was terrible and unfair, but they could do nothing about it. They were going to have a baby in April, and Will would go to Iraq in May, and they had no choice but to get ready. They would give up their home in Georgia, they decided, so that Sallie could stay in Knoxville.

She thanked God she had kept her psychiatric practice. If Will *had* to go, she pointed out, maybe it was better for him to be away now, so that their daughter—they planned to name her Savannah—wouldn't remember his absence when she was older. They agreed that separation would be so much harder on a three- or four-year-old child, who would be aware enough to miss her father every day.

Sallie had stayed in fairly regular contact with both Jen Bryant and Katie Moshier. Both offered to come to Georgia for the birth, and to help Sallie out with the new baby. Sallie appreciated the offer, but she politely declined; she was haunted by the image of herself holding her infant daughter, surrounded by Gold Star widows as her husband left again for war.

"I do not want to be a part of that club," she said to Will one evening. "I do not want to go there. I reject that on every level."

Will tried to turn the conversation to what would happen if he were to die. He was sure that Todd and Tim would have wanted Jen and Katie to move on, he told Sallie, to remarry and lead the fullest possible lives.

"They would not want Jen and Katie to live without the love of a man for the rest of their lives," Will said, "and Tim wouldn't want Natalie to live without the love of a father."

Sallie agreed but said nothing.

"Let's talk about it," he said. "I would want you to go on—"

"Stop!" Sallie said. "Stop. We're not going there."

"I want Savannah to have a daddy."

"She already has a father!" Sallie shouted. "You'll be home!"

HIS GLORIOUS VACATION OVER, Drew Sloan returned to work in his small office at Speicher, where twenty-nine memorial service programs now adorned the wall. On days when he and the general were on base, Drew had a steady stream of visitors. Iraq sometimes seemed to be an ongoing West Point reunion. Christine Ray was married now, and both she and her husband were stationed at Speicher. Two of Drew's former roommates from the Sunset House were there as well: Eliel Pimentel and Rob Anders, who had both served in Afghanistan. Drew even saw Shannon McCartan, who was now a staff officer for the division. Their conversations were cordial and professional; no one who didn't know them from West Point would have ever guessed they'd once dated.

Eliel Pimentel walked into Drew's office one day in late February. He and Drew enjoyed sharing investment tips and strategies. Inspired by Drew's success in Hawaiian real estate, they were talking about investing in another condominium together.

"XM and Sirius just announced they're going to merge!" Pimentel announced. He and Drew exchanged high-fives, and Drew logged on to a computer to check the report. They'd sunk a lot of money into Sirius.

General Bednarek, meanwhile, continued his tour of northern Iraq, always with Drew and Sergeant Abbott in tow. They spent a lot of time visiting Iraqi police chiefs, giving them private time with an American general and in turn making sure the local chiefs understood how central the revitalization of the Iraqi police was to the U.S. strategy. After a few such meetings, Drew could predict how the conversation would go, as surely as he'd been able to predict what village elders wanted when he had visited them in Afghanistan nearly three years before.

More people, the police chiefs would say, with George interpreting. More money. We need more vehicles.

The chiefs' offices were all the same. Couches stood along the walls below photos and mementoes presented by previous American visitors over four years of war. A television usually played at low volume in the corner, showing one of the Arabic news networks, music videos, or Lebanese soap operas. Once the movie *Sleepless in Seattle* played, with Tom Hanks and Meg Ryan speaking dubbed Arabic. The only real question was whether the meeting would be interrupted by an aide carrying a tray loaded with small cups of tea, or whether the aide would bring in cans of Pepsi. Once an aide made two trips, and brought both, and Drew and Sergeant Abbott had a good laugh about it.

SALLIE TUCKER HAD a due date of April 1, but that was unacceptable: She would never allow her baby to be born on the first anniversary of Tim

Moshier's death. She persuaded her doctors to schedule a cesarean section on March 22 at a civilian hospital in Atlanta. When the day came, Sallie gave birth, as planned, to Savannah Grace.

"Almost to the day," Will reflected afterward. "Four years ago, I was invading Iraq."

"Well," Sallie replied, "now you have a great memory to put with that memory." She checked out of the hospital after two days, in case the Army's medical insurance wouldn't pay for a third. The last thing she needed while Will was gone was to be embroiled in a fight about insurance coverage.

Will had five days off after Savannah was born, and then it was right back to twelve-and fourteen-hour workdays in advance of the deployment. Because his job involved logistics and supply, he was one of the staff officers most in demand. Each night, he came home to a newborn baby and an exhausted wife who was still in pain from the surgery.

When Savannah was ten days old, Sallie and Will went to the Army hospital on Fort Stewart to get the C-section staples removed. They were passed around from the ER to internal medicine, back to the ER, and then up to the OB/GYN section. After waiting for two hours in obstetrics, they were told they'd have to wait even longer until the medical personnel were all back from lunch.

They gave up and drove home.

"It's okay," Sallie said to Will. "I'll walk you through how to take these out."

She lay back in their recliner, and Will nervously, carefully used the staple remover from her nursing kit to do the job.

There was no longer any point in saving Will's leave, so he and Sallie took a vacation in April, planning to be gone for two weeks, much of which they'd spend at a resort in North Carolina. They had a great time, and Will loved being with their new daughter. But they were never quite able to push thoughts of the Iraq deployment from their minds. How could they? And, a few days into their trip, the phone rang.

"So this is for sure, sir?" Sallie heard her husband say.

Will got off the phone, and had to apologize to her yet again: 3-7 Cavalry would be leaving for Iraq ten days earlier than planned, so he'd have to cut the trip short. They stayed at the resort a few more days, then visited Will's parents in Alabama for a night before heading back to Fort Stewart.

There was still more difficult news. On April 12, the new secretary of defense, Robert Gates, announced that the Army didn't have sufficient troops to sustain the size of the force Bush had ordered to Iraq. To make up the shortfall, everyone going overseas would now deploy for fifteen months, not twelve.

Don't believe it, Will's squadron commander soon wrote in an e-mail to the soldiers' families. Plan on a year and a half.

Sallie explained the length of the deployment to her niece and nephew this way: "Imagine a whole summer vacation, then an entire school year, then another summer vacation, and then up until nearly Christmas again."

And she wondered: Would Will's service to his country never end?

AS THE DAY of deployment approached, the pace of Will's work quickened and his days got even longer. Even when he got a couple of hours off, he was often called back to the post to deal with one crisis or another. Sallie was endlessly grateful for their recliner. She was still in pain from the C-section, and when Will was gone it was the only place she could lie down with Savannah in her arms and feel confident she'd be able to pull herself up afterward.

Will had to work right up to the day of the squadron's departure, in early May. As the squadron's logistics and transportation officer, he would be extraordinarily busy during the week or two before his unit left Fort Stewart and for a few weeks after their arrival in Iraq. Even the morning of his flight overseas, he could only take a few hours to be with his wife and baby daughter. They posed for a final family picture. In his digital camouflage uniform, with his shaved head and dark mustache, Will looked older than his twenty-six years. Sallie, her sunglasses perched up on her blond hair, wore a white shirt and dark pants. Savannah, barely two months old, looked adorable in a baby's white dress with a red ribbon.

"I'm so sorry I have to leave," Will told Sallie, his voice soft and sad. "I feel like I'm abandoning my wife and daughter."

"You're not abandoning us," Sallie assured him. "You're defending our freedom and protecting Savannah's future." And, she added, "We will be okay."

By the time Will Tucker left again for Iraq, Eric Huss had been out of the Army for nearly two months. Like Will, he had saved his leave so that he could get off active duty on the first possible day; unlike Will, he had run very little risk of being sent to Iraq again. Eric was assigned to the armor school at Fort Knox, not as part of an operational unit, and as a result he had become one of the first D-1 Ducks to taste life as an adult civilian. He and his wife, Julie, had thought a great deal about where they wanted to start their postmilitary lives together, and they had settled on Denver. It seemed like a modern place, its economy was growing, and there were plenty of places to go camping and hiking—things they greatly enjoyed.

In April 2007, they bought a house that needed a lot of work, paying about half of what their neighbors' well-kept and refurbished homes went for. Julie studied for the Colorado bar exam, and Eric started work as a project manager at a construction company. He'd found the job through the Service Academy Business Resource Directory, an online network of 35,000 graduates of West Point, the U.S. Naval Academy, and other military schools. Eric thought of it as MySpace or Facebook for Old Grads.

His new job, Eric reflected, was a lot like his old one. The crews, vehicle operators, and laborers were like soldiers; the foremen were like squad leaders and platoon sergeants. Eric didn't know as much about engineering and construction as the men working for him did, but he knew how to motivate people and handle administrative details, so he often felt like a platoon leader again.

Each day, the company superintendent gave Eric his orders, and he led his workers out toward the tip of suburbia's spear, pushing into the surrounding wilderness. His crews excavated roads and laid the groundwork for electricity, sewer, and water connections, the first steps toward building million-dollar houses. In a residential development near the airport, they expanded an overflow basin to prevent a mountain creek from flooding the houses each spring when the snow melted. It was ironic, Eric recognized: The great outdoors and quality of life had drawn Julie and him to Denver, and now he helped to pave that same countryside. Such, he supposed, was progress.

Eric and Julie discussed starting a family—"talking about maybe thinking about having kids someday," was how Eric put it to a friend—but for now they were content just to play the part of the cool aunt and uncle for their nieces and nephews. With West Point precision, Eric talked about staying in Denver for seven years. If they did have kids, he reasoned, it would probably be in about three years, and then the oldest would be ready for school by age four. At that point, he and Julie would have to reexamine where they lived in view of the local schools, which hadn't been a concern when they first moved in.

Seven years. Not five years, not ten—seven. Until 2014, then, they seemed set. Eric felt blessed: Life was good, and he and Julie were happy. He had served his country honorably, and now they could get on with their lives.

JOE DASILVA was a true veteran. He had one of the longest tenures in 1-327 Infantry, and by late spring he was getting ready for his new assignment as an ROTC instructor. He had been holding out for an assignment to the University of Texas or Texas A&M, but when the Army offered him the same job at the University of Illinois instead, he decided to take it. He was glad to be getting a break from the Iraq deployment schedule, and he was looking forward to working with the cadets.

"Are you sure that's what you want to do?" asked the battalion operations officer, a major named Brad Mock. "You never wanted a command?"

"Oh, I've always wanted a command, sir," Joe said, and then explained his reasoning. Before he would have a chance at getting his own company, he would have to go to the advanced infantry course, be assigned to another unit, and very likely do a third tour in Iraq as a staff officer. That road was just too long.

Major Mock didn't say anything, but a few days later Joe's battalion commander, Lieutenant Colonel Peter Wilhelm, called him in and offered him command of the battalion's headquarters and headquarters company, which included all the soldiers assigned to staff sections in the battalion, along with mortars, communications, medics, and a scout platoon. He could get a command now, Wilhelm told Joe—no advanced course, no extra Iraq tour as a staff officer. The battalion was leaving for its next Iraq deployment in September, and if Joe wanted to, he could be a part of it.

What kind of officer would he be if he turned this opportunity down? Joe asked himself. True, he would only have been home for about eight months by the time he would take the company to the National Training Center for an exercise in June. And yes, this would be a fifteen-month tour, and it would surely be difficult. But Joe was still the same person he'd been back in Dr. Kozak's class at West Point: earnest, positive-thinking, the sort of soldier for whom there were never "frustrations" or "problems," only "challenges." Command was the challenge he had truly wanted to tackle, and this was his chance. He jumped at it.

Joe had a girlfriend, a teacher in Nashville, who wasn't thrilled with his decision, but he figured she had known the type of person he was when she started dating him. His parents thought he was crazy, and some of his friends agreed. As class president, Joe kept in touch with a lot of fellow alumni and he figured that roughly half of them would be getting out of the Army as soon as their five-year commitments were up. But not Joe: The military was where he belonged.

A few months after he deployed, Joe was stationed in northern Iraq, where his company manned a combat outpost near one of Iraq's three major oil refineries. He was enjoying command, he wrote in an e-mail. Sure, it could be frustrat—

Strike that. "It is definitely challenging."

TODD BRYANT'S CHILDHOOD bedroom at his parents' house in Riverside, California, was more or less the same in July 2007 as it had been when he had left it a decade before: Notre Dame wallpaper, golf and football plaques, and prom night photos covering nearly every inch of what he had once jokingly referred to as the Todd J. Bryant Memorial Wall. Resting on the bookshelf, in a see-through plastic container, was a copy of a 1958 comic book, "Cadet Gray at West Point." Linda Bryant had had that very comic when she was a kid, and when she found a copy on eBay after Todd's death, she thought it belonged in Todd's room.

His old clothes filled a cedar closet just off the bedroom. Linda thought Jen would probably want some of them, but so far Linda hadn't been willing to part with them. Someday Jen might remarry—Linda certainly hoped so—but Linda would never have another son. She wanted to keep Todd's things, though it saddened her to think that she'd likely never have anyone to pass them on to.

She and Jen had never been close, and these days they rarely spoke. They had very little in common except that they both missed Todd terribly. Linda and Larry were still active members of the California West Point parents' club, and they still moved in the social circles of soldiers and older veterans. Their home was thoroughly decorated with artwork and mementoes from the academy and the Army. October was the hardest month of the year for them, when it seemed Linda couldn't walk into a store without seeing a reminder of Halloween, the anniversary of Todd's death. But Linda still believed strongly in the war, and despite all her family had sacrificed, she felt she hadn't given enough. Sometimes, in fact, she said she was thinking of volunteering to go to Iraq herself. She worked for the U.S. Department of Agriculture and had experience in administering government contracts; maybe she could contribute in that capacity.

The Bryants' congressman, the same man who had nominated Todd for West Point nearly ten years earlier, sponsored a bill in Congress to dedicate the local post office in his honor. In July, in the midst of a punishing heat wave, about a hundred people gathered for the ceremony under a white canopy in front of the building. Jen Bryant flew out for the occasion, but even though they sat near each other in the front row, she and his parents barely spoke. As the audience applauded in honor of the new Lieutenant Todd J. Bryant Post Office, Todd's widow and parents were called up on stage again and again to receive plaques and certificates, condolences and congratulations.

Ryan Poe, Todd's childhood friend who had gone to college with Jen and introduced them to each other, sat in the front row as well. She was a lawyer now, and she had been asked to give a speech at the dedication. She did so without notes, speaking from the heart.

"Every time you drive by here," she urged the group, "remember Todd."

DREW SLOAN LEFT Iraq in April with his general's blessing, and arrived at Schofield Barracks to finish out his last few months of Army time. He found he had very few duties. He took a crash accounting class at the University of Hawaii in June, and studied corporate finance online at the University of Phoenix: Both courses were Harvard Business School prerequisites. And he worked out constantly. He competed in three triathlons, ran a half marathon, and did a one-mile open-ocean swim. Brian Oman and his wife, Ellen, came to visit—Brian had just gone on terminal leave—and the three of them toured Kauai and Volcano National Park.

"The Army," Drew acknowledged in an e-mail to friends, "or perhaps I should say certain people in the Army, were kind enough to . . . forget that I existed."

Harvard's B-school had a summer prep program for students from non-traditional backgrounds, meaning pretty much anything other than consulting and investment banking. Drew flew to South Carolina in July to visit his mother, then drove more than nine hundred miles in a single day, reaching Ryan Beltramini's parents' house in the Boston suburbs at two A.M., where he would be staying for the night. Happily, Harvard would reunite the friends: Ryan had also been admitted. He had spent his last two years in the Army with the 3rd U.S. Infantry at Arlington Cemetery and had led one of the honor guards escorting the body of former president Gerald Ford in December 2006. He and Alisha had been in town for a couple of weeks already.

The morning after he arrived, the first item on Drew's agenda was to visit the Boston office of the Department of Veterans Affairs. Though he felt fine, and was probably in the best shape of his life, Drew had to ensure that his benefits were lined up in case he ever needed more surgeries or follow-up care. Knowing how likely bureaucracies were to lose paperwork, he had carried his file with him to Boston.

He met with a counselor at the John F. Kennedy Federal Building, and they got to talking about why Drew had moved to Boston in the first place. Who was paying for business school? the counselor asked.

"Me."

Uh-uh, the counselor replied. No way.

Because of his injury, the counselor explained, Drew was entitled to be reimbursed for "vocational rehabilitation." Drew could hardly believe it, but his two years at Harvard Business School would qualify, just as if he'd wanted to go to nursing school or learn to fix cars. The government would pick up the cost of his tuition and all related expenses—a total of nearly $100,000.

The great news was still ringing in his ears as Drew drove across the Charles River from Boston into Cambridge. He got lost several times on the way, but finally reached Harvard Square, where he picked up the keys for his new apartment, directly above a Pizzeria Uno restaurant and a RadioShack. A few days later, he started the Analytics program—"math camp," to Drew and his fellow students—and found the experience humbling, a reminder of just how little he actually knew about the business world after nearly a decade at West Point and in the Army.

The converse was also true, Drew quickly realized: People in the civilian world knew very little about the military. The head of the program had sent a welcome e-mail to all incoming students, in which he'd referred to the Harvard Business School as "the West Point of Capitalism." And now, in Analytics, Drew was sometimes taken aback when classmates described their experiences over the past half decade. He and Ryan were hardly the only veterans; about six percent of his business school class had served in the military. Still, Drew wondered, when civilians heard the name "West Point," what did they think of? He couldn't imagine.

One day at lunch, a pretty, dark-haired girl struck up a conversation with him.

"So," she said, "you were in the Army?"

"Yeah," Drew answered, and gave her a thumbnail sketch of his military experience: West Point. Ranger School. Afghanistan. Iraq. He avoided mentioning Walter Reed, for now.

"Ranger?" the girl said. "Like a park ranger?"

"Yeah," Drew said. "Something like that." He found it funny. Besides, being a park ranger didn't sound so bad.

AFTER MATH CAMP, Drew flew back to Hawaii, where he still had to pack his things and sign out of the Army for good before business school started in earnest. He was in a hurry now, but one of the last things he did before returning to Boston was to attend the memorial service for Derek Dobogai, an infantry officer who had been one of the finalists to replace Drew as General Bednarek's aide. Dobogai had been a strong candidate— a Ranger, of course—and had been one of the top-ranked ROTC officers in the country when he graduated from college. As Drew remembered it, the only reason Dobogai hadn't gotten the job was that he was promoted to captain in the middle of the interview process; the aide to a one-star general was typically a first lieutenant. After his promotion, Dobogai had stayed with his unit, and on August 22 he'd been killed with thirteen other soldiers when their Black Hawk crashed in northern Iraq.

The service left Drew reflecting on his extraordinarily good fortune. Even being wounded had been a gift. The process of recovery had forced him to face hard truths about himself, years before he might otherwise have done so. The day in Afghanistan where he'd picked up the IED himself rather than order one of his men to do it, for example—he reflected on that now as the weaker choice for a leader, and one of the stupider ones he'd ever made. He could look back with a clear eye now and see the things he had done well, but he also knew he'd hurt people he loved along the way.

Asking his mother to help him plan his funeral the night before his aneurysm surgery, Drew saw, had been an act of selfishness. Just because he had made peace with the thought that he might die didn't mean she had, and he now understood she had been terrified of losing her only child. And, as important as it had been for him to go to Iraq after his recovery, it had been a self-centered decision, hard on both his parents.

Still, Drew did not have any regrets. Even the mistakes he had made contributed to the person he was becoming. But at age twenty-eight, he resolved to avoid repeating them.

MILITARY WIDOWS TYPICALLY went through three stages of identity, Katie Moshier had read, traveling from wife, to widow, to woman again. She lived for her daughter now. Natalie had grown into a cute blond toddler with Tim Moshier's blue eyes—"Kennedy blue," Katie called them. She and Natalie had gone back to Fort Hood after the funeral in April 2006. Texas had been their home, and besides, Maria Williams was pregnant again. John Paul Williams was still in Iraq, and long before Tim's death, Katie had promised to help Maria through the arrival of her new baby.

But she'd soon realized she couldn't stay. She went to a couple of FRG meetings, and when the talk turned to redeployment—the Army's counterintuitive term for a unit's return from overseas—it was even more painful than she had imagined. Katie needed to start over somewhere else, and especially to leave before 4-4 Aviation came home at the end of 2006.

She bought a house in Albany, not far from where she and Tim had grown up, enrolled in graduate school, and became heavily involved with a couple of charities. She signed on as chairwoman of a program called the Wounded Warrior Snowsports Event, in which volunteers taught injured veterans to ski and snowboard. Meanwhile, a friend in the hometown she and Tim shared had organized a five-kilometer benefit race in his memory. In April 2007, more than six hundred people ran in the First Annual Captain Timothy J. Moshier Memorial Run/Walk, raising money for a charity that benefited the families of wounded soldiers, among other causes.

Katie cherished the young and uninhibited love she and Tim had shared, and she thanked God for the child that had resulted from it. She had no doubt that she would have been married to Tim forever had he lived. But she was open to the idea that someday another man might become part of her life. She hoped that would happen, and she was amused that people wanted to know more about her love life than ever before.

Yes, she would say, she had been dating a little. No, she hadn't met anyone she was really serious about yet.

In August 2007, Katie and Natalie flew down to Knoxville for a few days to visit Sallie Tucker and Savannah. Katie really liked Sallie and could see that she was having a hard time. Will couldn't tell his wife much about where he was stationed—"eastern Baghdad" was all he was allowed to say—and Sallie was very worried. It seemed the war had faded into the national background noise, and she kept Fox News on all the time to reassure herself that somebody still cared about the troops overseas. But sometimes, Sallie said, the sensational coverage would scare the heck out of her. She would see a scroll at the bottom of the screen, or a brief news flash— Apache attack helicopters in air strikes on insurgents near Taji, say—then rush to her computer to send Will a short e-mail, just the subject line: "Please let me know you're okay."

A few hours might go by before she got back a quick "I'm fine."

Sallie was clearly struggling to manage her professional work and take care of Savannah all by herself; she was looking into selling her house and moving to Louisiana to be near her sister's family while Will was gone. A lot of people had left that area after Hurricane Katrina, she reminded Katie. There were good jobs there, and Will might find some appealing opportunities when he came home.

The women talked for hours and took their young children for little outings to the Babies "R" Us and the aquarium. But Katie realized that the last day of her visit was especially difficult for Sallie. Savannah was now almost the exact age Natalie had been when Tim Moshier saw her for the last time, and it was clear that Sallie couldn't help but wonder whether she might someday be in Katie's shoes. On that score, there was nothing Katie could say to comfort her.

IN SEPTEMBER, Katie took Natalie to Cape Cod, where they stayed with Tim's parents at their summer house for a few days. She found herself thinking back to early 2003, to how proud and excited her friends had been to serve their country and go to war. She felt now that they had been taken advantage of, and she regretted not having been politically active. She hadn't even voted in 2004; might history have been different if her peers had been more engaged in the debate about the war? Maybe Tim wouldn't have been flying that mission, on that day, in that place.

Katie's life had changed now, and she didn't normally dwell on the past. She still had her bad days. Once, she wound up in the emergency room after an especially bad anxiety attack. But "On to the next thing" had been one of her favorite sayings since long before she began dating Tim. She had no idea what might come next for her—but the beauty of life was in finding out.

NOW LIVING IN WASHINGTON STATE, Tricia LeRoux Birdsell felt as if she had finally found her niche. Law school was a notorious grind, but she enjoyed the opportunity to take whatever courses interested her beyond the required torts, property law, and civil procedure. Since she would soon be prosecuting or defending soldiers at courts-martial in the judge advocate general's corps, she loaded up on criminal procedure and trial advocacy; she also took a course on Islamic law. A scholarly paper was a prerequisite for graduation; Tricia wrote a primer on the Iraqi legal system. A colonel in the JAG corps read it, liked it, and had it posted on the JAG website as a beginner's guide for Army lawyers with orders to Iraq.

For summer 2007, Tricia was assigned to the legal office at Fort Lewis, about twenty miles south of Seattle. Tricia's mother, now an Army colonel, was stationed at Fort Lewis as well, as the inspector general for medical facilities in the western states. Their duties occasionally entailed working together; the Fort Lewis newspaper ran a story pointing out that they were one of the few mother-and-daughter officer combinations in the Army.

Toby was finishing his master's degree in urban planning that summer; he often came by the JAG office to visit Tricia or have lunch with her. Toby looked every bit the grad student—if a particularly well-conditioned one— but inside, he was pure soldier. Because he was trying to fit a twenty-four month program into eighteen months, he had no military duties and was not part of a unit. But as he looked around at the troops in Tricia's office wearing their camouflage uniforms, he sometimes grew nostalgic.

"I really miss the Army," he would tell Tricia.

In the fall, Tricia returned for her final year of law school. By October, she was pregnant, and she thought their baby daughter would be born not long before her final exams in the spring. She began swimming again for the first time in years, and she even competed in a couple of triathlons. Sometimes she and Toby would work out in the pool together; he was chagrined to find that, even pregnant, she could outswim him.

"Don't take it too hard," Tricia told her husband, reminding him that she had been part of the team that still held the West Point record for the 800-meter freestyle relay.

They would be separated again at the end of the school year, Tricia knew. Toby had orders to go to Fort Knox for his advanced course, and after their baby was born, Tricia would have to take the bar exam and report to the judge advocate general's school in Virginia. She was relieved to learn she'd be allowed to take their new daughter with her to the course.

Eventually, they would be reunited, probably sometime in early 2009. The Army's current plan was to send them both to Fort Bragg, North Carolina, home of the XVIII Airborne Corps and the 82nd Airborne Division— units with some of the highest deployment rates of any in the Army. And, Tricia understood that meant she and Toby would almost certainly be going back to Iraq.

VIRTUALLY EVERYTHING THAT could go wrong had gone wrong for Dave Swanson when he first left the Army. He had prepared meticulously for his bike ride across the United States, but at the last moment his riding buddy backed out. Then, long after Dave had started soliciting his friends and colleagues for donations, the cancer hospital he meant to benefit informed him that since he hadn't formally applied for permission to use its name, he couldn't mention it, even though he planned to keep no money for himself.

With time running out, Dave recruited a substitute companion for the trip—his uncle Paul, a retired mechanic living in Florida—and they found an alternate charity: the Lance Armstrong Foundation. They set out in early April from San Diego, with Dave riding his bike and Paul following in his truck. Paul turned out to be an excellent partner, putting up with Dave at his crankiest after long, hard hours of riding. Most days, they would stop for lunch in small towns, where they'd seek out a locally owned restaurant. Paul would walk inside first, announce what Dave was doing, and ask the manager if he or she would be willing to let them eat for free, so they would have more money to donate to cancer research. At one restaurant in west Texas, a waitress thanked Dave for his effort and explained that she had lost her two-month-old baby to cancer. That moment made Dave even more certain that the challenge was worth it. He was proud to have raised nearly $18,000.

After the benefit ride—the two men had made it across the country in thirty days—Dave and Reyna bought an older house in Austin, a fixer-upper. Dave had lined up a job with Bradley-Morris, a headhunter specializing in finding employment for former members of the military, but he'd taken the job just to have something—anything—waiting for him after his bike trek. Now he discovered that the position was mostly cold calling, trying to recruit companies as clients. He was paid straight commission with no benefits; worse, the company had hired two other people to do the same job, and all three started at the same time.

The place was like a factory, and Dave soon found he hated working in a cubicle all day. He needed to find something else, but he wasn't at all sure what. He had thought about applying to the FBI or some other federal agency, but really, he thought, how different would that be from the

Army? All such enormous bureaucracies promoted people on the basis of time in grade rather than aptitude and performance.

Dave was discussing all this on the phone one afternoon with an Army friend who had been with him in Sadr City. Mike Beckner had been an armor platoon leader, and Dave's platoon had come to his aid one day during a particularly violent battle. Beckner's tank had hit an IED and was knocked out of action; in the heavy fighting that ensued, U.S. soldiers killed seventy or more insurgents. Mike lived in Connecticut now, working for a company that developed wind parks, giant fields of windmills that generated electricity.

Mike told Dave that the company was looking for someone in Texas. "If I could get you an interview, would you quit that job?"

Of course, Dave said.

Mike called Dave back five minutes later.

Come on up, Mike said. "You have an interview Tuesday."

Dave flew to Connecticut and met with the CEO and cofounder of the small company Mike worked for. The man on the other side of the desk seemed brilliant, and also incapable of doing only one thing at a time. He fidgeted with his pens and paper as they talked; he checked his e-mail. For all that, he picked up quickly on the gap in Dave's résumé. He'd been out of the military since April. Now it was July.

What have you been doing since the Army? the CEO asked.

"I rode my bike across the country to raise money for the Lance Armstrong Foundation," Dave said.

The CEO perked up. "Really? I did that." He pointed out a picture from his trip hanging on the wall. "Where are you from?"

"Near Cincinnati," Dave said.

No kidding, the CEO said. "I'm from Cincinnati."

They talked about biking, about the Cincinnati Bengals, and a little bit more about wind power. Dave got the job. It required him to spend more than a week every month on the road, but he enjoyed the work. He was good with people, and now he spent most of his time identifying locations for wind park projects and negotiating real estate deals. Before long, he was working on developing a four-hundred-turbine wind park in eastern Texas.

LATER THAT SUMMER, Dave learned that Matt Mercado, one of his section sergeants in Sadr City and a great friend, had been badly injured in Iraq. At first, all he knew was that Mercado was at Brooke Army Medical Center in San Antonio, but the more he learned, the more amazing the story became. Two insurgents had ambushed Matt as he walked around a corner; one of them pointed an AK-47 directly at him. Matt had leaped at the man and strangled him with his bare hands: the Army's first confirmed, unarmed, hand-to-hand combat kill in Iraq, Dave was told. But the second man had hit Matt in the head repeatedly with a shovel, and Matt had suffered traumatic brain injury.

The news hit Dave hard. Reyna offered to go to the hospital with him, but Dave didn't want her to come along. When he announced a few days later that he was heading out the door to go, she couldn't believe it. They had been planning to work on their house that weekend.

"You're leaving right now?"

"Yes."

"Okay," Reyna said, angry. "Whatever."

"I'm sorry that I have to go visit my friend who was wounded in Iraq!" Dave yelled back.

Reyna felt terrible.

A few hours later, he came home.

"How did it go?" Reyna asked.

Very hard, Dave replied. Matt's hands had been shaking throughout the visit, and he had a tough time remembering even basic things. Dave didn't know whether his impairments were a result of the injuries or a side effect of medication.

Reyna could see that the visit had upset Dave terribly. He'd returned from Iraq two years ago, but he was still struggling with the experience and found it hard to talk about. One night, in bed, he told Reyna a story.

There was this one mission, he said, a mission he kept thinking about.

He'd been in a Bradley, and they'd opened fire with the 25-millimeter cannon on some men who had been shooting at them from a building. Afterward, he had targeted the gun sight on the building, zeroing in on the spot where they had seen the men.

"And I saw this hand. Just this hand, lying there. I can't get that image out of my mind. I can't erase it."

That was just a small taste of his grief, Reyna thought, only one of the painful memories he was carrying inside. She was sure there were many more. She could envision being eighty years old, lying in bed next to Dave wherever they might be living, listening in the dark as he described yet another new detail.

A FEW MONTHS LATER, Dave was traveling through east Texas on one of his many road trips. He pulled in for gas at a convenience store and saw two soldiers in green class A uniforms filling up at the next pump over. One, Dave noticed, had Christian crosses on his lapels.

"How's it going, Chaplain?" Dave asked. "What brings you guys out here?"

"Death notification," the chaplain replied, his tone abrupt.

"Oh, man," Dave said. "I'm sorry you have to do those. I was over there with 1st Cav, '04 to '05."

The chaplain's demeanor changed immediately. "How are you coping with it?" he asked, now seeming genuinely interested and concerned.

"I talk about it," Dave replied. "It's all I can do."

∗ 25 ∗

Will Tucker was tired and irritable all the time, ready to go home just a third of the way into his third Iraq tour. Back home, the conventional wisdom seemed to be that the "surge" of which he was a part was working. The number of casualties each month had been falling: In May, 126 soldiers had been killed, but in September only 65 died, and in October, the number fell again, to 38. In keeping with the new strategy, Will was stationed in a small combat outpost in Baghdad—not one of the giant forward operating bases—and the austere conditions did not help his morale. Now, in fall 2007, he lived less comfortably than he had on his second tour, in 2005. His job was to oversee Iraqi contractors; the vast cultural differences made that task frustrating, as did the language gap: Will still spoke barely a word of Arabic, while few of the Iraqi workers spoke any English.

A few things kept him going. He'd posted photographs of Sallie and Savannah on the wall next to his workstation, and when he could feel himself on the verge of blind fury, he would study the pictures until he calmed down. Once a month, Sallie sent him videos of their daughter, as well as CDs full of photographs. Before he left, Will had recorded videos of himself reading children's books to Savannah, and it comforted him to think of Sallie playing them for her, so his daughter would know her daddy's face and voice. He also took up woodworking. Will spent his off hours building tables, shelves, and other simple furniture. It kept his mind occupied, and made him feel he'd accomplished something at the end of each day.

Will and Sallie exchanged instant messages or e-mails most days, and they talked on the phone a few times a week. Sallie had established a new ritual, an update of the "Who are you coming home to?" mantra they had employed during his second tour. Whenever they talked, she would say: "Forever and always—"

Will would respond: "With all my heart."

And then she, or he, or both, would say: "I love you."

But sometimes Will was just too angry to talk, or the Internet and phones wouldn't work, and then Sallie might not hear from him for several days. She would sign into his online bank account to see whether he'd spent any money at the PX. If he had, she could be confident he was still alive. She worried, as well, about what he might volunteer to do. On his second tour, Sallie knew, he'd kept going on missions even after being made an executive officer. He'd admitted that only after he was home, when he thought he wouldn't have to go back.

This time, Will promised, he wouldn't volunteer. "I love you and Savannah too much," he told her in one conversation. But, as Sallie also knew, he didn't always have the choice.

The Army was now offering captains $30,000 or more to stay on active duty past their commitments, but most junior officers considered that a paltry incentive compared with the money they believed they could make in the civilian world. Virtually every captain in Will's squadron told their commander that they planned to get out of the Army as soon as possible. Sallie, meanwhile, proceeded with her plan to leave her psychiatric practice in Knoxville and move to the small town just north of New Orleans where her sister lived. She had a few job leads there, and Will told her the prospect of a move was fine with him. Sallie waited anxiously for his two weeks of leave, now scheduled for early 2008; she planned to have Savannah christened and celebrate her first birthday while Will was home. (The birthday party would be a few months early, but she figured Savannah wouldn't mind.) Sallie and Will had thought about holding a wedding ceremony—a restatement of vows—on their third anniversary. Will had been in Iraq for their first, and the second had fallen during the time when he had been saving his leave, trying to get out of the Army before they learned about the surge. But a squeezed-in ceremony during Will's two-week leave had little appeal, so they decided to wait. Maybe they could do it at the four-year mark, Sallie thought. They could have the ceremony at one of the chapels at West Point, invite their family and friends. . . .

Their friends. Todd and Tim were gone; so were Tony Mitchell and too many others. But Sallie hoped and believed that when Will came home it would be for good. She could be bitter about the Army but still proud of Will's service and of all that he had given; and she knew that, as much as she and Will had sacrificed, others had given infinitely more. She made a choice to believe. Someday, she, Will, and Savannah would get their chance to be together. Despite all they'd been through, despite knowing that many others had held tight to exactly the same certainty only to have it snuffed out in an instant, she clung to the belief—the hard-as-rock conviction—that Will would come home.

He would survive. They would survive.

ONLY ABOUT TWO DOZEN members of the West Point class of 2002 signed up to attend the five-year reunion over homecoming weekend in October 2007. The low turnout was not necessarily the result of disillusionment with the military or the war. Most of the class was either just out of the Army and couldn't take the time away from their new lives, serving in Iraq or Afghanistan, or preparing to deploy. But one of the few who did attend was interviewed by a blogger for *Newsweek* magazine. Matt Mabe, an engineer officer who had served two tours in Iraq, said he was struck by how little some things had changed. Cadets wore the same uniforms and still shouted out the same cheers at the football game against Tulane. But he saw a major difference: He and his class had committed to the Army during peacetime. The cadets now attending West Point knew from their first day that they were probably going to serve in Iraq—or some other war zone—after they graduated.

"It is one thing to have to go to war," Mabe said. "It is quite another to volunteer for it."

The class of 2002 had suffered more casualties in recent months. Captain Drew Jensen, an infantry officer in the 3rd Stryker Brigade, had been extended in Iraq because of the surge, and was shot by a sniper in Baqubah in May. Mentally intact, but paralyzed from the neck down and unable to breathe on his own, he asked doctors and his family to turn off his life support; they granted his wish in September 2007. Less than a week later, another 2002 graduate, a helicopter pilot named Scott Shimp, was one of three soldiers killed in a Black Hawk crash in Alabama. But these days, West Point death notices were more likely to be for more recent alumni. It was the classes of 2004, 2005, and 2006 who now supplied the Army's lieutenants and platoon leaders. They were the young officers who went out on missions every day and bore the brunt of the war.

IF JEN BRYANT had been asked in the first two or three years after Todd's death whether she might ever find someone else, her answer would have been an emphatic no. After Todd died, she'd felt guilty just for living. According to her grief-warped logic at the time, to be happy without him would constitute disrespect for his memory. Todd had been her soul mate. Meeting him had reordered her world, and she could not imagine ever feeling that way about someone else.

It's all right, she would tell herself. Plenty of people never got married, but lived fulfilled, successful lives.

But in October 2007, as the fourth anniversary of Todd's death approached, Jen was finally willing to acknowledge that she didn't want to be alone forever. She was living in the Virginia suburbs, sharing a townhouse with her sister Erin, two cats (Mokey and T.J.), and a golden retriever named Caya, adopted from a rescue league. She still considered Todd's older brother and sister part of her family. Tim Bryant was married now. He had been promoted to lieutenant colonel in the Marine Corps, and it seemed likely he would eventually go back to Iraq. Tiffany had moved to Atlanta; she was dating an Army major and studying to be a teacher herself, having given up on the corporate world in search of something that would feel more like selfless service. But even as she stayed close to Tim and Tiffany, Jen was increasingly living her own life.

Now teaching AP high school biology, she was working on her master's degree and busy with school activities. When she went out with friends and colleagues, she usually volunteered to be the designated driver. She had been working out and had lost most of the weight she'd gained in the first year after Todd's death. She looked good.

Every few months, she would visit Todd at Arlington. Many more markers now filled Section 60, rows of graves that hadn't been there a year or two before, bearing silent witness to other soldiers' stories, other families' grief. Silver tour buses rolled through. Hearses and limousines pulled in routinely. Work crews interred more bodies every day. Sometimes Jen would find evidence that others had visited Todd as well—flowers, coins, or stones set on top of the headstone. Once someone left a plastic toy in the shape of a cheeseburger; another time, there were little packets of salt and ketchup from In-N-Out Burger.

She had stopped wearing her wedding and engagement rings, and she had even gone out on a few dates. Maybe it was unfair to shut off that part of her, she had decided—unfair not just to her, but to Todd and his memory. She felt as if she'd lost years after his death. Ask her in an unguarded moment how old she was, and she would still say "Twenty-four" or "Twenty-five." In fact, she had turned twenty-seven in September. She felt out of step, not in the same emotional place as her single friends, but also not quite fitting in with those who were married. Jen wanted badly to be a mother someday, and she started to think that if she didn't find someone else, she might adopt a child on her own.

Most of Todd's things were boxed up now. But Jen had had many of his plaques and awards framed, and she kept his letters protected in a binder. She read them from time to time and always marveled at what a witty, soulful writer he had been. But she rarely looked at the "last letter." It had affected her deeply, had contributed to her feeling that moving forward from her grief would mean betraying him. Todd had said in that letter that he wasn't even sure he should write it, and perhaps he shouldn't have. For, despite all he'd said about wanting Jen to live on, he hadn't included the three most important words. Not "I love you." Instead: "Find someone else."

But Jen now understood that the Todd Bryant who wrote that letter had been very young—a kid, really, twenty-three years old—who simply had not lived enough to comprehend that he would one day die and that the greatest gift he could give his widow would be to let her go. Jen forced herself to remember that he'd actually written the "last letter" in Kuwait, before he'd experienced the horrors of war. Afterward, he had written Jen every day for nearly six more weeks.

Maybe, she recognized now—even *probably*—Todd would have wanted her to move forward. He would have wanted her to be happy.

AFTER A FEW MONTHS AT HARVARD, Drew Sloan had concluded that business school was almost as rigid as West Point and the Army. Among the students, though, the class dynamic quickly turned into something like high school, with cliques forming and all kinds of rumors and gossip about who was dating whom. Roughly a third of the students were women; for the first time in his adult life, Drew was working and living in an environment that wasn't almost completely dominated by men. He made friends easily, and his page on Facebook was quickly full of photographs of himself at bars, parties, and formal events.

Freed from military grooming regulations, Drew grew his hair to his shoulders, and he stopped shaving until he had a reasonable facsimile of a beard. Oddly, he and Ryan Beltramini observed, almost none of the students with short, Army-style haircuts had been in the military.

Although Drew occasionally wondered whether he'd done the right thing in getting out of the Army, for the most part he thought he had. He kept many reminders of what he had been through and seen, from albums full of photographs to the digital watch he'd been wearing in Afghanistan on the day he was wounded, which had an alarm that went off each day at eight thirty P.M. Drew still wanted to serve. He began thinking seriously about politics; perhaps he'd run for office someday. He loved his country and was proud of what he'd accomplished in the Army. The work he'd done and tried to do in Afghanistan—helping, however inefficiently, to improve the lives of people there—was thus far the greatest honor of his life. Without the U.S. government, he could never have done any of it. Drew believed that individuals could inspire change, but that it took governments to effect progress on a wide scale.

He had a plan for the near term; of course he did. His credentials— experience in the military and a decent understanding of foreign policy— were solid, he thought, and his work at the so-called West Point of Capitalism would shore up his economic and financial background. His only real concern was that he felt like a man without a home state. He had been away from Arkansas for years, and although he loved Hawaii, he didn't feel like a Hawaiian. Massachusetts was fine for school, but he didn't want to settle there. Colorado seemed especially promising. Drew had decided that he wanted to work in environmentally friendly energy consulting, and Colorado was home to groups like the Rocky Mountain Institute, which did exactly that. Maybe that was where he could go.

IN NOVEMBER, Drew's terminal leave from the Army ran out and he officially became a civilian for the first time in nine years. Two days later, he drove to West Point for the wedding of his classmates and fellow Hawaii soldiers Rob Anders and Emily Wnuk. With his long hair and light beard, people Drew had known for years barely recognized him at the rehearsal dinner on Saturday night. Later a friend told him he looked like a cross between Jesus Christ and the actor Matthew McConaughey. Despite himself, Drew was flattered.

A Harvard classmate who worked for John Edwards's presidential campaign had asked Drew whether he would be willing to introduce the senator at a series of Veterans Day appearances later that week. Drew had agreed, on condition that he not be asked to say anything negative about the war. Before the wedding that Sunday, he spent a couple of hours at a Barnes & Noble in Newburgh, New York, working on his remarks for the Edwards campaign appearance until he came up with the perfect language. He did not want to see a perpetual U.S. presence in Iraq, he wrote, but he also didn't want to see a Saigon-style withdrawl. What America needed was a president "who ends the war in Iraq in a way that honors the sacrifices of so many and leaves Iraq and her people with a fighting chance."

After he finished writing his speech, Drew drove to the Old Cadet Chapel at the West Point cemetery. Three years had passed since he'd last visited the campus, and he wanted to pay his respects at the grave of Mike Adams, his Beast Barracks roommate, who had been killed on the last day of his Iraq tour in 2004.

Drew looked through the directory in the empty chapel, then went out to the cemetery. He walked in the low light among the thousands of similar white headstones until he found Mike's. Drew knelt on one knee in front of the marker and put his hand on it.

I'm proud of you, Mike, Drew thought. *Really proud.*

He stood after a little while and walked down the row of graves, looking at the ground, imagining what might have been.

An inch to the left or the right in the Humvee in Afghanistan . . .

A few more days before the doctors at Walter Reed discovered the aneurysm . . .

An extra second before the insurgent near the Olympics building in Baqubah triggered the IED . . .

It so easily could have been me lying here, Drew thought. It could so easily have been another friend or classmate visiting him for ten minutes on a lonely November afternoon.

Drew left the cemetery and went to Emily and Rob's wedding, but he spent only a few minutes at the reception. He had to get back to Boston. He had his life to live.

IN FEBRUARY 2008 Will Tucker came home for two weeks of leave, the eighth time he had crossed the Atlantic either going to or coming home from Iraq. Sallie picked him up at the airport in New Orleans, and they drove across Lake Pontchartrain to their new home. Will had been in the neighborhood before, visiting Sallie's sister, but this was his first chance to see the house Sallie had bought. He heartily approved: four bedrooms, three bathrooms, and it was located just down the street from baseball fields, tennis courts, and freshly stocked fishing ponds.

Will and Sallie spent the first few days of his leave basking in normal life. Will doted on Savannah. They unpacked boxes and spent a small fortune at Home Depot. They took Savannah to the doctor. Will kept his head shaved, but he grew a goatee. He hung his fishing poles in the garage, and called Sallie in to see his handiwork—and to point out that he'd left two hooks vacant at the bottom for Savannah's pole when she was old enough to go with him.

It was bizarre to be back in the United States, Will thought, and to see how little the war in Iraq affected most Americans. He kept looking at Savannah, marveling at how much she had grown. She was talking now, saying things like "Da-da" and "apple," and he was thrilled that she had recognized him immediately from the videos he'd recorded. Will and Sallie talked about what work he might want to do once he was out of the Army. He'd been on exactly one job interview in his life, and he felt out of touch with the civilian world. He wasn't sure who would want to hire a West Point graduate who had spent thirty-five out of the previous sixty-six months in Iraq. But at least all the leave he'd saved up would finally do some good: He'd be able to take more than two months of terminal leave when he got home. He'd still be getting a paycheck while he figured out what he wanted to do.

And it helped that Sallie was confident he'd find a good place to land. "Trust me," she assured him. "You won't have any problems."

SAVANNAH'S BAPTISM WAS on the second Sunday of Will's leave, at St. Timothy on the Northshore United Methodist Church. The minister asked Will to wear his dress blues, so he had to shave off his goatee, since having anything more than a small, neat mustache while in uniform would violate

Army regulations. He wore four full rows of ribbons now, including a Bronze Star with a combat V and an oak leaf cluster on the ribbon because he'd been awarded the medal twice for valor.

The night before the christening brought thunder and a torrential downpour; in the church parking lot, Will dodged giant puddles and rivers of red clay mud. The previous service had just ended, and parishioners pushed toward the exits. St. Timothy's took a modern approach to services, playing contemporary music and providing two large TV screens for the benefit of churchgoers in the back. In a few minutes, Will would hold eleven-month-old Savannah Grace, adorable in her white christening dress with a white bow in her hair. She would play with the braided cord on Will's uniform—a fourragère, a French emblem worn by all 3rd Infantry Division soldiers commemorating the division's service in World War I. They would baptize the child, and the minister would give a sermon on John 3:16, the so-called Gospel in a Nutshell: "For God so loved the world that He gave His only begotten Son, that whosoever believeth in Him should not perish but have everlasting life."

For now, Sallie held the baby, and the three of them stood in a small vestibule just off the main entrance. People were mingling, walking in and out, some introducing themselves to Will, others looking curiously at the man in the blue uniform. To the uninitiated, he could have been a cop or firefighter in formal attire.

A young boy, freckle-faced with curly brown hair, knew the difference. He and his father walked up to Will, holding a small notebook with a camouflage cover that read "Army Reserve." The boy introduced himself: His name was Reese Cooper, and he was seven years old. Will saw immediately that he was totally enamored of the military. All week, his father explained, he had been excited about the chance to meet a "real American soldier" at church on Sunday. (Reese, Will later learned, drew a distinction between what he called American soldiers—anyone who'd worn the uniform—and *real* American soldiers, those who had actually fought overseas.)

"Could I have your autograph?" the boy asked.

Surprised, Will obliged. His was the twentieth autograph the boy had collected.

"Than you for fighting for our freedom," Reese said, and walked away.

The christening went well, although the minister misunderstood Savannah's name, and introduced her to the congregation as "Samantha" Tucker. That afternoon, Will's parents and sister visited for a few hours, and later Will cleaned the gutters of their house, joking that he hoped he would fall off the ladder and get hurt so he wouldn't have to go back to Iraq. But Sallie knew he would never do something like that; instead, he just spent as much time with his wife and daughter as he possibly could in the time that he had left. He took Savannah fishing in one of the little ponds in the neighborhood, and she was excited when he let her touch the fish he'd caught before releasing it. He bought her a little toddler-sized slide and swing set, and sang "Happy Birthday" when he gave them to her. And he read more bedtime stories into their video camera, so she wouldn't forget him after he returned to Iraq.

ON THE DAY in late February when Will's leave ended, he had to fly first to Atlanta, where he would board a military charter for the trip to Iraq. Sallie still had loose ends to take care of in Knoxville, so she decided that she and Savannah would accompany him on the first leg. Then she would rent a car at the airport and drive up to Tennessee.

Their tears started flowing just after takeoff from New Orleans. In Atlanta, they had to split up for a few minutes while Will checked in for his overseas flight and Sallie went to wait for their luggage. There were soldiers everywhere, and Savannah perked up at the sight of each one. Finally Will made his way back to them, and despite the fact that he was dressed identically to all the other soldiers in his digital camouflage uniform, she recognized him from far away and grew excited as he walked toward them.

They had only three hours together before Will's flight. They picked up Sallie's rental car and drove it to the short-term garage near the terminal, then went back inside and looked for someplace to sit together until Will had to leave. They chose a Houlihan's restaurant, ordering food more to justify occupying a table than because they were hungry. Soon after they sat down, a piano player near the bar started playing an up-tempo version of the Beatles song "Eleanor Rigby."

Ah, look at all the lonely people . . .
Ah, look at all the lonely people . . .

Savannah fell asleep, despite the music and the airport bustle.

"I'm sorry," Will said softly.

"It's okay."

"I feel like I'm abandoning you and the baby."

Sallie started to cry. They held hands.

"I don't want to go back," Will said.

"We can do this," Sallie reassured him. But it didn't help that Will wasn't sure when he'd be home again. He had completed ten months of what was supposed to be a fifteen-month tour, but he worried the term might be extended again. About 1.3 million American service members—in all branches—had served in Iraq; about 350,000 had served two tours. Will was one of only 111,000 who had served three or more times. But that didn't mean the Army couldn't extend his tour again if it decided he was needed.

"We have already done the hardest part," Sallie said. "We will not have to do this ever again."

"I know."

An hour passed, then another. The tables in the restaurant were close together, and Sallie became aware that an older couple next to them was watching them. They were European, she thought, or maybe French-Canadian—their style of dress and the fact that the man wore his wedding ring on his right hand gave them away.

Finally, Will asked for the check.

"Are you going back to Iraq?" asked the man with the ring.

"Yes, sir," Will said. They talked for a minute or two; Will offered a brief summary of his life with Sallie. Married three years; in Iraq for two of them. Father of an eleven-month-old girl; away for all but two months of her life.

"We've been married thirty-nine years," the woman said.

"What do you think about the surge?" the man asked.

"It has achieved a lot," Will said, but then added that he was worried that the next president might be unreasonably optimistic about how quickly American troops could be withdrawn. Iraq seemed to have all but disappeared as a political issue. In polls, far more people now said their chief concern in the 2008 election was the economy, or health care.

"In Bush's defense—" Will started to say. Sallie was amazed to hear these words come out of his mouth.

But the man started speaking at the same time. "Everyone wants the war to be over," he said.

"Americans want everything instantly," Will agreed, shaking his head. Then he added: "I think we'll be there for ten years or more."

It was after four P.M. now; Will had little more than half an hour before he had to start making his way through security. He insisted on walking Sallie back to the parking garage. It was cool outside. While Sallie got behind the wheel and started the car's heater, Will settled their daughter in her car seat. Then he walked around to Sallie's open door.

She put her arms around him. They both cried as they embraced.

How can we do this again? Sallie asked herself. But what she said out loud was "Forever and always—"

"With all my heart," Will finished.

"I love you," they both said.

"It's going to be okay," Sallie said again. "We can do this."

"I know," he replied. He kissed Sallie once more, and then walked around the other side of the car to say good-bye to Savannah.

"I love you, Savannah," Sallie heard him say. She looked at the dashboard clock. It was 4:41 P.M. She heard the sound of Will kissing his daughter on the forehead, and then the car shook gently as he shut the door.

Sallie put the car in reverse. She backed out and turned to look for her husband one last time.

But he was already gone.

AFTERWORD

By early 2009, as the Iraq War slipped into its seventh year, there was a pervasive sense in the United States that the story was over. The financial crisis that gripped the world in the fall of 2008, the U.S. presidential election, and the inauguration of Barack Obama (who had spoken as forcefully against the idea of invading Iraq as George W. Bush had argued for it) had long since crowded Iraq out of the news. All three of the major television news divisions stopped sending full-time correspondents to Iraq, and the *New York Times* reported that evening newscasts devoted barely a quarter as much time to the Iraq War in 2008 as they had the year before.

But for those who were still paying attention—not to mention those still serving in Iraq—the conflict continued. Violence was down, but not by any measure snuffed out. Just over three hundred American troops died in Iraq in 2008; one of them was Captain Torre Mallard, a member of the class of 2002 who was killed on his second tour, when an IED hit his armored Humvee in Diyala province. In January 2009, there were still more than one hundred thirty thousand U.S. soldiers in the country, to say nothing of another fifteen thousand or so in Afghanistan. Several members of the West Point class of 2002 were among them, including a handful who had finished their five-year active duty commitments only to be recalled from civilian life and sent overseas.

IN A TIME OF WAR is primarily a book about those early years in Iraq— before the surge, before the reduction in violence, before America changed the channel. When I began writing it, members of West Point's class of 2002 would sometimes tell me I should consider writing a second book, one about the later West Point classes who had chosen to attend the academy knowing full well that the nation was at war. I thought that a valid suggestion, although I found it more than a little ironic to visit the academy and hear current cadets express faith in the odds that the war would be over before they graduated.

The men and women of the class of 2002 are still young, and their stories have many chapters left to be written. Will Tucker came home safe and sound in mid-summer 2008, and finished out his military commitment by the start of the new year. He is a civilian now for the first time in eleven years, enjoys life with Sallie and Savannah, and works for Textron Marine and Land Systems, where he has helped build a tougher, more modern armored car that the Army often uses now in place of Humvees.

Jen Bryant remained in Virginia, where she is still teaching high school and doing well. Katie Moshier lives in Albany, where she works in nonprofit development. Katie recently became engaged to Nick Suhr, a West Pointer from the class of 2002 who had been a friend of both Tim's and Todd's.

Drew Sloan finished his first year at Harvard and decided to pursue a joint degree, taking classes at both the business school and the Kennedy School of Government. Joe DaSilva returned home from his third Iraq tour in November 2008. And Tricia LeRoux Birdsell finished JAG Corps training. She and Toby are now stationed together at Fort Bragg, North Carolina.

· ★ ·

WHILE RESEARCHING AND writing this book, I became completely absorbed in the lives of the men and women depicted in these pages. But I never forgot that each of them represents tens of thousands of others—the soldiers and families whose stories we don't know. Every one of those stories matters, and my hope is that readers will take away from this book a better understanding of the kinds of sacrifices we ask our soldiers and military families to make.

In a Time of War is, among other things, a book about leadership. It's also about the so-called millennial generation and how its members deal with great challenges. Finally, though, it's about something more fundamental. Not long after the book was published, I spent some time with another West Point graduate who doesn't appear in the book, a husband and father of two. We talked about how hard his two Iraq deployments had been on his family. He'd recently made a commitment that meant that he would probably spend a full twenty years in uniform. When I asked him why, he used the common officer's slang for enlisted soldiers.

The thing is, he told me, "I love Joe."

And there it was. Those simple words helped me understand that, at its core, *In a Time of War* is a book about love. Love of country, love of soldiers, love of service.

Later, reflecting again on that conversation and several others like it, I found myself wondering how we can repay those who choose to serve. Since I now had the e-mail addresses of several hundred young military officers, I decided to ask them directly what they thought the rest of us should do.

The answers were varied, but I heard a few themes over and over. *Find your own way to serve*, was a common refrain. *Exercise your rights*. And finally, most important: *Pay attention*. If civilians want to "support the troops," the troops believe they should start by paying attention.

The reason is simple. When we ask our young men and women to join the military and serve overseas—and to risk and sometimes give their lives in the process—we make a commitment. We tell them that we appreciate and respect their remarkable sacrifice. We tell them that we've got their backs. And if we don't follow through on our end of the deal when they go abroad—if we send them to a distant battlefield to fight and then stop paying attention—we suggest that we think they are fools.

What's worse, we break their hearts.

Bill Murphy Jr.
Washington, D.C.
February 2009

A NOTE ON SOURCES

This book would not exist if it were not for the nearly two hundred people who sat for interviews with me over nearly three years of research. Some endured a dozen or more grueling, emotional sessions, patiently going over the same important details again and again. Others gave me copies of their journals, official military records, and many hundreds of pages of e-mails and letters that they sent home from Iraq and Afghanistan. The vast majority of sources spoke on the record. Where dialogue is presented in quotes, they reflect conversations that were described to me by either the person speaking or someone who heard it firsthand, that were captured on audio- or videotape, or that I witnessed personally.

During the seven years and counting of the wars in Afghanistan and Iraq, the names of some places, including American military installations, have changed. In general, I referred to places in the narrative as they were known at the time.

In a Time of War is a work of nonfiction. However, I have changed the names of two characters in order to protect their privacy. Chloe Hayes and Ronald Seaver are pseudonyms. Additionally, where I learned details of tactics that have been used successfully against American soldiers in

Iraq and Afghanistan, and which have not been widely reported in the past, I declined to include those details. Otherwise, everything in this book is as close to the truth as I could possibly make it.

Among the specific additional sources I used are the following:

Pages 5–6: My understanding of the strategic challenges faced by the late-twentieth-century U.S. military comes from interviews with many military officers, government officials, and scholars, both as part of this project and others. For an excellent discussion of this period, I recommend Andrew Bacevich's *The New American Militarism* (Oxford University Press, 2005).

Pages 6–11: I had the good fortune of being the third author to write about the West Point class of 2002. Much of my understanding of what the academy was like during this time is derived from two books: David Lipsky's *Absolutely American* (Houghton Mifflin, 2003) and Ed Ruggero's *Duty First* (HarperCollins, 2001). The quote from General Abizaid on page 7 is from *Duty First*. I am also indebted to Rick Atkinson's *The Long Gray Line* (Henry Holt, 1999). It is difficult to imagine how Atkinson managed to write his book, about the West Point class of 1966, in an era before the Internet and e-mail.

Pages 32–33: I obtained the descriptions of Branch Night and Post Night from the participants themselves, but Lipsky's book was invaluable in filling in some details. The exact text of General Olsen's speech also comes from *Absolutely American*.

Page 42–44: Many of the details of what President Bush said and did on Graduation Day came from contemporaneous newspaper accounts, including Mike Allen and Karen DeYoung, "U.S. Will Strike First at Enemies," *Washington Post*, June 2, 2002; and Elisabeth Bumiller, "U.S. Must Act First to Battle Terror, Bush Tells Cadets," *New York Times*, June 2, 2002. Presidential speechwriter Michael Gerson's thoughts and actions were described in Bob Woodward's *Plan of Attack* (Simon & Schuster, 2004). Gerson declined to be interviewed for this book.

Page 55–56: The general background of the planning for the invasion of Iraq is well documented in Woodward's *Plan of Attack* and his 2006 follow-up, *State of Denial* (Simon & Schuster, 2006), which I worked on as a research assistant. The "cakewalk" editorial was "Cakewalk in Iraq," *Washington Post*, February 13, 2003, by Ken Adelman; it was Brent Scowcroft, friend and former national security adviser to President George H. W. Bush, who wrote the "Don't Attack Saddam" op-ed in the August 14, 2002, edition of *The Wall Street Journal*. The allegation that every U.S. senator had been briefed on the existence of Iraqi drones was made by Senator Bill Nelson of Florida, a Democrat, in remarks entered into the *Congressional Record* on January 28, 2004.

Page 66–80: The narrative describing the initial weeks of Operation Iraqi Freedom comes primarily from interviews with soldiers involved in it. However, I was assisted in figuring out how their stories pieced together by a number of sources, including *On Point* (U.S. Naval Institute Press, 2005), an official military account of the invasion. With regard to the planning for the invasion and its aftermath, I was guided by Woodward's *Plan of Attack* and *State of Denial*. The "transition period" quote on page 78 was from General Richard B. Myers, then chairman of the Joint Chiefs of Staff; the "hooray" comment on the same page came from Morton Kondracke on Fox News.

Page 93: Kevin Sullivan, a reporter for *The Washington Post*, obtained the "sitting ducks" quote, which he used in his article "Soldiers Standing Guard Duty Are Sitting Ducks," on July 21, 2003.

Page 96: Fernandez's discovery that he was wounded by friendly fire was reported by Meg Laughlin, a reporter for the Associated Press, in her article "Soldier Who Lost Feet Optimistic About Future, but Puzzles over War," on March 19, 2004.

Page 112: My understanding of the long history of the recently renamed Camp Manhattan was greatly enhanced by the work of the RAF Habbaniya Association, and from the group's secretary, Dr. Christopher D. E. Morris.

Pages 142–43: Part of the description of mortuary affairs at Dover Air Force Base came from reporter Mike Dolan's November 24, 2003, article in *The Virginian-Pilot*, "A Final Transfer as the List of Fatalities from Iraq Grows."

Pages 171–77:   The description of the April 4, 2004, battle in Sadr City owes much to Martha Raddatz's *The Long Road Home* (Putnam, 2007). The exact text of radio transmissions on page 171 and descriptions on page 174 of what happened to Captain Lewis came in part from Raddatz's book. Riley Soden's thoughts were described in Ben Poynter's "A Tale of Two Soldiers," *The Pitch (Kansas City)*, March 2, 2006.

Page 185:   The *Time* article cited was Tim McGirk and Michael Ware's report, "Remember Afghanistan?" from the March 8, 2004, issue.

Page 188–89:   Besides the recollections of people involved, certain quotes and descriptions of Dave Swanson's combat experience with the battalion personnel officer came from reporter Toby Harnden's article "Fighting the Mahdi with Iron Deuce Platoon," in the May 18, 2004, edition of the British newspaper *The Telegraph*.

Page 212:   Todd Bryant's letters appeared under the headline "The Things They Wrote," in the March 21, 2004, edition of *The New York Times*. Major John Nagl was profiled by Peter Maass in "Professor Nagl's War," *New York Times Magazine*, January 11, 2004.

Page 262:   Vice President Cheney's oft-cited "last throes" comment came in an interview on CNN's *Larry King Live* on May 30, 2005.

Page 277–78:   The description of Camp Taji was greatly enhanced by reporter Greg Jaffe's insightful and contemporaneous article "A Camp Divided" in the June 18, 2006, edition of *The Wall Street Journal*.

Page 304:   The two articles cited were Ann Scott Tyson's "Army Offers Incentives to Try to Retain Officers" from the February 12, 2006, edition of *The Washington Post*, and Thom Shanker's "Young Officers Leaving Army at a High Rate" from the April 10, 2006, edition of *The New York Times*.

Pages 315–17:   I visited the ERF headquarters in Baqubah, Iraq, in February 2007, about three months after the events described in these pages, and interviewed many of the soldiers who were involved in the battle.

Page 356:   Thom Shanker of *The New York Times* reported the statistics about the number of American servicemen who had served in Iraq in his

April 6, 2008, article, "Army Is Worried by Rising Stress of Return Tours to Iraq." Among active-duty soldiers in the U.S. Army (as opposed to mobilized reservists and members of the other services), Will Tucker was one of an even more elite group: By spring 2008, only 53,000 active-duty soldiers had deployed three or more times to Iraq, according to the *Times*.

ACKNOWLEDGMENTS

A complete list of people I need to thank would fill another book. At the outset, I am grateful to the nearly two hundred soldiers, friends, and family members who shared their stories with me, especially: Mike Baskin, Alisha and Ryan Beltramini, Toby Birdsell, Tricia LeRoux Birdsell, Jen Bryant, Larry and Linda Bryant, Tiffany Bryant, Tim Bryant, Earle Bundy, Caleb Cage, Joe DaSilva, Michael Gunther and Heather McAfee Gunther, Matt Homa, Mike Lee, Jim and Mary Ellen Moshier, Katie Moshier, John Nagl, John Novalis, Brian Oman, Kara Pond, Dana Scherry, David Sloan, Drew Sloan, Vicky Sloan, Carter Smyth, Matt Stauffer, Dave and Reyna Swanson, Randy Tucker, Sallie Tucker, Will Tucker, and Verle Wright.

In a Time of War was born as a footnote in a memo that I wrote to my former boss, the author and reporter Bob Woodward. Working for Bob was the best apprenticeship in journalism, and I am fortunate to consider him a true friend and mentor. Though mentioned elsewhere, I would also like to call special attention to two books: David Lipsky's *Absolutely American* and Rick Atkinson's *The Long Gray Line*. I highly doubt anyone will ever be able to write about West Point and its graduates again without referencing these two works.

My parents, Bill and Pat Murphy, were convinced long before I was that I had a book like this in me somewhere, and my four brothers and sisters—Jim (a Marine Corps veteran of Iraq), Chris, Seana, and Michaela—read early drafts. They were joined in this by Caleb Cage (USMA class of 2002), Jamie Diaferia, Jeff Himmelman, John Nagl (USMA class of 1988), and Christine Parthemore. The book you hold in your hands benefited greatly from their advice. Also, Jason Amerine, Steve Boehm, Rich Ducote, and Matt Stauffer read certain sections for technical and geographic accuracy. I am grateful for their help. Of course, whatever errors remain are my responsibilty.

One of the smartest decisions I made was to put my trust in Esther Newberg, my agent at ICM. She understood this project immediately and championed it in the world of New York publishing. John Sterling, my editor at Holt/Macmillan, did excellent work and cajoled a much better book out of me than I otherwise might have written. (I knew he would do so, as he was also Atkinson's editor on The Long Gray Line and other books.) I also thank his colleagues at Holt and Macmillan, including Jolanta Benal, Denise Cronin, Dan Farley, Lisa Fyfe, Vicki Haire, Emi Ikkanda, Tara Kennedy, Claire McKinney, Tom Nau, Maggie Richards, Kenn Russell, and Kelly Too, for their hard work.

Jeanne Murie, Evelyn Duffy, Sheri Prager, and Jessica Smith were immensely helpful in transcribing hundreds of interviews and tracking down thousands of facts. While I intentionally did not ask West Point or the Army for any official sanction or cooperation in writing this book, Theresa Brinkerhoff and Lieutenant Colonel Brian Hilferty of the academy's public affairs office were always professional and helpful. I thank them.

I was able to go to Iraq as a reporter for The Washington Post in 2007; this book is better because of it. Thanks to Lieutenant Jason Brinkley, Sergeant Benny Alicea, Specialist Jeremy Anderson, Private Stanislav Mykhaylichenko, and the men of Alpha Co., 1-12 Cavalry and the other units I was embedded with, for showing me the truth and not letting me get killed in the process. Thanks to Len Downie and Phil Bennett, the Post's editor and managing editor, and David Hoffman, assistant managing editor for foreign news, for making the fantastic opportunity possible in the first place. Assignment editor Cameron Barr has my gratitude for greatly improving my writing; reporters Josh Partlow and Ernesto Londoño for showing me around Baghdad; and Kate Agnew and Terissa Schor for providing the voices of sanity on the other end of the satellite phone, back on the desk in Washington. I'd also like to thank another *Post* reporter, Baghdad veteran Karin Brulliard, for her friendship and serendipitous career counseling.

Much of what I knew about military life before writing this book was the result of having served in the Army Reserve and the Army JAG corps. I would like to thank the 10th Mountain Division soldiers and Boston-area reservists with whom I spent the better part of 2003 on active duty at Fort Drum, New York; the soldier-lawyers I was with at the U.S. Army Legal Services Agency in Virginia from 2004 to 2005; and the hundreds of other soldiers I was privileged to know and serve with in reserve units in California, Maryland, and Massachusetts in the late 1990s and early 2000s, for their past and continued service to the nation.

Finally, saving the absolute best for last, my wife, Melissa, the principal of a District of Columbia public elementary school, is the hardest-working person I know. She put up with more than three years of my work on this project—the reams of paper taking over our apartment, the trips to Fort Benning and Fort Hood (to say nothing of Iraq), the ups-and-downs of living with a writer. She rarely complained and always gave me her support. She deserves my thanks and love, of course, but she also deserves the following public acknowledgment. Years ago she gave me the best advice any writer ever had: "Pick one project and stick with it." Well, Melissa: You were right!

ABOUT THE AUTHOR

BILL MURPHY JR. worked as Bob Woodward's research assistant on the bestselling *State of Denial*. A lawyer and former Army Reserve officer, he reported from Iraq for *The Washington Post* in 2007. He lives in Washington, D.C.